MAN'S QUEST FOR AUTONOMY

A Background for Modernization

Other Books by DAVID RODNICK

Essays on an America in Transition—1972

The Strangled Democracy: Czechoslovakia 1948-1969—1970

An Introduction to Man and His Development—1966

The Norwegians—1955

Postwar Germans—1948

The Assiniboine of Montana—1939

MAN'S QUEST FOR AUTONOMY

A Background for Modernization

DAVID RODNICK

The Caprock Press
1974

To

The Present and Future Young Generations

PREFACE

In the following pages I have woven a story with some threads that are strong and others that are quite weak. I have tried to reinforce the latter by using a relative amount of feedback to serve as warps as well as woofs. By connecting the threads and trying to make them into a coherent whole, I have had to employ a good deal of speculation to fill some of the many lacunae in the story of man. I hope that the reader will see the overall cloth and not the isolated and connecting threads: I am more concerned with trying to determine where we are at the moment in the never-ending story of mankind, where we have come from, and where the next possible directions tend to point. The story of mankind is like a cloth that is in the continuous process of being rewoven when threads weaken, snap, or wear out—and when the cloth needs to become ever larger to cover the extremely complex body that is mankind.

The book is dedicated to the present and future young generations, too many members of which become either discouraged or indifferent to the magnitude of national and global problems when they feel that there is nothing they can do to help solve them. But it is possible that *Homo sapiens* may occupy this world for a long time to come if the species so chooses. Clearly there is no one here to assure that outcome but ourselves. Hence the increasing importance of each generation understanding its place in the continuum of the story of mankind.

In putting this account together, I have greatly benefited from the willingness of my wife, Elizabeth A. Rodnick, to spend many hours carefully editing and re-editing. Much discussion and efforts at clarification have, we both hope, made this into a coherent record.

D. R.

Region 4
Blacksburg: Smithfield Plantation

Region 5
Big Stone Gap: John Fox, Jr. House
Blountville: Derry's Inn
Bristol: Edward Cox House
Bristol: Acuff Chapel
Pocahontas: St. Elizabeth's Catholic Church
Pocahontas: Pocahontas Baptist Church
Rocky Mount: Booker T. Washington's Birthplace
Wytheville: The Rock House

MUSEUMS
Region 1
Culpeper: Culpeper Cavalry Museum
Front Royal: Thunderbird Museum & Archeological Park
Front Royal: Dinosaur Land
Front Royal: Confederate Museum
Leesburg: Loudoun Museum/Visitor Center
New Market: New Market Battlefield & Hall of Valor
Paeonian Springs: Work Horse Museum
Strasburg: Strasburg Museum

Region 2
Charlottesville: Michie Tavern Museum
Harrisonburg: Harrisonburg-Rockingham Historical Society Museum
Orange: James Madison Museum & Information Center
Staunton: Statler Brothers Complex & Museum

Region 3
Bedford: Bedford Museum
Lexington: George C. Marshall Museum & Library
Lexington: VMI Museum
Lexington: Lee Chapel & Museum
Lynchburg: Lynchburg Museum

Region 4
Christiansburg: Montgomery Museum & Lewis Miller Art Center
Roanoke: Transportation Museum

Region 5
Big Stone Gap: Harry W. Meador, Jr. Coal Museum
Galax: Jeff Matthews Memorial Museum
Newbern: Newbern Museum
Tazewell: Crab Orchard Museum & Pioneer Park
Wytheville: Rock House Museum

Table
of
Contents

I   Prologue

It has been ten years since I first began to write *An Introduction to Man and His Development,* a book which aspired to view mankind's progress from its feeble beginnings through the present. Much has happened in those ten years: not only have new fossil discoveries been made which have changed past conceptions as to how mankind got its start, but also my ideas about man (and woman) have been affected by further study and reflection. More is now known about the developing nations (but not nearly enough) than was possible ten years ago. Much has happened in Africa, South America, India, China, Japan, and even the Soviet Union to provide a more perceptive understanding of trends in those areas — though not enough to let one feel sanguine as to what they will be in the next three decades.

Ten years ago, Japan was fifth in industrialization in the world: today it is second only to the United States. None of the developing countries has been able to find short-cuts to the processes of industrialization that have not been tried before. In Latin America, Africa, India, and China, the vast majority of the populations are still outside the Secondary civilization with its culture of industrialization and scientific studies. And, though the Communist nations have entered Secondary civilization, there is no evidence that they have discovered any different techniques that would enable them to increase their production of wealth or new knowledge. Indeed, the data of the past ten years seem to indicate that the promise of a new social world is still one to be met in the distant future. China remains in the throes of a revolution which endeavors to keep that country within the confines of a nineteenth-century peasant movement, this at a time when the modern world has made the peasant obsolete. In the Soviet Union, there is no indication that a more efficient or freer economic and political system has been able to displace the mixture of government and business that is still in control in the non-Communist world. The developing areas of the Third World seem destined to repeat the mistakes made by the developed nations, as they encourage the growth of wealth among a small portion of their citizenry while doing little to bring their large populations into the mainstream of the new civilization. In fact, the developing countries face problems that the developed nations have also not solved in the fields of agriculture, industrialization, urbanization, education, and health.

◇   ◇   ◇   ◇   ◇

An embryonic mankind spent millions of years lying virtually dormant in its narrowly restricted cultural chrysalis awaiting the moment when it could leave its self-made cocoon with a mental capacity that would enable it to cope with problems of nature's and man's own making. The adjustments to these worlds came slowly, sometimes inefficiently and many times irrelevantly, but still there was an accumulation of knowledge that enabled feeble and naked man to defend himself against his enemies — or those he thought were his enemies — and that enabled him to create more powerful extensions of his arms, his teeth, his shoulders, and his legs. From a poorly endowed physical creature whose nails were not equivalent to the claws of a tiger, whose teeth could not compete with those of a wolf, whose strength was not equal to that of a bear, and whose legs could not carry him as fast as the limbs of an antelope, man has been able to outperform all the physical assets of all other animals. No animal can kill so readily or so many in so short a period of time. No animal, including the powerful elephant, can lift as much as a man-made crane, and no bird can fly as fast as man in the planes and space ships he has invented. Through the frontal hemispheres of the brain that have slowly been evolving over millions of years, mankind has been able to create great strengths while exhibiting enormous weaknesses.

Man's greatest promise lies in this brain which he is still unable to use to the fullest. An extremely complicated machine, easily equivalent to the energy of more than five billion transistors, it is his creator and yet one whose depths he is unable to fathom or to understand. It is this brain which has enabled him to perform something which no other animal can do: to change his way of life and his technology every few generations. Animals lower than man in the evolutionary scale can live from generation to generation only as their ancestors did. No matter how long dogs may live in close proximity to human beings, they will still not be able to develop a canine civilization, nor a canine culture. Bears, lions, cattle, and horses are unable to effect changes in their lives every few generations, as man does. Dogs have no control over their fate, as man can. Dogs are as affectionate and as receptive to learning as they undoubtedly were ten thousand years ago, but they are unable to pass on to their descendants any knowledge which they might have accumulated in their lifetimes. The descendants of monkeys 20,000 years hence will be more like their ancestors in terms of the way they view life than will be true of our descendants 20,000 years from now when compared to ourselves, or even as we are contrasted with our own ancestors 20,000 years ago.

Yet, though man has begun to change his way of life in almost every generation and though he is also in the position of being able to change himself (through his ideas about himself and the world he lives in), his strength in being able to create a culture that can guide him can also lead to his self-destruction. He has no instincts to fall back upon, so he is forced continuously to set up guidelines for himself without knowing in advance which ones will be best over the long run. Man's written history contains thousands of pages extolling mediocre leaders (with mediocre ideas, or worse) whose evil deeds have taken tens of generations to even partially undo. Man's written history is still that of men who make decisions that they believe will enhance their status at the moment rather than to concern themselves with ones that will improve the well-being of mankind. The options that were available to men but which they never considered have seldom haunted those leaders who made important but ill-fated decisions. The pages of written history have little to say about those who sought more security for mankind through more efficient means of work, production, and thought; but they have much to say about those who spent their lives needlessly competing with others for high rank in the human pecking order. Men have spent little time seeking new options in behavior which could have been usable, but a great deal restricting themselves to continuing traditions from the past.

Although man has continuously been a seeker after knowledge, he is limited by his ignorance and been forced by expediency to assume a non-existent or an erroneous knowledge for the decisions which he has had to make in his daily life. This contradiction between not being certain but still having to make decisions often based on faulty knowledge has been man's administrative fate from the earliest days of his organized history. It has led to mismanagement, war, bloody repression, and intellectual stagnation—whose effects are still felt today in large parts of the world. Animals below man are unable to engage in generational change, but man is in the unusual position of being able to mold himself at will. To change himself deliberately, however, requires a more comprehensive knowledge of human behavior than he has possessed thus far.

The story of man's quest for autonomy, then, is that of a long-term struggle for knowledge, for guidelines, for options, for expanded areas of permissable behavior, and for the freedom to know one's self as well as one's society and culture. For most of the time in his story, man has been unable to see himself as he actually was. Until comparatively recent times, he was unconscious of himself as being a self-manipulator. The development of his brain to the stage where he could see how naked he was both actually and symbolically is much more a part of man's recent past than of his ancient beginnings. And the slow accumulation of knowledge that enabled him to understand the behavior which he internalized is an event in the most recent of yesterdays. Man is conditioned to seek the mythical security of a non-existent idyllic past, while at the same time he tries to establish a way of life based upon his pursuit of that will o' the wisp of the immediate future. He is continuously frustrated by having his dreams confronted, and then refuted, by the growing bits of knowledge which become established in his day-to-day world.

Like Sisyphus, the Greek king condemned to roll a huge stone up a hill in Hades only to have it roll down again on nearing the top, men seem destined to continuous frustration in selecting masters who know even less than they do as to what leadership they need. Perhaps over a period of time men may become educated to govern themselves and to select those options which they need in order to continue their search for personal fulfillment. While pre-men in the distant past were content if they had enough food, men's goals began to widen (and become ever more complex) as man's increased intelligence put forth new demands to be fulfilled. Men were no longer satisfied merely to have food at the end of the day: they wished to make certain that there would also be food tomorrow, the day after tomorrow, and even the next week and next month. They were motivated to put out feelers, seeking ways to assure themselves of even more. As men were able to satisfy their hunger and to shelter themselves from the elements, they began to develop new expectations. They were no longer content to sleep as animals when their simple demands were met; they began to push themselves with goals for greater personal fulfillment, to stay the void inside which told them that they were part of a chain that merely repeated other links, that men were born to die. This continuous struggle to prove themselves unique encouraged some men to organize themselves for warfare in the performance of heroic deeds, to fulfill the orders of the deities above them, and eventually to create civilization with its bureaucratic organization of men, its traditions, and its compiling of records. Later, men felt free to compete with their social superiors for feelings of importance, and thus set in motion a new type of civilization that is with us even today.

Men, it is true, are part of a continuous chain of life that may have begun more than three-and-a-half billion years ago (and if the theory of the exploding universe has some validity to it, there may have been high forms of life of an unknown variety that may have existed tens of billions of years ago and more). The chain of life that began with the first single-celled organisms has continued unbroken to this day, for if the chain had been broken at any one point, most of us would not be alive. We live, as we hope our descendants will, because the chain of life has come down to us unbroken. And though the chain stretches back in time to the earliest of life forms, it may continue on into the future in a way that none of us can possibly foresee at present. For, although men can go back a few thousand years in their written history and a few million years with their archaeological diggings, we still do not know the centuries that lie ahead. Men are satisfied to peer no further into the future than the extent of their own lifetimes. The year 2000 still seems far away, though to a man in his fifties 1945 was only yesterday. While we portray previous centuries in the movies or write about them in detail, we find it almost impossible to visualize the ideas that men will have even 500 years from now. The attempts of science fiction to tear away the veils of the future have tended to be projections of conditions that we see in our own society.

If the less-educated leaders of mankind do not manage to blow us off the globe during the next few decades, we may perhaps continue to live on this planet for a long time to come. Our descendants may possibly be around for the next thousand or even two thousand years. Perhaps they will even continue to propagate and develop new concepts for their everyday life 10,000, 100,000, and even 500,000 years from now. It is difficult to know what men will look like so far in the future, just as we have no conception of what their way of life will be, how they will spend their days, what they will think of themselves and their fellow men, how they will govern themselves, and what sort of family life, if any, might exist then. We can only speculate on the changes that will separate our day from those that will follow, but I believe that there are few who assume that men in the future will possess the same religious or political views that exist today. Yet, there are large numbers of men who are convinced that mankind has reached a plateau beyond which it cannot go, that the guidelines for future living have already been delineated.

◇   ◇   ◇   ◇   ◇

It took at least two to three million years before *Homo erectus,* our early tool-using ancestor, was able to develop a brain which permitted him to speculate, to draw analytical conclusions, and to ponder the mysteries of nature and human existence. Man the philosopher was evidently co-existent with man as *Homo sapiens,* which means that we cannot put Man the thinker back more than 300,000 years at the most. But in that 300,000 years he began to speculate about the existence available to him, for it was necessary to survival for him to understand why things were as they were. He may have no longer been content to while the time away, and he may have derived pleasure in carrying on speculative conversations or ones that were concerned with the origins of things and the reasons for their existence. Man's day-to-day accumulation of knowledge which he could pass on to his descendants must have increased enormously from 80,000 to a little more than 10,000 years ago. And this knowledge began to increase at an ever faster pace from 10,000 to a little over 3,000 years ago.

From about 25,000 years in the past to the present, men have thought more, speculated more, invented more — with large parts of this activity taking place in the past 200 years. Trying to project these trends into the future merely indicates that in succeeding decades larger numbers of men may change their ways of life and their lives in general by the interactions of their thoughts.

While men developed an agriculturally-oriented civilization in order to organize men more effectively for warfare and religion, the Industrial and Scientific civilization also came into existence through an improved technology for warfare and a new viewpoint on religion, the latter creating the incentive for men to know God's handiwork better. (Perhaps in the Tertiary civilization which seems to be around the corner, men may begin to devise a civilization for the future which is concerned less with warfare and religion, and more with creating cultural inhibitions against taking human lives or turning to the past for inflexible guidelines. Perhaps among our descendants of the next 10,000 years, there may be a fourth type of civilization, a fifth, a sixth, and perhaps a twentieth, all concerned with solving problems that none of us are vaguely aware of at the present time.)

With all of its defects, the Primary or Agricultural civilization brought literacy into the world and induced men to think of social justice, though little was put into operation. But the Agricultural civilization was unable to do much about poverty, mass illiteracy, and the inequalities and diseases which existed among men living under its aegis. Although the ancient Greeks may have talked about democracy, little of it was practiced in the Greek city-states. At the present time, the vast majority of the world's inhabitants have never lived under it. The Agricultural civilization was not a promise but only the organization of men for the benefit of small groups of elites. Before the seventeenth century, there was little in Agricultural civilization which benefited the mass of Egyptian *fellahin*, most Chinese, Indian, or European peasants. On the other hand, it is most unlikely that the Industrial and Scientific civilization, with its later increases in standard of living, levels of health, areas of literacy and intellectualism, could have arisen out of the Neolithic folk village. Rather, its growth required the milieu of the literate urban centers in the later Agricultural civilization. Dissatisfactions with the pace of the Agricultural civilization encouraged the development of revolutionary goals in urban Europe: egalitarianism, progress, personal fulfillment, and individualism (with its aims of both democracy and philosophical anarchism). Although the actual workings of the Industrial and Scientific civilization owe more to the need of absolutist European kings to possess larger and more efficient armies and weapons of war, the growth of social mobility — stoked by the long-dormant underground currents of egalitarianism — had much to do with the reaction against the institutions and knowledge of the past, and made possible the growth and encouragement of the scientific spirit.

The Primary or Agricultural civilization did not solve the problems that it created when it organized men into administrative urban centers. Because its organization could not solve pressing social problems, men turned to ideas that sapped the foundations of the old and led to the creation of other institutions. With the greater urbanization and wealth derived from the new industrial processes (even though they had been created by the need to build better weapons and the trappings of war), the new civilization was able to work on the problems of the old: its poverty, illiteracy, inequalities, and diseases. At the same time, however, it produced newer conflicts which it could not solve — creating ugly cities, despoiling the natural environment, inventing horrendous weapons of mass destruction, and developing a spirit of nationalism which could only lead to the Stalinist, Nazi, and Japanese holocausts whereby tens of millions lost their lives in Europe and untold millions in Asia. As of this writing, war still goes on in Asia, while the colonialism of the preindustrial era has continued with the Russian Colonialism enunciated by the Brezhnev Doctrine. Although the dream of man's eventual self-fulfillment has been repeatedly enunciated both in Europe and Asia since 1917, in actuality those regimes sponsoring man's "liberation" have been most repressive of his freedom to criticize or to innovate in the realm of ideas. In most countries of the world, the twentieth century has been marked by authoritarianism and totalitarianism.

As the Primary or Agricultural civilization could only go so far before hitting a blank wall, so the Secondary civilization of industry and science is also limited in its direction without running into a cul-de-sac. The latter can out-produce Primary civilization but it can also out-pollute it. It can raise immeasurably the standard of living of most of its inhabitants, but it can also cause larger numbers to lose their lives through automobile accidents and the fortunes of war. No king living in the past had at his disposal the millions of armed men or the weapons that are now under the authority of the top executives of the world's two superpowers. Although the Black Plague may have wiped out one-third of the European population in the fourteenth century, a human error or the pressing of the wrong button can now unleash destruction that might easily wipe out the entire population of the globe. Despite the growth of literacy and the increase in universities, heads of governments still operate on the assumption that a political conflict between nations can best be solved by putting weapons of war into the hands of drafted 18-year-olds so that they can kill other drafted 18-year-olds. The nation that can kill and destroy the most on the other side wins the political argument.

◇   ◇   ◇   ◇   ◇

Because the Industrial and Scientific civilization can solve certain simple problems but not more complex ones, mankind will be pushed into the arms of a Third civilization, a Tertiary one, that will not look upon production as its chief goal, but rather the solving of man's inconsiderate behavior toward his fellow men. Men learn slowly, but when they acknowledge that they have reached a blind alley, they can either accept the situation as one they can do little about, or a few can begin to consider the available options that could get the civilization moving again in a new direction. Thus far, most ideas about what needs to be done concerning the future tend to be part of an eighteenth- or nineteenth-century ideology. Even the mentality under Communism tends to remain in the nineteenth century as it seeks to erect a new world order for the twenty-first. This mounting pressure upon men's minds to get mankind moving in new directions will eventually push us into a new civilization oriented toward solving problems—one whose roots exist at present but whose infrastructure may not come into being for another 30 to 50 years. The ideas for working out the details of this civilization are still not in existence. They can only come to the fore of men's minds when the latter develop an irresistable motivation to try to resolve an impassable situation. At present, this problem-solving motivation is daily becoming stronger, much as the incentives for creating the Industrial and Scientific civilization began to develop in the centuries before the acceleration of our contemporary civilization.

Although the lives of most men have been frustrated by events beyond their control, only a few individuals have moved mankind forward. It is difficult to estimate how many men have ever participated in the invention of basic tools, in the selection of plants and animals for domestication, in the development of ideas that led to the making of pottery, of the plow, iron-smelting, the wheel, writing, building in stone, the blast furnace, transportation by steam, the factory assembly line, the fundaments of electricity, and eventually the development of the sciences and growth of knowledge in the arts and related fields. Out of the billions of men who have lived on this earth since man developed into *Homo sapiens,* how many have taken part in the discovery of knowledge? Perhaps one million? I believe that even this might be an exaggeration. The vast majority of men and women who have lived on this planet have added little to the accumulation of knowledge during their lifetimes. Most have been content to live passive, conservative lives existing much as their parents did, sharing much the same ideas and work, and tolerating authorities over them who knew little more than they did. It is possible that at no time has the percentage of creative and innovative individuals approximated one-half of one percent of the total world population. Even in a global population of over three-and-a-half billion individuals, it is highly doubtful whether as many as 5 percent are even carriers of the Industrial and Scientific civilization without whose specialized knowledge the entire industrial and scientific order might wither away.

Rulers of men have always been indifferent to the utilization of the potential creativity that exists in most human beings. Despite the talk about "quality" education, it is highly doubtful whether those who use that term mean the encouragement of *all* kinds of creativity in *all* men (and women). No civilization can be considered efficient that condemns most of its population to work that can best be done by machines, and yet permits very few of them to enjoy their labor. The tiny percentage of those who are permitted to be creative will increase with the decades and with successive civilizations. Perhaps one day in the future there may evolve a civilization whose most important aim will be the development of creativity among all individuals. The future will need to be concerned with the implementation of such a goal, for at the present time we do not know how to utilize the potential which exists in most individuals—just as we seem helpless to improve the intellectual quality of those who make the decisions for mankind.

At the moment, the trends that the future world order may take are very dim, but of one thing we are sure: the world of tomorrow will not be like the world of today or even like the worlds of yesterday. Mankind has not yet reached that plateau beyond which it cannot go. In our present primitive state of civilization, it is highly doubtful that mankind will reach such a plateau even in the next million years. Men have much to learn about themselves and the universe they inhabit. As they learn more, the benefits will not be centered so much in technology as in better interpersonal relations and in more freedom for the individual to grow. Freedom to develop one's potential is prerequisite to the growth of human knowledge.

First, however, it is useful to know something of our beginnings and how far at the present time we have come intellectually.

II   The Beginnings
of Man

It has taken almost three-and-a-half billion years to fashion man out of the first one-celled creatures: thus, one can say that we represent the epitome of three-and-a-half billion years of evolution. If astronomers are correct in surmising that the sun will not explode until more than five billion years from now, then mankind still has time for growth. Nature and man have both wasted a good deal of time in their development: nature has the time, but man has not.

The first one-celled forms of life may have begun after the earth had passed through perhaps one-and-a-half billion years of gradual cooling. It might have taken almost two-and-a-half billion years for the simple one-celled forms of life to evolve into more complex forms of invertebrate life. About one-half billion years ago, even before the first coalfields were laid down and the continents first began to separate from one another, the earliest vertebrates must have darted back and forth in the ancient seas around the new continents seeking food. A little over 300 million years ago, land plants must have begun to cover the continents as they spread slowly to their present positions. It took another 100 million years for the amphibians to take over the swamps and tidal basins, to be followed by the dinosaurs and other large land reptiles who ruled unchallenged by mammals until about 60 million years ago. Despite comic strips to the contrary, the large land and sea reptiles were unaccompanied by man. Although man's primate ancestors may have existed at that time, the apes who later evolved into man followed millions of years after the disappearance of the dinosaurs.

It is difficult to say when the first of man's primate ancestors separated from the other primates. None of the apes living today are ancestors of modern man. The primate ancestors of man evolved into man and in the process disappeared. There is no link connecting, say, the chimpanzee or gorilla with contemporary man. The links are between their ancestors and those of man, and the separation took place at least 20 million years ago. The contemporary apes have gone their way of development to a cul-de-sac that can perhaps never lead to the development of manlike species. Even if some holocaust were to destroy all living men, leaving only a few hundred wild chimpanzees or gorillas alive in remote corners of tropical Africa, it is very unlikely that the descendants of these apes could evolve into thinking men millions of years hence. Their development has carried them beyond the point where they could become such men, and whatever evolving would take place might only bring them further along the ape road. Man is most unique and his path may not be duplicated again by any animals living on this earth. It is also likely that man is alone within our solar universe, that there are no duplicates of him on the sun's more distant planets. Perhaps somewhere off in space, hundreds and thousands of light years away, there may be thinking species on unknown planets around unknown suns. But for the moment we must assume that man is not only unique in the animal world, but that he is alone, and will not meet others with whom he can communicate on other solar planets for a very long time to come, if ever.

Our development has been somewhat unsteady as our primate ancestors evolved from less complex to more complex levels. And here we know more and can speculate more than we could 10 years ago, though we shall know more 10 to 20 to 30 years hence. And obviously our descendants 500 years from now will be able to write a more complete story of man than we can at present.

Dryopithecus, a fossil found in East Africa who is about 17 to 18 million years old, was evidently the ancestor of the modern chimpanzees; he in turn was preceded by a primitive ape, Aegyptopithecus, who may have lived some 28 million years ago in Northern Africa. Man's ancestors could have been both or neither of these, since doubt still exists as to where these two can be placed in the line of man's ascent. On the other hand, there is little doubt that a series of fossils termed Ramapithecus and found in India between 1915 and 1950, and another series of similarly related fossils found in East Africa in the 1960's and called Kenyapithecus, could be part of man's ancestry. Drs. David Pilbeam and Elwyn Simons of Yale are convinced, however, that Ramapithecus was more of a hominid (or manlike) than Kenyapithecus, who was considered hominoid (or apelike). Ramapithecus may have lived in India between 8 to 14 million years ago, while Kenyapithecus could have lived in Kenya as early as 19 million years ago. Dr. Simons is also convinced that Ramapithecus was more advanced, had a slower maturation than contemporary apes, and that his molars permitted him to grind his food with manlike side-to-side movements rather than to chomp in apelike fashion. Both Ramapithecus and perhaps Kenyapithecus walked on their hindlegs. Although the late Dr. Louis Leakey of East African fame was convinced that Kenyapithecus is in direct line of ascent from modern man, Drs. Pilbeam and Simons believe that that honor belongs exclusively to Ramapithecus, whom they consider more man than ape in contrast to Kenyapithecus whom they consider an ape (advanced though he was). It appears that Ramapithecus was perhaps the first primate to move across the border that separated the hominoids or the apes from the hominids, or the manlike creatures. On the other hand, Kenyapithecus, though older and more primitive, might be in man's line of descent—unlike the older Dryopithecus and Aegyptopithecus, who are more the ancestors of contemporary African apes (though an ape such as Aegyptopithecus could conceivably have been a common ancestor of both).

Ramapithecus, who evidently lived in the savannahs of northern India around eight million years ago, could also have been the ancestor of primitive manlike creatures first found in South Africa in the 1920's by Drs. Dart, Broom and Robinson and termed Australopithecines, or Southern Apes (though they lived in Southern Africa, they are not seen today as apes but as pre-humans). We do not know how or when the Australopithicines evolved, but present thinking is that they may have developed out of Ramapithecine ancestors, since less than three million years separate the later Ramapithecus from the first of the Australopithicines (there were at least three and perhaps four species of these early hominids as they evolved from about seven million to a little more than two million years ago). Perhaps the evolving Ramapithecine, who became the ancestor of the first primitive Australopithicine, may have lived about six to seven million years ago (but he is certainly not the giant ape which Dr. Simons found in India, whose jaw indicated teeth that were closer to the Australopithicines than to the apes, and who may have been one of the sidelines that developed as apes evolved into men). At any rate, when an advanced Ramapithecus who walked on his hindlegs and who is no more than six million years old has been found, we will be closer to filling out the gaps in man's genealogy.

It is possible that such an individual has been identified in part of a jawbone found in 1967 at Lothagam Hill in northwestern Kenya, and in 1971 was given a date of some 5.5 million years. The jaw fragment has been identified as belonging to a female, since it appeared somewhat smaller than the jaws in other Australopithicine finds. The hominid was evidently mature and the single tooth was well worn, indicating perhaps an omniverous individual with a somewhat abrasive diet. It is believed that the jaw fragment represents a species very close to Australopithecus Africanus. The dating was done with the use of the Potassium 40 technique on the volcanic sands in which the fragment was found (over a period of tens of billions of years radioactive Potassium 40 breaks down into Calcium 40 and Argon 40). An armbone fragment found in northwestern Kenya in 1966 by Prof. Bryan Patterson, and tentatively given a date of some 2.5 million years, has now been identified as being almost two million years older. The armbone fragment is definitely human and by no means apelike, thus suggesting that the 4.4 million-year-old possessor of this elbow fragment could have had an apelike head and perhaps a human body.

◇   ◇   ◇   ◇   ◇

For millions of years, these pre-men engaged in a way of life that is virtually unknown to us at the present time. We do not know what their social life was like, though it could perhaps be close to that of contemporary great apes. We know nothing of what they ate, but it is more than likely that the earliest of these pre-men were divided into two categories: herbiverous and omniverous. It is very unlikely that the latter did any organized hunting, but it is more than possible that they were scavangers of a sort, eating the remains left behind by the larger carniverous animals. It is also unlikely that they used tools in the early part of this period, though it is possible that sticks, branches, and even stones may have been employed to pry, to kill, and even to defend themselves against other animals. Organized toolmaking does not begin until almost three million years ago. There is little question that from Ramapithecus on, these early pre-men were able to walk and even run on two feet and to use their hands for carrying and throwing. Although some sort of communication existed, no language was used at that time. It is also doubtful that the later social life of early man with his norms, kinship system, and organized sense of group life existed then.

In 1969, a group of French paleontologists, working with scientists from Kenya and the United States along the shores of Lake Rudolf in northwestern Kenya and on the banks of the Omo River in nearby southern Ethiopia, were able to uncover a quartz "pebble tool" which was tentatively dated at 2.2 million years. Though this pebble tool had little in common with the more elaborate stone tools produced by early men 10,000 to 100,000 years ago, yet it was evidently fashioned by early pre-men rather than by nature, for the pebble was chopped on both sides and had a curved cutting edge.[1] The fact that this quartz hand tool was dated at over 2.2 million years suggests that the idea of making stone tools must have occurred to some enterprising pre-man even earlier than this. Conceivably toolmaking could be as old as pre-man himself.

The French scientists also unearthed a small jawbone with 16 teeth, dated at almost two million years, which had one rather interesting characteristic: the wisdom tooth was somewhat smaller than

---

1. A little later in 1970, Richard Leakey found stone flakes chipped from these pebble tools in the Lake Rudolf area of Kenya. The flakes were given a Potassium 40 date of 2.6 million years.

its neighboring molar, thus suggesting an ancestral line to modern man. At the same time, Richard Leakey, the son of the late Dr. Louis Leakey, found an almost complete skull of a pre-man similar to the one found by his mother, Mary Leakey, in Olduvai in Tanzania in 1959—then given the name of Zinjanthropus—which was over 1,750,000 years old. Richard Leakey's later find is almost one million years earlier, or almost 2.6 million years old.

In early November 1972, Dr. Richard Leakey found fragments of a skull bearing what he felt to be striking resemblances to modern man, with a brain capacity of some 800 cc, compared to Australopithecus's 500 cc, and modern man's 1500 cc. The fragments were found in a layer of material that had been deposited more than 2.6 million years ago. It was Dr. Leakey's belief that his new find seemed to displace both the Australopithecines and the later *Homo erectus* as representatives of the early stages of man's development. Dr. Leakey's conclusion, as reported by the *New York Times* of 12 November 1972, was, "There is now clear evidence that in Eastern Africa a truly upright and bipedal form of the genus *Homo* existed contemporaneously with Australopithecus more than 2.5 million years ago."

If Dr. Leakey's conclusion holds, it implies that man's direct ancestor could have been neither Australopithecus or early *Homo erectus,* whom Dr. Richard Leakey considers as sidelines to man, and that man's ancestors existed side by side with other species of pre-men and of men until about one-quarter of a million years ago. If so, we can only hold this development in abeyance until further evidence accumulates, though Dr. Leakey's find at this moment seems to be more of an early Pithecanthropus, or early *Homo erectus* sub-species, rather than that of any *Homo* species related to modern man.

◇   ◇   ◇   ◇   ◇

Here it is necessary to go back and digress to what we know about the early Australopithicines so that we can put some order in this incomplete story of pre-men. The first find, a skull of an infant and named Australopithecus Africanus, was found in 1924 in a limestone quarry some 200 miles southwest of Johannesburg. In succeeding years, four other important Australopithicine sites were found within a radius of 300 miles of this cave. Two separate species were then tentatively identified as Australopithecus Africanus and Australopithecus Robustus, or Paranthropus. The species were then differentiated on the basis of their jaws and molars. Australopithecus Africanus appears to have been omniverous, while Paranthropus with his larger jaw appears to have been herbiverous. The two species may have become differentiated rather early, for the Lothagam Hill jawbone, which has been given a date of 5.5 million years, appears to have belonged to an Australopithicine rather than to a Paranthropus. Zinjanthropus with his large jaw was evidently a Paranthropus, for his worn molars indicated an abrasive roots and vegetable diet. Evidently Australopithecus also seemed to have been the early toolmaker rather than Paranthropus, and both species seemed to have lived side by side for millions of years. Australopithecus Africanus appears to have been the ancestor of a more advanced Australopithicine, first found in 1964 by Dr. and Mrs. Louis Leakey and given the name of *Homo habilis*. The latter was evidently a third species of Australopithecus. He has a very venerable age, for several almost complete skulls have been dated from 1.8 to over 2.2 million years.

If the earliest of the hominid finds, Lothagam Hill, was omniverous, if Paranthropus was vegetarian (though we have no evidence for this)[2] and if *Homo habilis* was a descendant of an advanced Ramapithecus, then we have a link not between Ramapithecus and modern man, but between Kenyapithecus and Paranthropus. It appears now that both of the latter ended in blind alleys, while Ramapithecus and Australopithecus Africanus could have led to *Homo habilis,* or an advanced Australopithecus (or some unknown advanced species that could have been a direct ancestor of modern man), who in turn could have been the ancestor of the earliest *Homo erectus*, who (if present indications are correct) might have been the ancestor of *Homo sapiens* or modern man.

The sizes of all these pre-men or proto-men were all of a small variety. Ramapithecus may have been about four feet tall. Australopithecus Africanus ranged between three-and-a-half to four feet, *Homo habilis* was roughly four feet, while Paranthropus with his heavier jaw was also heavier in weight and ranged about five to five-and-a-half feet tall. As far as we know now, and this may change during the next ten years, Australopithecus Africanus and the later *Homo habilis* were both toolmakers. Paranthropus was evidently not, though Mary Leakey found pebble tools near the site in which Zinjanthropus or Paranthropus was first discovered in 1959. Even Australopithecus Africanus, the early type, was first

---

[2]See Geza Teleki, "The Omniverous Chimpanzees" (*Scientific American*, January 1973) for evidence of meat-eating and hunting among wild chimpanzees in Africa, as well as for material on social sharing of meat. Also Jane Goodall, who in her observations on wild chimpanzees (*Intellectual Digest,* July 1972), reported seeing three chimpanzees eating the meat of a small piglet that they had hunted and killed.

For further evidence of meat-eating, see Irven DeVore and S. L. Washburn, "Baboon Ecology and Human Evolution" in *African Ecology and Human Evolution*, edited by F. C. Howell and F. Bourliere (New York, Wenner-Gren Foundation for Anthropological Research, Inc., 1963).

found near bones of other animals that had been broken for the marrow, and near baboon skulls evidently shattered in order to scoop out the brains. This led Dr. Raymond Dart, the discoverer of the first Australopithicine skull in 1924, to the belief that man comes from a long line of meat-eaters.[3]

There is some speculation today that the separation of the two lines of Paranthropus and Australopithecus could have taken place on the basis of food habits: Paranthropus feeding upon fruits, nuts, and roots had few challenges to his feeble brain. Though he was certainly more advanced than any ape living today and though he might have been able to defend himself and his family by utilizing broken boughs and boulders as weapons, still he might have had little interest in being aggressive toward other animals as long as they left him alone. Australopithecus, on the other hand, had to compete with the other carnivores — learning their habits, snatching part of their kill, driving them away, or separating the young, crippled, or old to kill at water holes. Because Australopithecus was slight or small, he had to learn to utilize his brains and special learning skills in order to compensate for his physical weaknesses. Hunting, stalking, working with others to add to individual strength, learning to utilize tools of various kinds, and making simple stone weapons may have had an effect in increasing the mental capacity of the Australopithicine. Paranthropus evidently became extinct a little less than a million years ago, perhaps made obsolete by the descendants of the later Australopithicines who had already evolved into *Homo erectus* at that time.

Both the earlier and the later Australopithicines were evidently toolmakers, but since stone is the only substance that can survive over millions of years, we have no way of knowing whether the Australopithicines also made tools out of some other material — wood, for example. The pebble tools which have come down to us could be made in a few minutes. When held in the fist, they became effective substitutes for claws and canine teeth. With them, one could wound other animals, sever meat from a freshly-killed animal, and cut up fruits and vegetables. The fact that tools were made perhaps as early as three million years ago suggests that the preliminary invention and first use of them must have evolved long before that, possibly as long as five to six million years ago, with the further inference that toolmaking may have gone hand in hand with the development of the first Australopithicines some six million years ago.

Thus far, Australopithicine and Paranthropus fossils have been found in the Union of South Africa, Tanzania, Kenya, Ethiopia, and Chad — all in Africa. Yet, there seems to be little reason not

---

[3]*Science News*, 23 November 1968, Vol. 94, p. 523.

to expect Australopithicine fossils to be found in the area stretching from Southwest Asia to India, where Ramapithecus first came to light in 1915. Some pebble tools have been discovered in the territory extending from Israel to India, but no fossils that can be readily identified. If the Australopithicines roamed over a larger area than their discovered remains, Paranthropus must perhaps have kept pace with them. But so far no Paranthropus remains have been found outside of Africa.

There is very little we can add to these bare-bone beginnings. We can speculate that the Australopithicines had larger brain capacities than the Paranthropine fossils; that the toolmakers were Australopithicines, though it is likely that Paranthropus might easily have used items that he could pick up, but not make, as weapons of defense. While the Australopithicines were hunters as well as gatherers, the Paranthropicines seemed to be gatherers. Australopithicines might have used the skins of animals, after the flesh had been scraped off with pebble tools, either for softness or for warmth. The Australopithicines had a brain capacity less than half that of modern man; Paranthropus's brain was even smaller than that by 50 percent or only a little larger than that of a chimpanzee. Did either one of them have language as we know it? The answer is probably no. Yet, the Australopithicines were able to fashion their pebble tools generation after generation in very much the same way, indicating a higher form of communication than existed among the apes, along with a greater learning capacity. Although individual apes may be able to fashion a tool of sorts from tree branches, still each individual needs to reinvent the form himself rather than have it come down from generation to generation as a primitive form of cultural learning.

Paranthropus may have been closer to the great apes in his social life, but even here we do not know. The later Australopithicines must have learned the value of banding together in order to fend off larger carnivores and to hunt more successfully. Still, it is doubtful that kinship terms existed or that the Australopithicines had become aware of the important social values of having incest taboos: that is, the addition of new relatives and the subtraction of any divisiveness and hostility between the older and younger males. It is likely that the early as well as late Australopithicines could have developed a rudimentary division of labor in which the males did the hunting, and the females did the gathering and killing of small animals who were within arm's reach. Did fire exist for the later Australopithicines? The answer must ruefully be no. Fire did not come until hundreds of thousands of years afterward when the last Australopithicine was gone and forgotten. As with many of the hunting animals of the present day, it is likely that the Australopithicines slept their empty hours away, ever watchful that none would be the meal of larger carnivores lurking nearby. Darkness must have been a frightening time for both the Australopithicines and the early men who followed. Probably both the Australopithicines and the Paranthropithicines had bodies more similar to modern man than to any of the great apes existing today. We do not know whether they were hairy then or whether as hunters the Australopithicines had begun to lose some of their body hair. We have no idea how many Australopithicines or Paranthropicines there were on earth at any one time, and one guess is as good as another, but one can speculate that there were very few — perhaps no more than 25,000 at any one time of either species, or even of both. The frailties of the Australopithicines make it one of the great mysteries of the past that they survived at all: one can assume that the death rate must have been high at all times and that the young and the old often became prey to the large number of carnivores that hunted either singly or in packs. Like later men, the Australopithicines could survive only by stressing the social and the cooperative. Few could survive living by themselves.

III The First Man: Homo Erectus

While the first Australopithicines have now been pushed back to more than five-and-a-half million years ago, we may also have to place the first men further back than we would have expected ten years ago. We must assume that by one million years in the past an early type of man had evolved from the later Australopithicines. Although these early men were not yet thinking men, they were no longer pre-men or proto-men, but nonetheless a species of men (they must be differentiated from modern man with whom they evidently had little in common). These Pithecanthropines, or *Homo erectus* men, had moved a long way from the Australopithicines, who could have been their ancestors.

While we do not know the exact steps through which evolution takes place or the ways through which genetic drift and change occur over a series of generations, we do know that the end result after hundreds of thousands of years is a changed physical specimen. The changes that brought about the first of the *Homo erectus* fossils must have occurred over a long period of time. This means that, when we date a fossil as having lived a million years ago, we do not imply that a sudden series of changes brought about that living-being a million years ago, but rather that the specimen is a random sample out of a total universe of beings who were similar to it and who lived within hundreds of thousands of years of that date.

We seem to have only one early *Homo erectus* who can compete for the honor of having lived almost one million years ago. He was found in China in 1964 and given the name of Lantien man (since he was found in Lantien county in Shensi Province). A more doubt-ful *Homo erectus* find, a fragment of skull (an occipital bone), was discovered in 1965 in a quarry near Vertesszöllös, 30 miles west of Budapest, Hungary, and given the name of Vertesszöllös man: it seems highly unlikely that the latter fossil is as old as Lantien. This last is evidently older than Pithecanthropus Erectus, first found in 1891 by Eugene Dubois and many years ago given a tenta-tive age of 700,000 years. We are not on very sure ground with Vertesszöllös, for there is still some controversy regarding his age and whether he was *Homo erectus* or a very primitive herald of a later *Homo sapiens*. At any rate, we must assume that, though *Homo erectus* was more advanced than the Australopithicines who were his ancestors (for there may have been more variety even among those who became his ancestors than we can assume at the moment), he was still quite a primitive form of hominid. Another Pithecanthropine fossil was found in Java in the 1930's and still another in 1972 — though little is known of the latter at this writing.

The Pithecanthropines, or early *Homo erectus*, seem to have occupied a larger area of the Old World than did the Australopithicines. Thus far, their remains have been found in Europe, Java, China, and Africa. By the time they disappeared, say about 200,000 years ago, they may have spread into most of the known world. (There is still a good deal of controversy as to whether they survived until about 25,000 years ago in Australia, Java, and Africa. There is also some question as to whether they may have been present in the New World some 200,000 years ago. Until the latter point is proven, it must remain speculative, although the late Dr. Louis Leakey insisted that *Homo erectus* was making his stone axes in California at that time.) We know that the Pithecanthropines, or the early varieties of *Homo erectus*, lived from about one million to about 500,000 years ago, and that more advanced varieties came in approximately during that period. In the Olduvai site in East Africa, a *Homo erectus* skull about 500,000 years old was unearthed: fragments have also been discovered in other parts of the Old World. In the famous cave of Choukoutien near Peking, China, parts of at least 40 individuals were found in the mid-1930's. Although a uranium-thorium date gave a range of from 300,000 to more than 500,000 years, the estimate today is that the *Homo erectus* individuals who lived in this cave may have been there more than 500,000 years ago.

Other *Homo erectus* fossils in Asia and Africa have been given dates of more than 500,000 years. One example in Europe is a hominid jawbone found in the village of Mauer near Heidelberg and given an age of more than 500,000 years. Finds in Hungary indicate thus far that *Homo erectus* must have wandered over that area more than 600,000 to 700,000 years ago. In France, Spain, and Israel, *Homo erectus* left reminders that he had also been there more than 300,000 years ago.

Although the Pithecanthropine fossils seem to indicate that their possessors had a brain capacity of about 900 cc, some 200 cc more than the late Australopithicines and about double that of a chimpanzee, they were still a long way off from the far greater brain capacity of *Homo sapiens* — ranging from 1200 to 1500 cc. Evidence seems to indicate that, though the making of handchoppers or hand-axes changed little over a period of two million years, *Homo erectus* later became a user of fire (it is doubtful that he knew how to make it because of his limited intelligence). Choukoutien man, unlike Java man, evidently used fire, but we do not know whether this was solely for warmth or possibly also for cooking. The sites in which *Homo erectus* fossils were found in Hungary indicate that about 500,000 years ago their tenants also used fire, while fire-blackened hearths associated with *Homo erectus* have been found in France and Spain.

◇   ◇   ◇   ◇   ◇

It is not unreasonable to speculate that the social group among both the Australopithicines and the Pithecanthropines might have been a small hierarchy of dominant males who may have shared the females, at the same time seeing to it that the immature and the less dominant males remained away from the females and dependent upon themselves. The dominant males may not only have tolerated one another within the group, but successfully endeared themselves to the females by being more attentive to them and their young. The young males may in turn have gained by having mothers who were also more dominant, thus assuring that they were tolerated more easily by the older males. The latter may have felt that they could not afford to be tyrannical or aggressive, but had to exercise self-control and cunning in order not to encourage aggressions against themselves by others (at the same time remaining relaxed in order not to threaten the other male and female members of the group).

A social group may have numbered no more than 25 to 40 individuals, consisting of the hunting males, who had worked their way to the top of the pecking order; the females, attached to these males; the young; and the young males, who stayed at the edges of the group and who could in turn challenge the older males only by being more cunning, controlled, and ever-watchful for opportunities. Any young male within the group who may have attempted to challenge the top males stood in danger of not only being driven away from the group, but also of being injured and possibly killed. The young male may have learned to stay within the group by being non-threatening to the dominant males.

Yet, within the social group (and this may have been even truer of the later *Homo erectus*) most individuals must have been taken for granted, were relaxed with the young as well as the old, and cooperated in hunting and fending off danger. At the same time, there could have been a certain amount of group cannibalism, as is indicated by the human bones found at Choukoutien, broken to get at the marrow or at the brains. (Even the Australopithicines appear to have been fond of animal marrow and brains, as revealed by the large number of baboon bones and skulls found nearby.) Since solicitude toward the young doubtless elicited good will from the females (thus permitting early man to handle the problem of longer maturation), the groundwork may have been laid for a later family system with its complex kinship terms based upon role behavior.

Although not many *Homo erectus* fossils have been found thus far outside of Africa (East Africa and Morocco) and the Far East (Java and China), it is more than likely that Europe was also an area of wanderings. Crude pebble tools dated at one million years have been found in France, along with fire-blackened hearths that go back to almost a half million years ago. We know that *Homo erectus* was in Spain and along the southern French coast some 300,000 years ago (or were these primitive *Homo sapiens*?). *Homo erectus* may have lived side by side with *Homo sapiens* until about 35,000 years ago in both Java, where Solo man (who was undoubtedly *Homo erectus*) lived until that date, and in the Omo Valley of southern Ethiopia, where fragments of a *Homo erectus* skull in a stratum dated some 35,000 years ago were found in the latter part of 1969 by Richard Leakey and his colleagues of the Kenya National Museum. (It is possible that the sites may have been disturbed at an early date and that both fossils may be as much as 70,000 years old, but these dates still indicate that *Homo erectus* lived until comparatively recent times.)

Most of the *Homo erectus* fossils found thus far seem to indicate that this species lived between one million to about 350,000 years ago, and that its tools were quite primitive. It seemed to use fire starting around 500,000 years ago, though we do not know how the fire was received (the fire could have come from brush set afire by lightning or even from fresh volcanic lava, or it may have been kept "alive" through feeding for long periods of time). What we do not know is how new forms of fire were obtained once an old fire died out.[1]

---

[1] It is conceivable that the use of fire may have produced revolutionary changes in man's thinking as he became more observant of what it did. *Homo sapiens* would have been required to make the observations, for it is unlikely that *Homo erectus* was intelligent enough to be a perceptive observer, though he certainly knew how to use fire. As *Homo erectus* evolved as an early *Homo sapiens*, he may have learned how fragile fire is. He may also have found that it suggested clues in defining life and death. Fire had to be fed or kept alive, and it could die quickly in high winds or rain. Though pure speculation, it is possible for us to conceive that the death of fire could have given rise to the vague spirits of the winds, the rains, and even the directions from which they came. Perhaps these spirits might also have been considered destructive ones that had to be placated.

With the use of fire, early men were able to drive fierce animals out of caves, and herds of large mammals off cliffs or into swamps. If large animals charged a man with a spear, he could deter their advance with a flaming bough. It is more than likely that being able to tame fire might have given early man supreme self-confidence, for with this superior weapon he could conquer even the largest animals.

We can also assume that the social life of *Homo erectus* was fairly simple. He was evidently not a speculative sort of man. He did not bury his dead, though he may have eaten them — not for religious reasons, but perhaps to allay hunger during times of famine. He was a hunter, but it is doubtful that he attacked animals larger or more aggressive than himself. The Choukoutien cave was found filled with piles of deer bones, thrown to the rear over hundreds of generations (perhaps along with the dead). If he had language, it was certainly primitive and limited, and it may not have included sounds of symbolic meaning. He may have had an elementary form of culture that permitted him to make roughly the same sort of stone tools (and perhaps wooden, bone, or shell ones) generation after generation, indicating that he was receptive to learning from those who preceded him. There may even have been vocal expressions, similar to the lip-smacking and friendly grunts employed by the apes in greeting one another, and similar in sound to the vowels used by man; to be followed later by consonants and glottal stops and also combined with the previous grunts, lip-smacking, and clicks modulated by tongue retraction. Communication of a sort within a band must have existed along with expressions that permitted the young to learn from their elders the techniques of toolmaking, hunting, and the proper social behavior toward members of the band and those outside the band.

◊   ◊   ◊   ◊   ◊

Until we arrive at about 300,000 years ago, there is no evidence of hut building. Even tools are still primitive and there appear to be few changes in them over hundreds of thousands of years. We seem to draw a blank as far as most of *Homo erectus* social activities are concerned. He must have lived generation after generation doing much the same things that his ancestors had done. He made very much the same tools. His social life must have been quite rudimentary, and though he must have enjoyed the company of his fellow *Homo erectus* band members, it is highly doubtful that they held stimulating conversations. Language must have been more complex than that utilized by contemporary great apes, but certainly not to be compared with the ability to symbolize sounds that is used by modern man. There may also have been communication that was more than mere grunts or warning signals. Some rudimentary sort of culture must have existed, based upon simple communicating of knowledge and behavior as well as of the socialization necessary to make the young receptive to this communication.

The bands may also have been small in numbers with perhaps no more than 30 to 40 in a group, containing a core perhaps of about four to six dominant males, ten to sixteen females, and the others children and immature males. The death rate must have been quite high, almost equaling the birthrate for hundreds of thousands of years. The increase in population must have taken place over millenia rather than on an annual basis, with the expectation of life at birth quite low. There was no burial of the dead. The latter were either eaten or left where they died for other animals to devour. Shelters may have been mere lean-tos composed of brush and boughs open to the elements and easily put together. It is doubtful whether *Homo erectus* would have dared to compete with cave lions and cave bears for shelter, except perhaps in winter when the bears hibernated and could easily be killed. It is unlikely that early men lived in caves until they learned to use fire, which they could utilize as a weapon to keep large carniverous animals out.

Homo erectus over a period of 500,000 years must have traveled long distances. Even if one assumes roundabout annual movements of only a few hundred miles, the distance traversed in a thousand years must have been tremendous, and in 5,000 to 10,000 years a good deal of mileage could have been covered. One must assume that *Homo erectus* traveled over a good part of the Old World. If one also assumes that the Chinese varieties of *Homo erectus*, who lived near Peking 500,000 years ago, could have been acclimated to the cold winters that may have existed then (just as their contemporaries in Europe must have met cold on the plains of Hungary and in southern Germany), one must be prepared to admit that in their wanderings *Homo erectus* could have left family hearths near Choukoutien and wandered along the coast northward, perhaps to Kamchatka and to the landbridges that may have covered the present Bering Sea 400,000, 300,000, or even 200,000 years ago. Hunting with the primitive tools of the Pithecanthropine *Homo erectus* of 500,000 years ago may have enabled them to go thousands of miles, even without maps and compasses to tell them where they were going. Northward and eastward may have meant just as much to them as southward and westward. We do kr that *Homo erectus* covered a large part of Africa, Europe, and A a except for the areas then under glaciers. But for most of the time that *Homo erectus* was on earth, there were as many interglacial periods as glacial ones. The population was probably small, and it is possible that the total *Homo erectus* population never numbered more than a few hundred thousand throughout the known world at any one time. *Homo erectus* could have been dispersed over large parts of the globe, perhaps in areas not suspected at present.

Whether there was a division of labor between men and women in the society of *Homo erectus* is unknown, but it is easy to speculate that there might have been some rudimentary division, though by no means the stratification that occurred later. Men could have done the hunting, the defending, and the killing perhaps of strangers or aggressive intruders. Women and children did the collecting — gathering wild fruits, vegetables, roots, eggs, edible insects, and small animals that were easily caught. Everyone must have been kept busy in the eternal quest for food and in the perpetual wandering that must have taken place in seeking it. There were very few possessions as we know property at the present time. Weapons could be fashioned in a few minutes, as could tools for cutting, chopping, and hammering. It is doubtful that *Homo erectus* had clothes at any early period, but it is possible that he may have used skins of animals at a later time, along with fire to keep himself warm. It is possible, however, that he may have learned early to tolerate a good deal of cold. In general, we can assume that until *Homo erectus* began to merge into *Homo sapiens* some 300,000 to 500,000 years ago there was little thought, very little speculation or innovation. Most of the gradual changes that revolutionzed the life of man did not begin until *Homo erectus* passed over the threshold to become *Homo sapiens.* Man, the killer of large animals, did not come into being until that barrier was crossed. And man, the eventual carrier of both complex societal organization and culture, also did not evolve until he passed the border and moved into the everyday life of *Homo sapiens,* with the latter's basic need to articulate through his newly-found symbolic sounds the concepts that would direct his life.

Homo erectus had a culture of sorts. He learned over a long period of time to become an efficient hunter, but unlike other hunting animals *Homo erectus* had to learn more than how to be stealthy and how to hunt certain animals that were plentiful enough to form part of his regular diet. He also had to make certain tools and weapons, and to learn how to get along with members of his group. He evidently had no ideology concerning the kind of world that he lived in with its spirits, magic, and compulsive rites that needed to be employed in order to keep nature moving in a proper arrangement. It is also most unlikely that he told stories around a campfire about his hunting exploits or about those of his ancestors (who could have been forgotten after less than one generation). *Homo erectus* certainly knew the members of his group, with whom he may have interacted in a friendly fashion. Did he know who his ancestors were? Was he conscious of social kinship? Although we do not know and perhaps may never know definitely, we can only speculate that he did not. Music, the dance, myths, magical rites of sorts, philosophical speculation about the universe, its origins and the end of man — all these would have to wait until a later day when *Homo erectus* slowly but surely took the first steps that led him across the threshold that separated him from the then evolving *Homo sapiens*.

IV   The Pathway To Homo Sapiens

We do not know how or whether *Homo erectus* evolved into *Homo sapiens*. We assume that he did, but this is only speculation about a period of time that is gone forever — a period we view with blurry vision in terms of a few hundred pieces of fossil bone, some stratified hearths, old postholes, and thousands of stone tools scattered along river valleys (where these implements were made from the pebbles of chert, quartz, or flint to be found there). We can guess that the transitional period that led to *Homo sapiens* may have started less than 500,000 years ago. Toward the end of that period, it might have been difficult to tell an advanced *Homo erectus* from a primitive *Homo sapiens* — the borderline was by no means distinct. *Homo sapiens* did not wake up one morning after having gone to sleep the night before as a *Homo erectus*. No magic was involved, nor any good fairy present to effect an abrupt change. The biological movement toward changes must have been almost imperceptible over a period of hundreds of generations. During hundreds of thousands of years, mutations accumulated which indicated a fairly important difference in the physical makeup of the human skull. *Homo sapiens* in his earlier form appears to have had a larger brain capacity than *Homo erectus* in his primitive form. In the borderland between the two as they began to approach one another, there may have been little physical differences, with members of one band perhaps having as many varieties of skulls as existed among both *Homo erectus* and *Homo sapiens* at that time.

The border may have been crossed when most *Homo erectus* individuals began to possess skulls with a capacity of more than 1000 cc. The threshold was left behind when their descendants began to develop spines that carried skulls with capacities of more than 1200 cc. The transition was complete when the new *Homo sapiens* began to use frontal hemispheres that had grown enormously in faculty and function within a maximum brain capacity that ranged from 1400 to 1600 cc. But we know of no distinct period of time in which this evolution took place, or of any specific area where it happened.

We suspect the beginning of this transitional period may have occured about 500,000 years ago when *Homo erectus* began to use fire. The Villefranchian or Oldowan simple tools, that were made in similar fashion for almost two million years, now seemed to change. Tools dated around 500,000 years ago were turned out with somewhat more skill and in slightly greater variety. This period, the Acheulian, is named after a site in France, Acheul, that appears to have been an important workshop for *Homo erectus* and his more advanced descendants for a period of hundreds of thousands of years (the period is also referred to as Chellean and Abbevillian after two other French worksites used during a related period of time).

Homo erectus had learned in the course of hundreds of thousands of years to choose the stones that would make the sharpest and the easiest-to-work tools. Through the years, the individual toolmaker became highly skilled at turning out efficient tools in a matter of minutes. An astute *Homo erectus* could have made hundreds, if not thousands, of stone tools in his lifetime. The museums of Europe are filled with tens of millions of stone tools made by perhaps more than a million men over a long period of time. The works of early man have been discovered in innumerable sites in Africa, Europe, and Asia, where he wandered hundreds of miles in his lifetime. But tens of thousands of more miles could have been traversed during the more than 100,000 years of searching for food and exploring river valleys for better flint or obsidian in washed-down river beds. Acheulian tools differ from the more primitive Oldowan by being chipped all over rather than only at one end or on one side. The flakes were evidently used also as cutting tools. The core was prepared in a few minutes by using another stone to make the proper fractures that would open up the rough core; then, with the use of a bone or a piece of wood, chipping off the flakes until one got a core that could be trimmed until, like glass, it became a most efficient chopping, cutting, or cleaver tool. These Acheulian stone tools are longer, larger, and sharper than the Oldowan ones.

The Acheulian tool industry could have produced transitional types of men who may have used fire on a more permanent basis, indicating perhaps that the Transitional Man between *Homo erectus* and *Homo sapiens* knew how to make fire. He may have even learned how to strike two stones together in such a way as to get a fracture in one stone that would lead to a rude core. In his experiments he may have struck chert or flint with a stone containing a larger amount of iron pyrites, or some other ore, which might have set fire to nearby moss or dried grass. Perhaps some such accidental discovery, though repeated often, was not focussed upon for hundreds or thousands of years. It may have taken a long period of time before early man (or, for that matter, modern man) drew the proper practical conclusions. (Though modern man has known about the skeletal similarities between man and other animals for hundreds if not thousands of years, it took a long time before men made deductions based upon these observations.)

Evidence is now appearing that about 300,000 years ago Transitional Men (for want of a better term) made huts for themselves along the coast of the French Riviera, especially at a hunting site near the present city of Nice. At some time between late spring and early summer, a group of hunters spent time seeking elephants, boars, oxen, rhineroceros, and stag. They evidently hunted the young rather than the older, more mature members of these species. At their campsite, they built a large oval hut out of tree branches 26 by 49 feet long with a sunken hearth at one end and a workshop at the other. Here they worked the stones they found along the beach. A variety of volcanic rock found only 30 miles away indicated the boundaries of the hunting territory in which these Transitional Men wandered. The site seems to suggest that the band arrived in late spring, built their huts and hearths, did some hunting, made tools, and then departed, returning evidently at almost the same time during the following years. The fact that the trips tend to coincide at almost the same date year after year may indicate a certain stability of social life in a round of repeated activities. The sunken hearths and the small workshops for making tools suggest this possibility: the weather in late spring along the Riviera does not necessitate the use of fire for warmth alone.

We have very few fossils of this transitional period: part of a skullcap of a young woman who lived along the Thames River some 250,000 years ago, and called Swanscombe after the site; a skullcap and a large part of the frontal area minus the jaw of a similar fossil found in Germany, given a similar age of about 250,000 years, and referred to as Steinheim after the site in which it was found; another crushed skull found in southern France in 1971 and assumed to be about 200,000 years old; parts of two individuals found at Fontechévade in southwestern France, with the skull of one smashed as if he had been the victim of violence (both skulls were given an approximate age of about 175,000 years). In Ehringsdorf, Germany in 1925, fragments were found of men who lived about 150,000 years ago. Fossils of men who lived in Yugoslavia and Italy some 150,000 to 200,000 years ago have also been found. Two skulls discovered outside Rome at the site of Saccopastore indicate a type of early man much like Steinheim, who lived almost at the same time. Although the skulls of these finds leave much to be desired in terms of completeness, they do indicate man who had much of the primitiveness of *Homo erectus* but with a much larger brain capacity, running almost to 1440 cc, or approaching the brain capacity of modern man. If it were not for the larger and longer brain cap, one could say that the facial features of Transitional Man must have changed little from his early ancestors. The larger brain capacity, however, certainly made an enormous difference in the way he lived.

Men in the Acheulian period appear to have been better hunters, had a greater variety of tools, knew how to make fire, and were evidently hut builders — even when they stayed for only a few days. The small bands, probably consisting of no more than 15 to 20 adults, evidently enjoyed more social life — especially around the hearths of their temporary hunting huts and workshops. It is also realistic to assume that a more complex means of communication existed, although it is unclear whether language as we know it was possible then. We can assume that culture played a greater part in their lives than in those of their ancestors several hundred thousand years before.

Transitional Men some 200,000 to 300,000 years ago seem to have used fire for driving animals into traps or a pound. Perhaps they had the ability to make fire since they appear to have used it so readily. Without fire, men would have placed themselves in a trapped position by occupying caves where they could not have escaped more powerful carniverous animals. With fire, men not only drove out animals living in a cave, but kept out those who were searching for a meal. Fire was evidently used as a weapon, as a means of keeping warm, and as a medium for sharpening wooden spears (apparently used at that time, with the charred parts scraped off with stone tools, leaving the hardened and sharpened core underneath to serve as a spearhead). Professor Clark Howell has suggested that men at that period may have used fire to drive larger animals into a swamp, where they were despatched after becoming exhausted trying to set themselves free. Animals were also driven over cliffs through the use of fire, thus assuring that few would survive.

Although Transitional Man was intelligent, a better hunter than his ancestors, a toolmaker creating varieties that early men could not make (including the use of bone tools for fracturing flint in making hand-axes), it is more than probable that he had not yet become a mythmaker. It is unlikely that he was speculative. Yet, our Riviera bands must have had some inkling of the seasons, some rudimentary way of tracking time in order to know when to make their migrations to certain areas, and a primitive calendar to retain in their minds. We have no way of knowing how Transitional Man viewed the universe about him, but we must doubt whether he had any religious or even magical views. The fact that he did not bury his dead may justify the assumption that he did not associate the breath of life with living, or the lack of breath with death. (Later, the breath of life became part of the soul which left the body at death, though it returned to it for rest.)

V   Over The Threshold

Somewhere in the Old World, Transitional Man became more adept at hunting, more socialized, more the speculative animal aware of his insecurities and quite conscious of himself as being temporary, or as one born to die. In the process of becoming *Homo sapiens*, or Thinking Man, Transitional Man left *Homo erectus* far behind and became a more intelligent creature. One can say that he not only crossed the threshold separating modern man from the ancient forms of pre-men and early men, but he became modern man himself — even though physically he looked more like Transitional than like contemporary man. *Homo sapiens* came on the scene a little over 100,000 years ago after tens of thousands of years in the making. He may have been a mixture of *Homo erectus* and Transitional Man, as suggested by Professor Carleton Coon, or he may have evolved out of a large number of different types. We must assume a good deal of variation among ancient man and his descendants, for even in a small population there is enough genetic drift to develop sometimes rather striking morphological differences over a period of hundreds, let alone thousands and tens of thousands, of years. One cannot expect even a small isolated population to remain unchanged physically over a long period of time, say, 5,000 to 10,000 years. (While this may seem like a long time to those of us living in contemporary civilization, it is only a fraction of time when one attempts to view the development of man.)

The earliest *Homo sapiens* populations seem to be associated with the Neanderthaloid types, who in turn are associated with the Mousterian material culture in Europe, beginning about 100,000 years ago and ending somewhat abruptly about 40,000 years ago (though the term "abruptly" may again have been a transitional period of about 10,000 or more years in which a new type arose between the more deviant Neanderthaloid types and the evolving physical types of modern man:(in the Mount Carmel cave near Haifa, Israel, Neanderthaloid skulls were found which have been associated with evolving modern skulls in roughly the same period of time, Skhul I to Skhul V.)

Neanderthaloid man, the new *Homo sapiens*, was more widespread in the Old World than the Transitional Men who preceded him, or the more ancient Pithecanthropine *Homo erectus*. His remains have been found in southern as well as northern Europe, including northern Russia, Czechoslovakia, Germany, France, Italy, and Yugoslavia. He has been found in Israel, Iraq, Iran, and North Africa. Similar physical types have also been found in southern

Africa and Java. His total world population may not have numbered more than one million at any one time, for the increase in growth must have been fairly small over long stretches of time. (Population explosions had to await the inventions of husbandry, agriculture, public health, and the eradication of epidemic diseases — the latter not coming until the end of the nineteenth and the first half of the twentieth centuries in the modern era.)

Although Neanderthaloid man seems to have occupied large parts of European Russia during the warm Eem or Riss/Würm Interglacial period, he appeared to have also been in existence in the colder Glacial Würm phase which followed. We are not sure whether he had clothes, but a Russian archaeological expedition claims to have found in 1969 two human skeletons of boys, aged 9 and 12, in a site 100 miles east of Moscow. The rock strata in which the skeletons were found gave the estimated age of the two skeletons at about 100,000 years, which would put them in the Mousterian Age, or the period in which Neanderthal man flourished. The boys, according to a report of the Academic Institute of Archaeology of the Soviet Union, were dressed in leather pants and shirts trimmed with beads made from mammoth tusks and wore fur-lined leather boots.[1]

◇   ◇   ◇   ◇   ◇

A recent archaeological report from the Soviet Union, which needs to be validated, claims that Neanderthal fossils have been found near Pechora, slightly below the Arctic Circle in European Russia, and that they lived there around 70,000 years ago during the warm Eem Interglacial period (Riss/Würm in Alpine terminology). There is little doubt that Neanderthal man lived in southern Russia, the Balkans, Germany, Czechoslovakia, France, Yugoslavia, and Italy — though there are no finds as yet from the Iberian Peninsula. (This may be due more to the paucity of archaeologists working in Spain than to other factors.)

---

[1]The report of the clothing and the tools found nearby, including arrows, a spear, and a finely-carved needle (all made of mammoth bone), raises a question as to the age given. The use of clothing, arrows, and fur-lined boots suggest a date of about 25,000 years ago. If this is the date intended, then the boys were not Neanderthal. If the date 100,000 is correct, then arrows and tailored clothing were made first in the Middle Paleolithic or Mousterian rather than in the Upper Paleolithic—which began some 40,000 years ago. On the other hand, it is possible that the bow and arrow could have been a late Neanderthal invention along with tailored clothing and harpoon points. If it were Neanderthaloid, it is doubtful that the site is as early as the Russians claim. But again, anything can happen and anything can be true in the still unclear story of man's climb to a more secure existence.

What little we know about Neanderthal indicates that he was not only more intelligent than his predecessors, but that he had succeeded in fashioning a human culture of sorts. We still do not know why the Old Man of La Chappelle-aux-Saints, found in 1911 and evidently suffering from crippling arthritis, was permitted to live long after he was so severely handicapped that he could no longer hunt. We still do not know why a 40-year-old Neanderthal, who was killed by a limestone ceiling which fell on him during an earthquake in Iraq tens of thousands of years ago, was permitted to live even though he was born with a withered right arm which was evidently amputated (but healed) after he was an adult. His teeth, on the other hand, were quite worn as if he had used them as a substitute arm, perhaps for holding heavy objects. His left eye was evidently blinded and, though he could do no hunting, he must have been kept alive by his fellow men some 44,000 years ago. Almost at the same time, a group of Neanderthals in the same area buried one of their fellow humans (perhaps a kinsman) in a grave dug out of the cave floor; the body had been placed on woody boughs covered with large quantities of flowers. Other graves indicated that Neanderthal placed his dead in graves decorated with red ochre, under hearths, with offerings of meat, evidently to accompany the dead. Can it be that these findings indicate the presence of human compassion among bands of Neanderthal men in both France and Iraq some 44,000 to 55,000 years ago? Was the Old Man of La Chappelle-aux-Saints a man who could arrange rituals of a sort, or possessed some needed skill? Was the 40-year-old Neanderthal a keeper of rites, a teller of tales who was kept alive because of his special knowledge, or because he was loved by his parents and fellow men? We do not know, but it is intriguing to recognize definite social traits so many tens of thousands of years ago.

At the same time, Neanderthal had other human qualities: he was speculative and perhaps even concerned with the problems of life and death. He buried his dead for reasons which we do not know, though we can guess at their significance. Evidence indicates that he was cannibalistic, that he ate his fellow man in some sort of ritual, cracking the skull to get at the brains. Here we do not know whether Neanderthal was perceptive enough to believe that the source of intelligence lay in the brain, and that eating the brain of a dead elder or wise man of the band would transfer the wisdom and memory of the elder to the one who participated in this ritual. (Or perhaps the cannibalism was done on enemies who had been captured or killed.) Neanderthal was certainly a religious philosopher, otherwise he would not have buried his dead. He may have concluded at an early date that breath was the essence of life; that the difference between being alive and being dead was the absence of breath, which might perhaps return to sleep or rest in the corpse when it was tired of hovering about. It is possible to speculate that the ghost theory, in which the soul lingered around the area in which it was buried, may have started with the Neanderthal inhabitants of some 60,000 to 70,000 years ago. It is also possible that the spoken wish for good health when one sneezed may go this far back — an expression of hope that the soul will not leave the body during the sneeze. It is possible that Neanderthal man recognized breath as the source of life and was concerned that it stay as long as possible in the body. The burial of meat, food, and flowers in Neanderthal graves suggests a belief in souls that return to the body to eat and to smell.

There seems little doubt that Neanderthal man had clothes, perhaps even tailored clothing, made of skins (leather) and fur boots to allow him to withstand the cold winters in northern European Russia (the winter evenings during the Eem Interglacial period and before the last Glacial must have been close to if not below freezing even in Czechoslovakia and Yugoslavia). In the last Glacial period, the weather in most of Europe where Neanderthal man lived must have been below freezing at least six months during the year. Even in the Israeli and Iraqi areas the weather must have been cold for at least three to four months.

Neanderthaloid tools were on a higher technical level than existed in the previous Acheulian period, and were improved upon in the period which followed. There were bone tools for dressing skins, and in the last period possibly needles and arrows. Spears were made of wood and in the Skhul IV skeleton found in 1939 in Mount Carmel, Israel, wounds appeared which had been made by wooden spearheads penetrating the left thigh bone hip socket. A thin stone blade had also entered the left rib of Shanidar III Neanderthal man some 45,000 years ago during a fight in Iraq.

Caves in Italy where Neanderthal man lived and buried his dead indicated that he was also a believer in magic. In one cave a human skull was found on the floor surrounded by a ring of stones. The skull had been opened at the base, evidently to extract the brains. In another cave near Genoa, an apparent animal-like stalagmite was found surrounded by rounded clay pellets in what could have been a hunting ritual of some kind (whether or not it was will remain uncertain). But Neanderthal man was by that time *Homo sapiens*. He had crossed the threshold that separated earlier man from Thinking Man. He had become a thinker, a speculator. He was a better toolmaker. He was evidently able to articulate his feelings of compassion and empathy. He was able to carry on a primitive sort of surgery in which the patient survived, as is indicated by the Shanidar of Iraq skeleton with its crippled right arm amputated above the elbow. He was also cannibalistic, though we will never know whether this was due to ritual, to magical reasons, or to humiliate his enemies. To engage in these activities, to speculate about life, death, and magic, and to carry on complex hunting and warfare operations must have necessitated the use of a spoken language containing symbols. Neanderthal man in contradistinction to those who lived before he arrived could have had almost a modern form of linguistic communication, though again we shall never know the sounds used to describe everyday activities.

The fossils of Neanderthal man found in Europe, Israel, Iraq, and Africa indicate great variation in features and morphology. In general, one can say that Neanderthal man had facial features that separated him from modern man, but showed his affinity to Transitional or Acheulian man. Some of the skulls found in the Mount Carmel caves in Israel, however, show a progression of features that link Neanderthal with contemporary types of men.

And yet, there is no way of knowing what sort of social bond kept Neanderthal men together. Anything one says is speculation, for there is little data to fall back upon. It is possible to assume that with Neanderthal man's ability to out-think his predecessors, with his compassion, and with his empathy for fellow relatives, he may have developed a rudimentary kinship terminology to indicate to himself the degrees of responsibility and obligation that he owed to those in his band. Altogether his level of accomplishment probably reveals not only a warm degree of relationships within the band but also a sense of unity against the outsider or the enemy.

It is possible too that this sense of a "we" may have led to a development of the incest taboo, otherwise the band would have been torn apart by jealousies, hierarchical struggles, and hostilities against the more dominant males. With incest taboos it was possible to strengthen the relationships of parents and children, even after they were grown, and to keep brothers from struggling against one another. The strength of the band was increased by identifying with a nearby band that might have been closely related to it, so that one can speak of common ancestors that united both. Perhaps nearby there might have been three or four small bands that had split off over a period of years or over one or two generations. Common descent and the seeking of mates in the other band tended to increase the number of close relatives that one could call upon for large-scale hunting, or for help when outside invaders threatened one's hunting territory. Since Neanderthal man, like *Homo erectus*, wandered in his search for game, it was difficult to know whether one's family had wandered hundreds if not thousands of miles since one was born. In traveling, there was always a chance that one could move into territory where non-related bands were also hunting, and conflicts could arise among hostile bands following large mammal herds. Although it is likely that many Neanderthal men were peaceful, others may have been aggressive in resisting intrusions of their hunting territory.

◇   ◇   ◇   ◇   ◇

   With all of his apparent virtues and vices, Neanderthal man evidently reached a cultural level containing a good deal of group or social consciousness, also language (else there would be no burial of the dead), a rudimentary type of religion based perhaps upon magic, cannibalism, and/or possibly a hunting ritualism that predicted success through imitative rites performed in advance.
   Neanderthal man was also a skillful hunter, who evidently decimated both mammoths and cave bears by an aggressive use of fire and by killing hibernating bears in winter. He appears to have been compassionate, but we do not know the reasons for this compassion (modern man has shown very little of it to his crippled young until comparatively recent times). He was also cannibalistic (as is modern man), but this may have been connected with his ritual hunting rites or guarantees for social living. He was evidently a maker of huts and perhaps skin tents: the construction of huts was known at least 200,000 years before he arrived on the European scene. He may also have known how to make tailored clothing and fur boots to withstand the severe cold of the Glacial period. It is also possible, though there is no evidence for it, that he may have used bows and arrows and even harpoons during the last stage of his existence in Europe. All in all, Neanderthal man was able to increase the small sum of knowledge which he inherited from Transitional Man, and may have added social items for which we still may not give him proper credit.

VI The Revolutionary Age of Modern Man

Sometime around 35,000 to 40,000 years ago, Neanderthal man apparently disappeared and modern man (modern in every physical sense) emerged in Europe, Asia, Africa, and the New World. Most of the modern subtypes of men were already in existence some 40,000 years ago, and by 30,000 years ago every conceivable place where men could live was inhabited by modern *Homo sapiens sapiens*. He lived in Australia, North America, probably South America, and almost all of Europe. As the Ice Age receded and the rains moved northward, he followed them — and in doing so permitted new deserts to separate him from other subspecies. Modern man has evolved over a long period of time, and it is possible that his physical beginnings and developing morphology extend back at least 70,000 years. He is mixed with Neanderthal, though he obviously evolved beyond Neanderthal with roots which may be separate and which may go further back than 70,000 years ago. His origins are clearly more mixed than we are aware of at the present time.

Even 40,000 years ago, the mixture of individuals from isolated groups and between groups must have produced a wide variety of physical types. The severe dry cold of Siberia required individuals who could adapt to its winter climate. Those living in high altitudes had to adjust to the thin air and the difficulties of expending energy in high elevations. Others hunted in flat savannah country under year-round sunshine. Others for tens of thousands of years lived and died under cloudy skies near the edge of glaciers and lost a good deal of their ancestral pigmentation. Over a period of at least 70,000 years in such areas of Europe, men became white (or pinkish tan) with light-colored eyes and hair.

Other individuals living in the green savannahs of the Sahara came under sun-burning rays in temperatures that were perhaps higher than those of the body. It was necessary for the latter to develop mechanisms to cool the air brought into the lungs and to help the physique evaporate large quantities of heat. In the mountainous areas where the air was thin and cold, the nostrils had to heat the incoming air. In the cold dry Arctic air of Siberia, there was a need to protect the eyes and cheeks with fat padding and to conserve the heat of the body.

All the above does not mean to imply that the morphology of modern man functioned in a one-to-one correlation to the changing environment. A good deal of physical evolution must have taken place that had little or nothing to do with the physical environment in which one was placed. Adaptation to nature's whims should not be seen in a deterministic cause-and-effect relationship irrespective of many other factors. Despite the loss of pigmentation that may have occurred in individuals along the edges of the European glaciers (Asia with its intense cold had almost no glaciers because of its low rainfall), there must have been a continuous mixture of genes from those who wandered into their areas from other climates — and who possessed other pigmentations and hair forms.

One can assume that even along the glaciers of Europe, there was no pure 100 percent "Nordic race" 40,000 or 30,000 years ago. Perhaps the admixture that occurred each century might have affected almost 20 percent of the population. Over a period of tens of thousands of years (the period we are concerned with here), there was probably no single individual who did not have ancestors of varying heights, head shapes, pigmentations, and hair forms. Certain characteristics may have been dominant over others, and a good deal of genetic drift must have taken place. The mixture of genes with those from outside Europe was doubtless ongoing, though at present we have no way of ascertaining specifically how this took place.

Bands that moved into new territory must over a period of years have been accepted as near-relatives by their neighbors, thus permitting mates to be exchanged. Children may have been adopted in order to bring the bands closer together. It is probably safe to assume that there were many blondes in a darker population, and dark-headed dark-eyed individuals in a blonde population. Kinship and a sharing of common goals rather than physical appearance must have determined a band's friendliness or hostility. (In the modern world, possession of the same skin color does not inhibit bloody civil wars or massacres, whether they are of Turks against Armenians, Hausas against Ibos, Hindus against Moslems, or Poles against Ukrainians. Color prejudice is a modern rationalized reaction and is generally associated with class or slavery.)

It is also possible that bands composed of blondes could have moved into other regions hundreds if not thousands of miles away, and their descendants in time could have changed their physical types. It was only in the early twentieth century with the spread of the blonde racist myth that an original "blonde" and "blue-eyed" people was postulated. Perhaps bands of individuals moved thousands of miles from, say, Asia or Africa into Europe, where they mixed with bands already in existence. Bands of men moved across the landbridge of the Bering Straits, mixing as they moved along. (There is still no evidence that men may not have been in the New World before 40,000 years ago.) It is also possible that individuals whose ancestors came from Asia or Africa moved across the fields of Jutland 40,000 to 60,000 years ago, or ones whose ancestors came out of Western Europe moved into Indonesia or Australia to mix with those who came from somewhere else.

This random and continual wandering makes it virtually impossible to try to find the original "human nature." Over a period of tens of thousands of years, men have evidently never been isolated from one another. Diffusion of behavior, beliefs, material objects, hunting techniques, and other aspects of living must have gone wherever there were people who could move them, and men and women who were receptive to them. Ideas may also have traveled to areas where men did not need them, either because they felt that their own were superior or because they could not see how the new tools or ideas would benefit them. Study of primates may help us guess at the life led by our proto-men ancestors. But once man learned to speak in symbols, once he organized himself socially, and once he began to experiment in producing new or more efficient tools, he became influenced by the ideas that slowly diffused around the known world of human society. At present, the contemporary social scientist can only ask, just how does one get underneath the layers of diffused ideas, techniques, and models of behavior? How does one dig down layer by layer to try to determine the original pristine quality of the human being as he emerged into a cultural world that continually shaped him to the ideas developed by the elites that governed him and thought for him?

On the same basis, it becomes narrowly ethnocentric to assume that the centers of man's ideas and development took place within the confines of contemporary Europe. Men must have developed ideas in Southwest Asia, Southeast Asia, along the Asian coast, in the Indonesian archipelago, Australia, Africa, and even in North and South America. Why should we assume that ideas developed first in Europe and then spread to Asia, Australia, and North America? Why not assume that a good many ideas and concepts came to Europe from Africa, Asia, Australia, and North and South America?

Over tens of thousands of years, *Homo sapiens sapiens* had slowly been accumulating ideas about hunting, the making of tools, the family, the band, and the outside world of souls, ghosts, and unknown forces. These became the basis of a human culture that was increased and diffused over a period of tens if not hundreds of thousands of years. The core developed by Acheulian and Mousterian men were added to by the men who lived in the Upper Paleolithic in Europe who created what are called the Gravettian, the Perigordian, the Solutrean, and the Magdalenian cultures. But men in other cultural areas also made contributions. The basis of human culture goes back before the arrival of modern man. As we have seen, the making of fire, of human habitations, of a rudimentary social life, and perhaps even of a rude language go back to the Acheulian period of 200,000 to 300,000 years ago — if not before. Neanderthal man made contributions which were more than mere additions or accretions: he perhaps added a whole new dimension in man's thoughts about himself, about life, death, the purpose of existence, and about the world that man had created in his attempts to adapt to the reality that he had defined as existing around him.

The presence of less or more pigmentation goes back before the beginnings of modern man to ancestors who lived under a hot tropical sun in the savannahs of Africa, or under cloudy skies along the edges of European glaciers. By the time modern man came on the scene, the mixing with men of other pigmentations must already have taken place. Along the Mediterranean by the second millenium B.C., the mixing with darker Australoid-appearing individuals must have been going on for quite a while. Europe is a peninsula of Asia, and in the period of the last glacier was connected with that immense continent and with northern Africa. Before the seas were created as a result of vast glacial melting, Asia was connected with the huge continents of North and South America. There was little to stop migrations from Western Europe over the steppes of Siberia to the highlands around Lake Baikal, thence northeastward to Alaska, and thence southward down the continents. Conversely, migrations no doubt occurred the other way. There was little to hinder men from south of the Sahara migrating through the grasslands of that area to the lands now occupied by the Mediterranean, and thence northward into present-day Europe.

Since men tens of thousands of years ago had no compasses and since animals and men were continually on the move seeking better hunting or grazing, one can assume that no boundary markers were encountered to forbid them from continuing further. The separation of men into restricted areas is comparatively recent. In modern times, new artificial borders have not prevented Europeans from moving into Africa, Asia, and North and South America; Africans from moving into Asia, Europe, and North and South America; and Asians from moving thousands of miles away from their homelands. Just as contemporary migrations have had little effect upon the receiving populations, so we must assume that the total number of genes exchanged perhaps never formed a majority of the population in any particular region. Even a percentage of gene mixture as low as 20 to 25 percent is all that is necesary to keep human beings on the same potential biological level throughout the world. No group can be considered deviant in mental ability or in the biological faculties that make possible human learning and living. One must assume that man has always been part of a world-wide social fabric that has interconnected him with his fellows living elsewhere. Isolation may take place over hundreds of years, but not over thousands or tens of thousands. This is why collecting ethnographic data on primitives around the world gives us an idea of human cultural variety, but it adds nothing to our understanding as to what the "original human nature" was—if such a thing ever existed.

Once men acquired complex language with thousands of symbols, they were able to develop hypotheses about the world they lived in (even Neanderthal man was evidently able to do this). Language permitted a complex system of kinship, utilizing terms and roles with reciprocating behavior and expectations. Men were able to talk to one another about their ideas and dreams. They could observe and articulate their observations. They had the means for socializing their children in greater detail. They developed an empathy for other men. And their need for security encouraged them to identify with the spirits of the animals they had killed, begging their forgiveness — on the assumption that animals had been put on earth to feed men, as parents feed children.

In the need to find hope for the future, magic began to play a greater role. Attempts were made to imitate nature in art, music, and dance in order to control it. Perigordian and Magdalenian men in France some 20,000 to 30,000 years ago tried to create reality for themselves by drawing pictures on walls in almost inaccessible recesses of caves. The more animals one painted, the more there would be to hunt and be killed by the men who first brought them into existence on the walls of caves hundreds of feet away from the outside openings. The caves represented the wombs of life, and the men were attempting to imitate what they felt went on in the dark wombs of the females. They identified the animals with man's social reality by postulating fathers and heads of animal families who could be appealed to, placated, and encouraged to supply their human children with animal flesh.

The dance was also a form of imitative hunting magic. Men undoubtedly dressed in the skins of dead animals, and imitated their behavior in order to bring them into a close interacting relationship with the hunters. Music may have begun when men imitated the whistles of birds, the cries of mammals, and the roar of thunder — in the belief that imitating would give them the power to control the living things of nature and nature itself.

Men were also aware of changes in the seasons, as they had been for hundreds of thousands of years before. But now they evidently began to keep careful records of the number of days which elapsed between changes in the moon by carving small dots on pieces of bone. There existed an awareness of the first quarter moon and the full moon. By observing the heavens in greater detail, they began to wonder what brought about daylight and what the night. Perhaps daylight was correlated with life, and night with its absence — which would mean that there was a compulsion to keep life going, possibly through the use of sacrifices, rituals, or taboos. Magic presupposes cause-and-effect relationships, and men who were dependent upon the vagaries of nature had to engage in acts which would ensure a predictable rather than a random order in nature.

Upper Paleolithic man was modern in almost every sense of the term. Through the exercise of his large brain, his understanding of the forces around him was continually growing. He had picked up a good accumulation of human learning that had developed hundreds of thousands of years before, and had added his own contribution. He felt insecure in a world in which he and his family were continuously threatened. He needed to know why he loved, why he became ill, and why he died. He needed to understand his own behavior and that of those around him. He needed to know why there was enough food some of the time, but little or none at other times. He had to know the behavior of the animals that he depended upon for food, where he could find them, and how he could assure a supply. He had a compulsion to know why the weather changed: why there was rain and snow, heat and cold, and who or what were responsible for the erratic changes of nature. Although he may not have known the exact reasons for any of the insecurities that bothered him, he could at least develop explanations that sounded rational to him. What he did in the past, man is still doing at the present time; for careful scientific research on these problems still has not provided adequate answers, and we must too often say that we do not know. But Upper Paleolithic man could not live generation after generation, millenium after millenium, in the belief that he did not know (without becoming overwhelmed by his daily insecurities). He had to operate as if the answers were known, as if he could find the reasons for the insecurities that he faced.

And so, we find Upper Paleolithic man drawing his beautiful murals on cave walls that are difficult of access in France and Spain, and on rocks in North and South Africa, Australia, and North America. We find him working on small statuettes of female torsos with exaggerated breasts and hips, but with faces that are featureless (a few have been found with noses and braided hair, though no other features). These small figurines have been found by the thousands. Did their sculptors look upon them as magical forms of creating life, as the murals could have been? With a high birth rate but with an equally high death rate, babies were needed to keep a band alive. Perhaps the statuettes of pregnant women were expected to help bring about pregnancy. Although Upper Paleolithic man may have understood the process of mating in producing the young, he may also have believed that insuring the success of the mating act was as important as performing it. Religion and magic were means of ensuring success in what one attempted to do.

At the same time, Upper Paleolithic man must have been aware of unknown forces in the universe which were dangerous if the human being came into contact with them. It was as if there were high-amperage hidden wires surrounding one, which needed to be charted by someone with the gift of X-ray vision who could see them when most others could not. Death, illness, and famine were all part of the invisible forces which existed and had a reality of their own. One invited them to work their evil if one let down one's guard or failed to create a protective armor to keep one safe. Seeing and identifying the unknown forces and creating encircling shields required an exploration of the invisible universe and the nature of the dangers that existed within. Perhaps this need led to the role of the early shaman, the individual with power to see the unseeable, a talent which he had received as a reward, or in exchange for a gift, from the forces that manipulated the dangers of the unknown world.

Further, men were beginning to create a more diversified division of labor. In Acheulian and Mousterian days, the division of labor was probably simpler: men did the hunting and women the gathering; men did the protecting and women the caring for children. Men made the simple tools for hunting, skinning, and chopping; perhaps women made the tools that were concerned with simple housekeeping. As human society became better organized, certain individuals were freed from the cares of hunting to engage in magic in order to ensure the success of the hunters. Perhaps such a division of labor may have existed in Neanderthal days, which could explain why Shanidar and La Chapelle-aux-Saints might have been kept alive, despite their apparent inability to hunt.

In Upper Paleolithic times, bands became larger. Possibly the genesis of the clan and the concept of shared ancestry among many bands may have been in existence. While the incest taboo, resulting in the selection of mates outside the band, may have started in Acheulian or Mousterian times, it was certainly in existence when Upper Paleolithic man roamed his known world some 30,000 to 40,000 years ago. By that time, it had become evident that exogamy, or the acquisition of mates from the outside, strengthened the band by doubling the number of relatives (since the mate and the mate's relatives then became part of one's kinship group). There may have existed a series of prohibitions concerning whom one could mate, based upon the experiences of the past as well as upon the expectations of reciprocal behavior then in existence. Role behavior, or learning the group's expectations of how one should behave as a male, a female, a father, a mother, a grandfather, an uncle, aunt, or cousin may have become quite fixed by the time man had evolved as far as 20,000 years ago.

We know nothing, of course, about the myths, legends, or stories that could have been told around camp fires 20,000 to 40,000 years ago. But language and memory by that period had become important characteristics of the human mind, and verbal accounts of great events must have been passed down through successive generations. Over thousands of years, the earthquakes, floods, extremely cold winters, hot dry summers, and human as well as nature's catastrophes inspired stories which with a certain amount of modification over the generations eventually developed a morality of their own to explain why these events happened. Hundreds and possibly thousands of years after the events, the tales and myths gradually became edited to make them more exciting and to retain human interest. But a germ of authenticity probably continued which could have provided the observer of 20,000 years ago a certain amount of insight as to what might have happened in the past.

Over a period of generations, the bands met strangers coming into their areas, and they themselves may have moved into other regions where their ancestors had never been. We know little of how the contacts took place, or whether they were hostile or friendly. We can assume that these meetings were friendly when bands exchanged mates, and that they were hostile when the other band was withdrawn and refused to exchange goods, women, or children. One must also assume that migrations were south to north as well as the opposite, and east to west as well as west to east. Man could well have persisted in holding on to his culture, as he slowly changed his physical characteristics in moving from east to west and then the reverse; and in his migrations could have left a good part of his genes as well as part of his culture with bands with whom he had had friendly relations.

We cannot assume that the large game animals moved only in one direction unless we also postulate that there was a line of men advancing behind them, thus making it impossible for the mammoths and woolly rhineroceroses to reverse their directions. This could have happened, of course, but one must also posit a more random moving of men and animals without definite direction, for men in all parts of the world were too few 20,000 to 40,000 years ago to be able to destroy everything in their path. (Even the buffalo in the territory now comprising the United States was not wiped out by the more numerous Plains and Woodlands Indians: it took the building of railroads and the arrival of nineteenth-century European and American "sportsmen" to accomplish the near extermination of this species.)

There is more known about the material culture of European and American men who lived 20,000 to 40,000 years ago than there is about their social way of life. We know that they built huts in the south and skin-tents in the north. They had developed an amazing variety of stone, bone, flint, obsidian, and wooden tools. Their workmanship had become more specialized, as is indicated by the Solutrean spearheads and arrowheads, and the Clovis and Folsom points of later men in North America. Men also learned to fashion stone awls and bone needles. They were able to make thread out of the sinews of the animals they killed. They could survive the frigidly cold regions in the tailored clothing which they sewed from the skin and furs of Arctic animals (tailored clothing, awls, needles, and thread may have also arrived before modern man developed). The world of the Eskimo, with his complete self-sufficiency despite Arctic isolation and polar cold, seems to have existed 20,000 to 30,000 years ago. Few modern men could learn to adapt to a world where they had to make everything themselves, though the men who preceded us tens of thousands of years ago were able to do so. Self-sufficiency was what the children learned from their parents: how to get their own food, how to make necessary tools, how to build their own shelters, make their fires, tailor their clothing, and adapt themselves to a world in which few men were their friends (most could be their enemies).

Thirty to 40,000 years ago, modern men existed in all climactic areas capable of habitation, even in regions then covered by glaciers. They adapted themselves to intense winter cold and long dark nights: also to burning heat, and warm and humid evenings filled with insects that brought diseases and discomfort. They were able to make adjustments to severe cold that were not improved upon until fairly recent times — also to tropical heat as well as arid and semi-arid regions (though it took the domestication of the horse and camel before man was able to manage both steppe and desert conditions comfortably).

It is difficult to say what sort of social controls existed 20,000 to 40,000 years ago. One can postulate that the bands were autonomous and that such a political organization as the tribe had not come into existence. Yet, the latter was functioning 10,000 to 15,000 years ago. The band could have been governed by those in hierarchical position over others, either the old who were the successful hunters, or the middle-aged (but probably neither the young or the women). Possibly one or two men were viewed as father-figures possessing the father's authority. We must assume that democratic or egalitarian behavior is recent in time, that 10,000 to 15,000 years ago hierarchies and authoritarian behavior were more the norm than the exception. Later, the strong authoritarian father-figures might also become the deities or the latters' high priests. At this period, however, the apparent authoritarianism and rule by strong hunter-warrior figures do not necessarily mean that the band had deities upon which it felt dependent or which it worshipped as important father-figures. Deities may have come later with the development of agriculture and the growth of a pastoral economy. At this period, we can assume that a network of spirits was fantacized which it was necessary to placate or manipulate through magic rituals of various kinds.

One must also assume that the roots of a later agricultural and domestic pastoral system could have been in existence 20,000 years ago; that men were experimenting in planting seeds that required human help; that instead of killing young animals with their mothers, they saved the little ones to rear them in a human setting as pets, either to be killed later or to be freed at adulthood (though the latter seems unlikely). Perhaps necessity or experimentation in eating wild plants might have eventually led to the domestication of specific plants. Perhaps returning to sites visited the year or years previously could have led to the discovery that certain plants can be duplicated if their seeds are collected and placed in the ground. A receptivity toward keeping certain young animals as pets and later as food may have encouraged someone to perceive the large-scale consequences of reserving particular animals for breeding purposes rather than killing all of them for food.

At any rate, there is a vague possibility that somewhere in Southeast Asia about 20,000 years ago, faint observations were made that could have led to the later development of a garden horticultural economy; that in the same area and perhaps also in Southwest Asia along the Zagros Mountains near the present border between Iraq and Iran, a pastoral economy (based upon the domestication of certain types of animals that are receptive to living under man's control) could have come into being first as observation and later as concept. The institutionalization of these concepts into workable social systems perhaps came into being 10,000 to 12,000 years later. Southeast Asia could have been the center for this agricultural experimentation since it was probably on the crossroads of diverse cultural influences, just as the Zagros Mountain area could have been the center for the domestication of the goat and the sheep.

Apparently by 20,000 to 40,000 years ago, all institutions of modern man were in the first stages of growth — though their birth may go back to the beginnings of the Acheulian and Mousterian periods. Men at that time might also have been experimenting with basketry, after having in certain tropical areas fashioned vines into fishnets. Using clay as a water-proof lining for baskets may over thousands of years have led to the discovery of pottery-making, again in those areas that were located on the crossroads of diverse peoples and ideas. Men also learned to make efficient bows and arrows, and spear-throwers (it is not known whether the latter may have come first and triggered the invention of the bow and arrow). We also have no way of knowing whether the invention of the bow and arrow, the spear-thrower, or the harpoon might have preceded the arrival of modern man. These could also have been developed slowly by Neanderthal man, but until more archaeological information becomes available, we will not know which came first or where.

◇   ◇   ◇   ◇   ◇

It is possible that modern men crossed the Bering Straits from Siberia to Alaska some 40,000 to 50,000 years ago, and perhaps even before that if we can assume that men learned to adapt to a cold climate for tens of thousands if not hundreds of thousands of years before. It is not unrealistic to speculate that men of the Acheulian period might have made that migration time after time. We must assume that migration is a two-way street and that those who crossed the land-bridge from Siberia to Alaska unwittingly could have returned without moving southward into the present-day territory of the United States, Central or South America. One can also speculate that those who moved into South America could have reversed their line of march and over thousands of years returned to North America, Alaska, or Siberia.

Modern man by that time was walking rather than shuffling, just as he had learned to shuffle after crawling and creeping. In the next revolutionary phase he jogged, while in the one following that he ran, then rode on horseback, and finally in our period moved in cars and airplanes. In the days to come he will move at the pace of space ships, and who knows how fast he will race in the next few thousand, let alone the next few hundreds of thousands, of years? Man after a long period of slow development is now on the move.

VII   A New Food Supply And A New Civilization

At one time we used to refer to the second great revolutionary age of man as the Neolithic. This was the period in which man began to polish his stone, flint, and obsidian tools. But today we need a more descriptive term because the importance of the period lies not in polished stones but in the fact that man invented almost all the forms which are used in modern tools, learned to domesticate animals, and to cultivate his crops in a settled village existence. The period once referred to as Neolithic preceded the growth of civilization. It contained that phase wherein men first began to develop the ideas and institutions that led thousands of years later to the organization of men under bureaucratic administrative, priestly, and military hierarchies that continue even today.

By the time men had come to this period some 10,000 to 12,000 years ago, they had already learned to live in groups, develop norms and values, organize a complex language with its symbols of kinship and role behavior, create a body of beliefs that attempted to explain the mysteries of life, death, disease, misfortune, and chance. Neolithic man had done a good deal of moving about by this time, but settling also slowed him down, although mass migrations continued through the twentieth century. The small organization of the band expanded to include many bands, and these in turn subdivided to include descent either through the father, the mother, or both. Above the complex of bands was the tribe, which when too large or unwieldy split into branches or segments which retained the former's kinship system, including lesser obligations to distant relatives. Later, the tribe did not split but became even larger as it was headed by a complex bureaucracy using a common language and a common set of myths which traced not only descent but the development of common goals. Government may have come into being as the new complex, organized tribe began to conquer non-tribal peoples and incorporate them within the hierarchical set-up as social inferiors to do the bidding and servile work for the good of the new complex.

We are, however, getting ahead of our story concerning man's entry into the second great revolutionary period of rapid cultural growth. For thousands of years, men not only experimented with developing new forms of tools, new types of materials for clothing, and new sources of food, but they were also beginning to ask themselves about the purposes involved in living. While *Homo erectus* was satisfied with merely living, and Acheulian and Mousterian men with getting through each day with enough to eat, a good shelter, and a certain amount of social and sexual companionship, men in the Neolithic period began to ask themselves whether there wasn't more to life than just hunting and eating. Some men were becoming more concerned with their social identity, and there must have been a few who wanted to know who they were and what they wanted out of life. Goals for most individuals in the Neolithic Age were still based upon having enough to eat, a dry warm place for shelter, and enough clothing to protect against the elements. But a few men were also looking at the skies at night and wondering whether those points of light were live spirits which moved to different positions at different times of the seasons. By 20,000 years ago, men had probably developed a calendar of sorts wherein they noted that changes in the heavens coincided with the waxing and waning of the moon, and that there were differences in the sun's heat in winter and summer. Perhaps they gave names to the seasons. Though men might not have kept an exact track of time, they were aware of events occurring in terms of the number of full moons that had passed since a fixed point. Perhaps they noted the numbers of winters or summers that had elapsed. We will probably never know what names men gave to the periods in which the full moon occurred or the seasons of the year. One must assume, however, that since men had a notational calendar 20,000 years ago, they could have named the periods for which they made the notations. (They might have had such a calendar as far back as 40,000 years ago. We also have the archaeological puzzle of Acheulian men coming to the seashore for a few days between the end of spring and the beginning of summer 200,000 to 300,000 years ago.)

The original simple social hierarchies existing among the men who preceded modern man were evidently continued, but modern man began to consider that warrior behavior by young men held special virtue. One suspects that modern men with their love of warfare were more violent than Upper Paleolithic or Neolithic men. But the latter two could also have been warlike. Perhaps there were gradations in status based upon warrior-role behavior, with the highest status possibly going to middle-aged and old men who were warriors, above-average hunters, and authoritarian heads of large families. If this were so, then young hunters might have felt social incentives which approved their becoming aggressive and stealthy not only toward the four-legged animals whom they killed but also against the two-legged ones, who if they were outside the band occupied the same category. Young men were trained to be hunters and their status was based upon how efficient they became. It is only a step from hunter to warrior, however. One can easily imagine the status of a young man becoming so dependent upon his ability to kill both animals and men that death was preferable to the ignominy of ineffectiveness in this all-important masculine social characteristic.

One can also imagine that, though men 20,000 years ago were still concerned with finding enough to eat, entertainment in the form of rituals, dances, specially organized hunting parties, and social occasions with friends may have made life fairly pleasant at times.

Family life may also have been organized, and opportunities available for young adolescents to carry on romantic episodes with girls from related bands. Although nothing is known of any social contracts existing between men and women living together in those days, it is possible to assume that some sort of ritual probably cemented a relationship among the families of the partners. Friendships may have held high social value, and mutual aid between men may have stemmed from the social intimacies of their families.

As for the lives of the women and children, again we can only speculate. Marriage as a social contract must have taken place early when the bride and bridegroom were barely above puberty. Life was short and children most important if the band was to survive. Girls were important to the band as future mothers. They possessed highly developed skills, such as skinning animals and preparing their leather for clothing—probably a female task from the beginning. Though men made the implements employed in hunting and fighting, it is possible that those tools that women used in preparing skins and sewing clothing, along with vessels for storing, eating, and carrying might have all been made by women. It is not known whether 20,000 years ago a bride-price was demanded for giving up a girl, or whether the making of clay "Venuses" was intended to make it easier to obtain certain girls from nearby bands.

It is possible that among both men and women certain individuals were reputed to have the powers to cure and even to kill, and various men and women were the band's repositories for myths, songs, dances, genealogies, and rituals.

Who were the men and women who roamed the earth some 20,000 to 30,000 years ago? It is difficult to say, but one can speculate that they were well mixed and belonged to no "pure" races. The contemporary subtypes of men largely represent the result of men becoming fairly stationary in agricultural villages beginning with 12,000 to 15,000 years ago. Two thousand years ago, men were far more isolated from one another in terms of potential breeding than they were, say, 10,000 to 12,000 years before the present. What we term "European," "Polynesian," "Mongoloid," "American Indian," "African," or "Australoid" may be products of the last 20,000 years rather than of the 20,000 to 40,000 years before that.

At any rate, enough isolation existed to produce startling changes in groups that were fairly isolated over hundreds if not thousands of years. There were enough familial variations, even when intermarriage with other bands took place, to develop certain local characteristics. These must have been of more than one kind, with facial characteristics blending with those of neighbors to pro-. . . . . duce conspicuous differentiations if compared, say, with the local characteristics of bands who lived 2,000 to 3,000 miles away.

Despite the exchange of genes, we must assume that no more than 10 to 20 percent of all the genes available to man were ever brought in from the outside, and this slight exchange would certainly not have affected local characteristics too much. Even a continuous exchange of genes from darker-skinned groups would not have been reflected in a population of blondes along the glaciers in Western Europe. There would have been a small percentage of redheads, one or two dark-headed and dark-eyed blonde-skinned individuals—or conversely, individuals with blonde hair, blue eyes, and a brunette skin. A few could have had thick straight blonde hair, and a few would have had curly, wavy, or even peppercorn hair. At the same time, a migration of blondes into a dark-haired and dark-skinned area would only perceptibly have lightened the skin of the descendants, and would not have had too great an effect upon eye or hair color.

Like the proverbial iceberg, the facial features or hair forms that one sees are only a slight indication of the genes that exist in all human cells. Since man shares more of his genetic structure with even the most distant specimens of mankind than not, we can assume that all of the mixing and interbreeding over hundreds of thousands of years have tended to make men throughout the world more alike than unlike. Certainly as a domesticated animal, man shows fewer of the differences that divide dogs, cattle, or indefinite subspecies. So the answer to the irrelevant question: were there "pure" races 20,000 to 40,000 years ago must be negative, just as the same question asked of today merits the same response.

There were mixtures in Asia that roughly shared the characteristics of those who today are termed "Mongoloid," but there must have been many individuals in these groups who shared characteristics that could have been termed "Australoid," "Caucasoid," or even "Negroid." In a very generalized fashion, one can speak of "Negroid" physical characteristics (that may have developed only in the last 40,000 to 50,000 years), or one can speak of "Caucasoid" in the sense that an Iranian may share a large number of his features with a Frenchman or a German, though also with his neighbors to the East. On the other hand, one can say that most of the generalized characteristics of the broad mass of men in the contemporary world may have been in existence 20,000 to 40,000 years ago: that is, the depigmented "Caucasoid" of varying color and features; the high-cheeked and broad-nosed "Mongoloid" with his epicanthic eyelids; the "Australoid" with his dark brown to black skin, his broad nose with large nostrils, his hairiness, and varying hair forms; the "Bushmanoid" with his large everted lips, his yellow skin, and peppercorn hair; and the various mixtures of all three — plus other local groupings that have since become submerged. All could have developed into the populations of Southeast and East Asia, southern India, and into the varying populations in North America, along the Mediterranean, and East and West Africa.

Although a good deal of interbreeding continued among all the populations of the world, the mixtures took place over thousands of years rather than in the few generations that affected the people of China, the population of Rome and its empire (as a result of an influx of slaves from North Europe, Africa, and the Middle East), the physical differentiations in Europe (as a result of the enormous migrations from the fourth to the thirteenth centuries), and those taking place in the United States, Canada, Australia, and the Soviet Union today.

The present paucity of archaeological evidence makes it difficult to trace the migrations as well as the diffusion of ideas and material objects (though these two may have gone hand in hand with the first) from one part of the world to the other. Yet, over a period of hundreds if not thousands of years, the development of material and cultural ideas appears to be on roughly the same levels. As animals are domesticated, the ideas of how to domesticate are diffused perhaps by those who practice them. As horticulture develops, the concepts behind the tilling first of gardens and then of small farms are likely to spread in certain directions, again perhaps by those who themselves are engaged in farming.

Even the Old Testament in its story of Cain and Abel expressed the conflict that may have existed for thousands of years between the two ways of life (which later were joined)—between the agriculturist tilling the soil, and the shepherd herding his animals from one grazing area to another. The farmer evidently came from regions where there were ample rainfall and fertile soils; the pastoralist from semi-arid and arid areas. But the story in Genesis was apparently written down thousands of years after the conflict first erupted, after men from different cultural areas met in class conflict as they crossed one anothers' paths.

The evidence is somewhat tentative, but men in Southeast Asia may have been the first to experiment with horticulture. Perhaps around 13,000 to 14,000 years ago or even earlier, men in that area began to cultivate peas, beans, and various root plants thousands of years before wheat and barley were grown in the region of Southwest Asia in the Fertile Crescent. The cultivation of special plants from seed must have taken place over thousands of years. Men first drew conclusions on what they saw, hypothesized on what had happened, and speculated as to whether they could make it happen again.

At any rate, it was thousands of years after the first use of domesticated seeds (as found in Spirit Cave in Thailand) that we find agriculture with wheat, barley, and peas developing in the area of Southwest Asia. At almost the same time, a primitive horticulture with squash and pumpkins arose in the Mexican Valley of the New World (though corn or maize was not grown until thousands of years later). Here we must pause to point out that there is no evidence to suggest how the concepts of agriculture spread. We can only speculate, hoping that new archaeological finds and the fertile imaginations of archaeologists will provide us with partial answers.

In Thailand, a primitive horticulture arose around 12,000 to 14,000 years ago. The possibility exists that experimentation with plants to be eaten may go back another 6,000 years. In Southwest Asia, agriculture began after the domestication of goats and sheep some 12,000 years ago, with evidence from the ancient sites of Jericho and Jarmo that wheat and barley were grown domestically from 9,000 to 10,000 years ago. In the Mexican Valley, archaeological sites appear to indicate that the hunting ancestors of Mexican Indians began to grow squash and pumpkins in small plots some 9,000 years ago. Agriculture in these areas utilized quite different plants, having domesticated ones native to the area. The animals domesticated in the northern area of the Fertile Crescent in Southwest Asia were native to that area. In Southeast Asia, those domesticated were the jungle fowl, the ancestor of the modern chicken, and the forest pig (the pigs we eat at the present time are descended from the domesticated Southeast Asian hog rather than the wild swine of Southwest Asia or Europe). The contributions of Southeast Asia to the culinary accumulations of the modern world include the pig, the chicken, and rice—which means that we owe our enjoyment of fried chicken, chicken soup, ham and eggs, peas, beans, and rice to the domestication of animals and plants that first began to develop in Southeast Asia more than 12,000 years ago. We obtained our wheat and barley from Southwest Asia, and squash, pumpkins, and later, our maize, beans, tomatoes, potatoes, chocolate, and vanilla from the horticulturists in the New World. We obtained sorghum from Africa and soy beans from China.

Evidence seems to indicate that settled villages of hunters preceded the domestication of animals in Southwest Asia. This development along with the later domestication of plants became part of a farming complex. In Thailand, no evidence appears to exist as to when the pig and the chicken were domesticated, though evidence does seem to indicate that the domestication of plants came first—thus suggesting that the controlled breeding of animals did not take place until thousands of years later. In the New World, the domestication of the turkey and the llama evidently did not occur until comparatively recent times. In all three areas, the plants and animals that had been domesticated eventually spread around the world (with the exception of the llama which appears to have remained localized).

Were the ancient inhabitants of Thailand (who were evidently not present-day Thais—the latter, along with the Burmese, started their migration southward into this area somewhere around the beginning of the Christian era) the sole inventors of the agricultural complex? Or is it possible that the latter represented an independent development in all three areas (the way in which sorghum and watermelons were first domesticated in West Africa)? The answer is still very indefinite, but my own opinion is that it was undoubtedly a mixture of the cultural diffusion of ideas from Thailand plus the independent discovery of certain plants locally that could be domesticated. The discovery that seeds, spilled during the grinding process in various seasonal campsites, could reproduce themselves must have occurred hundreds if not thousands of years before some curious individuals saw a connection between the eating of these wild plants, the spilling of their seeds, and the growth of duplicate plants the next year. Even after the connection was made intellectually, it must have taken quite some time before an enterprising individual (a woman, perhaps?) experimented with those plants that required a human midwife to open the pods. Otherwise, they would have split when ripe and scattered their seeds everywhere. Perhaps preceding the discovery, there had been a long period of grinding wild seeds into some form of paste. (As a result of their early socialization, most men are too traditional and conservative to let us assume that some individuals everywhere see causal effects immediately and work upon them pragmatically.)

There appears to be no way in which we can connect Mexico, Thailand, and Southwest Asia at about roughly the same time period, unless we assume that there may have been a continuous migration of men in all directions, generally taking the easiest routes—which in Southeast Asia meant the coastal areas. One can posit moving southeasterly and then northeasterly along the Asian coast, and over a period of thousands of years coming in some way to Mexico (which may explain the development of pottery at an early date along the eastern coast of Asia)—then moving westward along the coast, arriving in Mesopotamia thousands of years later with the ideas rather than with the pottery, the plants, or the animals themselves. On the other hand, we can assume a partially independent development of both the pastoral life and the rise of agriculture in Southwest Asia. But perhaps one of the reasons why Southwest Asia seems to play such an important role in human culture may be because geographically it was on the crossroads of men and ideas migrating in all directions. Because of its location, it benefited enormously. Similarly, Mexico also profited from being on the crossroads of men and ideas moving north to south (and perhaps south to north as well).

We know only one thing definitely about the development of this new age in Southwest Asia; that is, that somewhere before 9,500 years ago men learned to engage in the raising of animals and food while living in settled villages. The ideas behind such a complex could have developed there independently, they could have come up from Southeast Asia or somewhere in between, or they could have been diffused as a rumor after having been rejected by other peoples. The fact that it took thousands of years before this complex spread from Southwest Asia to Central and Western Europe indicates that migrants served as the intermediaries, just as Roman administrators and legionnaires diffused Roman law and culture into Western Europe and Great Britain, and technicians and scientists are today carrying the ideas of the Industrial and Scientific civilization into the developing nations.

At any rate, men 10,000 years ago in certain areas of the world no longer worked fulltime as hunters. A new economy based upon production rather than collection was slowly being created. One can say that the period from 10,000 to a little over 6,000 years ago was part of the first really great cultural revolution that man has created. For a long period of time, he was a collector and hunter of food, migrating seasonally with the animals, carrying everything he owned on his (or his wife's) back, making simple tools, and suffering from the perpetual insecurity of scarcity. About 10,000 years ago (after an initial trial period of perhaps thousands of years), he came up with a new way of life in which he got more food over a given period of time than ever before—but still not enough (he had to await the modern period for that).

Not only has man organized the production of food for himself and his family, but he has also developed the kinship network to its present level as a social institution. Over a period of hundreds of thousands of years, a gradual social development occurred in which men who were more attentive to the young were in somewhat greater demand as mates by the females than the males who were indifferent if not downright hostile to the young. As a result of this preferential mating process, men gradually assumed more obligations in caring for the young—in time even acting as substitute mothers in socializing their offspring. By this period, men had already created cultural roles for themselves as fathers and husbands, and ritually they had also become concerned parents.

Fatherhood with its series of obligations toward the young was in existence at least 10,000 years ago.

The composite of ideas surrounding the family complex, the kinship patternings, the development of role or socially expected behavior, the norms, the social hierarchy existing within each band, plus the relationships between bands, could have been highly developed by 10,000 years ago. The rise of agriculture and the pastoral economy, coupled with fixed villages in the region of Southwest Asia, were all leading to the development of a religious complex with pastoral as well as agricultural deities. The pastoral deities were perhaps projections of headmen as protectors and herdsmen. The later rise of an agricultural economy could have given settled communities the mother-earth figure, whose body when inseminated gave birth to a son—or grain. Just as there were deities connected with the hunt, the weather, pastoral life, and warfare, so there were also other gods and goddesses that supplied men with their grain, their vegetables and fruits, and protected them against death, disease, and famine. The religious identification of an individual with various guardian spirits could have occurred in this period, as men became concerned to guarantee themselves the surety involved in getting deities to reward them for their efforts rather than to punish them with failure.

◇   ◇   ◇   ◇   ◇

We know the Southwest Asian area slightly better than other regions of the world primarily because of its larger number of archaeological sites, a result of the traditional belief that this area played the greatest part in the rise of civilization.

For tens of thousands of years, Southwest Asia was on the crossroads between Asia, Africa, and Europe. Its location assured that it would receive cultural currents from all directions. This region appears to have provided the different physical types who were transitional both to Neanderthal and modern man. And modern man himself may have moved from Southwest Asia into Europe by a succession of easy steps some 40,000 years ago. Continuous migrations must have affected this area as large numbers of bands came seeking game on its broad green savannahs. The increasing semi-arid and arid conditions in this part of the world did not develop until a little more than 10,000 years ago.

Although North and East Asia contain barriers of mountain ridges vis-a-vis Southwest Asia, with even higher mountains in the Caucasus, there are passes in the mountains that men used during early periods of time. With few barriers in their way, men were also able to move slowly along the seacoast from India and Pakistan, along southern Iran, and then up the Persian Gulf to the Tigris and Euphrates Rivers. Until the end of the last glacial period about 12,000 years ago, there was a land-bridge connecting Southeast Europe (the Balkans and Greece) and Anatolia (Turkey). Men evidently moved in both directions, into and out of Europe. Until the end of the last glacial period, Europe and Southwest Asia almost merged (as did South Europe and North Africa).

With rains gradually moving northward at the end of the last glacial period, Southwest Asia may have been invaded by hunters coming from areas then under water, or from humid grasslands that were turning into semi-arid or arid lands. Beginning about 13,000 years ago, men no longer appeared to be nomadic hunters, but seemed to live in fixed villages from whence they hunted and collected within a radius of miles. Sometime after 12,000 years ago, these settled villagers evidently learned to domesticate the sheep and the goat, both native to the region, perhaps at first in the mountainous area between present-day Iran and Iraq. Wild cereals were collected and perhaps pounded into some sort of meal in stone querns. Within a few thousand years, the settled villages became centers for small-scale farming and a domesticated pastoralism. Ten thousand years ago, the people who lived along the Fertile Crescent, the area of present-day Israel, Lebanon, Syria, Turkey, Iraq, and parts of Iran seem to have been somewhat different physically from their descendants, as civilizations began to emerge about 6,000 years ago. Little doubt exists that extensive and continuous movements of people took place into and out of this region even during the period of settled villages.

⬦   ⬦   ⬦   ⬦   ⬦

By 7000 B.C., farming had become a fixed part of the Neolithic way of life, along with parttime hunting, collecting, and raising of animals. Villages dotted the area along the Fertile Crescent and along the various river beds, including those of the Tigris and Euphrates Rivers. Men used rafts and primitive kinds of boats to travel up and down streams. As the area became drier and the population larger, farming as a way of life became more important. There may also have been continual conflict as individuals seeking more farmland to till came into areas in which the available land had already been preempted. By 7,000 years ago, the structure of the later urban state had been set. Trade had taken on an extensive network of exchange as individuals in Southwest Asia who lacked resources went far afield into contemporary Iran, Anatolia, and perhaps as far as Southeast Europe looking for copper, obsidian, flint, and gems. In return, they bartered their finished copper, flint knives, obsidian tools, and polished gems.

It is difficult to know when the modern city-state began to function, but it must have been even before the first of the Sumerian city-states recorded its history. The origins of the state may lie in the twin social institutions of religion and warfare. The period in which the state slowly evolved may have occurred over an epoch of more than a thousand years. Just as we need to refer to pre-men, so it is necessary to speak about the age before the beginnings of Sumerian civilization as a period of pre-civilization. It must have taken many hundreds of years to organize tribes into city-states with all the social systems of administration, codes, division of labor, and the recording of accounts and administrative orders. It is impossible at present to know the immediate background of the first civilization or how the immediate pre-civilization period functioned. But one can speculate that it may have stemmed out of the insatiety of the village deities for more tribute, plus the increasing shortage of farmland needed for a burgeoning population.

At this time, men may also have become acutely aware of how fragile, ephemeral, and temporary life is. Because it was believed that the gods who made man had it in their power to withhold life (and thus send men to worlds of limbo), it was necessary to discover what the gods demanded in return for giving this great gift of life. It was apparent that the gods insisted upon shelter and food, but they may also have demanded human life itself—a life for a life. Villages that expected to continue to enjoy life had continuously to exchange a symbolic life for the collective one that the group found agreeable. Perhaps the capture of nearby or other tribal villages (in order to bring captives for sacrifices under the sovereignty of the tribal gods and thus make the collective more powerful) may have been one of the first steps in achieving religious legitimacy. The need to enforce the instructions and decrees of the deities required not only a tribal priestly administrative class, but also a group of men behind them who could enforce their orders— thus giving rise to the development of policing or soldier power. The two evidently combined to form administrative centers. Within these centers of the tribal deities it was necessary to keep records of the decrees, the instructions, and the laws of the gods as well as of the accounts owing them. Perhaps symbolic notations were made of the quantities of wheat, barley, and sacrifices paid to the deities. Accountings with the deities were made upon demand.

It is difficult to say when writing first developed in Mesopotamia, but there must have been a proto-Sumerian writing that began even before there was a Sumerian administrative center. Indications are that the Elamites, who were contemporary with the

Sumerians, may have developed a form of writing by 4000 B.C. In the city of Tepe Yahya, clay writing tablets in a proto-Elamite or proto-Sumerian script have been given a Carbon 14 date of around 3560 B.C. Since Carbon 14 dates are generally 20 to 30 percent off on the conservative side, we can speculate that writing may have developed sometime before 4000 B.C.[1]

The trade between Mesopotamia and distant regions must have developed before the Sumerian tribal city-states became important administrative centers. Religion may have played an important part in this trade through the need of the deities to have a high standard of living and their desire to have a military force that could compel obedience to their demands. Trade required writing and the compiling of records, and Sumerian writing tablets dated as early as 3500 B.C. have been found as far afield as Rumania. Even before the period of writing, which may have started at the end of the fifth millenium B.C., there was an active trade in obsidian and copper which was carried on with regions hundreds of miles away. Before the development of writing, the crude smelting of copper ores containing many impurities was evidently known from the eighth millenium B. C. on.

Cultural influences from the Sumerian and Elamite cities must have been disseminated by traders and other early travelers within a short period of time after their rise as administrative and technical centers. By 3200 B.C., the dissemination of administrative and technical knowledge evidently influenced some tribal chieftains along the Nile River. These may already have learned to expand their power by becoming special agents of their own deities who demanded more wealth, power, and status—again reflecting the social conditions and the ambitions that may have been in existence at this time both in the Mesopotamian-Elamite area as well as along the fertile region in the Nile Valley. The generational conflicts between the various high priests of the deities and the more secular paramount chiefs of a group of tribal villages may have led to a high receptivity to technical and administrative knowledge among both sides, along with the development of military and judicial systems. The victims of this spreading aggression may gradually have taken over the aggressor's political and social systems, thus leading to even more diffusion of ideas from the new administrative urban centers.

One can speculate that almost immediately after the establishment of the first urban states, newly-organized urban clusters proliferated, spreading slowly outward from the core, borrowing a great many of the characteristics of the first centers, and as a result of

---

1. See, for example, "An Early City in Iran," C. C. and Martha Lamberg-Karlovsky, *The Scientific American,* June 1971.

their experiences adding many of their own. (These early administrators doubtless found that they had to solve local problems which
had not been handled before.) Towns evidently spread from the
Sumerians to the Elamites in present-day Iran, to the Semitic-
speaking Akkadians, to the Egyptians, to various areas of the Fertile Crescent, to Anatolia (present-day Turkey), to the Indus River
Valley, to Crete, and thence to Greece.

The urban administrative center (with its organization of men
in a bureaucratic hierarchy, its military and administrative tenta-
cles spreading out in larger and larger radii, its writing and records
accumulating, and its codification of past human norms turning
into supernatural decrees stemming from the founding deities)
slowly swept through most of the Neolithic world. As it moved from
Mesopotamia and Persia eastward to the Indus River, it gave birth
to the Harappan civilization around 3000 B.C., then moved eastward to the New Delhi area, southward to the Bombay area and
beyond, and then jumped north and eastward (how, we still do not
know) to the Yellow River of China about 4,000 years ago. Other
points of civilization appeared thousands of miles away as the
Olmecs began to develop their administrative urban centers around
1500 B.C. along the Mexican coast of the Caribbean. From the
Olmecs, who were overthrown in the fourth century B.C., came the
new victors, the Mayas and their successors, leading in time to
the Aztecs, who in turn were overthrown by the Spaniards (with
the aid of Indian allies who were thirsting for revenge after previous
defeats).

Civilization 2,000 years ago also spread into South America,
especially along the coast of Peru, setting the direction for a succession of cultures from the Mochicas to the Incas. Civilization with
its organization of men in fairly large units also moved with Roman
colonization and the sword into Europe, and by the twentieth century most men living in most parts of the world had come under
its bureaucratic, traditional, religious, and elite social controls.
Although a great many local varieties of this civilization would
exist, a good many similarities were to be found almost world-wide.
This first stage of civilization, that spread as the Neolithic and
covered the world from 4000 B.C. to the present, I call Primary
civilization. It brought into being the peasant and the noble, the
artisan and the scribe, the priest and the soldier. It existed as various forms of feudalism, but it also came under absolute monarchs
to whom the peasant paid his obligations directly rather than
through the mediary of the noble.

◇   ◇   ◇   ◇   ◇

Primary civilization was a much more highly organized social system than the Neolithic village that preceded it. The first village was the settled abode of a group of hunters and food collectors that slowly developed into the folk agricultural and pastoral village, with its roots in the soil and in the past. Primary civilization, on the other hand, was based upon the administrative center, and could have been the trading temple town containing a division of labor among men and women serving the deities along with their servants; or it could have been the temporary abode of the priest-king with his growing retinue of hundreds and then thousands of followers—as later took place in Egypt, China, and Europe. The legal organization of the inhabitants was initially started to protect the welfare of the deities on down to their representatives. It was not a civilization concerned with the well-being of the mass of inhabitants, except insofar as the well-being of the community was viewed as being identified with the interests of the top administrative elites. The obligation of the community was considered to be that of protecting the high social status of the local deities and their representatives. The substance that the community could produce— the temples, the artisanal treasures of precious stones and metals, the palaces, and even the urban fortifications—went to the glorification of the deities and the well-being of their representatives on earth. It is probably no exaggeration to speculate that the standard of living of the priests, administrative officials, nobles, and king (as direct descendant of the gods, or their most loyal vicar and servant) was immeasurably higher than the standard of living enjoyed by the village chiefs or headmen within the Mesopotamian, Egyptian, or Elamite villages in Neolithic times. Although the peasants gained little from the organized civilization of the urban era, the increase in wealth enhanced both the social status and living standards of those who governed the administrative centers.

The new civilization also developed special artisanal skills, for the division of labor went further than in the Neolithic farming and pastoral village. No longer was the urban dweller able to make his own textiles, pottery, furniture, baked bricks, tools, or weapons: now there were artisans attached to the temple, the local palace, or independent workers in the marketplace who spent their days making the items which were in demand by the nobles, by the servants of the nobles, and by the priests and the townsmen. The artisans traded their goods for food grown by the peasants, who lived in or on the outskirts of the urban center. Early barter soon gave way to a money economy in which silver was the medium of exchange. Many of the urban artisans also tilled small plots of land outside the town, kept goats or sheep, and later even a cow in their courtyards. Specialized artisanal work was combined with subsistence farming. Though weavers made fine cloth for the nobles, it is more than likely that the peasant's clothing was made by his family in the home on a wooden loom constructed by a neighboring carpenter. Pottery was made by a specialized potter rather than at home by a member of a family during spare time: pottery required an oven for baking and not all houses possessed suitable large bake-ovens.

There was a good deal of receptivity toward innovation in all of the early civilizations. The strides made were quite phenomenal in the first few hundred years of the Sumerian towns, the Egyptian kingdoms, the Harappan civilization, the Anatolian city-states, and by the Phoenicians and the Cretans. The development of the Olmec, the Mayas, and the Mochicas also seem to indicate a good deal of innovation and receptivity to new ideas during the early periods of their civilizations. But in subsequent periods, tradition and con-servatism became fixed in the administrative machinery of the civilization; no longer was ability rewarded, but innovation was replaced by seeking solutions chiefly in terms of what the past had done. The pottery made in the late Harappan or Cretan periods indicates a deterioration in quality. Instead of innovating ideas or continuously increasing new techniques in technology, there was a conventionalization of previous art forms and a slight modification of techniques. Later bureaucracy seems to have been based upon the inheritance or purchase of posts rather than upon the selection of those with the most talent or ability.

All this does not mean to imply that there are few differences between the early Sumerian or Egyptian civilizations with the later Greek or Roman civilizations. There are many changes which took place in the more than 3,500 years that separated the beginnings of the first two with the levels of the last two. A good deal of diffusion occurred in the more than 3,000 years that elapsed, and much was created from these borrowings. The early mud-brick dwellings gave way to buildings of stone and marble. Unpaved streets and roads were later paved with stone and brick. The population of cities increased, and more provisions were made for supplying the larger population with food, water, and sewage. In both the Harappan and Cretan sites, there appears to have been plumbing of a sort with water piped into the houses. In the Roman period, large via-ducts were built to bring water from nearby streams to important population centers.

Intellectually, much had changed between 3000 B.C. and the second century B.C. There was more sophistication in the expression of ideas. Men were thinking more about the changing norms and values which should guide them if they were to interact with one another peacefully in urban settings. Religion in organized forms became more important as a unifying factor in the politics of the city-state as well as in the proliferating empires. Technology had improved immeasurably and had become more complex. Greater wealth was in the hands of the few who could draw upon more skillful architects, sculptors, painters, goldsmiths, technicians, and artisans to create their homes and luxuries. Early traders around 3000 B.C. traveled a good deal, but in the second century B.C. there was more awareness of the known world, travel was more extensive, a bit more curiosity existed about people not far away, and some attempts were made to speculate about differences (though ethnocentrism was as pronounced in the second century B.C. as it undoubtedly was in the third millenium B.C.) Little interest existed in trying to understand different cultures. The study of foreign people had to await another 2,000 years before any intellectual curiosity about people different from one's own came into being.

The world of the urban city-state, of empire, and of written religious literature was by no means a world of science or of reason. Men at that time were satisfied with any kind of explanation for natural phenomena if the explanation came from a revered or respected source. Men were also satisfied with simple explanations. Their curiosity had not been sharpened by any large amounts of contradictory knowledge, and what was perceived as being contradictory was immediately put out of mind. Tradition and the wisdom of the ancients were seen as adding intellectual weight to belief.

Men were convinced that they lived to serve and to flatter the gods and goddesses, who had provided man with technology, laws, and discipline. In an absence of fear, men would not willingly obey but would live only to please themselves. The gods needed to be reassured of man's loyalty to them through continuous worship and fulsome praise, as kings needed to be lauded for their great achievements.

Observing that the deities were irrational, whimsical, and quite unpredictable in their behavior encouraged worshippers to fear that even their prayers and offerings would not prevent the gods from becoming angry with them for no reasons that they could understand. The Job theme appears often in the mythology of ancient Sumeria, wherein ill-fortune is visited upon innocent worshippers by unpredictable gods and goddesses. Because men believed that they could not control the behavior of irrational deities, their behavior had to be accepted with resignation: after all, what mortal man could understand what the gods did or why they did it? A fatalistic acceptance of divine will as final also led to the concept of complete submission to the deities, their representatives, and to kings. In this concept, the gods needed man to respect and worship them, while man needed the gods to govern him (he, like an immature child, needed the firm hand of strong parents, since he did not know enough to govern himself). To man, knowledge came from the more mature gods and goddesses.

Early civilizations encouraged the belief that man as a perpetual child could never break away from the ties that connected him with the deities. The world was viewed not as being ordered or rational, but as filled with fears and anxieties that anything could happen. Therefore, it was best to be prepared for the unexpected. Implicit in organized religion was the cult of authority wherein one became dependent upon a more powerful figure to remove the uncertainty from ephemeral life and to provide a modicum of security — a cult which appeared to arise from the concept of a world one could not understand but had to learn to accept nonetheless.

◇   ◇   ◇   ◇   ◇

Little is known of the religions that developed in the Harappan civilization or in the intervening Persian city-states of the period. We assume that in all of the early civilizations, including those of the New World, the requirement of complete submission to the will of the gods was accepted. The role of the priests was not to understand the personalities of the deities, but to anticipate their will. An understanding would have assumed a superiority toward the deities which early priests could not accept because they did not believe that men could become like gods. In the Biblical story of the Garden of Eden, Adam and Eve were severely punished because they tried to be like the gods by eating the fruit from the tree of knowledge. The Golden Age represented a period of nostalgia for a happy childhood that rarely existed. If men presumed to believe that they knew as much as the deities, they could expect to be exiled from their homes. With exile came punishment that followed them and their children until the end of time. Although men dreamed of deities that would make them independent, superior, and secure, still their daily lives made them feel that they would be better off if they did not expect too much, lest they be sorely disappointed. Buddhism as a religion developed a mass following through teaching the restriction of desires and wishes. These led only to unhappiness and violence in the competition for the scarce treasures of life.

Though men cursed the tyrants who ruled them and dreamed of worlds in which social justice would prevail, there was little freedom for the individual in any of the early civilizations. Freedom is a growing concept rather than an absolute one, but even in its relative meaning one can say that it is of comparatively recent evolution. Although in ancient Israel the people had a tradition of governing themselves through the medium of elected judges, and though the prophet Samuel is purported to have warned them as to what would happen if they transferred their power to the hands of a king, still the masochistic desire to have a king rule them and assume responsibility for them was strong. Whether or not judges existed in the post-Exodus period or whether there was a Samuel to voice his warnings, the tradition continued that men at one time were free. That men could govern themselves was something that priestly writers in the early civilizations could only conjecture about.

Later, men created the myth of supernatural forces, sympathetic to human justice, who would help overthrow the evil parent or tyrant by conferring the power to do so on a savior, a warrior-figure or a political organizer.

One advantage in having a large number of deities to pray to was the belief that at least one among them would listen to pleas for mercy and justice, and be moved. The disadvantage in having only one powerful deity was that he could not be replaced if he failed in his protection of those who worshipped him. In order for hope to exist, it was necessary to have intervening figures who could prevail upon the single powerful deity. The choice was either that or suffering in silence. A lone individual could not change the behavior of the powerful deity upon whom he was dependent, just as he could not affect the behavior of a powerful parent or superior: non-acceptance would suggest violence. The murder of a parent-figure implied a sense of guilt which one was unable to assuage except through worship of the assassinated tyrannical parent-figure. Men can destroy their gods through displacement, but with a deity who by definition cannot be killed, one can only try to ignore his presence and operate by falling back upon one's own resources. Single powerful deities can lead to their followers' agnosticism and increasing individualism when they become displeased with supernatural behavior.

Early civilizations had only their past experiences to use as references in developing their bureaucracies, religions, and social systems. Men seeking new ideas of organization fell back upon the family, both nuclear and extended, and projected the interpersonal relations already existing within it as a basis for the larger extended family which became the city-state, and later the empire-state. Family life in periods prior to the beginnings of civilization may have been based upon an authoritarian status hierarchy of elders operating as patriarchs, in which the female and the younger males played submissive roles. This may go back to early stages of mankind when the band was led by a small group of dominant males, with the females occupying an inferior position. Social hierarchies are part of the inheritance from our primate biological past which men since then have rationalized culturally. Deities became powerful because the early hierarchy of dominant males within the village had more status than the rest of the population. Those who had power used it for personal enhancement. As deities were invented, they too expected men to grovel before them, worship them, and to make them feel important through their homage and sacrifices. Men, it was held, cannot rule themselves but must be governed by the more intelligent deities by way of their representatives. The gods ruled through high priests and kings, and it was through them that one received behavioral norms and values, even though these norms and values may have been derived from those originally used by other neighbors. Men were punished when they attempted to cease being dependent children. Kings, like deities, also had to be flattered and reminded continuously of their superhuman greatness by those who accepted social inferiority to them.

Authoritarianism is the mark of most early civilizations. Perhaps as villages changed through conquest and the development of the city-state form of government, the loyalties of the headmen also changed. No longer was the village headman concerned with what the villagers or the village deities wanted, for his obedience had been transferred to those above him who ruled him from the new administrative centers. A good village headman was judged by his superiors, and not by his social inferiors, on how well he carried out his orders from the top even though doing so might mean conflict with the villagers. He then became the man in the middle. Since he could be destroyed by the men above him, he had to choose between punishment from the less powerful villagers or from the stronger administrative center. His obedience to the administrative center became the choice that marked the beginning of an organized bureaucracy—though initially there may have been more feedback from him to his administrative superiors than was the case centuries later.

As the first Neolithic villages were conquered and put under the rule of the deities of the larger village, the first level of bureaucracy may have been created. As this larger village later became the priestly and military administrative center, a second level of bureaucratic officials came into being. When the administrative center became superceded through conquest by still another center, a third level might have been put into operation. As the various centers became seats of regional power, resulting from new empires being created out of the conquered centers and placed under the distant authority of a king, levels of authority were organized in which the loyalty of each administrative level was to the one above it. With the development of bureaucratic rules of operation, authoritarianism in all of its modern aspects was born. Although there may have been some feedback from the bottom to the top, this too became lost as the administrative officials saw that disobedience to the ones above them only brought punishment. It was easier to oppress those beneath them. Taxes had to be raised, even when it meant getting blood out of a stone; laborers had to be drafted for public works; temples to house the gods had to be built with forced labor; and warriors for the king's army had to be drafted from each village.

The concept of authoritarianism, or the obedient acceptance of all authority emanating from the top and requiring blind loyalty from those below, has continued from the dim past to the present day. It has played an equally important part in twentieth-century authoritarian government, corporations, and industries. In government bureaucracies, the final loyalty of the employee is not to the theoretical public weal, but to the hierarchies immediately above.

Civilizations not only brought in organized religions on more than a regional scale, but enhancement of the deities went hand in hand with the development and spread of these civilizations. Although it may be undoubtedly true that the Neolithic Age may have developed fertility and storm gods and goddesses, the behavior of the latter was seen as subject to control through magical rites and incantations as well as human and animal sacrifices. It is very unlikely that Neolithic or village deities were looked upon as superior but irrational human beings; the behavior of these deities was considered to be predictable. One had to wait for civilization to take the step of clothing deities with human frailties, vices, arrogance, and lust for power. Gods and goddesses lived in human fashion, jealous of one another's prerogatives, competing for social status, and insisting upon an ever-higher standard of living. Pastoral gods looked down with contempt upon the agricultural deities with their fertility rites and sexual-magical ceremonies. The Old Testament reflects this age-old prejudice in the story of Cain and Abel, in which Cain, the agriculturist, has his grains and vegetables refused as sacrifices. (The story in its final form was not completed by the priestly scribes until the end of the fifth century B.C.)

◇　◇　◇　◇　◇

Even as the Primary form of civilization developed, its leaders found themselves prisoners of the culture of power which others before them had created. They became victims of the regal "machismo" which evolved from the honorific hunter complex of the past (which continued to exist side by side with the pastoral and agricultural social complex for thousands of years). The former hunters-turned-leaders who chased four-legged animals became the pursuers of the two-legged ones, though the name of the game was no longer hunting but warfare. Young men, chiefly of high hierarchical lineage, could no more farm or herd sheep than they could weave or make pottery. They were socialized to believe that life for a male was not worth living if he could not compete with strangers for the honor of seeing who was the stronger and more daring, and who was willing to die in order to determine who was the victor.

The need to force others to accept one's deities, one's village, one's people, and even one's nation as stronger and more powerful became ends in themselves, thus leading indirectly to changes in the cultural structure. Men fought to the death generation after generation, dynasty after dynasty, to prove that they were men, independent and masterful. The role of being a male implied that one could not be defeated in battle. Defeat meant becoming a slave—or a counterpart of the female. The fear of defeat at the hands of others, the fear of being emasculated into a slave, the fear of being humiliated in one's conception of one's male status became important in the literature of the classic civilizations. Their histories provided endless accounts of kings defeating or being defeated in battle, of monuments and poems reciting the brave masculine deeds of kings and their masculine armies as they swept across hostile areas, ending threats to their male power or their "machismo." Peaceful villages and quiet areas were conquered just as weaker nations were later subdued by men who had a pressing need to achieve the status of supernatural gods, demanding power and adulation. They too were haunted by the fear that their power was a passing phenomenon.

Because power could only be retained through a military bureaucracy, the man on top feared those beneath him in the escalating hierarchy of power. Though these may have been suitably rewarded, they still needed to be doubly watched. As civilization expanded, those in the low ranks who occupied no threatening positions could appeal for justice to the top individual over the heads of those in the middle ranks. The peasant appealed to the king for justice over the heads of the feudal lords, just as priests entreated the gods to avenge them against the king. Tyrants lost the protecting power of the gods, just as barons could lose the support of their liege lords. Tyrannical stepfathers and overlords might be found out by those above them. These were jealous of any who tried to alienate them from the ranks of those who formed the balance of power. The king who tyrannized his subjects created a power vacuum that others tried to fill. The king who punished his tyrannical nobles, on the other hand, created future support for himself in the ranks below the nobles. Since the armies of early civilization were made up of conquered village headmen and tribal chiefs leading their draftees into battle, their fighting morale reflected how well they were rewarded by those who originally had conquered them. Memories of injustices lasted long in the annals of ancient civilizations. Many empires went under when they persisted in unfair treatment toward those defeated, who were required to display unflinching loyalty to the conquerors but received no mercy or magnanimity in return.

Early civilizations spent much of their people's energies in battles that attempted to perpetuate the memory of their short-lived kings, and also devoted much of their limited wealth to erecting public works and temples to commemorate their temporary leaders and deities. Whatever wealth there was had to be spent immediately lest neighboring peoples take it for embellishing and preserving their own self-esteem. Wealth was based upon exploitation of the peasant, plus the labor of conquered peoples and slaves. Although technology from 4000 B.C. to the end of the Roman era slowly increased the fund of knowledge (and thus of wealth), the end results went into creating large massive buildings for the emperors and deities, into acquiring more soldiers and weapons of war, and into supplying limited luxuries for those who served the emperors and deities. In all the early civilizations, the vast majority of peasants gained little in a standard of living superior to what their ancestors had possessed in the era of the Neolithic village. Though there had been an extensive development in metallurgy from 5000 B.C. on, little filtered down to the village tiller, except for the few special possessions of his headmen. While land for the Neolithic family had been sufficient to grow all of its food with a small surplus left over, under civilization the expanding bureaucracies and the swollen armies managed to take whatever surplus was grown by the later peasants. In fact, as the Roman Empire spread, its major source of food came from the conquered areas whose peasants were compelled to give most of their limited supplies to their conquerors.

The innovative aspects of the early civilization were brief in time. Although the inventors of the early phases were motivated by promotions in social status, social rewards went later to the non-innovators, to the manipulators of men, and to the keepers of the court records and sacred traditions. Men may have been concerned with trying to understand the worlds they never made in ancient Greece, India, and China, but they were more intrigued by what the fathers had said than they were in trying to be founding fathers themselves. Scholars and scribes were few in number. Even in Athens of the fifth century B.C., only a few thousand were able to engage in intellectual pursuits, and this because hundreds of thousands of others served as their menials, artisans, and slaves.

Slavery went hand in hand with the agricultural civilizations, where the few could exist only by exploiting the many. Even the ancient Greek freeman feared conquest and enslavement, with all the symbolism that that implied: loss of one's masculinity, and thus of one's freedom.

◇   ◇   ◇   ◇   ◇

One may talk of the organized city-states, the public works, the literature and art of ancient Primary civilization, but the vast majority of the population were still illiterate inefficient peasants, even though many lived near the walls of the administrative centers. Poverty on the subsistence level was endemic; wealth was limited and available only to the few on top. Illiteracy was the rule. The few scribes or clerks coming mostly from the lesser noble class were connected with the priestly temple and the administrative center. It took years in the temple and administrative schools to learn the art of writing and to create the tools of one's trade: the parchment, the papyrus, the clay tablets, and the writing paper. Later, artisans were trained to lighten the work of the scribes. But only the children of the moderately well-to-do could be spared from agricultural or artisanal labor to spend most of their days in learning how to become literate in the knowledge of the day. Because schools were essential in the training of scribes, lesser administrative officials, priests, and judges, the curriculum tended to emphasize the traditional, the status quo, and the conventional. The models were from the past, and those who deviated were punished, while those who emulated them were rewarded. The few innovators were mainly those who were aware of past knowledge and who attempted to refine the crudities they found.

Since few were literate, the emphasis was upon the sacredness of the written word. When written down, words developed an eternal soul of their own. They possessed a magic which turned them into reality rivaling that of monuments and public works. Words written down became the sacred breath of the gods, with a potency which could ward off unfriendly gods or unknown demons. Written words were the commands of the gods which brought about all changes that took place in human society. It was through the written word that kings were able to move the bureaucracies and that men hoped to change the evils of the world into something better.

Because men believed in the sacredness of words, both oral and written, verbal symbols used in formulas could also be used to perform magic, to transform both man and nature. Words inscribed on metal or on stone monuments developed an immortality of their own, and the magic implied in the ability of men to put abstract symbols into records suggested that the same symbols would transmit information to those who might read them thousands of years afterward. Because words did not die, unless obliterated by defacement, the acts lived on that the words commemorated. Writing and the need for immortality became the basic necessity of those who proclaimed the intentions and deeds of both the gods and the king-gods. Poetry, literature, and history go together in the annals of the early civilizations whose writings have come down to us. In China, the group of practitioners of the various words became the elitists, or the Mandarins, while in Israel, Rome, and the Hellenic world their status became comparable to our modern upper-middle class.

It is difficult for us to know how the vast majority of the populations in the ancient civilizations lived, for most of them were illiterate peasants who left no records about themselves. Those who could write generally described themselves or their liege lords; they had little interest in recounting what for them were the boring lives of the peasants. Clearly, the peasants with their wives and children must have worked hard. In succeeding millenia, cultivable land undoubtedly became scarcer as families slowly proliferated—despite incessant warfare, invasions, and enslavement—and as more mouths had to be fed from smaller and smaller plots of land. Although little was known of scientific agriculture, crops slowly increased by the use of more intensive labor, and tools became perceptibly more efficient. The skilled artisans lived in the administrative towns and temple centers, but many peasants became parttime artisans to supply needed goods for themselves and their neighbors. Slowly, of course, new crops came into cultivation and oxen were soon used to pull primitive plows in place of the labor of the family members. Irrigation was employed whenever conditions permitted and where and when the governments were able to utilize the labor of the villagers to impound flood waters that were used during the dry season. Over a period of time, traditional crops along with new ones from afar were planted on every available piece of land.

Thousands of years ago, young sons who sensed that the family lands were too overtilled and insufficient to help each child migrated to areas where they could work for others and eventually obtain a bit of land to cultivate—either through purchase, marriage, or adoption in the new village. There was also land which could be cultivated if one could move far enough and receive permission from those who were hunters or pastoralists to settle in their midst. Immigration was not a peculiarly nineteenth- or twentieth-century phenomenon; it existed on a large scale thousands of years ago.

Land could also be obtained through warfare, and one received it along with the slaves to work it from one's military superiors. Land belonged to the victor and could be given or taken away as reward or punishment. Entire villages with their inhabitants and common lands could be given to those whom the conquerors wished to favor. When in turn the old warriors were conquered by new ones, the land could be again distributed to deserving captains or nobles who had been of assistance. To the victor belonged the spoils was also the favorite dictum of warrior states in the past, as they took treasures, land, slaves, and concubines from those who were not able to fight back successfully. The weak deserved to be mastered by the strong. There was little pity for the defeated and enslaved, since the belief was held that, if one did not win, he in turn would be defeated and enslaved.

◇   ◇   ◇   ◇   ◇

So, as the nobles and the kings fought and hunted other two-legged animals generation after generation, millenium after millenium, the peasants who formed the vast majority of the early civilizations lived as best they could in what we today would call abject squalor. Their huts were small, windowless, without chimneys, having floors and walls of earth through which heat, cold, wind, insects, and rodents found it easy to enter. Men lived short lives both as peasants and as nobles; and most peasants, men as well as women, died by the time they were forty. Men who could live to be 50 or 60 were considered fortunate sages who could dispense wisdom to those younger than they. Women died in large numbers as a result of overwork, childbirth, and disease, while children who survived to the age of five were considered lucky. Infants who died were not given names or identities. Food was scarce between harvests, during the dry seasons, and especially in times of drought. The large storage bins for grain in the small administrative towns were perhaps the product of a later time. It is more than possible that the grain was reserved for the king and his large staff rather than for the peasants who either starved or sold their children or themselves into slavery for the security of meals that they could count on. Men in most of the ancient civilizations ate little meat or fish. Their diet was monotonous and composed mostly of cereals. They ate few fruits or vegetables, and not more than one meal a day. Slaves subsisted on a marginal starvation diet for most of their lives.

Little is known about the techniques used in agriculture between 3000 B.C. and one A.D., and it is quite possible that a system of letting land lie fallow for a season or more may have been in existence at that time. We do not know whether fertilizers of any kind were used, although it is likely that household garbage as well as human and animal wastes were spread on the land (we find a primitive use of fertilizer in Europe at that time). The villages must have been governed by headmen with a good deal of authoritarian power to extract surplus grain as taxes for the king's granaries—also the power to draft young hunters as soldiers for the king's armies (though as time went on hunting became the prerogative only of the nobles and kings).

There was probably some form of ancestor worship even before the agricultural deities came into existence. There may have been special village deities or spirits, though it is more than likely that the development of a pantheon of deities and temples had to await the coming of the urban states and the rise of advanced Primary civilization. After the Sumerian period, the villages adopted the deities and their worship from the priestly class in the temples in the city-states. With the rise of Primary civilization, the village lost its autonomy and the agriculturists became a definite class of peasants, subject to the laws and control of the administrative centers wherein they had little or no voice.

Although the peasants continued to live as their ancestors had in the past Neolithic period, they were restricted in the amount of land they could till and in the free utilization of their own produce. They were subject to taxes and their sons and daughters could be taken away to serve the nobles and kings in various ways. And yet, there must have been festivals in which the villages could participate, as well as councils in which the individual heads of families could express their points of view. There may have been various rites of passage for infants, adolescents, men and women. The seasons and the harvest may also have been celebrated, and the social life must have been pleasant enough to permit the villagers to obtain their relaxation in meeting and talking with their fellowmen.

Despite the existence of the nearby administrative center, the villagers could say, as the later Chinese peasant did, that the king was far away and the peasant could still regulate his life much as his ancestors had. Parents could still rear their children to be as much like themselves as possible. Whatever knowledge the young needed, they could obtain it within the family circle from parents and close relatives. Disasters were part of the usual order of things, including conquest by invading kings, periodic droughts, continuous incursions of bandits recruited from the sons of broken families, unemployed landless tenants, and orphans whose families had been killed in battle or natural events. Diseases were rampant. Though one may have prayed and made proper sacrifices to the deities, one had to accept the fact that other unknown deities who were more powerful had conquered the deities of the peasant and even those of the urban administrative center. One had to learn to accept one's fate passively. Thus, religion became more and more important in letting the individual in the Bronze and Iron Ages chart the unknown and unseeable worlds in which the deities, the demons, and good and evil spirits moved.

◇   ◇   ◇   ◇   ◇

Men in this period of Primary civilization needed counseling based upon knowledge in order to make the right decisions and to avert the ill-fortune which lurked around them. But knowledge obtained from any critical examination of the world, from assessments of the various options which were open, or from attempts to hold common assumptions up to the light of reason was not available. Instead, a series of assumptions about the real world were made which were accepted primarily because there were few other statements that men could hold to. These were accepted as substitutes for knowledge of the unseen world, of men's motivations and anticipated behavior, and of the mysterious ways in which the deities and lesser forces operated.

Men in Primary civilization were not yet ready for critical thinking and for experimental feedbacks to test the assumptions of the day (any more than we are in the twentieth century), but it is most unfortunate that men were unable to build more rapidly on the knowledge inherited from the Neolithic Age. Primary civilization, on the other hand, lasted as long as the Neolithic, and in many parts of the world continued until the end of the twentieth century in its mentality, its assumptions, and its dogmas.

For an understanding of the unknown world that they lived in, men first began to observe the heavens where the deities lived, in order to determine which of those living there was responsible for the seasons, for the daily rhythm of day and night, for the floods, for famines, warfare, illnesses, plus all the rewards and punishments that human beings were heir to. Men were believed to be born under the protection of guardian deities who dwelt in the stars. If one could discover under whose aegis one lived, one could identify the deity and attempt to win his favor. (Later, men believed that knowing the fixed behavior of these astral deities let one anticipate what they had in mind, and the religion of astrology was further expanded.) Men also turned to oracles of various kinds to ascertain what the fates (in the person of deities) had reserved for them. The deities directed everything, which meant that there was definite purpose in life. Even those things that seemed to be random in appearance were in actuality effects of definite, although incompletely known, causes. To know the latter, men believed that they needed to seek this other world of knowledge through revelations and insights obtained directly from the deities.

Men looked upon the world not as being one of change, but as one that had been fixed from its earliest days. They believed that they could have no effect upon the world surrounding them for everything had its place, everything its cause. It was a world that impinged upon man, but he could not influence its movement any more than he could influence the behavior of the sun, the moon, and the stars. Though the universe existed outside of man, man had been given the right to enjoy its fruits. Men believed that, while the deities made and controlled this universe, they could benefit from it if they were willing to serve the deities loyally and submissively as servants and favored slaves. In return, bits of revelations as to how the universe worked might be slowly leaked to them as rewards for their loyalty.

Men could not attempt to understand the universe, it was believed, because knowledge belonged only to the deities and men's attempts to do so could lead to severe punishment. (Later Deists asked questions, however, in an effort to understand God's handiwork.) Men were thrown into confusion by being unable to cooperate with one another or to communicate knowledge to one another. They had to understand how inferior they were to the gods, how lowly, how inadequate, and how humble: men could not compete with the deities for understanding or insights.

The world of the Primary civilization was static, and men were taught that whatever knowledge was needed already existed. With the help of the gods, men had reached a plateau beyond which they could not go without courting disaster. The parable of men being children to the deities was to be repeated in succeeding centuries and millenia: unless men learned like little children to trust those who gave them knowledge, they would be unable to achieve the rewards which theoretically were open to them. This authoritarianism would still be around even at the end of the twentieth century.

VIII   Technology, Civilization, and the Urban Administrative Center

Civilization as it appeared first in the Sumerian city-states, then in Egypt, and next in the Harappan culture was a matter of organizing men in order to get them to accept government passively or submissively. It spread its concepts of record-keeping, of respect for the written word, of urban administrative centers, of laws (which had a sacredness of their own), of bureaucratic rigidities, and of a moral code in which loyalty to legitimate authority was all-important. Even in its earliest days, civilization spread fairly rapidly, for it had more to offer than the single autonomous Neolithic village. Because of its complex organization, it was able to manipulate men as well as resources. It could husband wealth, even great wealth, in a comparative and relative sense, and could command a more developed technology than was possible in a Neolithic village, where the few artisans worked only parttime at their crafts.

Civilization used traveling merchants to bring rare ores into urban workshops which paid for them in finished goods. Though trade had existed in Neolithic days, it was not in the hands of specialists but was part of the everyday barter that villagers engaged in with other villagers. Neolithic chieftains and headmen coming in contact with Primary civilization were evidently impressed by the goods, the power, the self-confidence, the writing, the keeping of records, and the urban way of life which it manifested. Though slow initially, this way of life was able to infiltrate large areas both in the Old and New Worlds.

The Neolithic Age could be spread by simple agriculturists and pastoralists, but the forms of Primary civilization could be transmitted only by the literate merchant, the administrator, skilled full-time artisan, scribe, and priest—with the aid of professional soldiers. Though it is not known specifically how ideas were carried from one area to another, it is suspected that the complex of civilization spread from Mesopotamia both eastward and westward, and from the Caribbean coast of Mexico westward and southward. Civilization is far too complex to have developed in one area independently of other centers. We must assume that—like the later Industrial and Scientific civilization which had its generalized origins in Western Europe—it could spread only with the assistance of those who were the original carriers. We know that the Industrial and Scientific civilization did not have multiple origins on various continents, and we must assume (though complete information is lacking) that the Old and the New World civilizations (like the Neolithic Age) also had common origins.

At any rate, Primary civilization with its urban centers based upon a large-scale peasantry began in Mesopotamia slightly before 4000 B.C. It spread to Egypt by 3500 B.C. and to other points in Southwest Asia by 3000 B.C. By 3500 B.C., it had moved to the Elamite cities of present-day Iran, and through the various Elamite city-states along the Persian Gulf diffused to the Indus River by 3000 B.C. By that time, it was spreading to Anatolia, to the first of the Trojan cities, and to Crete. From the Harappan cities, civilization moved slowly eastward and southward to present-day India, covering an area from present Delhi and Agra to contemporary Bombay. By 2000 B.C., civilization had covered all of Anatolia and Southwest Asia and had spread to China (from what direction we still do not know). It moved to mainland Greece roughly at the same time, where it stalled until later Greek colonists took it to Italy and southern France. The Phoenicians, who were carriers of the Primary civilization from 2000 B.C. on, spread it further to North Africa and Spain. Primary civilization came to the New World by 1200 B.C. (from where we still do not know), and very slowly moved into the Yucatan, the Mexican Valley, and Guatemala. Later, the New World civilization jumped to Peru, where the beginnings of a Primary civilization were founded during the first century of the Christian era.

The technology of the Primary civilization went hand in hand with urban settlements and the development of professional classes of artisans, military officers, scribes, administrators, and priests. Though pure copper was hammered out cold by 7000 B.C. in Anatolia (and in the New World somewhat later), the smelting of copper with various impurities to form bronze began with the first city-states in Southwest Asia around 5000 B.C. The smelting and casting of gold and silver was coincidental with the existence of city-states both in the Old and the New Worlds. In Thailand, bronze-casting was known as early as 2500 B.C., before the process was used in China. Iron-smelting came later: the first sign of it archaeologically is in northeastern Anatolia in the vicinity of contemporary Armenia, where it appears to have been developed around 2700 B.C. Iron-making became universal in Europe by 1000 B.C. and moved into Africa south of the Sahara in the first millenium of the Christian era. It was virtually unknown in the New World, indicating that those carriers of civilization who came to the New World must have arrived before iron-smelting was widely known in the Old World.

◇   ◇   ◇   ◇   ◇

The wheel was invented somewhere in Southwest Asia by 5000 B.C., but it appears to have been associated with plains country and the establishment of an extensive transport system between urban centers. The boat is Neolithic in origin; but the boat-with-sails, designed to utilize the energy of wind to propel it far distances along the coast, was associated with the trade complex that appears to be part of Primary civilization. Extensive trade utilizing sea transport did not start until after 4000 B.C., although short distance travel by boat may have preceded this date by a millenium or so. Horses and asses of various types (including the Onager used by the Sumerians) became part of the urban scene soon after the invention of the wheeled carriage or cart somewhere between 3000 and 3500 B.C. (The horse was not domesticated until about one thousand years later in the steppes of southern Russia and also in the area of what is now Central Asia.) Somewhere in the region where the wheel was first discovered (seemingly the area north of the Sumerian towns), someone had learned that a castrated bull made a docile source of animal energy to pull plows and carts. The horse, though faster than the ox, was not used for transporting bulky goods until after the invention of the horse-collar (the ox-yoke choked the horse) by the Chinese sometime around the beginning of the Christian era. At approximately the same time, the Chinese invented the short stirrup, which also increased the usefulness of the horse. Neither the wheel nor the wagon was known in the New World (though wheeled toys have been found in Olmec graves). There were no New World equivalents of the horse or the ox which could have been used to pull a wagon, even if one had existed. The llamas in Peru were not able to carry more than an average-sized porter could transport in a day on the roads of the Incas. In the civilizations of Mexico, men were the chief source of transportation power. (The preceding may perhaps indicate that the civilizations of the New World were encouraged initially by ideas diffused from Southeast Asia that may have started around 2000 B.C. and moved eastward: the steppingstone islands of the Pacific seem to have been inhabited as early as that date.)

The blast furnace for increasing heat in the iron-smelting process did not come into existence in Europe until the fifteenth century of the present era, but piston-bellows for this purpose were used in Southeast Asia by 1000 B.C. and in China soon after. In

Iran, goat-skin bellows may have been used roughly around 1000 B.C. to develop a temperature of over 1,300 degrees centigrade in order to reduce the iron oxides which had been added to the lead and copper flux—and which may have led to the later development of an iron industry. Silver and gold reduction appear to have gone hand in hand with the smelting of copper and iron. (It is possible that all the metals used by early men may have been found close to one another, and accidental or experimental smelting may have produced an extensive variety by 1000 B.C.) In the New World, copper was used in its native state by the Indians around the Great Lakes as early as 9,000 years ago. The actual smelting of copper, silver, and gold may not have occurred until the beginning of the Christian era, with the processes first discovered in South America. Metal-smelting did not take place in Mexico before 1100 A.D.

Glass-making may have been discovered in the process of reducing metals. In this, Egypt and the area around the Phoenician coast (present-day Syria, Lebanon, and Israel) may have been co-equals in discovery sometime in the second millenium B.C. Glass-making spread from these two centers to the other urban regions. Glass-blowing was not discovered until just before the Christian era in the Syria-Lebanon-Israel area. On the other hand, glass-making was unknown to the civilizations of the New World, though obsidian, a form of volcanic glass, was known and used in ornamentation.

In dealing with the technologies of these early civilizations, it is difficult to know how many of the items found in archaeological sites originated there and how many may have come from areas and sites that are still undiscovered. Recent evidence indicates that Stonehenge in England, for example, is older than the pyramids of Egypt; that many of the megalithic passage graves found in Brittany are older than those found in Mycenean Greece. This means that it was as great an innovation for men living in the beginning of the third millenium B.C. in Britain to float tons of stone from Wales to the site of Stonehenge as it was for the overseers of the first pyramids to transport enormous quantities of stone down the Nile River. Whether the two are interrelated we do not know, though we can assume that certain ideas could have been in circulation over regions of great distances and over a long period of time before they were put into practice. In general, it is safer to assume today that the pyramids were an Egyptian invention just as Stonehenge was an ancient British one, though the pyramids could have stemmed from a technology first worked out at Stonehenge— even if this seems very unlikely at the moment.

The Sumerian and Harappan towns were built of mud-brick (though the latter used baked brick more than the former), but the Egyptians learned to use stone at an early date. In Britain, the building of Stonehenge around 3000 B.C. required the transporting of four-ton blocks of stone hundreds of miles from the mountains of Wales by sea and land. In early Egypt shortly after 2600 B.C., two million blocks, each weighing more than two and a half tons, were transported by raft and primitive boat 600 miles down the Nile from quarries situated near the present Aswan Dam in order to build the Great Pyramid. The building was then surfaced with newly-developed white polished limestone, which was removed by the Arabs a little over one thousand years ago (much as the citizens of Rome stripped their ancient monuments of marble and polished stone in order to use them again in churches and palaces).

The Great Pyramid, like the later pyramids and temples, was a memorial to those early geniuses of management and technological innovation who planned the work of thousands of men (perhaps as many as 10,000 at one time), who were then organized into work groups, fed, motivated, taught, and supervised. Materials and men of widely varying skills had to be brought together. Copper tools had to be virtually invented on the spot to cut the stone to its proper length. Accurate measurements using very primitive tools had to be devised to make certain that each block would fit into its proper place. On the Pyramid itself, there were scribes at work who devised techniques for measuring what had already been completed and assessing what needed to be cut. The large blocks of limestone and granite had to be separated and transported without any knowledge of the wheel or block and tackle, but with knowledge of a primitive see-saw to hoist the stones, a simple type of lever, a roller, and an inclined plane. All these techniques were invented less than one century after men in Egypt had first learned to cut stone. The men who devised the Stonehenge monument in Britain were faced with challenges as great. Not only did they need to design a monument to fit their purposes, but they had to learn to quarry large blocks with primitive tools (it is possible that copper tools were present in Britain around 3000 B.C.), they had to learn where the best stone could be cut, had to devise techniques with their customary or new tools to transport these huge blocks by water and land, and then had to erect them in a pre-arranged fashion using unskilled labor. The organization of men and their energies were thus the goals of all the early builders as they pushed their way toward more sophistication beyond the achievements of previous cultures.

◇   ◇   ◇   ◇   ◇

The cities of Harappa and Mohenjo-Daro in the Indus Valley began growing as urban administrative centers somewhere around 2500 B.C., and evidently reached a high level of technical development within a few hundred years. By 2200 B.C., it is possible that the average resident in both these cities may have had better housing and sanitary facilities than the town-dwellers of the Tigris-Euphrates and Nile River Valleys. Houses of the Indus Valley (especially those of the administrators and the subordinates who worked with them) were made of plastered baked brick (though plastering was also known to the Sumerians), were large and roomy, two-storied, had bath facilities, latrines, and semi-open drains leading to clay cisterns in the alleys for waste disposal.

⋄   ⋄   ⋄   ⋄   ⋄

The civilization in Crete which began around 2500 B.C. received cultural influences from both Egypt and Mesopotamia (also possibly to some extent from the Balkans, the route that some of the Myceneans and the later Dorian Greeks took, since there seems to have been an interchange of persons between Anatolia and the Balkans even before 5000 B.C.). Crete made its great technical contributions chiefly in the form of three palaces in different parts of the island. The largest and most luxurious of the palaces, at Knossos, had broad stairways, central halls leading to private suites, and a large central court around which there were two levels above and two below. The royal suites had small rooms with earthenware bathtubs and drains proceeding from these small bathrooms to a central drain which in turn led into a nearby river. Drains also led from the roof within the walls to an underground open drain which connected with the main sewer. Water to the palace was piped in through terra-cotta pipes, slanted at various sections to prevent the accumulation of sediment. An open channel was built next to the main stairway leading from the central court to the river. The Cretans had to know the basics of hydraulic engineering in order to construct the channel with parabolic curves to slow the rush of water, thus preventing it from overflowing and turning the stairs into miniature waterfalls.

The Cretans even more than the Sumerians and Egyptians lived off trade, and the three palaces represented the three important business centers on the island. Knossos appears to have conducted an extensive trade with Anatolia, the Balkan coast, and within the Black Sea area. Phaistos seems to have been the center of trade with Egypt, while Mallia was evidently the chief port exporting and carrying on an import trade with the coastal areas of present-day Syria, Lebanon, and Israel. Smaller towns containing wharves cut into their rocky coasts have been found that may have traded with the western Mediterranean area. Some Cretan traders may even have sailed along the Atlantic coast to England and perhaps to the German coast, looking for those metals that were rare in the Mediterranean area. The small traders with the larger merchant-king and merchant-prince were evidently the carriers of Primary civilization to far away lands. Although after 2000 B.C. the Myceneans as conquerors appear to have been changed by Cretan culture, it is likely that they were also equally influenced by social currents coming from Anatolia and the Balkans.

◇   ◇   ◇   ◇   ◇

The Anatolian city-states may not have been sources of empires, but they were centers of extensive trade and a high degree of technical achievement—though they did not match the levels of the Egyptians, Sumerians, or Cretans in arts and craftsmanship. Perhaps among the oldest of these city-states was Troy, which began to grow within a few hundred years after the rise of the Sumerian city-states. By 2400 B.C., or at the time of the Cretan apogee, the city had arrived at a stage of development in which it possessed stone palaces, immense stone fortifications, large dwellings, and complex monumental art. It is possible that the famous legendary Trojan War may have been fought more over trade routes to the Black Sea than over the abduction of Helen. As a center for trade and cottage industries, Troy could have competed with Crete as well as the other Anatolian city-states for the Balkan and Black Sea trade. Thousands of years later, the Greeks followed their trade to the Black Sea and built colonial centers to carry on barter with the Indo-Iranian-speaking Scythians and perhaps even with the Finnish-speaking tribes to the north.

Troy and many little city-states nearby were basically small centers ruled by a minor king, advised by a small elite of merchant-aristocrats controlling the labor of thousands of peasants within a 20 to 30 mile area, and acting much as the small principalities did within Germany before 1871. The merchants with the protection of their mercenary soldiers carried on trade over extensive land and sea routes that became almost monopolies. They conducted their own workshops with fulltime supervisory artisans and skilled workers making the bronze axes, daggers, spears, pottery, finely woven cloth, and carpets which they traded for metals of various kinds, uncut jewels, slaves, and goods which they could not make themselves. Troy was not the only city-state in Anatolia. There were dozens, all having their origins at the beginning of the third millenium B.C. At Dorak near the various cities of Troy, archaeologists have uncovered sites going back to before 2500 B.C. Royal graves have been found containing scepters of pink-veined marble encased in gilt with silver handles, along with fragments of red carpet (similar to ones made today in this region), a silver dagger, and a sword with an iron blade (indicating that the smelting of iron was known even before 2500 B.C.).

◊   ◊   ◊   ◊   ◊

The Hittites, an Indo-European-speaking people who settled in Central Anatolia around 2000 B.C., brought with them from the north (they evidently came down from the Caucasus over a period of hundreds of years) domesticated horses, the use of iron, complex war chariots, and complicated metal tools. The evidence seems to indicate that some unknown people to the north of them, perhaps in present-day Soviet Armenia, were the makers of iron long before the Hittites came in (but newer evidence in the future may indicate that the knowledge of iron-smelting was known to more than one people: its origins are still unclear).

◊   ◊   ◊   ◊   ◊

In the Levantine area south of Anatolia along the eastern end of the Mediterranean, cultural influences emanating from both Sumeria and Egypt began to play important parts in their urban development from about 3300 B.C. on, though written records started around 2700 B.C. Two important groups, the Amorites and the Canaanites, both speaking roughly the same mutually understandable Semitic language, were the chief actors: the Amorites being influenced from Mesopotamia, while the Canaanites on the coast were more affected by cultural emanations arriving with the trade from Egypt. The Amorites had descendants known to history as Babylonians, Assyrians, and Hebrews, while the Phoenicians and also the Hebrews were descendants of the Canaanites. The Amorites learned a good deal from the Sumerians, but they also influenced the latter in architecture, astronomy, and technical achievements. The Phoenicians carried on an extensive trade within the entire Mediterranean region, perhaps even venturing up the Danube and along the Black Sea. Although we know little of Phoenician or Canaanite trading routes in the second millenium B.C., we do know that they reached the Azores by the seventh century B.C., and that they might have circumnavigated Africa by the sixth century B.C. There is a faint possibility that they may have reached the coast of Brazil as a result of storms off the west coast of Africa, which may have scattered a few ships westward in the sixth century B.C. It is also in the realm of possibility that Phoenician ships may have reached England and the northwest coast of Europe at an early period, but here the evidence is scanty. The Phoenicians carried on an extensive trade in their craft specialties: purple-dyed woolen and linen textiles, multi-colored textiles made of various materials, olive oil, cedar wood, fine pottery, and jewelry. They also carried on an extensive fishing industry and dried fish for export.

Although the Phoenician port cities were overrun by the Assyrians in the seventh century B.C., the Phoenicians had by this time already established extensive colonies on both sides of the Mediterranean. Carthage had been settled by the eighth century B.C., and when the Phoenician port cities of Tyre and Sidon were destroyed by the Assyrians, those Phoenician merchants who escaped made Carthage their new center of trade and craft operations. The Phoenicians also learned early from the Egyptians how to improve their skills at glass-making, and passed on this knowledge to neighboring Syrians and Israelis. Glass-blowing evidently originated in this area, and in Roman days the chief artisans working in glass were the Syrians and the Jews. It is also more than possible that large numbers of conversions to Judaism during a period of more than a thousand years of slow conquest brought many Phoenicians (or Canaanites) into the Jewish fold. If so, this may explain why the Jews taken away by the Babylonians in captivity in the sixth century B.C. quickly became well-to-do in the Babylonian urban centers as a result of their having special skills in crafts and trading. The large number of Jews living outside Israel by the second century B.C. merely indicated how extensive the number of converts to Judaism must have been in the Mediterranean area. Alexandria by the first century A.D. had a very large minority of skilled Jews living in their own sections of the city.

The Phoenicians referred to themselves as Canaanites; the name Phoenician is of Mycenean origin. As traders and craftsmen they were second to none, and their colonization efforts were on only a slightly smaller scale than those of the later mainland Greeks. Their colonies were composed of small groups of skilled artisans and merchants who usually settled among larger numbers of local residents, intermarried, assumed local leadership in matters of trade and craftsmanship, and soon influenced larger numbers than would have been possible if the colonists had segregated themselves. Phoenician trade was extensively based upon a wide variety of cottage industries in which individuals were employed fulltime to make objects for which there was a market. Trade as a daily occupation for the Phoenicians must have begun early, for there is evidence that by 2000 B.C. Canaanite metalsmiths were bringing their crafts and metallurgical knowledge to Central Europe, coming to the head of the Adriatic by sea and then moving by land northward over the mountains. From an early date, the Phoenicians were middlemen diffusing techniques which they received from other sources. Not only did they spread the art of metalworking to Spain, Portugal, and Central Europe, but after the thirteenth century B.C. they diffused the arts and crafts of Egypt to even more extensive areas. They were traders and explorers, as the Greeks and later the French, Spaniards, and Russians were. Their greatest gift to later civilization, however, lay not so much in their techniques and crafts which they disseminated, but in the phonetic alphabet which they received from other Canaanites (and which may have been derived from coppermine foremen working for the Egyptians, who used Egyptian hieroglyphic consonants sometime around the seventeenth and sixteenth centuries B.C.). The Sumerians had first used pictographic symbols (like the early Egyptians and the early Chinese), but by 3000 B.C. had changed their system into a phonetic syllabary (in which syllables were represented rather than consonants alone, as in the phonetic alphabet). The Egyptian hieroglyphics were modified after 2600 B.C. into a script that gave some phonetic value to initial consonants of words. The early Canaanites added new letters to those received from the Egyptians, but allowed each consonant a separate symbolic value. The Phoenicians evidently received their initial alphabet by 1500 B.C., and later by the ninth century B.C. disseminated it to the early Greek traders who then added vowels—though they kept the Semitic names for the consonants. The Greeks in turn diffused the phonetic alphabet to the Etruscans north of the Greek colonies in Italy, who in turn passed it on to the Romans, who as their inheritance passed it on to those whom they influenced culturally. The alphabet also spread eastward to India and Southeast Asia, influencing the growth of new alphabets there.

◇   ◇   ◇   ◇   ◇

The Chinese in turn were influenced by cultural currents stemming from Southeast and Central Asia (which had already come under the cultural influences of the Elamites, Sumerians, and the still unknown centers of urban civilization to the north and east of them). The Neolithic period, which preceded the first growth of Chinese civilization along the Yellow River Valley, was again affected by waves of ideas coming from the south and the west. Chinese civilization began its history with the rise of a group of peasant-warrior kings known as the Shangs, who encouraged the growth of both a military and urban technology (though the latter came initially from outside their kingdoms). As a result of the technical influences arriving from Southeast Asia, especially from Thailand, the Chinese were able to cast bronze in a more artistic and efficient fashion than the civilizations in the Mediterranean area.

The Chinese made many contributions to Primary civilization. In generalized form, however, Chinese civilization differed little from the other civilizations to the west and south which preceded theirs. Chinese innovations began fairly late, with such monumental public works as the Great Wall built in the third century B.C., and the extensive canal system which was expanded during the first millenium of the Christian era. The creation of populous urban centers occurred roughly about the same time. The crank was first discovered in China, from whence it moved slowly to Europe, reaching there about the ninth to tenth centuries of our present era. Printing was used in both Korea and China in the ninth century A.D., although the concept of imprinting with fixed blocks was known before that time. The crossbow was made in China centuries before it was used in Europe, and it was not until the eighteenth century that the Europeans discovered the Chinese secret of making porcelain from kaolin. The Chinese reached their apogee of technological innovation in the sixteenth century.

China received Buddhism from Southeast Asia in the sixth century A.D., but, though there was a receptivity to some of Gautama's teachings, most of these were transformed to become more Chinese in spirit. China influenced Korea and Japan after the beginning of the Christian era, but those influences were a one-way route, for China saw herself as the center of the world and the teacher of others rather than a willing pupil.

Few European nations equalled China in the first ten centuries of the Christian era in crafts, standard of living, and artistic levels. The Chinese added little new to the general repository of Primary civilization—despite the unusual building of extensive roads and canals from the third century B.C. to the eleventh century A.D., linking the coastal areas of China to the interior. China was ahead of Europe in using the equivalent of a blast furnace and the piston bellows; the latter, however, originated in Southeast Asia rather than in China. Marco Polo was impressed by the grandeur of technological China in the thirteenth century of the Christian era, but after that century Europe slowly forged ahead to widen the gap between itself and China. The industrial and scientific revolutions widened it even more.

Since Chinese philosophers before the beginning of the Christian era were convinced that Chinese civilization could go no further, they were concerned to keep the status quo. Like the Greeks, however, they were secular in their quest for knowledge. Rather than seeing it as being eternal and infallible (as the ancient Egyptians, Sumerians, Hebrews, and Hindus had considered it—since to them all knowledge came from the gods who could never be indecisive), the Chinese point of view was theoretically experimental (though the rigid elitism in which past knowledge was held prevented the quest for new varieties). Mathematics, engineering, and the sciences were looked down upon as compared to the eternal truths of the classics, discovered by the intellectuals who lived from the sixth century B.C. to the third century A.D. Unlike the Hindus, the Chinese saw knowledge as a consequence of thinking, and had little interest in trying to define original First Causes.

While China theoretically attempted to reward merit and ability through an extensive examination system, in actuality it merely perpetuated a literate aristocratic class. Poor peasants were unable to support their sons during the years of schooling necessary to let them qualify for civil service examinations. The family was all-important, and the wealthier the family the more its members were expected to help it continue to hold onto its riches and power. Though ancestral worship has always been important to the Chinese, the coming of Buddhism completely contradicted it, for in the Wheel of Life one's ancestors moved into strangers' bodies upon death. The Chinese solved this problem by keeping ancestor worship and changing Buddhism so that it was less contradictory. Chinese thought was too secular to permit new religions to propagate absolute truths among them. If one religion had some truth to it, a second might add even more substance to the truth, and a third still more. From the Chinese point of view, there was nothing contradictory in being a Buddhist, an Animist, a Taoist, and even a Christian, all at the same time. Chinese thinking was thus receptive to experimental scientific thought, even though Confucius and Mencius taught adherence to traditional doctrines and a respect for the status quo in all interpersonal relations within the family, the clan, and the empire.

As in the case of all the Primary civilizations, Chinese political legitimacy came from the deities. From the sixth century B.C., the rule of men came from the hands of the deity called Heaven (who permitted the king to act as its agent unless he fell into disfavor with the deity). The king, like other rulers further to the west, was the priestly intermediary between the mortal world of men, who are born and die, and the immortal world of spirits and deities, who suffer neither. Although the mandate to rule legitimately came directly from Heaven, that deity could easily remove its protection if it were irritated with the way the king governed his subjects. If he were overthrown by his nobles or by conquering invaders, this event only indicated that Heaven had previously withdrawn its protection of him (otherwise he could not have been defeated); his mandate was thereby revoked and his subjects owed him no further loyalty.

Chinese society was hierarchically organized. The king was loyal to Heaven, and the nobles owed obedience and filial piety to the king. Every official was obedient and loyal to those above him, and he in turn was expected to be benign, considerate, and fatherly to those beneath him. Society and the state were seen as extensions of the family. This hierarchy of statuses was transformed into classic moral codes by Confucius, Mencius, and other Chinese philosophers, and became the instruction for the examinations into the civil service, thus limiting the education of later Mandarin administrators. The status quo was fixed in Chinese society. It remained traditional in form and content until the entire system was overthrown through the conquests of European and Japanese invaders almost 2,000 years later. Technology slowly improved during these centuries, new emperors came, and dynasties were founded. Nomadic armies invaded looking for the treasures which had been amassed by the concentration of wealth by the few on top. And the peasants could only hope that they would be left alone by the rapacious tax collectors and the administrators appointed by an emperor living far away. Despite the moral code of Confucianism, the emperor was not too concerned with the well-being of the mass of illiterate and poverty-stricken peasants, who supported the entire hierarchy of officialdom which made up the operating arm of Chinese civilization.

◊   ◊   ◊   ◊   ◊

The New World civilizations never equalled the technological achievements of their contemporaries in the Old World. The Olmecs were the first pioneers in diffusing the organizational patterns of the urban-centered civilization. The Olmecs developed many of the glyphs and part of the calendrical enumeration used by the Mayas, the next-door neighbors who succeeded them. The early Olmecs began their urban development around 1200 B.C. and lasted until around 800 B.C., when their main ceremonial and administrative center was overthrown by their own peasants who may have reacted against supporting the enormous social overhead that appeared to be a concomitant of urban civilization. But, although they were able to overthrow a particular kind of ruling group, they were unable to overthrow civilization in general — thus preventing their return to a previous age of greater economic and political freedom. The destruction of San Lorenzo, the Olmec administrative seat centuries before the beginning of the Christian era, was a battle won but a war lost by long-suffering underlings — a war that continued to be lost by the later Indian peasants of Mexico, Central America, and the coastal regions of western South America. Although San Lorenzo was destroyed, Olmec chieftains built up La Venta and Tres Zapotes as later administrative centers. The Mayas followed with their theocratic rule and obsessions with calendrical dates. They were able to invent an abstract value, the zero, which was then unknown in the Old World. Though the zero seems to have been reinvented in India sometime after the beginning of the Christian era, there is a possibility that trans-Pacific cultural movements could have brought the zero to Southeast Asia, from whence it diffused to India and later to the Arab and European worlds. But this again is only speculation, for definite contacts between the Mayas and Southeast Asia are not yet known to have occurred.

As in the Old World at that time, religion and warfare went hand in hand in the New World as the Mayan theocracy forced masses of peasants to submit to their rule, erecting a large quantity of ceremonial monuments to mathematical deities whose will could only be ascertained through the magic of astronomy and' complex numbers in the billions. As in the Old World, cultural ideas spread and the Olmecs and Mayas influenced their neighbors, the Toltecs, who in turn affected the Zapotecs, the Mixtecs, and later the Aztecs. Large pyramidal tombs as well as temples were built out of cut stone, using the false arch and requiring the labor of thousands.

Mexican civilization moved slowly down the Pacific coast to Columbia, Ecuador, and Peru, where a succeeding number of civilizations were built on the bases received from the north. Although writing and dating were used by the Olmecs, the Mayas, and those who followed them, they were unknown to the Incas (some scholars believe that these did use a primitive form of writing and that some kind of record-keeping utilizing written symbols did in fact exist).

◇   ◇   ◇   ◇   ◇

It is difficult to compare the New World civilizations with those in the Old World, for despite the historical documentation and archaeological work which have been done, we still know very little about any of them except for records of religious rituals and monuments erected by kings and nobles to commemorate forgotten battles. Little is known of the daily life of the average inhabitant, and even less of the ideas which circulated among the leadership in all these civilizations. It does appear that in the fifteenth century the New World urban centers were in an earlier stage of development than the Old World civilizations in the first century of the Christian era, but both were so different that it is difficult to compare them.

The New World civilizations did not have the wheel, but even if the wheel did exist, it is unlikely that the cart could have been put to efficient use in the mountainous topography of Mexico, Central and South America. Although the Peruvians had the llama, it was not an efficient beast of burden (men were more docile and could carry more). There were no domesticated species of animals that could have been used, for only the guinea pig, the dog, and the turkey were domesticated by the other New World Amerindians. While there were cities, we know about them only through the exaggerations of the early Spaniards, who had to convince themselves as well as those in Spain of the enormous discoveries which they had made. None of the New World civilizations reached the technological or intellectual levels that were present in Egypt in the twelfth century B.C. or in Greece by the fifth century B.C. Certainly none was on the level of Chinese or Roman civilizations at the beginning of the Christian era. The New World civilizations were in the process of growth, and like those of the Old World each was able to stamp its organization with an individuality of its own, for diffusion is rarely imitative (Egyptian and Harappan civilizations differed markedly from the Sumerian). Mayan civilization with its theocracy differed from the later Aztec, just as both differed from the Incas in Peru. Like the Old World civilizations (with the possible exception of the Chinese, which continued on a fairly stable keel until the twentieth century), there were innovative periods with a flowering of the arts and crafts and the building of magnificent stone tombs, temples, and cities, followed by an age of conservatism with a lowering of guard — to be succeeded by conquest in which the civilization was taken over and carried slightly further by another people. Civilization is a matter of ideas concerning the organization of men and the keeping of records, and these are carried by only a small part of the population.

Kings and nobles may be overthrown, but if the scribes and administrative officials survive, the civilization will endure. For the vast majority of the populations under Primary civilization in both the Old and New Worlds, life went on century after century in roughly the same way, even though the men were drafted to serve in the armies and to build the monumental public works. The innovations were only those encouraged by the ruling groups. If the latter were non-achievers themselves, the particular form that the civilization took stagnated. And this evidently occurred among the Olmecs and Mayas in the New World, as among the civilizations in the Old World. Although Egyptian arts, crafts, and engineering reached higher levels by the twelfth century B.C. than those reached by any other civilization at that time, they had soon begun to stagnate. By the time the Hellenic influences came in during the fourth century B.C., Egyptian technology had already reached its nadir.

◇   ◇   ◇   ◇   ◇

From the eighth century B.C. onward, the various small Greek city-states learned to survive in the Mediterranean world of priestly, trading, and warring peoples. They learned to write phonetically (by taking over the alphabet from the Phoenicians and adding vowels to what had been purely consonants). They had accepted the gods and goddesses of most of their neighbors (Zeus's home was originally in Crete before the Greeks replaced it with Mount Olympus) and made them all part of their pantheon. Influences from other civilizations had preceded the Greeks by thousands of years. Even before the Dorian Greeks moved into this area from the Balkans, the Myceneans had been there for at least a thousand years (the Myceneans were a mixture of peoples who came from the Balkans and from Anatolia). And before the Myceneans there were other peoples who had also lived on this crossroads between the Balkans and the Middle East. Agriculture, the domestication of animals, and the settled villages had come into existence well before 6500 B.C., which meant that the motivations that had built up settled villages in Southwest Asia and that had turned nomadic hunters into a sedentary mixed farming and pastoral people had also taken place in Greece at a period of time that was not too far in the past.

The later Greek civilization was an evolutionary product of the civilizations that had preceded it. Greek art and architecture did not equal those of Egypt and of Crete until a thousand years later. As civilizations go, both Greek and Roman were Johnny-come-lately cultural growths, dependent for their technological and organizational levels upon the variety of civilizations that preceded theirs by an age that covered more than three thousand years — a period of time greater than that which separates us from the Greeks and the Romans. The latter's technology, art, and architecture were taken from the civilizations that preceded theirs, though they modified and improved much of what they took. While the Babylonians had used the arch for more than a thousand years before the Romans picked it up, the Greeks never used it at all, although they did use the column derived from the Sumerian, Babylonian, Cretan, and Mycenean models. While the mainland Greeks were a trading and an agricultural people, there is little we can say about their developments in technology. A few citizens in Greek colonies such as Sicily did work on the lever, the screw, and a primitive steam engine used for opening temple doors. Archimedes in Greek Sicily in the third century B.C. evidently invented a complex winch, a spiral conveyor, and parabolic mirrors. He looked upon his applied technology chiefly as being toys, however, and preferred to be remembered mainly for his mathematical theorems. Ctesbius, who also lived in the same century as Archimedes, may have been one of the inventors of the windmill. Hero of Alexandria has been given credit for having invented a primitive steam engine in the second century B.C., and is reported to have experimented with the energy developed by compressed air and waterpower.

The Greeks learned a great deal about urban planning from the Babylonians, who seem to have been pioneers in city planning. (In the early centuries of the Christian era, the Japanese picked up city planning from the Chinese. Roads that were intersected by straight streets at right angles were as much Chinese as they were later nineteenth-century American.) The Babylonians built their cities with sewage drains, paved roads, viaducts, and piped water — all long before the Romans adopted these ideas in the construction of their cities.

Although Athens has been given conventional credit for having created Greek civilization all by itself, in fact much of what we know as Athenian culture came from other Greek colonies and cities. Much of Greek philosophy, mathematics, political thought, drama, art, and literature came from cities in Southwest Asia, southern Italy, and Sicily. By the third century B.C., cosmopolitan Alexandria in Egypt had become a center of Hellenistic culture, and contributions to that culture were made by Hellenized Egyptians, Hebrews, Lydians, Phrygians, Syrians, and Greeks. Although Athenians talked of democracy, in practice Athens was never a political democracy. Rather, the city was governed by an oligarchy of aristocrats and supported by a large majority of non-citizen metics and slaves, the metics being foreigners who worked as artisans and traders but had none of the rights and privileges of free citizens. The few thousand who attended the street-corner academies, or who watched the plays of Aristophanes and Sophocles in the open air theatres in the fifth and fourth centuries B.C., were a small fraction of the population. Their leisure was made possible through the physical labor of the foreigners domiciled in Athens and the large number of slaves (averaging three to four to a family), who provided the free Athenians with their leisure, goods, food, and services.

Non-citizens also carried on the activities which enabled Athens to subsist by exporting the metal, the wine jars, textiles, and other goods which were used to import grain, the food, and raw materials for supporting the free citizens of Athens.

Despite the monumental buildings and temples which were erected in the market squares, Athens and Greece were always poor. Without the daughter colonies, it is doubtful that Athens, Corinth, or the other city-states could have existed for very long. Most Athenians even in the fifth century B.C. ate only one simple meal a day, and perhaps had fish or meat no more than once a week. Wine was drunk sparingly only by the well-to-do, who were owners of the crafted luxuries, patrons of the sculptors, the street-corner academies, the theatre, the proprietors of the stuccoed houses with tile roofs, and the tasters of the limited diversity of foods. Most of the peasants who lived in Greece at that time seldom drank wine. Their daily meal was generally a gruel made of coarse cooked grains seasoned with garlic and salt. Vegetables and fruits were considered luxuries and eaten rarely. Although the Sumerians and Egyptians brewed beer, we do not know what the average Greek drank with his gruel; it is possible that it was only water.

Much of what the Greeks possessed they borrowed from those who had preceded them. The columns used in supporting their buildings and the tile for roofing had been used thousands of years before. Their mathematics and elementary mechanical principles were derived from the Babylonians and the Egyptians. Their alphabet came from the Phoenicians. The Cretans and the Phoenicians founded colonies long before the Greeks. Although the latter encouraged the search for non-revealed knowledge that was based upon man's reason, still slavery was part of their everyday life. The city-states warred with one another just as ferociously and inhumanely as the "despotic Orientals" that ethnocentric Greek historians have described for us. Women were subordinate to men, and the greatest of all Greek fears was that of being emasculated or enslaved, of having one's wife and children held in bondage, and of being required to obey the bidding of other men.

Although the Greeks speculated about the universe more than other ancient people (not even the Chinese equalled them in this intellectual activity), still they were unable to unify themselves to achieve common goals, unable to work on their social anxieties, unable to give their women greater social equality, and unable to eradicate the institution of slavery. Man's inhumanity to man was as prevalent among the Greeks as among those whom they labeled despotic tyrants. Even when Greek philosophers speculated about poverty, slavery, and warfare, they still accepted all three as being normal in human affairs, if not inevitable among men. They viewed the world pessimistically, and when they postulated moral systems, the emphasis was upon an acceptance of hierarchy and authoritarianism. As long as there were enough peasants, slaves, and oxen to do the drudgery, the Greek (and the Roman) upper classes could not have cared less about the qualitative levels of the lives of the peasants and slaves. The Greek world was one in which those who held power and wealth intrigued continuously to keep them — though there was always the underlying anxiety that what the fates gave, they could also take away. Men were governed by forces beyond their control which set in motion decisions which were made even as the individuals concerned were being born.

◇   ◇   ◇   ◇   ◇

Despite their contributions, Greece and Rome for the most part were examples of Primary peasant civilizations. Their small urban populations had made strides in adapting to city living and their technology was on a high level, but the vast majority of their populations remained illiterate peasants, barely existing above a subsistence level, and subject to all the vagaries of life in those days — epidemics, slavery, famine, and warfare. Both civilizations continued and improved the organizational patterns of complex society which had been evolving for more than 3,000 years before they came on the scene. Neither Greek nor Roman civilizations was "Western" in any modern or organizational sense, or very different in form and content from the civilizations which preceded them. A Roman or an Athenian citizen had more in common with a Cretan or an Egyptian of two thousand years before than either could have with a twentieth-century citizen in an urban part of the industrialized European world.

◇   ◇   ◇   ◇   ◇

The Romans, like the Greeks, continued to a large extent the forms, ideas, and cultural content of all the civilizations in the Mediterranean area that had preceded them. Rome at its height built straight paved roads, but so did the Babyonians and the Chinese, and the Mayans, Mexicans, and Incas in the New World. Rome built viaducts to bring water into the cities, but so did the Babylonians. And almost one thousand years before the Romans, the inhabitants of Southwest Asia had built underground viaducts, the Qanats, which brought mountain ground water to their arid plains. Although the Roman viaducts today are tourist curiosities, the Qanats with their extensive underground tunnels still provide more than 75 percent of all the water used in contemporary Iran — three thousand years after they were first invented. The Romans built public buildings using marble-faced rubble in their construction, but so did the Egyptians more than two thousand years before then. The Babylonians employed the arch long before the Romans rediscovered its use in building; the Greeks had been unaware of its utility, while the Myceneans had used the corbel, or the false arch.

The Romans took over the ideas of civilization from those who had preceded them, but they added their own touches to this superstructure. They had learned to become better engineers, empire builders, and organizers than was the case of the civilizations to which they were heir. On the other hand, Roman administrators did little to encourage the growth of technological innovation. Whatever changes took place over the centuries were due more to the individual peasant and artisan who innovated the slight improvements which made life a little more comfortable and efficient for their fellowmen. Some agricultural changes took place as a result of the initiative of the land-owning patricians in Rome. These were encouraged by the ready market in wine, grain, and olives (due to the increase in numbers of the military in the Roman legions, to the greater wealth looted from those who were conquered, and to government subsidies for the unemployed in the cities) to begin experimenting with an increase in crop yields. They cultivated the grape and olive more intensively and added to their yields of grain by alternating the planting of peas with that of wheat. Although the production of grains was increased over the years, the net effect added little to the standard of living of most inhabitants of the Roman Empire. It is difficult to compare per capita incomes through the ages, but it is possible to estimate that the income in the Roman Empire in the first century of the Christian era may have averaged no more than $35 in 1973 dollars, compared to the average per capita income of about $1,400 for the citizen of Rome at the present time.

The Roman Empire with its professional military legions, its administrative officials, its cities, and its engineering works was supported by the drudgery of a huge peasant population of more than 40 million (or more than 90 percent of the inhabitants), who scratched the soil with inefficient wooden plows to supply a meager fare for the five million who lived in the cities. The conquered areas were obligated to send grain as tribute to Rome, most of whose citizens had to survive on a subsistence standard of living.

While the Roman legions required large amounts of grain, armor, swords, clothing, leather, and tools, their suppliers had little incentive, say, to increase their production through developing more efficient means of productive power, using the energy of water and wind power, both of which were known in theory to the Romans by the first century. Large fortunes were made by those who supplied necessities to the military and the government, but the market was limited and sales were based upon favoritism. The work of production itself was done by a never-ending supply of slaves as the military extended their conquests and captured large numbers of men, women, and children.

The Romans expanded the organization of empire from what it had been in previous civilizations, but their technical innovations were few and far between. It is doubtful, for example, that they improved much on iron-smelting from the fifth century B.C. to the fifth century A.D. The crank, which had been invented by the Chinese, was unknown to the Romans (it did not come into Europe until after the Roman Empire had breathed its last), though they did know how to use the wheel, axle, lever, pulley, the endless screw of Archimedes, the wedge, the cam, and three basic forms of gearing (which they utilized in mining, in building war machines, and in the construction of viaducts, bridges, roads, and monumental public buildings).

The Roman military, recruited from within the Empire, brought with them ideas which they knew at home, or which they were able to pick up as they served along the borders in areas away from their home bases. The waterwheel, for example, was picked up in the highlands of Anatolia and brought back to Rome in the first century B. C. The Roman military engineers changed the primitive horizontal water turbine into a vertical overshot wheel, and recommended that these waterwheels be used to harness the energy of swiftly flowing streams to grind grain and to operate simple lathes. Although the military used some waterwheels in grinding flour for their quartermaster trains, the usage did not spread because donkeys and slaves were cheaper.

During most of the Roman period, grain was ground by hand using the labor of slaves and primitive mills. Weaving was entirely a cottage industry, again using the skills of slaves. Woven cloth was bought by various merchants who used their own slave labor to finish and dye it, with the end products being sold in small shops. After the first century A.D., Alexandria was a more important center for cottage industry than Rome. By the third century A.D., window-glass as large as one by two feet was made in small workshops. (A recent excavation near Haifa, Israel, has disclosed an enormous block of colored glass weighing more than a ton, which had evidently been melted and formed into a large block of opaque glass — for what reason no one knows — with dating roughly before the sixth century A.D.) By the beginning of the Christian era in both Alexandria and Rome, Syrian and Jewish glassmakers almost monopolized glass-blowing in making bottles. But despite glassmaking there had been little change since Sumerian days in the ways in which the artisans performed their labors. Blacksmithing, woodworking, weaving, spinning, glassmaking, and leatherworking were all performed in small workshops by a few free artisans with slaves as helpers.

The Chinese were still ahead of the Romans technologically by the first century A.D. The water turbine and the waterwheel had both spread from Anatolia to China along the Silk Road by the first century B.C. Soon thereafter the Chinese were using a horizontal waterwheel to drive a triphammer in the process of milling rice (the vertical waterwheel did not come to China from the West until centuries later). This last was not used much by the Romans because it required streams where water flowed the year round. In the Mediterranean area, the rains came in the winter and the summers were fairly dry. When the waterwheel moved north of the Alps, it arrived in a region where streams flowing swiftly the year round made it useful.

In Roman days, accepted belief did not hold that all men needed to have their standard of living raised, that men should be saved from laborious drudgery, or that their life goals should be elevated from generation to generation. These aims had to await the development of a new civilization in Europe in which men would assume that there are earthly goals which men need to strive for; that men are basically equal in what they want out of life; that men should have opportunities for achieving their individual goals; that men must have the right to make choices which affect the direction of their lives; and that men should have the means to regain the earthly Garden of Eden that had originally been lost — or, in other words, to possess ways of achieving happiness and well-being instead of having to live with sadness and hopelessness.

Although men in the Ancient World undoubtedly dreamed of these goals, in a later Europe they attempted to realize them, and in so doing created a new civilization, one as different from that developed in Sumeria and continuing through the Greek and Roman, as the latter differed from the settled village of the Neolithic period. But as we come to the end of the Roman era, there was no belief that the world existed for man, and that man could improve it. When Christianity took over, it was more concerned with adapting man to the hereafter; the earthly life could look after itself. The peasants of Europe, Asia, or Central and South America held little hope that life on earth could be made better for them, or that life contained goals other than those of preparing for the next world. For them, the future merely repeated what had gone on in the past. Poverty was assumed to be fixed, eternal, and necessary. Men, no matter how thoughtful and empathetic, could not perceive the possibility of abolishing it.

IX   The Roots of Secondary Civilization

Until the eleventh century A.D., Europe north of the Alps was by no means an advanced area of the world. It was only during the twelfth century that the quality of European organization began to equal that of the Roman or Chinese civilizations. Although Roman architecture antedated the eleventh century, Romanesque was not used to any extent except after that date, and Roman type cement that hardened under water also did not become known until later. Europe north of the Alps by 1000 A.D. was backward as compared to Primary civilization then in existence along the Mediterranean, in India, and in China; but it was learning fast how to utilize the cultures bequeathed it from the past. There is no doubt that life in seventh-century Japan, China, India, Byzantium, Mesopotamia, or Alexandria was more comfortable than everyday existence in seventh-century Rome, Anglo-Saxon England, the little principalities of seventh-century France and Germany, or existence in Russia, Poland, the Czech lands, or Austria.

The life of the tiller of the soil (the overwhelming majority of Europe's population at that time) had not improved very much over what it had been, say, around 1700 B.C. or even 2700 B.C. Parents still reared children to be as much like themselves as possible, and the overwhelming number of Europeans remained illiterate until the nineteenth and twentieth centuries of our era. When civilization with its organization of men and compiling of records came to Europe north of the Alps, it appeared in those areas where the Roman legions had spent most of their time between military engagements. In general, civilization came to those settlements that had been influenced by Byzantium, Alexandria, Cairo, and Baghdad.

Although Primary civilization came fairly late to Europe north of the Alps, a high level of technical culture had begun to develop there even before 3000 B.C. Many of the stone monuments erected as tombs or as astronomical observatories had been constructed between 3000 B.C. and 2000 B.C. Bronze had come with wandering tribes out of southern Russia, North Africa, or Spain. The southern Russian Scythians, influenced by Anatolia, Mesopotamia, and the Aegean city-states, affected in turn an area extending as far to the west as present-day Hamburg. The Celts in Central Europe were the recipients of the technological ideas emanating from the

Aegean, the Balkans, Rome, and North Africa. The Scandinavians centuries before the Christian era were recipients of ideas and objects arriving from as far away as the Black Sea and the Italian Peninsula.

As in the case of the other Neolithic areas of the Ancient World, it is difficult to view Europe before the Christian era as being composed of a series of stationary tribes, each owning land in definite geographical areas from which all foreigners were barred, and living in isolation generation after generation. It is possible that a good part of the European population did remain stationary over thousands of years, but there may also have been a steady increment of settlers arriving from areas where there was a shortage of agricultural land, or where there was temporary drought. Until modern times, the population of Europe was fairly small. At the height of the Roman Empire, the European areas may not have contained more than about 23 million (including all of France, Spain, Italy, Great Britain, and areas of Switzerland, Bavaria, Austria, Yugoslavia, and Rumania). The rest of Europe may have had perhaps no more than 20 million.

Even by 1000 A.D., all of Europe may not have had more than 42 million, compared to 38 million in Southwest Asia (then fairly populous), 70 million in China proper, 48 million in India, 15 million in all of the Americas, and about 35 million in Africa south of the Sahara.

Until the sixteenth century, Europe possessed space for invading peoples coming out of Asia, North Africa, or from other parts of Europe; and the movement of poorer peoples to the more prosperous areas must have been as normal during the first centuries of the Christian era as they are today. Despite this large territory, most of it was not habitable because the continent was covered with dense forests, swamps, or mountains. Steppe country existed chiefly in southern Russia and parts of Central Europe: even the plains of Europe were covered with dense forests or impenetrable swamps, which were drained after 1000 A.D. The forests were made more penetrable with the cleared areas attracting invaders from the northland (the Vikings), the Slavic tribes after the fifth century A.D., and the Asian Avars, Magyars, Bulgarians, and later the Mongols and Turks.

Spain at the close of the Roman era was invaded by various Gothic tribes from the north and by Muslim armies and peoples from the south, who brought with them the religion of Islam. The new invaders slaughtered local peasants, but they also mixed their genes with the survivors. Almost everywhere the invaders were a minority compared to those who were invaded. It is doubtful that much drastic change occurred in the physical characteristics of most of the European populations over the centuries, although the diversity probably became more widespread. Even the Vikings in the period in which they devastated large parts of the northwestern European coast brought back to their settlements many captive slaves, both male and female. One can assume that the genes of the latter must have been added to the gene pool of the Vikings, as the latter added theirs to those of the Russians, the Baltic populations, the French, English, Scots, and Irish.

After the various invaders had preempted the best land available, the clearing of new land was encouraged. It was easier for invading warrior-peasants to snatch good agricultural or pasture land from conquered peasants than to laboriously reclaim land of their own. It was also more comfortable and agreeable for the victors to have the conquered till their land than to do it themselves.

Those who possessed good land had to fight to protect it, for there were always those from the outside who wanted it. Languages in various geographic areas of Europe changed as a result of conquest and intermingling — from Etruscan (an unknown language perhaps reminiscent of bygone European languages displaced by the Indo-European languages brought in from southern Russia or the Urals) to Latin, or from the various Iberian languages (of which Basque is the only survivor today) to the Carthaginian and later the Latin. Those spreading the new language were individuals who remained behind and who learned to speak the language of the conquerors, even intermarrying with them. In like manner, the Celts who moved into France and Great Britain had their languages adopted by those whom they took over. The Celts, on the other hand, adopted the languages of their Roman overlords or those of the Slavs who moved into Central Europe after the fifth century A.D., or those of the Angles, Saxons, and Jutes as the latter moved into Celtic Britain after the Romans left. The changes involved in speaking new languages occurred slowly, for the invaders came in small groups at different times, and the process of assimilation took place over centuries.

One must also assume that there was a sudden growth in European and Asian populations between the first and the tenth centuries A.D., which forced those who were surplus to settle elsewhere — as was the case with Celtic and Slavic speakers, or with those who were military invaders such as the various Goths, Avars, Magyars, Vikings, Angles, Saxons, Jutes, Bulgarians, and Tartar and Mongol tribes. It is also possible that the Arab push into North Africa and Europe may have been the indirect result of population pressures in Southwest Asia.

Northwest Europe was strongly influenced by the Mediterranean civilizations. Trade had been carried on between the Mediterranean commercial city-states and the rest of Europe from the third millenium B.C. on. There was a continuous diffusion of technical ideas and religious concepts from the Mediterranean centers by way of various European middlemen, the Scythians, Celts, Iberians, and later by the Northmen, or Vikings.

◇   ◇   ◇   ◇   ◇

Evidence suggests that even before the invasions of the early Christian era, European tribes and clans were continuously engaged in internecine warfare, fighting off neighboring invasions of their lands. It is difficult to know today what were the causes for this ongoing warfare, especially since we are dealing with a period containing mass illiteracy. Standards of living for the continent as a whole were extremely low, and poverty among most tribesmen was endemic. Articles of wealth that have been found in archaeological sites were generally the few possessions of the chiefs and had been buried with them: wagons, shields, axes, spears, glassware from the Mediterranean (or from the Rhine Valley in the early Roman era), and wine containers (an extensive trade in wine occurred from at least the seventh century B.C.).

Even before the second millenium B.C., a three-class system appears to have existed, composed of the nobles who were the warriors, the free peasants who carried on a mixed type of farming, and the slaves who were later the thralls and serfs. All wealth evidently belonged to the chief, who doled it out to his noble retainers. The peasants, like the cultivators in the ancient Mediterranean civilizations, were not even an afterthought. Their role was to support the petty aristocrats and the tribal chiefs; the latter were the extended family heads, in whose hands all wealth and power were concentrated. The petty nobles owed loyalty to the chiefs, and the peasants owed obedience and support to both the nobles and the chiefs.

As a result of technological diffusion from both the Scythians and the Romans, the Central European Celts developed a skillful metallurgical cottage industry before the beginning of the Christian era. It was not until well into this era, however, that the political organization of the Mediterranean civilizations was used. And it was not the Celts who then became the political organizers of men, but the Germanic subtribes and the Slavic groupings of Central Europe (though the legend later developed of a mythical King Arthur and his political organization in Celtic Britain).

By the end of the Roman era, Western and Central Europe had already been strongly influenced by Rome and its alter ego, or Byzantium — though Alexandria was still the technical center and continued so until after the tenth century of the Christian era.

The populations of Europe north of the Alps and away from the Mediterranean remained small and dispersed. There were no super-tribes that ruled their followers as Attila had the Huns, or with the discipline of the later Avars and Magyars. Each tribe or subtribe was almost self-sufficient, and the various autonomous subtribal chiefs must have put up much spirited defense against sharing their authority with others. Poets were rewarded to commemorate the petty rule of the chiefs, for emphasis was still upon the magic of the spoken, or sung, word rather than upon the written one. If there was any literacy before the arrival of Christianity in the fourth century, whatever was written down has since been lost. No records existed before the ninth century (except for the seventh- and eighth-century Vikings, who adopted Runic writing and kept records before they became converted to Christianity).

◇   ◇   ◇   ◇   ◇

We know little of the life of the pre-Roman Celts or the pre-Christian Slavs. There was some kind of fosterage among the Celts whereby nobles of various villages exchanged sons, but little is known of Slavic social organization at that time. There may have been large extended families among the Slavs in which both land and wealth were held in common, and it is possible that this system may also have existed among the Celts. Neolithic log houses found in Poland indicate that extended families may have been more common than the nuclear family, for the houses seem to have been built to accommodate large groups living together. The heads of extended families appear to have had a form of tribal council, which may have elected the tribal or subtribal chief. The social structure contained a few artisans who were neither nobles nor peasants, but whose social status may have come closer to that of the former than of the latter. The family was the protector of the individual, and the stronger the family the greater the protection. It was evidently the family that demanded "blood" money in case any of its members were injured, and it was the family that took up arms against another family if its honor or that of any family members were impugned. There must have been a good deal of competitive boasting of the strength of one's family, since it is doubtful that the individual would have seen himself as being distinct from his family. The strong families may have preyed upon the weak, even within the subtribe. Individual warriors evidently counted upon their women, the weaker families, and the serfs to do most of the farm work and to carry on most of the crafts. The highly skilled work was done by the artisans who may have occupied a slightly lower social level than the warriors and nobles.

Religion seems to have been concerned with witchcraft and various sacrifices to unknown deities and spirits. The offerings included those of human beings, who appear to have gone to their deaths with a certain amount of willingness — indicating some connection between the sacrifice and a possible future divinity. Even the Romans, who were not known for being tender-hearted, reported that the human sacrifices of the Celtic Druids were a bit too much for them to stomach. The bogs of Denmark have recently cast up their first- and second-century severed heads of men and women who seem to have gone to their deaths with serenity. There were also sacrifices to the sacred groves and trees, to the deities of the rivers, bogs, mountains, sky, and weather, along with those connected with the fertility of the soil and of women. A faint possibility suggests that a sedentary agricultural community may have existed side by side with a semi-mobile pastoral one with the two seeming to form a symbiotic relationship, though it is not clear whether we are dealing with the same community. Wealth was evidently in the form of cattle, pigs, sheep, and metal (as it was in the ancient pastoral world). The non-ownership of land made it difficult to consider the soil, which was tribally owned, or its fruits, as being equivalent wealth to herds of cattle or sheep, which were privately held.

Although we know little about the period before the seventh century in Central Europe, there appears to be some evidence for believing that the roots of the later social and economic changes in Europe may have begun to develop even before this time. The Europe that later gave birth to the Industrial and Scientific civilization was, in the period before the seventh century, mainly Celtic and Germanic — and strongly influenced by the recently defunct Roman political and technical civilization. The Slavs were still behind the curtain of history, and little or nothing was known about them specifically, though they also were influenced by the currents emanating from the Black Sea area — where the Greeks had established colonies more than a thousand years before and where merchants coming from Mesopotamia had trod three thousand years earlier. The two greatest forces to change the Germans and the Celts were the Roman legions and the ideas and objects they brought with them, plus the arrival of missionaries both from Ireland and from Rome. The Irish missionaries appear to be lost in a legendary history, but it is possible to speculate that they may have had a greater influence upon the Celtic-speaking peoples than the Latin-speaking emissaries from Rome or Romanized Gaul. Their activities, though now lost to view, may have been based upon a certain type of Christianity which they brought, a religion that could have had an influence in making the later descendants of their converts dissatisfied with the Roman Christianity of their day.

It appears that Celtic-speaking missionaries may have made inroads into the Celtic-linguistic areas of Central and Western Europe even before the fifth century A.D. (What follows is pure speculation, for we have no evidence, but it is possible that they may have made their successes in preaching an apocalyptic form of Christianity, wherein the emphasis was upon the coming end of the world because of the sinfulness of people — although the opportunity to reform was still available. Men had to listen to the glad tidings because they had no choice; the world was coming to an end, Jesus would soon appear, and men had to prepare themselves for this pending event — the same appeal that Jesus may have made as the Messiah, or the Messenger from God, to those who heard Him in His day. In a message of the coming millenium, the emphasis may have been upon performing now what God expected if one wanted later to be saved eternally. The implication was that those who were greedy, who engaged in injustices, or who lived in sin were basically endangering the possibility of the future eternal lives of those around them, and therefore their sinfulness had to be stopped.)

The Celtic tribes were soon overrun by Slavic speakers coming in from the northeast, plus various Germanic tribes (here again, we know little about the relationship of the Celtic and Germanic tribes: they evidently lived side by side in large parts of southern and central Germany). After the sixth century, a time vacuum appears during which there were apparently no traveling missionaries except those from Rome, who seemed to favor the more settled areas of Italy, France, and Spain. Byzantium filled this religious vacuum temporarily by sending special missionaries to those Slavic tribes that had infiltrated the Celtic regions (in present-day Germany, and in Central and Southeast Europe). As in the case of the Celtic missionaries who could speak to their brethren in a language which they were able to understand, the Byzantine missionaries used a generalized Slavic, or Church Slavonic, in which to carry on their religious teachings. By the ninth century A.D., however, new invasions from the northeast separated many of these Slavic (former Celtic) speakers from their religious sources in Byzantium. Rome began to fill this new empty spot with German-speaking, Latin-using missionaries who could have been seen by their new parishioners as incomprehensible "dumb" aliens, preaching wrong doctrines and employing ineffective magic in the words they used. With these shifts in religious rites and language, there evidently developed an undercurrent of scepticism in which men questioned whether these new missionaries and then the priests and bishops who followed them were obeying the word of God, or whether they were interested in enriching themselves.

What is being suggested here is that some motivation for the later revolts among the peasants and artisans, which led to the religious heresies of the Albigensians and the Waldensians in France, the Lollards in England, the Hussitic Taborites in Bohemia, the various pseudo-Messiahs in the Netherlands and Germany, could have been part of a continuing underground resentment within European Christianity wherein approval may have been given from generation to generation to scepticism about earthly aristocracies, priesthoods, and the Church in general. What is also being suggested, for we have no proof about any of these descriptions of life hundreds of years ago, is that the European credos of egalitarianism, democracy, and individualism began in the Medieval period. The beliefs that men could govern themselves and make decisions concerning their needs, that injustices could be removed if men returned to the idyllic stage of the Garden of Eden through living their lives as God — or nature — wanted them to, and that each man had the right to be the judge of what was expected of him and of what he needed to do (irrespective of the environment in which he lived), all these were part of the complex motivating forces that pushed Europe from the thirteenth century — slowly at first, but then more rapidly in the eighteenth, nineteenth, and twentieth centuries — into a new civilization, the Secondary civilization of science and industry.

Other roots of the new civilization produced the growth between the seventh and thirteenth centuries that changed the former conception of the purpose of life. Perhaps one of the more important changes derived from the work of the monasteries in making physical labor respectable among the learned. In the Ancient World of civilization, physical labor was viewed as being degrading; it was what slaves and the poor did. Gentlemen scholars were not concerned with physical work or lightening the labor of slaves, nor were they interested in helping to increase the wealth of society so that all would possess a higher standard of living. Wealth was looked upon as a rare commodity that chiefly benefited the nobles; it was not viewed as being limitless because efficient horticulture could make two plants grow where only one grew before, or because labor could be reduced by producing more thread or weaving more cloth. Markets were small. Most of a community's needs could be easily satisfied on the local level, and the international market was neither large or very important. Few merchants or artisans were required to satisfy the needs of the latter. Workshops on the local level were small, and only during the Roman period did slaves perform a good part of the urban and rural labor.

◊   ◊   ◊   ◊   ◊

Although Medieval Christianity looked upon labor as a punishment from God, the Judaism, upon which some of the early strains of Christianity was based, emphasized work as an obligation to God: "Six days shalt thou labor, and on the seventh shalt thou rest." Even learned Jews were expected to know a trade or a craft in addition to carrying on the study of the law. Jesus was reported to have been a maker of wooden agricultural tools, Paul was a tent-maker, and the later Maimonides was a physician. The rabbis who discussed the law in the Mishna and the Gemara of the Talmud from the third to the seventh centuries A.D. earned their livelihoods through a craft so that they would have the means to let them study parttime. The early Christian church thus broke with the Roman and Hellenic traditions, though not with the Jewish one, that men of learning should not dirty their hands with labor.

While Byzantium after the fourth century A.D. continued to exist as a second Rome, there was a gradual withdrawal of social identification from the more populated urban centers of Southwest Asia and Egypt. Numbers of individuals left the cities to form small communities where they could create their own godly societies, and thus avoid contact with the sinful secular world. They spent most of their time trying to save their immortal souls through good works, faith, and prayer, while at the same time acquiring their food through physical labor. Most of these individuals learned to organize themselves in a voluntary self-disciplined fashion, as others had done in previous centuries (the new Covenanters of Dead Sea Scroll fame being only one of many communes in ancient Israel).[1] In these rural communities, men worked and prayed together, and made rules that fixed a set routine to the daily round of activities. After the sixth century, the proliferation of these religious communes or monasteries created large centers in Central Europe (especially those that were attached to the Benedictine Order) wherein work was looked upon as being good and necessary. At the same time, however, no more than five hours per day were specified; the rest of the time had to be spent in contemplation, prayer, and the copying of sacred writings.

Despite the maximum of five hours of physical labor, the monasteries encouraged a cooperative sharing of work and ideas which made them receptive to more efficient techniques in farm and construction work, and later even to simple labor-saving machinery. The division of the monk's day into seven canonical hours encouraged the development of a means by which this time could be measured. The sundial was an ancient device, but it was

---

[1]It is possible that the various monastic sects of ancient Israel may have been influenced by ideas emanating from Buddhism, in the train of Alexander's conquest of northwest India and the subsequent Hellenization of Southwest Asia. Ideas generally travel a two-way street.

difficult to use in the endless cloudy days of winter in Central and Western Europe. As a result, the waterclock and hourglass soon displaced it.

Although we have no idea whether the clock was actually invented in the monastery, we do know that urban communities from the thirteenth century on paced their daily activities in accord with the time shown on the townhall clock, or with the bells in the cathedral tower which were rung in unison with the time intervals shown on the mechanical clock. It is possible that the monastic ringing of bells according to the canonical hour may have resulted from the obligation of the monastery to observe the passing of time. With the rise of the commercial spirit in the new towns of Central and Western Europe, the monastic order of ritual and routine (based upon the ancient military traditions of discipline, obedience, and set tasks) may have determined the pattern which governed the town's work and activities.

The monastery was receptive not only to the religious ideas stemming from Rome but also to those concepts and techniques coming to them from the classic past and from the territorial fringes of the trading and mercantile world of that day. Each member shared in the proceeds of the work, though the total profits went into buildings, libraries, and the purchase of new fields — with the monks constructing the buildings, tilling the soil, and adding to the manuscripts in the library. Although self-sufficient in food, the monastery needed to import from outside its local area furnishings for the chapel, special building tools, cabinetwork, and parchment for copying manuscripts. These last had to be adorned with semi-precious stones, gold and silver filigree work.

The monasteries of Europe north of the Alps formed a rich market for manuscripts from the Ancient World that were concerned with both the sacred and secular aspects of daily living. The few technological observations of the Ancient World found their way to the monasteries from the urban centers of the Hellenic and Roman worlds. The monasteries also became a model for practical Christianity by stressing the contrast in living standards between the nobles and the monks, and between the bishops and other Church aristocrats with the monastic order. This contrast in two ways of life — between men working for their living, studying, and modestly attempting to be well-informed, with those who exploited the labor of others, who lived luxuriously, and who shared neither authority nor work with those beneath them — may have encouraged many of the egalitarian trends which later led to reformist religious movements as well as to egalitarian and democratic ones.

The monasteries of Europe, together with the later universities composed of poor clerics, became centers for the budding scientific spirit, the searching for "God's truths." This led to many heresies, which the Church attempted to repress, and encouraged a receptivity to ideas which later produced millenarian reformist movements, peasant revolts, and revolutionary reactions to the status quos. This monastic competition for higher status with bishops and princes of the Church and with secular lords led to social movements of protest and revolution, and to a receptivity to new dogmas which held that men deserved higher standards of living, for all men were created equal and were descendants of the equality developed by God in the legendary Garden of Eden. Men now felt free to look back to a past when there were no yokes, no aristocrats, no exploiters, when men were brothers and no social differences existed between them.

Alongside the bureaucratic and hierarchical Roman Catholic Church, with its princely cardinals and aristocratic bishops (in whose ranks aristocrats formed the vast majority), there also existed a common man's, almost underground, religion. This contained a strong element of apocalyptic millenarianism wherein the rich were to be kept out of Heaven and those who misused their power were to be punished by spending eternity in Hell. A sullen reaction to authority was encouraged along with the establishment of a military and religious discipline. The roots of this religion may go back to the early millenarian and evangelical preaching of the first missionaries (who converted large numbers of former pagans to Christianity) as well as to later disappointment that Christ did not reappear in 1000 A.D. The struggle for social egalitarianism did not mean that the European village in the pre-Christian era was egalitarian and democratic, any more than Anglo-Saxon England was freer than Norman England. (The peasant revolts in fourteenth-century England and the seventeenth-century "Diggers" in Cromwellian Britain both used the legend that things were more idyllic before the Norman "yoke" was fastened upon them, a myth that is also part of the Garden-of-Eden-back-to-nature syndrome in which men were supposedly equal and free of social restraints. Rousseau in the eighteenth century continued this image.)

◇   ◇   ◇   ◇   ◇

A small middle class, living in the large village and in the small cathedral or marketing town, catered to the needs of the wealthier peasants, the feudal lords, the latters' retainers, and to the various Churchly officials above the rank of poor parish priests—the former providing a market for fine cloth, brocades, luxurious leatherwork, furs, and fulltime artisan work. While each

village may have had a parttime or small group of artisans engaged
in various skills to satisfy local needs, the regional or cathedral
towns had fulltime artisans working for the larger market (including areas hundreds of miles away) under the direction of a master-
artisan who was also a parttime merchant. The merchant-trader
had been moving about Europe from the fourth millenium B.C. as
a representative of the more advanced urban center seeking new
sources of raw materials and paying for them with finished artisanal goods. He was generally an outsider until after the tenth
century A.D., although a good many of the Norsemen were
merchants trading far and wide for the goods which their chiefs
desired and which would enhance their social status over that of
their retainers. Europe north of the Alps before the tenth century
was underpopulated and filled with almost impassable forests and
swamps, with village clearings in the forests only near navigable
rivers. The chiefs and petty kings of small regions moved continuously from one large village to another, living off the bounty of
the land, until their hosts let them know that they had outstayed
their welcome.

Compared to the wealth of India, Southwest Asia, or China,
Europe — excluding the few old Roman settlements — was still
very rural, isolated, and almost self-sufficient except for the few
luxuries which the chiefs, petty kings, Church lords, and a few
favored heads of well-to-do peasant families desired and which could
easily be satisfied with the annual visits of alien merchants from
Byzantium, Southwest Asia, or Muslim North Africa. Compared
to conditions one to two thousand years previously, Europe by the
tenth century A.D. provided no beacon of light in technological or
social progress. China was on a higher level at that time, as was
India and Southwest Asia. Life in seventh-century Nara in Japan
was far more comfortable than life in seventh-century England,
France, Germany, Czechoslovakia, Poland, or even Scandinavia —
let alone seventh-century Russia.

◇　◇　◇　◇　◇

Various technological innovations came to Europe from China,
perhaps along the land route of the old Silk Road (which connected
China and Rome in the first centuries of the Christian era). These
included the crank, the stirrup, the horse collar, and the blow gun
for iron-smelting, which in Europe soon became transformed into
the bellows. The Korean invention of printing in the eighth century
did not reach Europe until almost seven centuries later. The Chinese use of coal as a fuel for heating as well as for smelting was

not employed in Europe until the twelfth century, though coal as such was known centuries before. The various luxuries of the Classic or Chinese worlds did not come to Europe until after the tenth century. Between the fall of the Roman Empire in the fifth century until the beginning of the eleventh century, the small European population spent much time attempting to keep out of the way of invading peoples and trying to grow enough food to ward off starvation, especially during the long cold dark winters.

Somewhere among the Slavic-speaking peoples, the so-called "Saxon" plow was evidently developed in the sixth century. This was a heavy wheeled-plow with a coulter and an iron-cutting edge which turned over the swampy heavy soils of Northwest Europe. (The Slavic-speaking peasants of Europe at this time occupied swampy areas in East Germany, Poland, White Russia, and parts of the Ukraine.) Despite the use of the heavy plow in turning the drained soils and virgin land reclaimed from the vast forests, it is doubtful that Europe at that time produced as much food per acre as China, the southwestern Asian area, Egypt, or India. More centuries had to pass before Medieval and Renaissance Europe equaled and then surpassed the Ancient World in food production. Until an agricultural revolution of sorts occurred after the eleventh century, few towns and cities had an agricultural surplus to support large numbers of administrators, scribes, or artisans. Even the monasteries before the eleventh and twelfth centuries had to be self-sufficient until a trade in foodstuffs was developed between the various regions of Europe.

During this period, Italy, Spain, and Byzantium were in a slightly more advanced state of technological culture than were the rural areas of the rest of Europe. After the sixth century in Italy, smaller Roman cities and towns existed under the fertilizing social influences of Byzantium. Spain, however, was invigorated by currents coming from Southwestern Asia, Persia, and India through Arab conquest in the seventh century. The technical achievements of the Classical World, now augmented by objects coming from India, first resided in Italy. By the eighth century, Florence, the ancient city of the mercantile Etruscans, became a center for the new manufacture of brocades and textiles (under technical influences from Alexandria) that were far superior to anything Rome could have produced during the height of its power. By this time, the Lombards were also extending their authority over northern Italy with Milan as their trading center, while the Venetians were slowly building a prosperous artisanal manufacturing center on a group of islands at the head of the Adriatic Sea.

◇   ◇   ◇   ◇   ◇

The changes which we associate with a later Europe had evidently begun their development by the tenth century. At that time, most of the migrations had ended. Later, the Mongols and Turks made incursions into the center of Europe, and by their conquests inhibited the conquered populations from raising themselves to the technical levels of Italy and Western Europe. The Magyars had already taken over Hungary and split the southern from the northern Slavs. The Slavs had made conquests in northern Russia, taking over Finnish-speaking peasants in the area around Moscow. The western Slavs in turn were conquered by German invaders. The pillaging raids of the Norsemen had ended by the tenth century, when Scandinavia became warmer and its inhabitants found that they could not only cultivate land at home but also in Russia, across the sea in Iceland, in parts of Greenland, and perhaps even in Newfoundland in North America. Along the Mediterranean coast, bands of Arabs had taken over Sicily, Malta, and the islands in between; but those who lived north of the Alps had little to fear from these southern invasions emanating from overpopulated regions. By the beginning of the tenth century, Europe north of the Alps was moving abreast of the ancient Classical and the contemporary Chinese and Persian civilizations.

It is difficult to compare the levels of culture in Europe or Asia with those in North America at that time, for the civilizations of the Mayans, the Mixtecs, the Toltecs, and the pre-Incas were at a pre-Iron Age level, or at the first stages of the ancient Bronze Age in Mesopotamia. Although the Mayans were highly specialized in their rituals which revolved around a complex calendar, it is still difficult to compare the cities and public temples of the New World with those of the Old. The high technical levels in Egypt during the second millenium or the Middle Dynasty period, the architectural levels of Babylon and Assyria in the beginning of the first millenium, and the technology of the Chinese during the early Han era expressed a more complex basis of development than those in the New World. And while a stage of early Primary civilization was occurring in parts of Black Africa at that time, still the early Axum, Songhai, or Mali were by no means at the levels of sophistication that saw the beginnings of the Romanesque period in architecture and the bare glimmerings of the complicated Gothic cathedrals as they were built later in the twelfth century.

By the end of that century, the receptivity of monasteries to efficiency in labor techniques had made agriculture more productive than it had been in the past few centuries. Europe had begun to move ahead of the Ancient World by using horses and primitive agricultural machines to increase the productivity of the soils. The Baltic and later Slavic heavy plow with its coulter, share, and mouldboard, plus the more efficiently harnessed horse (thanks to the Chinese horse collar), along with the inventions of the scythe, primitive reaper, and horse-drawn tools for breaking up the soil after it had been plowed, all tended to raise the productivity of the earth. By the beginning of the thirteenth century, one could say that productivity per acre more than equalled what had been grown in Classic and Mesopotamian times.

Concurrently after the tenth century, there was a shift in farming wherein the cooperatively organized village system (which had previously led to the feudal manorial system) slowly began to shift to individual farming, in which free yeomen owned their land and tilled their soils by using only the labor of their families. Serfdom continued to exist, however, until the middle of the nineteenth century (it was abolished only in 1848 in Austria and Prussia, and in 1861 in Russia). The strident protests of the serf that he be permitted to own his land and be master of his life became a crescendo by the beginning of the fourteenth century, with millenarian religious movements serving as a catalytic agent. The number of independent peasants slowly increased as many purchased their freedom from feudal obligations to the lord of the manor. (Under feudalism, there were two sides to the concept of obligations: the right of the lord to the labor of the serf, but the right of the serf to protection, justice, and free consent — he owed nothing to the lord if the latter did not fulfill his obligations to him.)

◇   ◇   ◇   ◇   ◇

All these strivings for social justice, which Medieval man tended to believe were part of God's plan, encouraged the development of "rights," which many peasants believed their superiors were obligated to acknowledge as well as to defend. The "right" to a private individual existence was based upon the conviction that men were born "free" in the Ancient World before military conquests yoked them to "feudalism." The gradual improvement in agricultural technology and in resultant yields led Medieval men to want this surplus for themselves rather than to give it over to feudal lords and bishops. As a result of draining swamps and felling large forests, enough land had become available to satisfy the needs of the twelfth-century peasant, if he could also have had the private "right" to till his land and grow his food without having so much of it entailed to feed others.

Monks, frustrated by incompetent abbots and bishops, disseminated Biblical teachings that stressed the original as well as future equality and brotherhood of all men. Peasants, who were upset by the greater exactions of the feudal lords, and artisans who reacted against the despotism of the guildmasters, were most receptive to teachings which envisioned a society where men were equal, where all men were free to own property, and where no hierarchy of social classes existed.

Merchants and bishops in the free urban centers encouraged opinions that were unfavorable to feudal lords, with whom they were competing for status. This status conflict between social classes motivated men to seek out their God-given "rights" which they considered came down to them from Adam and Eve, and which had been taken away by later generations of usurpers. The later refusal of petty kings, feudal lords, and merchants to honor traditional unwritten laws between themselves and those dependent upon them helped to break down an internal system of social interactions which had never been strongly entrenched in the first place. Feudal lords were later seen as conquerors rather than as heads of an extended family, clan, or subtribe. Frustration at their authoritarian behavior led to feelings of alienation and a belief that social superiors had broken the unwritten but traditional contract which regulated behavior between social classes, and thus had become unworthy of being trusted or respected. If superiors also appeared weak and unable to enforce their power to extract obedience from their social inferiors, revolt often ensued. One can say that there have never been idyllic periods in the history of Europe, despite later attempts to resurrect them. Conflict and alienation have long been a normal part of life in most areas of Europe.

◊　◊　◊　◊　◊

After the eleventh century, Europe began to make economic and technological progress which by the fourteenth century (along with an almost doubling of the population) had raised technology to such a level of sophistication that Western Europe for the first time forged ahead of the Ancient civilizations and above the levels of India and China. The Europeans after the fourteenth century became the new vanguard of the advanced Primary civilization; the seeds of the later Industrial and Scientific civilization had been sown and were slowly taking root. In no areas of the world between the eleventh and fourteenth centuries did populations increase as much as in Europe. During this period, China increased her population by about 35 percent as contrasted to 75 percent in Europe. Africa, India, and Southeast Asia barely held their own, while only in the New World with the rise of civilization in Central and South America did the population increase as fast as in Europe.

In the Ancient World, merchants had lived in special sections of urban port settlements, which could not be called ghettos: the tradition of living separately from the local inhabitants goes quite far back. Myceneans, Cretans, and Phoenicians lived in their own quarters in foreign ports (as the English did in seventeenth-century Russia, and later in India, China, and Egypt).

The Romans formed their own encampments around which arose many of the early administrative centers of Gallic Europe. In the early Middle Ages, many of these centers attracted the merchants. Towns began to grow in Europe not as fixed administrative centers (these came later), but from the trading activities of the merchants who generally resided near important transportation points, such as river junctions, natural harbors, or the edges of mountain passes. As the merchants widened their markets, these small towns became the sites of workshops for the artisans who manufactured items for the former. Later, small numbers of administrative employees were added, to be followed by monks, priests, and teachers. Churches and religious orders were financed by the bequests of merchants who wished to secure the assistance of the Church in helping them get into Paradise. Small foundries were established in these towns along with various services. There were also large numbers of peasants who lived slightly outside the town walls but who tilled the lands for the subsistence of the town dwellers. Their children often swelled the ranks of the artisans and their helpers, sometimes even rising socially to the lower orders of monks and clergy. Since the peasants sold food to the town dwellers, they owed almost no feudal obligations to the towns. Hence the peasant proverb that merely breathing the air of the town made one "free;" free of stagnating social ranks, free of possible repression, and free to encourage one's children and grandchildren to rise in the world, even to compete socially for status with the feudal lords and the latter's descendants.

The peasant in Western Europe was aware of the social progress and technical prosperity that had come to him between the eleventh and fourteenth centuries. Iron, which had been a very scarce commodity in the Ancient Roman World, was used in large quantities in eleventh- and twelfth-century Europe. The plowshare was made of iron; the horse-drawn harrow with iron teeth replaced the wooden mattock and rake; more diversified tools of iron were made for both cultivation and handicrafts (though machines and gears were made of wood as late as the seventeenth and eighteenth centuries).

In the tenth century, many peasants had owned small watermills for grinding corn. In that century, however, feudal lords began to insist upon their right to grind all grain in their mills, thus reinforcing the dependency relationship between peasant and manor house. Later, the peasants attempted to regain their former autonomy over their lands and their labor, but the feudal lords (with the aid of petty kings) persisted in demanding their right over the labor as well as the lands of the village. The strife between peasant and lord lasted into the nineteenth and even into the early part of the twentieth centuries.

In the Medieval period, most livestock in the colder regions of Europe were killed in the autumn, for not enough forage was grown to carry the animals through the severe winters. The plow team was spared, but even these animals were fed near-starvation rations of straw and hay, and by the time spring came they were mostly skin and bones (like their masters). It was not until the fifteenth and sixteenth centuries that the manorial system of letting certain lands lie fallow was changed to one of alternating crops and growing root vegetables plus legumes. At the same time, forage was increased so that most farm animals were not slaughtered in the autumn. (The slaughter of young animals has continued through the twentieth century, for it has been too difficult and expensive for veal to age into beef or lamb into mutton.)

By the sixteenth century, agricultural productivity had increased by more than 50 percent over what it had been in the eleventh and twelfth centuries. Instead of one bushel of seed growing two bushels of wheat, as in the past, one bushel began to produce four to five bushels, thus surpassing the agricultural productivity of the Ancient World and Southwest Asia.

The Moslems had already introduced into their areas of Europe such new crops as buckwheat, rice, hops, sugarcane, flax, and cotton. With the growth of an urban market, the feudal lords, the urban peasants, and the monasteries had a motivation to increase their yields. The merchants also encouraged a greater diversification of crops, including the cultivation of more fruits and vegetables for the urban market. Various areas in Europe began to specialize in raising sheep, thereby providing wool for the export market. By the fourteenth century, England along with Spain and Italy had become the most important wool-producing areas. In that same century, the feudal lords and merchants of Prussia, Poland, and Hungary were also increasing their wealth by exporting large amounts of grain to the new and growing urban centers of Western Europe, including those of England.

◊   ◊   ◊   ◊   ◊

Although the amount of inter-European trade was slowly multiplying, the merchant towns were still small and sparsely populated. No settlement had as many as 100,000 people until the sixteenth century: towns were small in population and with 10,000 to 25,000 people were reminiscent of the urban centers of the Sumerians. Even Florence in the fifteenth century had no more than 70,000 inhabitants, while the great Flemish and German trading towns contained less than 25,000 each. The merchant town had its stone walls, its gates, clock, a wide ditch surrounding the wall (which could be used for defense), and vegetable gardens, stables for horses, cattle, and hogs behind each house.

European technical knowledge was slowly increasing as a result of the more frequent interactions between the Italian cities and the smaller towns north of the Alps. Until the fifteenth century, the Moslem world and Byzantium remained the chief manufacturing centers for glass, sophisticated textiles, and such highly developed crafts as jewelry and metal working. Venice became an important trading center by the ninth century, and a great many of the innovations from Byzantium, Southwest Asia, Egypt, Persia, India, and China came to the Venetians before they moved northward. By the early twelfth century, Venice had become an important center of artisan crafts for the rest of Europe; most of the stained glass windows for later cathedrals were made in Venice. In the following centuries, the architects, sculptors, and masons of the other Italian cities were employed in constructing most of the cathedrals, palaces, and public monuments of Europe.

It was not until after the sixteenth century that Northern Europe began to compete with the Italian cities in wealth, levels of technological achievement, and innovations. The great Italian trading cities of Florence, Venice, and Genoa — along with lesser ones such as Pisa, Bologna, and Ferrara — funneled the technical and trading knowledge of Byzantium and the Moslem world into their workshops and counting houses. The manufacture of fine textiles built up the wealth of Florence, its largest customer being the Church. The Papacy in Rome was interconnected as well as interrelated with the Florentine bankers and merchants. Glass and ships developed Venice, while Genoa traded on its ability to obtain spices in large amounts for the growing urban communities north of the Alps. Milan remained an important manufacturing city until the beginning of the seventeenth century with the rise of the Protestant manufacturing centers in Northern Europe. The Italian cities lost their preeminent rank after the seventeenth century as a result of many social factors, chiefly among them the repressions of the Catholic Counter-Reformation.

◊   ◊   ◊   ◊   ◊

Perhaps the greatest contribution to the growth of European technology and marketing after the eleventh century was the introduction of the Hindu zero and numerals via Moslem middlemen. The zero, along with place decimals, were unknown to the Classical World (though known to the Mayans from the beginning of the Christian era). Both were invented somewhere in India about the sixth century A.D. At the same time, the Hindus had developed algebraic equations and a system of simplified numerals, square roots, cube roots, and trigonometry. All these were disseminated by the educated Moslem merchants as the result of the Islamic conquest of northwest India in the eighth and ninth centuries.

The new mathematics proved to be of great value to Moslem traders, lawyers, builders, and administrators who lived in the highly developed urban areas between northwest India and the Mediterranean during the ninth to the thirteenth centuries (that is, before the invasions of the Mongols and the Turks, which almost turned this area into a desert). The improved arithmetic, numerals, and simple algebra were used as valuable tools in assessing legacies, settling lawsuits, handling complex matters of interregional trade, building canals, monumental edifices, quanats, irrigation ditches, and measuring land for tax and selling purposes.

Mathematics came to Italy and France via the Moslem world through the extensive trade in manuscripts. The European monasteries were an important market for manuscripts dealing with knowledge about the Ancient World. (The wealthy cathedrals also became customers of the Moslems, buying untold nails that purportedly came from the True Cross, innumerable bones of the Three Wise Men, as well as hundreds of pieces of wood from the Crucifix.)

The Moslem world had already painstakingly translated into Arabic the large numbers of Greek manuscripts and others of the Ancient World that came to their attention. These manuscripts were then sold to middlemen who had them translated into Latin, though there were many monasteries where monks themselves could translate Arabic into Latin. In most cases, the translators were Jewish rabbis and scholars, who earned their livings in the Muslim and Christian worlds by translating and inscribing manuscripts that dealt with the water clock, trigonometric tables, technology, and the medicinal and surgical practices of the Ancient Hellenic World, which had been added to in the urban Moslem centers of Baghdad and Cairo. Even Aristotle's natural history, which played such an important part in changing educational and theological directions in the later Middle Ages, first came from the Moslem world via Italian traders. The do-it-yourself system of education through reading was evidently in full force in Europe by the end of the twelfth century, and may have played an important part in encouraging the growth of scientific reasoning and observation after the thirteenth century. Both found acceptance and social approval among many of the educated members of the Church.

◇   ◇   ◇   ◇   ◇

The thirteenth century was the watershed for Medieval Europe; the *before* and *after* segments of this period were entirely different cultural eras. Almost all of Europe before the thirteenth century was culturally backward in comparison with the Ancient Classical civilizations of China, India, Persia, and the Moslem world. But after this century, Europe developed a commanding lead which was not taken away from it until the United States became an industrial nation in the nineteenth century. Western Europe from the fourteenth to the eighteenth centuries gave birth to a new organization of increased production and knowledge that swept away the past, just as Mesopotamia had originated a civilization that became disseminated throughout the Old World. Although technological improvements were still taking place in the non-European parts of the globe, Europe began innovating more technology at a faster rate, accumulating more knowledge and speculating more, all leading to greater change in the course of human history than events in Asia, the New World, or Africa.

More than in any previous period in history, Western European men were trying to solve practical problems. Innovations were taking place in a few regions, monasteries, and workshops by a tiny number of men, for the vast majority of Europeans — at this time from Russia to Sicily and Spain — were unaware of any new trend in the development of human knowledge. Even if they had known about it, they might have felt quite indifferent, for this was a period in which almost no one was curious or well-informed as to what was happening near his own village — let alone in the world a few hundred miles away.

The watermill which came out of Southwest Asia at the beginning of the Christian era could be employed only where there were swiftly flowing streams. In the Mediterranean area where the wheels and mills were first imported, seasonal variations in rainfall meant that many of the mills could not be used in the summertime when rains were absent and streams were either sluggish or dry. If dams were constructed along the Mediterranean where the rivers were shallow, the heavy rainstorms of autumn and winter might cause flooding of low-lying areas. In Western Europe, and especially in the Low Countries of present-day Belgium and Holland, a solution to the problem of flooding had been devised by redesigning the Persian windmill, evidently toward the end of the twelfth century.

The redesign of the windmill allowed it to pump water out of low-lying areas, grind grain, and even act as a source of energy to turn simple wooden machinery. The Chinese took to the new European windmill as quickly as it was received from the West sometime during the middle of the thirteenth century.

At the end of that century, monks and artisans in England, Flanders, France, Spain, and Italy were using their spare time to experiment with optics, and it may have been in the last area, perhaps in Florence, that eye spectacles were invented and first used. Here was an invention that immeasurably lengthened the scholar's working life, for it was no longer necessary for a scholar over the age of 45 years to have someone else read to him; he could continue writing and reading until a ripe old age. Spectacles spread rapidly from Italy throughout the known world where literacy was a requirement, even coming to China as early as the fourteenth century, where the new invention was carried by Venetian merchants (Marco Polo and his father were only two of the many who traveled the old Silk Route from Anatolia to China).

◇   ◇   ◇   ◇   ◇

The scientific spirit, though weak and very much influenced by the traditionalism and irrationality of the day, was beginning to spread by the end of the thirteenth century. There may have been many others like the English monk, Roger Bacon, who sought to eat the apple of the new tree of knowledge and to be like the gods in their understanding of the world they lived in — even when conflict existed between the monks themselves as to how this aim could take place. Some insisted that this knowledge and understanding could come only through revelation via theology and philosophy; others, and here Roger Bacon was one of many, insisted that man could learn chiefly through his experiences and his senses, that one could not reason without the former. Although men could reason on the basis of what they thought they observed, Bacon insisted that they needed to go further by experimenting and later by validating their conclusions. Roger Bacon saw philosophy and science as complimentary rather than as contradictory, and hoped that men in the future would learn to carry on continuous observations and experiments, and attempt to verify their conclusions by even further testing. Experience and inquiry were seen as being necessary if man was to build up knowledge about his world and himself.

This thirteenth-century glimmer as to the true importance of scientific reasoning was pushed into the background and repressed, however, by those in authority who felt that an inquiry into all things might develop an opposition to Churchly dogmas and thus be translated into heresies. The scientific spirit, which was evidently present in the mind and thought of the thirteenth-century Roger Bacon, went underground for many centuries before it was resurrected in the seventeenth century, this time against the opposition of the Church. From this period on, the scientific spirit became accepted and practiced by larger and larger numbers of men within each succeeding generation — though the vast majority of the world's population still reasoned as men did in the Medieval period before Roger Bacon.

The monasteries had become not only the centers of learning by the thirteenth century, but were also laboratories of technological efficiency. A contemporary technological account of a thirteenth-century monastery in France described the different ways in which energy from a river could be utilized:

"... gushes first into the corn-mill where it is very actively employed in grinding the grain under the weight of the wheels and in shaking the fine sieve which separates the flour from the bran. Thence it flows into the next building, and fills the boiler in which it is heated to prepare beer for the monks' drinking . . . But the river has not yet finished its work for it is now drawn into the fulling-machines following the corn-mill. In the mill it has prepared the brothers' food and its duty is now to serve in making their clothing. This the river does not withhold, nor does it refuse any task asked of it. Thus it raises and lowers alternately the heavy hammers and mallets, or to be more exact, the wooden feet of the fulling machines. When by swirling at great speed it has made all these wheels revolve swiftly, it issues foaming and looking as if it has ground itself. Now the river enters the tannery where it devotes much care and labor to preparing the necessary materials for the monks' footwear; then it divides into many small branches . . . seeking everywhere for those who require its services . . . whether for cooking, rotating, crushing, watering, washing or grinding . . . At last, to earn full thanks and to leave nothing undone, it carries away the refuse and leaves all clean."[2]

---

[2]As quoted by Lewis Mumford, *The Myth of the Machine* (New York, Harcourt, Brace and World, 1967), p. 270.

Not only did heresies begin to abound in the thirteenth through the fifteenth centuries, but men also dreamt of building secular Heavenly cities on earth wherein labor was efficient, luxuries flowed, transportation functioned by means of horseless carriages, flying machines, and underwater boats, and communication was instantaneous through the air. Men also dreamed of achieving the wealth they needed, and visualized materials being transmuted by chemical elements. In their imaginations, monks in the monasteries took the lead in exploring the world of the future. The Italian monk, Campanella, had his principal character report in his book, *City of the Sun*, that men would make more history in the next 100 years than they had in the past 4,000 (as they actually did).

This sense of optimism about man and his future among the monks and lesser clerics was a millenarian antidote to the prevailing pessimism encouraged by the secular lords and princes of the Church that man was basically evil, that human nature could not be changed except by God, that the status quo existed because it had withstood the test of time, and that man had reached a plateau beyond which he would not be able to advance. Most of the latter believed that it was more important for individuals to prepare their souls for the pending eternity than it was to be concerned with what happens in a temporary world filled with evil, sin, and suffering: only God could bring about change in this mortal life, but only if men learned to be completely dependent upon Him. Unquestioning obedience to temporal and sacred authority was man's only alternative if he wanted to be saved by the Grace of God. Man could not change nor save himself through his own efforts. And these two points of view have continued to battle one another even through the twentieth century.

The Middle Ages proved to be a period of enlightenment as well as of technological achievement. Inventions and innovations in technology were many. By the thirteenth century, inventions included the canal lock, sails that permitted tacking against the wind, rudders that were attached to the boat, revolutionary techniques in shipbuilding, and the use of the magnetic compass (which came from China at the end of the twelfth century and which permitted merchants to move with safety into the oceans, and from one point to another by taking advantage of different prevailing winds). By the end of the thirteenth century, Genoans and Venetians went far out to sea: the Genoans anticipated Vasca da Gama's later fifteenth-century voyage around Africa by experimenting with such a sea route to India at the end of the thirteenth century — a voyage that ended in failure. By the end of that century, men were becoming technically sophisticated enough to understand the theory behind rotary feed, the principle of the flywheel, and the belt-transmission of power. The fourteenth century brought a remarkable development in gearing, and by the end of the century the town clock had become a complex model for the later industrial machine. The arrival of the blow-gun from Malay during the early fifteenth century led to the development of the musket, and later in that century to the suction pump.

The technology which had come to Western Europe from Southwest Asia, Persia, India, and China, slowly began to spread to the rest of Europe by way of the various monastic orders. The Cistercian Order, for example, not only carried out the Benedictine concepts of hard labor combined with scholarly study and priestly duties, but disseminated technology as well. The technologies which had been profitably used by the monasteries of Western Europe began to spread to Eastern and Northern Europe. By the fifteenth century, Poland, Lithuania, Czechoslovakia, and western Russia had already been brought within the circle of influence emanating from the area between Paris, Antwerp, London, Hamburg, Prague, Nuremberg, Florence, and Lisbon. The monasteries in Eastern and Western Europe had by the late Middle Ages become centers of learning and technology. The manufacture of handicrafts for a larger market began to spread from the monasteries to the various European trading and artisanal cities, though the former still remained centers of instruction and learning.

⬦   ⬦   ⬦   ⬦   ⬦

What the monasteries had begun, the Medieval and Renaissance trading and cathedral towns carried further, the guilds then taking over the discipline, rules, regulations, and need for technological achievement which the monasteries had brought to Western Europe. (The guilds, like the later monasteries, became content merely to continue the status quo and to be concerned chiefly with their own narrow self-interests rather than with the good of the community as a whole — but this is true of all institutions that begin as innovators and end as social obstacles to cultural change.) The role of religion in developing technology and science in Europe cannot be underestimated: the Medieval monastery accepted the premise that man was weak and incomplete, but could be made stronger by nature. The latter was considered to be the means that led to the goal of knowing God. The growth of technology was stimulated by this attempt to understand and imitate nature. Everything that man discovered about his world became part of his growth, leading him to greater insights about the work of God. Human reason was thus seen as part of God's plan for man.

The clocks that told monks the time of the day became by the mid-fourteenth century the status symbols adorning the city halls of the merchant towns. Their machinery became the basis for the more sophisticated machines that appeared increasingly after the beginning of the sixteenth century.

The influence of the monasteries encouraged learning and the opening of schools. The merchants and artisans in the new towns were impelled by their increasingly important activities to keep books and records, and to educate their children in reading, writing, and arithmetic. All these developments led in the mid-fifteenth century to the first mechanized assembly line, the printing press. This development was only possible after metallurgy had been used to fashion better weapons of war (as, for example, a more efficient cannon and a stronger musket). In concept, the printing press was European for it was based upon the existence of the olive oil and wine press, but the movable type which it used was Korean and Chinese in origin.

The number of literate individuals had slowly increased during the fourteenth century so that by the middle of the fifteenth century at least 5 percent of the Western populations obtained their knowledge through the written word. The well-to-do merchants educated their children in the Latin schools of the day, which were attached to the cathedrals or monasteries. The lesser administrative officials serving the regional lords, princes, and kings also encouraged their children to acquire more than a bare literacy in the Latin schools in order to enhance their later employment opportunities. The increase in literate artisans, accountants, lawyers, notaries, and clerks created a growing market for products of the printing press, while the growth of schools and universities after the fifteenth century also added to the accumulation of consumer demand for books. The rise of Protestantism after the sixteenth century encouraged even more individuals to discover God's truth for themselves by reading the Bible. Even before Luther, the Hussite Taborites of Bohemia and the Waldensians of France had been convinced that one could determine which religious errors were being promulgated if one was free to go to the original sources of truth in the written word of God.

◇   ◇   ◇   ◇   ◇

Printing and the printing press stimulated the egalitarianism then existing in Europe. Literacy and the reading of books were seen as leading to the liberation of man from entanglement in the errors and falsehoods existing around him. There was even more magic attached to the printed word than to the handwritten one. The charges and countercharges involved in the growth of the Reformation and the Counter-Reformation were disseminated through the media of thousands of books and pamphlets. Printing diffused new forms of knowledge, and men in Europe became more aware of the ideas and knowledge that had been created by those living thousands of miles away. If the assembly line of the printing press had not turned out a steady stream of ideas and concepts, it is doubtful whether the Industrial and Scientific civilization could have been born.

The Industrial civilization and its scientific overtones could not have developed in the Moslem countries, in India, or in China, primarily because those countries lacked the cultural receptivity which motivated empirical theorizing about the universe, government, man, and a more "perfect" religion and religious organization. In the intellectual circles of Western Europe, students were encouraged to look upon the growth of knowledge as something that never ended, since it had to be continually discovered. Although the monasteries played a most important role in encouraging the spread of knowledge immediately after the eleventh century, by the fifteenth century the university had become the intellectual center for the diffusion of new knowledge. In the first 100 years of the printing press, it had been used mainly to diffuse religious and theological tracts, but by the seventeenth century it had also become a means for spreading knowledge about alchemy, architecture, astrology, metallurgy, medicine, and nontheological interpretations of the universe.

◇   ◇   ◇   ◇   ◇

From the eleventh century on, Europe slowly increased in affluence with each passing century. Agriculture gradually improved, as did the home or cottage industries. Trade had become something more than a few merchants leading 10 or 12 horses or donkeys on a pitted dirt path or sailing with goods in a ship of a few tons. The wealth that had slowly been created and accumulated between the eleventh and sixteenth centuries benefited the aristocracy, the Church, and the merchants. It scarcely affected the living standards of the peasantry. The increased wealth in the hands of aristocrats, churchmen, and merchants did, however, increase job opportunities for artisans, journeymen, and the unskilled in the small but burgeoning towns of Europe. As wealth increased, the gap between the upper groups of aristocrats, bishops, and merchants, and the lower classes of artisans, journeymen, and unskilled laborers slowly widened, thus increasing the frustrations of the latter who saw themselves steadily becoming poorer from a relative point of view. The sense of being pushed out of the mainstream of wealth, government, and the control of their own affairs acted as a stimulus to these townspeople to compete with the aristocrats by seeking more education for themselves and their children. As a result, they became more receptive to the knowledge of the printed word as well as to those egalitarian religious movements which emphasized the temporary aspects of the Medieval class structure and the millenarian equality based upon moral behavior which would accrue to all men with the Second Coming of Christ. The wealth which stimulated the growth of the cathedral classical schools and universities also encouraged men to build more elaborate buildings, to devise more varied consumer goods, to create more efficient means of obtaining the resources of the earth. At the same time, it also influenced men to seek that knowledge which would help them overcome the social frustrations of their daily lives.

From the tenth to the fourteenth centuries, the European population had slowly increased from about 43 million to more than 74 million. By the middle of the fourteenth century, however, the Black Plague had swept over Europe, killing more than one-third of the population within a decade. By the beginning of the fifteenth century, there were fewer inhabitants in Europe than there had been in the eleventh century. The sudden decrease in population can be correlated with the increase in international trade and the growth of towns, both of which built up a sellers' market among peasants, artisans, journeymen, and laborers. Wages went up as the accumulated wealth had to be shared with those who did the work. Jobs also became easier to get because master craftsmen and merchants bid against each other for the services they needed, thereby creating a higher level of self-esteem among the working town-dwellers. This higher level of self-fulfillment was disseminated to relatives who still lived as peasants under feudal conditions, thus serving to raise the latters' expectations. As the small towns began to demand autonomy and get it, first in Italy and then in Flanders, the Netherlands, the German principalities, the Czech lands, and England, workers became encouraged to demand more rights for themselves. From the fourteenth through the sixteenth centuries, religious rebels received a good deal of their moral and physical support from the poorer townspeople who wanted their social status to be raised vis-a-vis the merchants and master craftsmen. The evolution in standards of living and social status led to the later Industrial and Scientific Revolution, plus the rise of millenarian movements that soon became secularized when many followers despaired of the Second Coming of Christ and wanted to move ahead in establishing the foundations of the Heavenly City on Earth.

The egalitarianism which is so much a part of European aspirations has a long religious history whether one deals with the Lollards, the Hussites, the Taborites, the followers of Thomas Münzer, the Diggers, or any of the other European movements that encouraged their followers to hope that a day of reckoning would soon arrive which would let them become equal to the best of men. The desire for respect encouraged many to seek a means to close the gap that existed between themselves and those who felt that they were social superiors. We do not know if this trend existed in the New World, in Africa, China, India, or Southwest Asia at the same time, but we do know that it existed in Europe, that its traces were more apparent than in other parts of the world. We can accordingly assume that it helped make easier the rise of the new civilization of industrialization and science in Europe than elsewhere.

This desire for higher personal status could have taken the form of banditry (as it often undoubtedly did), and it could have led to the encouragement of small warrior gangs who used warfare to achieve higher status for themselves and their leaders — as occurred over and over again in Europe and other parts of the world. Or it could have taken the form of encouraging the creation of religious scholars, as among the Jews, or of holy men, as among the Hindus and Buddhists. But in Western Europe men turned toward the accumulation of wealth to increase their status and toward a commercial capitalism that arose in the urban centers. They engaged in cottage manufacturing, exporting to a larger market than the local one; they loaned money to nearby feudal lords or church officials for Church construction; they financed trade and trading companies; or they were the middlemen who supported new forms of industry geared to a ready market.

Money could be made in Europe by using other people's money, or by joining with those who had access to capital to organize new trade routes, or to purchase trading and coining monopolies from the princes of the realm. Although a merchant needed political connections in order to become successful in the city-states of Western Europe, an artisan had opportunities which let him become a master craftsman employing five to ten workers; a master craftsman found it possible to become a merchant on a small scale supplying goods to a larger market; and sons of well-to-do master artisans and merchants were able to expand the family's business.

Some descendants of artisans became dukes, while many grandsons of wealthy merchants became oligarchs. Princes encouraged the idea that money was the best means of enhancing one's social status, and that the man of wealth could become the social equal of the bishop or the aristocratic warrior; or, if he did not, at least his descendants would. As the numbers of men of wealth increased in the communes that turned into the towns and cathedral centers of

Western Europe, they slowly severed the ties that had kept them under the rule of feudal lords and bishops. After the eleventh and twelfth centuries, freedom from tradition and arbitrary rule became a part of town life, as the townsmen defended their right to be ruled by laws now made only by themselves.

The first and largest market for European merchants had been that of the Church, with its myriad of functionaries, its need for fine textiles, brocades, silver candlesticks, paintings, sculpture, and altars. The Church needed financiers to help it utilize the money that came from all corners of Western Christendom. The funds that flowed in supported a large number of Church bureaucrats in Rome, while the artisans and artists that the Church employed lived in nearby Tuscany, the urban center of which was Florence. Aristocrats and kings formed another large market, which grew larger and richer through the centuries — though in the eleventh and twelfth centuries nobles and kings were generally poor and had few possessions that could be translated into wealth. The growing cities were another expanding market for they needed wheat and other foodstuffs which they could not raise by themselves. Over the centuries, the Hanseatic League became strong and wealthy by supplying Prussian wheat to Flanders, England, Norway, and the Rhineland. The Italian cities acted as middlemen in the export of grain to Constantinople, Egypt, and Tunis, while Naples used the wheat of Sicily to expand her trade with other Mediterranean centers. The cities of the Po region and the western side of the Appennines were chiefly dependent upon cereal grown along the Adriatic or in Sicily. At the same time, many cities were outlets for the manufactures of other cities. Venice, for example, though a glassmaking and shipbuilding center in its own right, was also an outlet for Florentine textiles, not only buying the latter for its own population (which had reached 100,000 by the seventeenth century), but also re-exporting these textiles and brocades to distant areas at a profit. Florence was a workshop that made fine crafts for the Po Valley, Genoa, Pisa, and the smaller cities north of the Alps.

Beyond the Alps by the thirteenth century, various regions had begun to specialize in certain commodities. Hungary and Prussia produced a surplus of wheat for export, and both also sent meat to nearby areas. England became a wool-producing country, turning out thread for the Flemish weavers. Iron-making became a specialty of those close to large forests (where charcoal could be used) and iron ore deposits (since transport of iron ore over long distances was not practical in Europe until the beginning of the barge age in the seventeenth century and of the railroad age in the mid-nineteenth). By the fourteenth century, iron-casting had become a specialty in the Belgian Brabant area (we do not know whether this was an independent invention or whether the process came from the Chinese, who evidently had it a few centuries before the Christian era). The smelting of ore for casting required a higher heat than had been available in the Classical World. The ancient Chinese had used a blow-gun, derived from Southeast Asia, as a form of bellows; in Europe at the beginning of the fourteenth century, a bellows was invented which increased the heat of the charcoal fire to permit the complete melting of the iron ore so that it could be poured or cast in a sand mold. A primitive blast furnace (not to be confused with the Bessemer Process in the nineteenth century) had already been invented and certain centers in France and Bavaria had become important iron-making areas.

◊   ◊   ◊   ◊   ◊

After the fourteenth century, a significant motivation for improving metallurgy was the growth of warfare wherein primitive cannon and muskets were continuously improved to enable communes to fight other communes, feudal lords other feudal lords, and kings other kings. Although the cannon was a European invention (the first use of one appears to have been in England in 1319), the idea seemed to have come from the Byzantine copper tube that held the explosive "Greek fire," an invention that may go back to the seventh or eighth centuries. After the tenth century, the idea of mixing potassium nitrate, sulphur, and carbon in order to obtain an explosive gunpowder for use in warfare dispersed slowly in all directions. The Chinese may have received the formula for it from Moslem traders by the eleventh century. It became known to Europeans through returning Crusaders in the twelfth century. The scientifically-minded thirteenth-century English monk, Roger Bacon, described the explosive power of gunpowder when enclosed in a solid container and set afire. The first European cannon were wooden tubes held together by iron rings; the primitive gunpowder was used to propel against castle walls the stone balls inside the tubes. In the early part of the fifteenth century, wrought iron was used as the barrel when lead shot began to be utilized as the propellant. By the sixteenth century, bronze had replaced wrought iron, and iron balls took the place of both stone and lead shot. The growing need among princes, towns, and kings to obtain better cannon than their adversaries led to a knowledge explosion in mining, casting, and the growth of the mathematical physics of ballistics.

Many merchants in the sixteenth century became wealthy by seeking out ore deposits and then erecting small furnaces and artisanal smithies near them to manufacture cannon and flintlock muskets. The growing demand for ferrous ores (and more iron was then being produced in Europe than in the rest of the world combined) led to the exhaustion of surface iron ore seams, and deeper ones had to be worked. As the mines became deeper, water seepage became an almost insoluble problem and ventilation of the long shafts became difficult. Transportation of the ore from the mine to the blast furnaces became unpredictable as flooding interfered with the mining.

The increase in agricultural productivity among the peasants and the rising affluence among the townspeople encouraged the kings, princes, and town oligarchs to raise taxes in order to build up their military forces and use them to "protect" their trade and monopolies (as Venice, Genoa, London, the Hanseatic cities, Nuremberg, the Flemish and Dutch cities did) against what they felt to be "unfair" restrictions placed on their trade by others. (The use of warships to open up trade with China or Japan was not a nineteenth-century innovation; it was used in the fifteenth through the seventeenth centuries as well.) This defence led to increased military budgets to pay the costs of larger ships, more efficient cannon, new firearms of various kinds, and uniforms to clothe the armies. By the seventeenth century, warfare had become more devastating for civilians than it had been in the Ancient World. Despite the reputation of the ancient Assyrians, Louis XIV proved just as adept in laying waste large areas. The Thirty Years' War destroyed more towns than had the campaigns of the ancient empire builders chiefly because weapons had become more dangerous and Europe contained more wealth, more urban centers, and industries than had existed in the Ancient World. But the direct result of this useless destruction was that a market was created for the coming Industrial Revolution to fill.

Religion with its attacks first against the status quo and later in defense of the status quo, along with warfare, helped to push segments of Europe into the new industrial civilization, much as the linkage of religion and warfare had helped to establish the first agrarian civilizations of the Ancient World. More research was encouraged on warfare, one result being that granulated gunpowder, invented at the end of the fifteenth century, exploded with more violence than the earlier poorly made dust (or the original "Greek fire," with its mixture of naphtha, saltpeter, and sulphur). The appetite for iron, copper, tin, silver, and gold became almost insatiable among the petty rulers of Western Europe, who enriched the merchants when the latters' agents found new deposits of ore on the continent. A market was also created for the services of the adventurers who with financing from the wealthy merchants sought out the precious ores in the New World. By the sixteenth century, three to four tons of bronze were required to make an effective cannon, while an iron cannonball weighed from 100 to 150 pounds. Two tons of iron were required for the heavy bolts on the carriage, the chains, and the hook. Even the axles and wheels were made with large amounts of iron to strengthen their wooden framework, and wrought iron was used for the tires on the gun carriage wheels. As a result, the production of iron from the mid-fifteenth to the mid-sixteenth centuries more than quadrupled, reaching an annual production of more than 100,000 tons in Central Europe alone. This again quintupled during the next 100 years.

At the height of the Roman Empire, the entire world production of iron was perhaps no more than 10,000 tons annually. On the other hand, the European increase in production was tiny when compared to the present annual world production of more than 600 million tons of iron and steel. Copper, never a plentiful metal, was produced at a rate of 10,000 tons per year in Europe during the middle of the sixteenth century. Though this is little compared to the contemporary world production of more than 10 million tons, it was far higher than it had ever been in the ancient civilizations.

◇   ◇   ◇   ◇   ◇

In the sixteenth century, Europe was set for an expansionist period. It was in a better position to view the globe as a whole than the Romans, the Chinese, or the Phoenicians had been. While the Romans had occupied a large part of the Mediterranean area and most of Western Europe, they had felt little curiosity as to how those outside the Empire (or even within it, for that matter) lived and thought. Although the Chinese had engaged in trade with Korea, Japan, Southeast Asia, and even temporarily with the coastal areas of India and East Africa, there was little motivation to keep up the trading contacts over the centuries. Even during the fourteenth century when China sent a fleet to East Africa, it still remained isolationist rather than expanionist. The Phoenicians may have traveled great distances, but they left almost no records of where they went or what they had done. While ancient travelers and voyagers observed other peoples and their customs, the strangeness was apparently taken for granted because they appear to have assumed that all strangers were different from themselves, including their neighbors. One gets the impression that most Romans who traveled to the outskirts of the Empire accepted differences as being normal, though at the same time they held that human behavior should be based upon Roman norms and values. On the other hand, men during the sixteenth century in Western Europe were more curious about the world they lived in. In Europe from the thirteenth century on, the scientific method had been growing through investigations into the ways in which nature functioned. Men had become more curious about the physical world, about man's social relationships, about the differences between men, about the creation of the universe and the Heavens, and about non-theological causes of misfortune.

In Europe from the sixteenth century on, men benefited from more than 400 years of underground thinking which had challenged traditional explanations of the physical universe and of man's social world. Although Aristotle had been accepted by the Church in Rome, his unchanging universe was somewhat uncongenial to the thinking of many Europeans, as it was not to most Moslems. It was difficult for the Western Europeans, for the scholarly churchmen of Paris and Oxford to accept the Aristotelian world with its fixed laws that even an all-powerful God, who had created them to run the universe, could not change. Such a world tended to be too authoritarian and dogmatic for their tastes. Scientific-minded scholars were unable to engage in much speculation about a rigid and fixed universe, though there was much they could discover and think about in discussions of an infinite universe which expanded and changed over the years. More discoveries could be made by substituting observation for intuition, and mathematics for philosophy. Slowly at first but then more rapidly after the seventeenth century, thoughtful men in Europe began to transform their thinking about the universe, man's place in it, and the complexity of natural laws which made both the world and man function.

By the sixteenth century, scientific thinking which had begun slowly in the thirteenth century had advanced sufficiently to stimulate curiosity and to permit observations about the recently discovered New World and the differences which had been encountered there as contrasted to what existed in Europe. Although these observations were naturally not as scientifically sophisticated as contemporary ones, still a comparison of the writings of the sixteenth-century Spanish friars in the New World with those of Tacitus or Herodotus reveals how sophisticated men's thinking had become. Because of accounts left us by Spanish observers, we are better acquainted with Mayan and Aztec cultures at the time of the arrival of the Spaniards than we are with the world which Herodotus and Tacitus knew in the pre-Christian era.

Literacy had increased enormously after the first use of the printing press in the mid-fifteenth century. More literate individuals in the sixteenth century than had ever existed before formed a large market for both the printing presses and their output of learned observations, which were disseminated to all corners of Europe. Although wealth and urban settlements had increased in this century, few cities had as many as 100,000 inhabitants. Most of the European population was still composed of illiterate peasants working their lands as inefficiently as their fathers had done, plus a small percentage living and making goods for the local market in small towns. In the large towns of Western Europe, a few merchants employed craftsmen to manufacture for the larger market, acted as middlemen to bring scarce goods to where they were wanted, or bought grain, textiles, glass, and iron to ship where sales appeared most promising. In return for supplying Scandinavia with grain from Prussia, the League of Hanseatic Merchants received herrings, which were then pickled and sent to areas where there was a need for the protein which men could not obtain from the available meat supply. A steady market for fish and wine was encouraged by the Church as it commanded its followers to refrain from eating meat on Friday, and as priests used large amounts of wine for sacramental purposes. Feudal lords and bishops also bought large quantities of wine as a luxury drink.

The wealth that had come to Western Europe through the development of technology, the increases in agricultural productivity, and the opening of new mines was poorly distributed, however, with some areas being much wealthier than others. Since the new cannons, firearms, and gunpowder could no longer be made locally but became the specialties of certain metallurgical centers, feudal lords and petty kings found it necessary to obtain more gold and silver in order to buy the equipment they needed to defend their realms against those who desired them. Those who were isolated in areas where barter had been the chief mainstay of the economy were unable to amass the wealth that was needed in order to carry on even limited warfare. The Spanish and Portuguese kings were in a more favorable position because large amounts of silver and gold had been obtained by looting the New World or by carrying on trade to obtain these metals from India, the East Indies, the Philippines, and Japan. Later, the Portuguese, Danes, and English got their gold and silver by transporting thousands of slaves each year from the west coast of Africa to the plantations in the New World where their labor was exploited. In Mexico, the Spaniards deemed themselves fortunate for they found millions of docile Indians who worked for them as they had previously labored for their Indian chieftains and conquerors.

The large amounts of gold and silver that flowed into the treasuries of the Spanish kings were consumed in purchasing cannon, firearms, uniforms, provisions, and transport by sea and land for the growing armies. The preparation and execution of warfare created an ever-expanding market for the urban merchants, one far greater than any previously developed through supplying the Church, the feudal lords, or the growing artisan class in the small mercantile cities.

The Austrian emperors and the French kings also needed gold and silver in ever larger amounts to equip their armies to oppose the armies and ships of their brother Spanish kings. In the process of trying to compete, the smaller and weaker kings and feudal lords fell by the wayside. They were unable to receive from their subjects or to borrow (even with collateral from Italian and German merchant-bankers) the enormous amounts required to equip armies with trained manpower and expensive supplies.

Because money was loaned by bankers who either had the protection of the Church or blackmailing power over their fellow merchants (whether Hanseatic, Venetian, Florentine, Genoan, Pisan, or the smaller groups at Nuremberg and Augsburg), the merchant-bankers could press their claims even though they pushed their clients into bankruptcy, as many did, thus making it easier for centralized government to grow in Western Europe. Kings were able to defeat their weaker vassals, or the smaller armies of neighboring independent princes, dukes, counts, and barons. Only the wealthy merchant Republic of the Netherlands was able to survive successfully.

Since the wealth of Europe became more and more concentrated in the hands of merchant-bankers located in the growing industrial and commercial towns, the latter were able to increase their military strength. They hired mercenaries and used their shipyards to build warships, their foundries to manufacture cannon, and their skilled workers to construct better fortifications around the towns. They also enlisted the free citizenry plus the lesser artisans into fighting forces that were often more than a match for the armies of nearby feudal lords and faraway kings.

It was in the towns that the discontented artisans, journeymen, and their unskilled helpers became the mainstay of the revolutionary millenarian movements that swept through Western Europe from the fourteenth through the eighteenth centuries. It was from the towns that the emotional sparks came that ignited the movements of the Lollards, the Hussites, the Taborites, the various Anabaptists, and the "Diggers." The gap between the great riches of the few town merchants and the poverty of the artisans and their helpers caused increasing dissatisfactions among the latter. Most of these were sons of discontented peasants who had moved to the towns to breathe "free" air and to find opportunities for a better life. Although peasants revolted in England, in Germany, in the Czech lands, and in parts of France, the chief rebels were those who lived in the small but growing towns who wanted more humaneness in their lives.

◇   ◇   ◇   ◇   ◇

The towns had purchased their freedom from bishops or feudal lords who at one time owned their sites (almost all urban areas in Western Europe had obtained their freedom from extraneous control at fairly early dates). The Hanseatic League of Merchants stipulated in its agreements with the kings with whom they did business that their settlements and their quarters in foreign urban ports must remain free from any outside control. European kings had many difficulties with the towns in their midst, whether the urban settlements were London, Paris, or Prague. The Italian cities had freed themselves at an early date from too close a dependence upon their agricultural hinterlands, and had developed extensive trading organizations to import their foodstuffs and raw materials. The Hanseatic Leagues in Germany, Denmark, Sweden, and Norway had also arranged to be relatively independent of the surrounding countryside. They functioned as almost free communes or city-states in their own right, as the ancient cities were never able to do (with the possible exception of the Phoenicians, though here the evidence appears to be scanty).

Feudal lords found it difficult to exact unflinching obedience from their subjects when the latter knew that their relatives in the cities were free from such loyalty. Although the feudal lords resented their increasing dependency upon the centralized monarchy, they were able temporarily to offset the greater power of the king only through alliances with the town merchants plus the latters' artisans and helpers. And, as in the cases of the later Dutch, English, and French revolutions, the merchants were the ones who gained the most from these alliances. In the towns themselves, whether in the German ones of Augsburg and Nuremberg or in the Swiss ones, the Merchants' Guilds insisted upon their social and political equality with the nobles, and especially upon equal participation in the town councils.

Unfortunately for the continental merchants, the wars waged by the Hapsburgs impoverished the Fuggers and their fellow German merchants. The warfare undertaken by the French and the Spaniards offered virtually bottomless chasms into which money was poured to pay for the armaments and mercenaries who were hired to fight the wars between the various Protestant Leagues, the Austrian and Spanish emperors, and the French kings. If the soldiers were unpaid, they retaliated by looting. Rome and Antwerp took a long time to recover from the pillage inflicted by the mercenaries of Philip II of Spain. Although enormous wealth still came into Spain to pay for the wars against the French king, against the English queen, and against the pirates of North Africa, most of these military adventures ruined the Italian cities, impoverished Spain, and turned Austria, Bavaria, and Flanders into virtually bankrupt areas. The Reformation and Counter-Reformation in the sixteenth and seventeenth centuries also disrupted trade and censored innovations.

◇   ◇   ◇   ◇   ◇

The wealth that was gradually being built up in Western Europe after the eleventh century produced improved technology, larger public buildings, and cathedrals, castles, palaces, and other manifestations of splendor along with changes in the standards of consumption. The Italian and Flemish cities in the sixteenth and seventeenth centuries were larger, wealthier, and provided higher standards of living than men had possessed in earlier centuries. Changes in social thought were also occurring gradually, and when added to the past accumulation of knowledge became translated into increased wealth: better mining techniques, more efficient production, and discoveries in chemical technology. Innovations took place in improved techniques in smelting, in higher agricultural production (though the great agricultural revolutions which completely transformed the ancient trades of farming and husbandry did not begin until the eighteenth century), in the development of new crafts, and in the construction of a few isolated plants of large-scale manufacture.

Although great wealth had accumulated through trade, technology, and mining (plus the looting of treasures in the New World in the sixteenth and seventeenth centuries, and of Indonesia and India in the eighteenth), there was no guarantee that the period of economic development which had begun in Western Europe with the eleventh century would automatically continue. While scientific thinking had been in existence in the thirteenth century (mixed with mysticism, occultism, and irrational cause-and-effect relationships), its effect upon the thinking of most individuals in power (most merchants, artisans, scholars, churchmen, and literates) was quite minimal. A few hardy individuals were zealous to obtain new knowledge through observation, experimentation, and the testing of new hypotheses (that would attempt to bring order and comprehension into what appeared to be an incompletely known and understood universe); and these became the ones whose work pushed Western Europe into the new world of science.

The kings and the symbols of traditional authority in the seventeenth century frustrated most men who had to live under their governance. Although the commercial revolution from the tenth century on increased the manufacture and consumption of various luxury goods, the benefits went almost entirely to the upper classes composed of Church prelates, feudal lords, kings, and their courtiers plus the wealthy merchants in the new towns and communes of Southern and Western Europe. The artisans and their helpers gained very little and the peasants almost nothing. While Western Europe had progressed technologically beyond the levels of the Ancient World, it had maintained the same form of civilization as the latter until the beginning of the seventeenth century. The vast majority of the population were still illiterate peasants and the urban population was small — in most cases less than 10 percent of the total. Although manufacturing was on a cottage industry level, the numbers employed became higher than they had been in the Classical World: they did not approach, however, the numbers which the Industrial Revolution in the mid-nineteenth century required to work for the mass market. The roots of science had been laid, but the few scientists were mentally still part of the Medieval World. While they were interested in experimentation and observation, they carried around in their minds a good many ideas that had little to do with scientific observation, generally bringing to their studies assumptions and hypotheses that were completely unproven.

The European world had moved ahead of the Ancient World. Civilization by the end of the sixteenth century in Western Europe had advanced by becoming more complex and sophisticated, but it had not changed. The important transformations took place in the succeeding four centuries as mass education substituted for education within the family, as individual interpretations of the world replaced the teachings and dogmas of the Church, as adherence to revelations from God about the world He had made and His instructions for man became democratized so that new direction could come from those outside the Church. These included the teachings of the new sciences which were also seen as attempts to understand God and His handiwork. Men then secularized what had once been the sacred monopoly of the priesthood — the opportunity to know God through understanding His works and His laws.

Europe between the eleventh and sixteenth centuries gave the rest of the world new ideas about the equality of men, about the right of men to seek knowledge through their own initiative without recourse to traditional authority, about the need to make life pleasanter (though not for all men: this came much later), and about the necessity to create more wealth for society by harnessing the forces of nature more efficiently through new methods of work. By utilizing more productive processes, more grain could grow, more goods could be made, and more men could become wealthy — all redounding to the greater glory of God. Although changes were also occurring on other continents, one could say that the techniques and culture change which Europe brought about produced a far greater effect upon the rest of the world by creating a new civilization—

as new as Sumeria had been vis-a-vis the Neolithic world, but as different from Sumeria as the latter had been from the agricultural village in the pre-Sumerian past.

X   The Birth of Secondary Civilization

The seventeenth century begins the story of a new civilization, one whose roots were in the past but one that in ensuing centuries transformed its carriers and influenced those who were neither its adherents nor its designers. The Primary civilization had generally been regional in its influences (the Chinese and the Roman Empires had not affected more than a small population around their borders), but the new civilization interfered in the lives of Africans, Asians, North and South Americans. It engulfed the world as Primary civilization never did. The unchanged peasants had been exploited by Primary civilization, but the new one completely transformed them either into a farmer (dependent upon industry and science for the goods and knowledge he needed in order to earn his living) or into an unskilled laborer (pushed off the plot of land his ancestors had tilled, becoming propertyless and forced to move to the growing industrial city where he became a factory worker with another style of life).

The division of labor which had been fairly simple during the Neolithic period, but had become somewhat complex at the height of the Classical World, became even more subdivided into new categories by the beginning of the eighteenth century. New occupations were born and pioneering professions spread as men for the first time began to seek practical solutions to the problems that hindered increased production in agriculture, engineering, construction, and transportation. Men in the Ancient World had speculated about the universe and had experimented with the rudiments of science, but they were not even slightly interested to make work easier for the slave or the peasant. The purpose of Greek and Roman scholarship was not intended to add to the fund of practical knowledge for the benefit of men in general.

In the new world which came into existence after the seventeenth century, men were more motivated to solve everyday problems. They hoped that in trying to understand nature, they would be helping themselves. Science in its inception was eminently practical. It was interested in navigation, better agricultural techniques, improved breeding of farm animals, stronger watch springs, chronometers, magnetism, forestry, and so on. If science and industry did not live together compatibly until after the middle of the nineteenth century, the fault was not that of the man of science, but rather of the practical man of industry who felt apprehensive at his inability to live day in and day out with the former without succumbing to feelings of inadequacy.

Although the "impractical" man of science was most interested in astronomy, the derivatives from the study of the heavens led to a good many useful aids for improving navigation, for developing more accurate methods of measuring time and distances on earth. Experimentation in the theoretical aspects of the universe led later to improvements in metallurgy, chemistry, and engineering. Scholars also speculated about the origins of man's society, about explanations for "human nature," and about the differences within mankind in general—all without turning to Aristotelian or Biblical concepts. Reason, rationalism, and the individual's need to test concepts of truth for himself were all parts of this revolution in looking at the world with a new vision.

◊   ◊   ◊   ◊   ◊

The craftsman had little interest in learning from the scientist. He was much more concerned with making a quality product in terms of past guild prescriptions than in innovating something original. In fact, the guilds by the seventeenth century were restricting innovations: they opposed "unfair competition" through advocating longer working hours and through opposing price-cutting and improving the quality of the product. The craftsman or artisan was in the same position as the peasant in the Ancient World when civilization began: he gained little from industrialization and the growth of science. He and his workshop were not able to compete with the new mass production brought into effect by the technological revolution in the manufacture of various consumer goods. In the Medieval World, the artisan's market was that of the few rich; the Industrial Revolution operated separately by seeking wider and larger markets. By the early nineteenth century, it was easier for women and children to work at low wages as unskilled labor than it was for artisans whose skills had been displaced by the machine.

The Ancient World used the peasant, but it did not put him out of work. The Industrial Revolution and the new Scientific Age replaced hundreds of thousands of artisans, and continued to do so as the Industrial Age swept across Europe, North America, and Asia in the nineteenth century. The skilled artisan working in production was made semi-obsolete by the Industrial Revolution. The master craftsman, whether he was a master tailor, a master shoemaker, a master baker, or whatever, found that the new mass industries opened up markets that he never knew existed. While the master craftsman continued to make luxury goods for the rich, he was doomed by the arrival of mass industry. He would not become an important man of wealth nor a leading figure in the economic growth of nations.

After the seventeenth century, the number of scientists slowly increased. Although individual scientists made important contributions during the seventeenth, eighteenth, and nineteenth centuries, it was not until the twentieth that the scientist plus the industrialist came into their own. The industrialist was the artisan-turned-merchant who perceived what and where the markets for his products were and who was acquainted with the technical resources that could be utilized to fulfill his requirements. These occupations did not come into the world full-blown as Venus did from the sea, but had been slowly evolving from at least the thirteenth century. The rare industrialist who employed 200 or more workers under one roof existed in fifteenth-century Florence and Flanders and in sixteenth-century France, England, and Germany.

The early industrialist, unlike the contemporary professional manager of a corporation, created his plant from scratch, trained his workers and supervisors, and decided what product to make. As his own salesman, he traveled about and learned the extent of his market and the technical resources available to him. The unusual industrialist also did his own inventing and innovating.

Today, the professional manager takes few risks, is rarely an innovator, and in most cases is more of a manipulator of resources that already exist within the corporation. While many an early entrepreneur quickly went bankrupt, many times through no fault of his own, it is difficult if not impossible for the modern corporation to go out of business. A company in a bankrupt condition is attractive to a more profitable corporation that will purchase it for the tax deductions made possible by American tax laws. Credit from banks and governments is also more readily available to the corporation. Our contemporary culture subsidizes corporations so that profitability is assured; in the seventeenth century, the culture surrounding the small industrialist assumed none of his risks.

◊   ◊   ◊   ◊   ◊

Although much has been written about the motivations for the rise of the Industrial and Scientific civilization from the seventeenth century on, the explanations will not be very satisfying 100 years hence. Industrial societies have either been cast as individuals undergoing all the incentives and motivations which push men on, or else they have been clothed as various super instruments, behaving much like airplanes that take off and soar (but evidently never come down again). There is much agreement that Western Europe in the eighteenth century was more receptive to the new Industrial and Scientific civilization than were India or China. The New World, even before the arrival of the Spaniards, was by no means culturally ready for it. If it had continued to live in isolation, it would not have developed this type of civilization by the twentieth century any more than Africa could or did.

The Industrial and Scientific civilization had to be encouraged as a new way of life, with large numbers of individuals within its milieu encouraged, if not commanded, to act as its missionaries, carriers, and defenders. The Industrial and Scientific civilization operated almost as a religion, a creed, that insisted that a better society could be built on this earth rather than in Heaven; that men needed to become more efficient and knowledgeable; that learning was part of life; and that, in fact, without learning life would be empty.

Although heartened by the capitalistic spirit which developed in Western Europe from the thirteenth century on (roots of this capitalism also existed in various parts of the Ancient World), the destiny of the new civilization while linked with capitalism was still not part of the same patterned thinking. Both industrialism and science could be encouraged by absolutist kings, czars, Communist governments, plus endowed institutions of higher learning. Capitalism was motivated by monetary rewards that produced higher status, but industrialization and science had additional rewards: for example, the pleasures involved in discovery, in innovating, in creating and managing new complexes of people, and in ascertaining what stood behind hitherto unfathomable mysteries. Capitalism by itself as a system of private property working for profit could hardly have developed the new civilization. Without the technology, the broader levels of education, the investigations within laboratories, the free spirit of inquiry, and above all, the freedom to experiment, to learn, to apply, and to speculate, it is quite likely that the Industrial and Scientific civilization would have been stillborn.

Although great and wealthy merchants existed in the Italian cities and communes and although many citizens of the latter played pioneering parts in establishing the scientific spirit, still the Industrial and Scientific civilization did not find a comfortable home in Italy after the seventeenth century — any more than it did in Flanders in the areas of Bruges, Ypres, Antwerp, or in the German cities of Augsburg, Nuremberg, and Ulm. Western Europe contained many rich cities in which merchants piled up their wealth, traded with the entire known world, and directed hundreds if not thousands of artisans and their helpers in producing goods for the international market.

Lisbon was the center for the Indian and African trade, just as Seville was home port for the ships coming from Spanish America. Venice was not only an important glass center but a ship-building one as well. There was wealth in Lübeck, Hamburg, and Copenhagen, but this was not the chief prerequisite for pushing a population into the Industrial and Scientific civilization. For this, other factors were essential.

Although much is made of the need for achievement, the fact remains that Europe did contain many individuals who felt this need. While many highly talented individuals lived in such small cities as Florence (with less than 200,000 people), Venice, Genoa, Pisa, Padua, Ferrara, or Bologna, their presence did not push these cities toward building the foundations for the Industrial and Scientific civilization. It is doubtful that 10 or 20 or even 100 individuals can start a trend when cultural conditions disapprove of the expansion of a new civilization; when the Church represses them as heretics and thus dries up the source of intellectuals; when the merchants are unable to understand trends; or when governments do all in their power to discourage the growth of new ages. (Despite the capitalism of the Old South in the United States, it is questionable that the Industrial and Scientific civilization could have developed there.)

◇   ◇   ◇   ◇   ◇

Although it is not at all clear that the conditions which brought about the Industrial and Scientific civilization in Europe are the same as those that today act as motivating forces in industrializing a developing nation, still it is possible to list some prerequisites that may be necessary before a certain area can adapt itself to the new civilization. First of all, there must be a large number of individuals who are literate, who can read the products of the presses, who can learn the new technologies from the books in which these technologies are disseminated. There must be a certain amount of cultural encouragement for new ideas and for the concept of "progress" wherein a society moves toward stated future goals. The conviction needs to be present that men must be encouraged to experiment with new concepts rather than to be punished for the ideas which they hold (a highly centralized and authoritarian regime may not support the freedom necessary for this fragile civilization to grow). When certain avenues of traditional mobility in a society are closed, individuals should at least feel optimistic about developing new occupations for themselves and should be honored for their efforts.

There must also exist the conviction that men can appeal for and obtain justice; that arbitrary and whimsical decisions cannot be made that would affect their lives, opinions, or property without their having recourse to impartial courts of law. Men must be free to choose or not to choose their religious beliefs rather than be forced to accept the beliefs of the prince who rules them, or the employer who employs them. Countervailing pressure groups encourage more freedom of expression than centralized governments. In the middle of the seventeenth century in a divided England, Galileo would never have been forced to recant his conceptions about the solar universe, as he was forced to do in Florence (though he was given an opportunity to express himself freely under the patronage of Venice). By the eighteenth century, it had become virtually impossible for a scientist to work untroubled in Spain, Portugal, the Papal States, France, Calvinist Geneva, or in Counter-Reformation Prague, Vienna, or Budapest.

The independent industrialist threatened the power of kings and princes. Only when he was willing to be subservient to them, their military or commercial interests, was he permitted a modicum of security. His property could be taxed away or confiscated, however, and legal obstacles placed in his way in running his industry, seeking his markets, exporting his goods, and importing his raw materials. By the eighteenth century, there were few banks that readily gave credit, and the government was chiefly indifferent to the manufacture of any goods that did not have military importance or that did not enrich those in the court or those holding high positions in bureaucratic ministries.

For industrialism and science to develop in Western Europe after the end of the seventeenth century, something more was required: the self-confidence of the industrialist that he could master the technical know-how that was necessary, that he could obtain financing, that he could handle the competing guilds, unfriendly government officials, members of parliament or legislatures, and, above all, that he could manage, teach, motivate, and direct the workers that he hired so that they would do their best and learn the skills which were needed for efficient production. Men of this kind were chiefly absent in most of Europe, and certainly in Asia, in pre-Hispanic America, and in Africa. A few have always existed but have utilized their talents in ways other than in production. Many became warriors and leaders of warriors, a few organized their own political units, others became wealthy merchants, and some organized religions of their own. Seventeenth-century culture in Western Europe attempted to encourage their growth, and for various unknown reasons England until the end of the nineteenth century led in producing them in large numbers — though France, Italy, and Germany had more than their share of practical innovators (but not of free industrialists). In the eighteenth century, English colonists in New England, the Dutch in New York, and the various English, Welsh, and German colonists in Pennsylvania all produced different representatives of this enterprising industrialist, while the French in Canada, South Carolina, and Louisiana, and the Spaniards in the rest of America did not.

The enterprising scientist had to have the freedom to explore new intellectual horizons and the self-confidence to persevere in finding the answers to the questions he was asking. At the same time, unlike the industrialist, he had to feel that in seeking answers that went counter to tradition or the teachings of the Church he was not engaging in heresy or was not in danger of being ostracized by public opinion for his ideas.

The Industrial and Scientific Age required a receptivity to an everchanging all-embracing point of view which had been lacking in the Ancient World. As a frame of reference among the majority of those who live in the developing world in this century, this scientific yet ideological point of view is still absent. The freedom of most individuals to seek higher social status for themselves, to manage and direct, to explore new intellectual horizons, or to walk in areas not trodden before by their fellow countrymen, are either lacking, are greatly modified, or are even slightly repressed in almost all countries of the modern world.

The eighteenth-century industrialist and scientist had to break with the traditional ways of doing things, with the workings and restrictions of contemporary guilds, with the unscientific way of seeing the world, and with the blind refusal to let observational facts interfere with what had been taught in the past. To do so, they had to buck the conventional wisdom which held that men had to be taught humility by authorities — much as they had had to be taught at the hands of the ancient gods. Who was man that he thought he could know as much as the gods? The truths were already in existence, and new research or observations would only produce new heresies rather than further truths. Where such restrictions were placed upon human thought, thinking tended to be traditionl and conservative.

Perhaps no science was as important in changing men's minds about the universe and themselves as the astronomy developed during the seventeenth and eighteenth centuries. When men began to view the universe through the early telescopes, they beheld phenomena that shook their traditional ideas about the universe they lived in. They saw the planets and many had moons that revolved around them in much the same fashion that the moon moved around the earth (which suggested that the earth and the other planets might revolve around the sun in the same manner). For the first time, men were able to see that the number of stars then visible had increased at a high geometrical rate. From the few thousands that men could see with the naked eye, they could see millions through the telescope. And as this instrument was made larger and more powerful, the number increased into the tens if not hundreds of millions.

The new evidence destroyed the traditional concept that the earth was the center of the universe, that the sun and stars were entirely different phenomena, with the former furnishing light for the universe and the latter representing either holes in the heavens or the small abodes of deities who watched over those born under their aegis. The study of the heavens opened up new vistas for men and made them dimly aware of how much of past teachings had been based upon ignorance of the vastness of the universe. As the decades passed into the eighteenth century, men revolted against what they considered to be the erroneous precepts of the past; if the Bible was unable to provide men with a truthful scientific picture of the physical universe by means of revelations from God, how much of its picture of man was based upon human error and ignorance? The Deists of the eighteenth century were convinced that men could no longer accept errors from the past, but had to seek new truths continuously in order to discover more of the infinite universe as it began to unfold before their eyes. Men in the past had assumed definite knowledge, but, if their assumptions had been false,then they had not truly seen the real universe that the Supreme Being had created. And, if men had not seen the universe clearly, what made them think now that they could understand man and the social world which he had brought into being in the past?

The doubts, the scepticism, and even the frank denials of past knowledge encouraged men to try to make up for lost time by turning away from a tradition which insisted that in the past true knowledge had been revealed only to certain men. A new trend developed in which each man attempted to become an explorer in his own right. Eighteenth-century rational man insisted that there were no miracles involved in obtaining knowledge. Men could no longer say that they believed because they had faith: they believed because they had seen the evidence, had tested it, and had not found it wanting. Men were encouraged to use their own perception, intellect, and senses rather than to accept the thinking of those who had taught in an earlier time.

As men turned away from tradition, they discovered how little they knew about their own bodies. Although in the past dissections had taken place at executions and the human skeleton was known to men, few Medieval artists could have drawn the body accurately.

Men knew little of the grasses, the herbs, the flowers, or trees around them. Although they had seen the skeletons of fish, lizards, and animals, few during the eighteenth century were able to conclude that men and animals shared certain anatomical traits. It was the middle of the nineteenth century before men perceived the possibility that this relationship could be a matter of evolvement. In the past, men had not been trained to observe, and preconceived ideas had prevented them from using their faculty of perception. Even seventeenth-century astronomers had been unable to get away from Aristotelian preconceptions of the perfect order that had to exist in the heavens, and many described the paths taken by the planets around the sun as examples of the perfect circle, which of course they were not. Since men have always found it difficult to get away from past conceptions, or misconceptions, many of the discoveries of the seventeenth and eighteenth centuries were also combined with past or traditional concepts that were unverified by scientific reason.

◇   ◇   ◇   ◇   ◇

For the Scientific Age to begin, men needed the prerequisite of an optimistic self-confidence that allowed them to make an effort at understanding. Scientific thinking of the seventeenth century required first of all a deep respect for man's intellectual ability to pierce the dark and swampy forests of ignorance that operated as mental obstacles to his understanding of the world in which he had been placed by birth. Science requires man to reject the tradition that he is still an immature child who in the past had been incapable of receiving adult knowledge either from the gods, from the institutions created by man, or from a religious or centralized authoritarian government. Scientific thought assumes an optimistic belief in man, not as one who has fallen from grace but as one who is rising to it — a being with great capacities for learning, discovering, and understanding.

The scientific spirit went hand in hand with the belief that man could change his social world without waiting for God to give him the word when to begin. It assumed that the Deity expected man to grow up, stand on his own feet, assume responsibility for his actions, and use his reason and intelligence to resolve the problems that he faced. The spirit of free inquiry postulated that man needed more knowledge than he already possessed; that the quest for this knowledge was not only part of God's unfolding plan for man, but stemmed from the world of ideas that man had succeeded in creating for himself.

Pioneering thinkers, men such as Giambattista Vico of the latter seventeenth and early eighteenth centuries, were beginning to take fresh looks at man, and insisting that men everywhere had to invent their own social worlds, that myths and histories should be viewed as human inventions designed to help early as well as later men to understand themselves and the world they lived in. If mathematics and natural science appeared to be systems that were logical and insightful, it was because men had developed them to be logical, but at the same time they had only reflected the minds of the men who had created them. Though reason was extremely important, it was also necessary to see that reason like logic was based upon hidden premises and assumptions which might not be properly understood.

As the seventeenth century turned into the eighteenth, men became more sensitive about their thinking, more aware of their own preconceived assumptions as well as those of others. Although in the seventeenth and eighteenth centuries objectivity in observing human behavior was neither present or understood, men were at least moving away from faith as a reason for believing. Evidence was becoming a more important criterion in helping men to make up their minds. Though some were beginning to question just what was "evidence," others were insisting that because traditions had stood the test of time they were thus valid as "truths."

In the seventeenth and eighteenth centuries, men achieved a greater sophistication of thought about the physical world and about the environment they had built for themselves. Although it would be inaccurate to say that social scientific thinking existed during these centuries (this arrived in the nineteenth century), some men in England, France, Italy, Germany, and the Netherlands were beginning to take a hard look at themselves and to question previously held beliefs about authority, legitimacy, religious truth, and social dogmas. Even before the beginning of the eighteenth century, Baron Lahontan had used a mythological Indian in the New World to point up how men in Europe had lost their original freedoms as a result of the organizational straitjackets into which they had been placed by the development of civilization. Others, working parallel with the ideas developed by Vico, began to look critically at themselves in order to understand why man behaved as he did, to theorize about man's first organization of himself and the bonds that tied men to one another and to society. Neither the Ancient or the Medieval Worlds would ever have engaged in such speculations, but men in the seventeenth and eighteenth centuries were beginning to develop a culture that was more receptive to the critical scientific point of view.

It had taken more than 400 years for this mental receptivity to take place, helped along in certain parts of Europe by the divisions in government which prevented a highly centralized Church from using its power to suppress the heresies of scientific thinking. A highly centralized state also used the Church for perpetuating its political power, which meant that the state also punished heresies as severely as did the Church. Wherever scientific thinking existed freely, different varieties of religious thought also flourished amid governments that had to share their authority with landed aristocrats and urban merchants. In France, the need to support a highly centralized Church led some aristocrats to attack the Courts of Toulouse for protecting the peasant Bible-reading Waldensians in their midst. The need to protect the power of the aristocrats brought about the attempts to destroy the Hussites, and later to the actual destruction of the Anabaptist Taborites. In England, the power play of the English Crown designed to weaken the power of the Vatican encouraged the royal protection which John Wycliff received.

One could almost say that Henry VIII opened a Pandora's box in separating England from the Roman Catholic Church, for it meant that without the latter the power of the Crown became weaker and could not be used in suppressing heresies (as it was used against the Huguenots in France by a more powerful Louis XIV). At the same time, the closing of the convents by Henry VIII, as has been pointed out, led to later social changes for the aristocracy and the wealthy merchants. Parents could no longer put an unmarriageable daughter in a convent, but had to do something about her unmarried condition. Sooner or later these spinsters were permitted to marry beneath their social station in life, but when they did, the socialization processes became changed. No longer would the father of her children be held up for the sons to emulate, or for the daughters to see as a worthy model for a husband and future father. Instead, it was her father who was held as one worthy of respect, and whose higher social status became a goal for the sons to aim at. Although the mothers internalized in their sons their disappointment with the social status of their husbands, the opportunities for the sons to achieve higher status than their fathers was limited by tradition, by the condition of the economy, and by the lack of social mobility existing within seventeenth- and eighteenth-century society. The ambitions of the mothers for the sons to live above their lowered social position led to the development of men who sought other than the conventional avenues to worldly success.

The most important guarantee of social success in seventeenth-century England was aristocratic birth, which opened up conventional avenues of endeavor. Relatives of the royal family, titleless younger sons of earls and dukes, and holders of lesser titles and small estates were generally given preference for posts in the government, the Anglican Church, the military, and the universities.

Royal families, whether in England, France, or Russia had large numbers of impoverished relatives who had to be supported and given posts worthy of their rank. When positions were closed to other poor young men with ambitious mothers, they had to look to the new and innovative industries. By keeping one's ear to the ground and by training one's eye to perceive and recognize new opportunities, one could learn where it would be possible to bring workers, techniques, financing, and markets together. Since the city guilds saw the new techniques as harmful to their interests, one had to move further afield where no guilds were in charge — which meant that the smaller towns and villages of the Midlands became the industrial centers rather than London. The English merchants and bankers who knew the markets and arranged financing, however, remained in London.

Since the traditional avenues of opportunities and advancement were closed to these scions of the new middle classes, they had to create their own. Wealth by the seventeenth century in England, the Netherlands, and the Scandinavian countries increased one's social status and provided opportunities for advancing the social fortunes of one's descendants through intermarriage with the impoverished nobility. Wealth also increased one's self-esteem and enabled one to build a mansion that competed with those of the lesser aristocracy. In fact, some of the largest mansions in the seventeenth century belonged to rich merchants rather than to aristocrats, as had been the case among fifteenth- and sixteenth-century merchants in the Italian cities. With wealth one could educate one's children and subsidize learning. Industry attracted those who wanted wealth; the existence of markets and technical know-how were more in evidence in the seventeenth century than in previous ones. The markets were not only based upon the consuming needs of aristocrats and churchmen, now wealthier than ever before, but also upon the rising expenditures of artisans, of merchants, and especially of the increased budgets of kings at war. The seventeenth century was a century of war, destruction, and massive expenditures of silver and gold for provisions, uniforms, cannon, firearms, and means of transportation. The large amounts of silver and gold taken from the New World were melted down so that the Spanish kings could carry on their endless battles against France, Austria, England, and the Turks. The silver and gold eventually found their way into the pockets of merchants supplying the military needs of the various kings and emperors (the latter found that the task of keeping their authority intact was a never-ceasing one). As in the case of Primary civilization, the Secondary civilization was also fertilized by warfare and religion.

◊   ◊   ◊   ◊   ◊

All of Western Europe contributed to this new civilization. Discoveries and inventions increased at a geometric rate from the thirteenth and fourteenth centuries on, but after a slow start England took the lead in the second half of the seventeenth century. There are a number of reasons for this, though we are not certain which ones are most relevant to understanding. First of all, the culture changed and became highly receptive to money-making and technical achievement, coupled with an availability of workers and financing. Secondly, a good deal of knowledge had already been accumulated, starting in the thirteenth century, which led to the technical growth necessary to secure the foundations of industrial society. Thirdly, the culture popularized the belief that men could rise socially if they had what it took to make money, to study, to innovate, and to organize. Although only a few were able to overcome handicaps of social and economic backgrounds, still more were convinced that social mobility was possible for a poor boy who wanted to get ahead and who was able to acquire the education or to learn the necessary skills by himself. Self-educated seamen recorded their observations and studies of magnetism and navigation, curious artisans dealt with the designs of more efficient pumps and water-driven machinery, while self-taught agronomists wrote about the need to use crops as fertilizer rather than to let land lie fallow as was done previously. Many young apprentices dreamed of the fame that would come from their important mechanical discoveries. In the sixteenth century, the work done on pumps, vacuums, bellows, and valves led to a revolution in concepts of the human body and helped bring about the new sciences of physiology and anatomy. Both industrialization and science were viewed as opening up new occupational opportunities for the young, plus new wealth and prestige.

More than that, the merchants, educated craftsmen, and apprentices created a mental revolution whose effects would continue on to the present time. The reaction to traditional forms of authority helped produce the conviction that merit originated more innovations than bureaucratic inheritance of an office, that ability was an individual environmental matter and part of a man's learning necessary to the cultivation of his special talents. In the eighteenth century, the conflict betweeen the traditional aristocratic point of view (that ability and talents were inherited) and the "natural aristocratic" egalitarian point of view (that more talents are hidden by lack of opportunities than are present among those who inherit social rank and wealth) became even sharper. The two points of view emerged as the conservative and the liberal positions. The latter supported the development of a philosophy which encouraged social as well as economic egalitarianism, and the right of a man to decide for himself not only his religious beliefs (rather than accepting those of a prince or king), but also how he would like to be governed. The heretical concept that man could hire (and fire) governing officials was the basis of eighteenth-century democracy: the right of men to decide how they wanted to be ruled. (In reality, the democratic concept only applied partially to man in his society. He still was not able to affect or influence those who governed him at his work, at school, or within the various corporate and governmental bureaucracies.)

The social changes that trained men to become factory workers, urban dwellers, and white-collar employees evolved from past conditions. Even in the late Middle Ages, there had been individual factories with hundreds of artisans, helpers, and parttime home workers. Royal governments organized workshops to manufacture goods for kings, nobles, and their armies. Urban centers existed simultaneously with the first of the agricultural civilizations. In the eighteenth and nineteenth centuries, the percentage of those who were propelled into heterogeneous urban clusters began to increase until one could say that by the last third of the twentieth century the overwhelming majority of the population worked for others, and were completely dependent upon other organized men for their food, clothing, shelter, and the goods which they used. The percentage of those who still lived on the land in urban industrial societies had dwindled to a small fraction of the total population. The new civilization was pushed through by wealthy merchants who hired skilled staff members, and various assistants and supervisors who in turn trained and handled new types of workers. These then carried out the plans laid down for them by new occupations and professions that did not exist before the eighteenth century, and clearly not in any large numbers before the twentieth.

The Industrial and Scientific civilization requires that a large percentage of the population be its carriers; that the overwhelming emphasis reside in the production of goods, stressing volume and reducing costs to increase profits; that the training of men for different occupations and professions be outside the home; and that the population be literate. The worker must be able to read signs, blueprints, and other instructions; and the white-collar employee be able to amass information, consolidate it, and pass it on to the managers who need to know how the plant, the corporation, or the bureaucracy are functioning at any given moment. In contrast to organization in previous centuries, the Industrial and Scientific civilization is highly organized and functions through individuals with a high degree of self-discipline. While the early seventeenth-century industrial plants had complete control over their workers (being able to imprison them for insubordination if necessary), the later industrial plants had to motivate workers through rewards in order to offset the rising tide of unionism and its tendency to split the worker's loyalty, and thus his identity with the firm.

The quest for new knowledge, brought about by the printing press and the geographical explorations of the previous century which had made European man aware of a new world, encouraged many wealthy merchants, master craftsmen, and artisans (who had educated themselves through experience and experiments) to develop a new mental spirit or point of view. What had heretofore been deemed eternal truths gave way before new values concerning man's goals on earth and the role and importance of the individual. Men were beginning to see a universe and a globe that were entirely different from what previous generations had assumed them to be. This encouraged them to look upon themselves anew as pioneers and explorers trodding paths where no European man had set foot before and seeing the heavens and nature with a new vision. It was difficult for men to go back to Aristotle, Ptolemy, and Galen after beholding far more of the universe and the earth than they. It was also difficult to subject themselves to secular and religious authorities once they discovered how little knowledge these authorities had in contrast to what they themselves knew. While men in the Ancient World had accepted the authority of those whom they felt knew more than they, either because of their closer communication with the deities or because of special blessings by the fates, men in the late seventeenth and eighteenth centuries began to view themselves in a superior intellectual light — they now had better tools with which to look at themselves and the universe they inhabited. Not only had men learned much about navigation, other geographical areas, customs, and foods, but they had utilized the telescope and microscope to see macro- and micro-worlds that were hitherto unknown. At the same time, some of the scientific motivation in the fields of mechanics and physics was based upon devising practical instruments (such as the chronometer, perfected by Dutch, French, and English practical scientists and clockmakers) or the conception of using atmospheric pressure (thought about in the seventeenth century by Huygens and Papin, but put into operation by Thomas Savery in 1698 with his steam engine for pumping water out of deep mines).

On the other hand, it is necessary to see how little seventeenth-century scientists and industrialists knew in contrast to contemporary ones. Even in the eighteenth century, practical men in industry had to operate by rule of thumb. Science then contained little knowledge to help solve the problems involved in developing more efficient means of producing more goods with less labor and effort. But what the scientific method did was to inspire its users with enough confidence to believe that using certain techniques could help in resolving certain problems.

With this background, it is interesting to try to determine why England in the seventeenth and eighteenth centuries was able to push itself forward to become one of the leaders in the new Industrial and Scientific civilization. In contrast to both Italy and Spain at the beginning of the sixteenth century, England was backward. Its population was small, with no more than three million during the reign of Henry VIII. Techniques in mining, manufacturing, building, and merchandising had gone further in Flanders, in the Augsburg-Nuremberg-Regensburg area, in Venice, Florence, and Milan. But by the beginning of the seventeenth century, England had made great advances in all these fields, even though its population remained less than that of France or Italy, though somewhat more than that of Flanders and the Netherlands. At the beginning of the eighteenth century, England had little more than six million, and at the end no more than nine million. This is in contrast to a population almost three times as great in France at the beginning of the seventeenth, eighteenth, and nineteenth centuries.

Compared to Flanders, Germany, or northern Italy, England had few cities. London was the only city of over 5,000 in England from the thirteenth to the fifteenth centuries, having in the latter era about 30,000 inhabitants. By 1540, as English development began to increase, the population of London grew to almost 50,000. By the middle of the seventeenth century as England increased its trade with the rest of Europe and began to colonize the New World, the city's growth reached 300,000. By 1750, the metropolis had increased almost three times to a little over 800,000, though it did not reach a million until the beginning of the nineteenth century. In the eighteenth century, only nearby Paris and Yedo in far-off Japan equalled London in population.

When London was a small urban center in the middle of the sixteenth century, it was able to get all the supplies it needed within a 50 mile radius — its firewood, food, services, labor, and manufactured articles — although it imported luxuries for its upper class and mercantile groups. But in general one can say that London in the middle of the sixteenth century during the time of Henry VIII was almost self-sufficient in the goods and services it needed. Within a century, all this had changed when the city increased its population more than six times, and when it began to draw upon the rest of England for its needs. For example, coal upon displacing locally-cut firewood of a century before came by barge all the way from Newcastle in the northeastern part of the country. Food was no longer provided by the nearby farmers living within a 50 mile radius (or grown within the city by the individual citizens who raised their own chickens, hogs, and cows), but began to come from all parts of England and Ireland by barge, cart, and ship. The marketplace was no longer filled with traders and merchants handling spices, silks, brocades, and other luxury goods, but had become the meeting place for merchants, master craftsmen, craftsmen, and journeymen making household utensils, furniture, bricks, tiles, clothing, leather articles (including shoes), and other items for a small but growing mass market. While demanding luxuries that once went to the aristocrats, this new market was willing to accept them with some diminution in quality (furs which the rich nobles and merchants wore to keep warm in the unheated English houses became available to modest folk, though less fine). By 1650, the market for coal, grain, fish, meat, vegetables, timber, bricks, household utensils, and clothing far exceeded the supplies formerly required by the large-scale armies which had finished devastating Central Europe a few years before. The demands of a population growing faster than that of any other European city created an expanding market for wholesalers, jobbers, retail merchants, carters, bargemen, and petty suppliers of all kinds. Although the Industrial Revolution had still not affected England, the city of London was manufacturing goods for a market larger than that of all of England.

Though London grew in population from the sixteenth to the seventeenth centuries, growth by itself was not the reason for the late industrialization of England. Yedo, the predecessor of modern-day Tokyo, was also growing by leaps and bounds at about the same time, but Japan in the seventeenth century was not quite ready to move into the Industrial and Scientific civilization. The factors were varied and complex, and it is difficult to know which ones should be stressed in order to understand the transition that took place between the seventeenth and eighteenth centuries. This transition brought into being new means of production, greater efficiency in agricultural and industrial output, the complex hierarchical organization of men, an ever-larger percentage of the population living in urban areas, higher levels of literacy, and a point of view that saw movement to higher stages of consumption and technology as being worthwhile goals. This plus an attitude that viewed change as being both essential and necessary.

◇   ◇   ◇   ◇   ◇

England became the first modern industrial nation as a result of a series of fortunate circumstances. With the English Channel separating it from the continent of Europe, England had escaped the repeated land invasions that had destroyed the workshops of Flanders and northern Italy. Although the sixteenth and seventeenth centuries in England saw a number of civil wars, they did not ravage London, which became a refuge for those with skills and capital fleeing the Spanish armies in Flanders, the Spanish and French armies in Italy, and the French armies in Germany. The persecution of the Huguenots by Louis XIV sent tens of thousands of skilled refugees, small industrialists, and entrepreneurial merchants to Prussia, the Netherlands, and England, with London getting a large share of their accumulated knowledge and techniques. In the first half of the seventeenth century, highly skilled men tried to escape the wars in both Italy and Central Europe: the devastation left by the Thirty Years' War, for example, was so great that it took Germany and Bohemia almost two centuries to recover from its effects. The English civil wars increased the power of the new middle classes and, instead of repression and apathy remaining in their wake, the country acquired a state of mind in which achievement, goals of progress, and new forms of knowledge were looked upon as positive virtues. Although France after the middle of the seventeenth century was able to compete with England in the rise of science, only the Netherlands equalled England in permitting freedom for the human mind to use its imagination untrammeled.

From the fourteenth century on, the English kings had given their support and protection to men, such as John Wycliffe, who directly or indirectly favored royal power against the authority of the Church. The aristocrats, who prided themselves on their independence, gave both patronage and support to those writers who turned to them rather than to the Crown or to the Church. Although controlled by the Church in the beginning, the universities insisted at an early date upon their rights of autonomy. By the seventeenth century, the urban communes had also earned the right (rather than the privilege) of governing themselves. The merchants supported all attempts that increased their status vis-a-vis the aristocrats, and that legitimated and enhanced their king-pin position within English society. In England, science and industry owed their growth as much to the rich merchant class as to the aristocrats. The new middle classes insisted that they were entitled to play a part in governing England. Their insistence led to the rights of free speech, freedom of the press, and legal toleration of free and scientific thought.

The English Colonies in the New World around 1750 were the beneficiaries of the growth of literacy and the proliferation of skills in England during the sixteenth and seventeenth centuries. They had higher levels of literacy, more diversified skills, more capital, and more merchandising talents than the inhabitants of the French or Spanish colonies, or for that matter the inhabitants of France, Italy, or Spain at that particular time. England was ready for Adam Smith even before 1776, as France was not, primarily because in the latter country the centralization of royal as well as governmental power implied that everything was forbidden which was not expressly permitted. In England, the reverse was the case. A Baron Lahontan, who though a Frenchman had been influenced by the English revolution in individual freedom, had to spend much of his life as a refugee, as did Voltaire almost a half century later. While Thomas Paine was also a refugee of sorts, he could have remained in England easier than Voltaire could have lived in France. In the latter country, it was the aristocratic class reacting against the greater power of the king which supported many of the philosophical, scientific, and humanistic ideas of the eighteenth century.

In France, the enterprising Huguenots had been driven out by the revocation of the Edict of Nantes; in England, the various nonconformists, though prevented from finding employment in the government, could at least open up new employment possibilities for themselves. Financing was also easier in England through the development of a non-centralized banking system, the support of various London merchants, and the attraction which various European banking houses found in the English free market. The growth of technology, the awareness of markets both in England and abroad, and the opportunities available for catering to these markets encouraged bright young men to seek their fortunes in industry and their fame in science. By the beginning of the seventeenth century, the culture in England was probably readier to support a new civilization more than that of any other country in Europe.

By 1640, only the Netherlands was a close competitor to England, which had already become the leading industrial country in Europe. (The Dutch Republic encouraged the growth of industry and science as much as England. Both industry and knowledge were considered to aid the production of wealth, and wealth represented one of the more important aims of the Dutch Republic.) Although the Netherlands had created far-flung trading outposts in areas from which it was not removed until the twentieth century, England was not far behind, and in fact was moving ahead rapidly. By the beginning of the nineteenth century, it had outstripped the Netherlands, France, and Spain in the amount of its income from trade.

England in the seventeenth century had been able to forge ahead of a European continent at war, or already devastated by war. In many fields the English artisans were becoming more efficient than their French confreres, and had gone ahead in learning from experience. The English were becoming increasingly interested in the large mass market both at home and on the continent. On the other hand, the French ignored the mass potential of their local market: large-scale manufacturing was done by the state for the benefit of the king, his relatives, the aristocrats, and their retainers, the Church, the military, and those connected with collecting taxes and governing the country. The merchants had to obtain both their necessities and their luxuries through the cottage industries set up for them and the other well-to-do burghers and rich peasants. Quality in production was considered more important than quantity.

England had learned a great deal from the Flemish and Italian refugees who came to its shores after the fifteenth century. From the manufacturing cities of Milan, Turin, Ferrara, Bologna, and Venice, and the textile centers of Bruges, Ypres, and Antwerp, the English learned to build a few large factories where labor was supervised, trained, and guided. In the first half of the sixteenth century, for example, John Winchcombe owned a woolen factory which employed 200 weavers, 100 female carders, 200 girl spinners (spinning was done by hand on the recently invented spinning wheel, for various kinds of spinning machines were not invented until the eighteenth century), and 150 sorters — a total working group of over 850, not counting the various supervisors and clerks. Although the large-scale factory was a novelty in the sixteenth and seventeenth centuries, there were a few around to act as precedents for the later large mid-eighteenth century industrial enterprises.

In England, the move toward becoming an industrial society had started early. The putting-out system of cottage handicrafts had been developed by the Florentines from the fourteenth century onward; this system spread to Flanders in the fifteenth century, and by the end of that century to England, where it found a home. An observer in the late seventeenth century pointed out that one village in southeastern England had fewer than six out of sixty small farmers who derived their total incomes from working their lands; the majority supplemented their incomes by working at home with their wives, daughters, and sons as spinners and weavers or as leather workers. The pre-factory putting-out system, which became a chief source of employment for many Jewish immigrants arriving in New York in the nineteenth century, was also a means for keeping body and soul together among peasants in seventeenth-century England. In both that and the eighteenth century, agricultural production was increasing, but mostly on the large estates of the aristocrats and well-to-do yeomen farmers; little came from the inefficient small farmers, who had to turn to other work to make their living despite growing most of their own food.

England thus forged ahead of the European continent not because of any special abilities which were inherent in its population, but because it contained a large number of individuals who, perceiving a continent at war, took advantage of the greater techniques, financing, and markets which this situation created. Accompanying this change was a cultural phenomenon wherein larger and larger numbers of people increased their self-confidence (though the total number affected still remained a small percentage of the English population). Spanish and French troops fighting one another over the length and breadth of Flanders had by the end of the sixteenth century destroyed most of the sugar refineries of Antwerp. The sugar merchants and their skilled workers left for London and Amsterdam (the only two centers that seemed unlikely to be destroyed by invading Spanish or French armies). The cloth makers of Bruges, Ypres, and Antwerp also fled to the safety of Amsterdam and London, Rouen, or Hamburg — with the merchants and their clerks following.

At the beginning of the sixteenth century, Spanish Flanders had been one of the leading manufacturing regions of Europe, but this top position was lost in the interval between that and the seventeenth century. By the first half of that century, even more Flemish industrial capital and technicians moved to England than to Holland, thus laying the foundation for later English technological development.

Another advantage that accrued to England was the relative weakness of the king, the Church, the aristocrats, and the merchants throughout the seventeenth and eighteenth centuries. This meant that ideas inimical to one branch might be supported and even encouraged in the other three. For example, scientific agriculture was aided to a large extent by the aristocrats who saw in the improvements to husbandry and horticulture opportunities to improve their financial position vis-a-vis the king and the merchants. Mercantilism was supported by the king and his administration, who saw in an ideology of state support to the economy opportunities to increase taxation, armaments, and the wealth of the Crown. Science was encouraged by the aristocrats and the merchants, although the results of science and the thinking it engendered tended to run counter to that of the Church of England. On the other hand, the merchants identified themselves with the anti-mercantilist (or free enterprise) thinking of Adam Smith. Later, the aristocrats sympathized with the problems faced by child workers in the early nineteenth-century industrial and mining enterprises, although not with the penniless peasant adults who were forced to leave their common lands (so that regional landlords, who claimed them as a right they had never relinquished, could take them over).

While a small percentage of the English population became the carriers of a new civilization that was largely urban-based, middle-class, and technologically oriented, most individuals in Great Britain in the seventeenth and eighteenth centuries were still living mentally in a peasant world, sharing more of their ideas with their forebears of the past few hundred years than with members of the various Royal Academies, with the few wealthy merchants in the large cities, or with the even fewer entrepreneurs existing at that time. The agricultural revolution inaugurated by the aristocrats in England and by the Physiocrats in France during that period had produced some improvements in agriculture, but most peasants continued to farm as their ancestors had, accepting the prevailing mythology as to how nature and human society worked.

Most individuals in the eighteenth century were either indifferent or else saw the rise of the Industrial and Scientific civilization as a personal threat to their sense of security; few were interested in such abstract concepts (to them) as freedom of speech, press, or religious belief. Few in the eighteenth century were affected or influenced by the new scientific or technological discoveries. The new civilization did not redound to the benefit of the vast majority of men in Europe or North America until the end of the nineteenth century: most individuals in Asia, in the rest of the Americas, and in Africa were not affected by it until well into the latter part of the twentieth century. In the beginning, the new civilization appeared little different from the old one that had developed in the Ancient World: it benefited a few, but seemed to be of little value to the vast majority.

Each decade of the eighteenth century saw more men attempting to satisfy the demands of a small but growing mass market. The increasing need for metal meant that existing mines became ever deeper, with the difficulties of getting underground water out of deep mines becoming a pressing technological problem. Throughout the second half of the seventeenth and the first half of the eighteenth centuries, many French, German, Dutch, and English devoted themselves to the problem of improving the sixteenth-century pump in order to mine more ore. The results were the inefficient steam engine, designed in 1684 by Denis Papin, a French Huguenot, but never built; the wasteful steam engine first built by Thomas Savery in England in 1698; and the somewhat improved steam pump devised by Thomas Newcomen in 1720 (which lasted until a more efficient one was invented by James Watt in 1764). The use of more metal in machinery encouraged ironmasters to seek better methods of producing stronger iron with more efficient puddling techniques. In the early eighteenth century, English ironmasters learned to smelt iron by using coke (as against the more inefficient use of charcoal, which was wasteful of forests and softened the iron by combining with the smelted metal).

As early as 1701, men were wondering in print whether one could mass produce pocket watches or pins if the item to be manufactured were reduced to component parts with one worker making one part by using machines especially designed to cut down on the amount of labor expended. By the end of the century, these early ideas had led to the development of the system of the manufacture of interchangeable parts.

Although England pioneered in developing the Industrial and Scientific civilization, initial support had already come from a cultural acceptance of the importance of money, of the growth of wealth as an absolute good, and of profit-making as an important motivating force in getting men to become innovators and entrepreneurs. With each century, more men internalized the cultural need to get ahead, to achieve higher social status, to be equal to those above them (which meant more competition leading to ever more inequality), to have strong feelings of guilt if one did not achieve one's goals, and to struggle continuously against feelings of uselessness or powerlessness if one did not continue to advance. Those in the eighteenth century who were closer to the merchant class, who were au courant with what was happening in the fields of technology and science, who were aware of markets at home and abroad, who had internalized the new ways of thinking about the universe, technology, and human behavior, and who could self-confidently correlate markets, techniques, and financing, were more able to become the carriers of this new civilization than peasants on farms or workers in cottage industries who were physically isolated and mentally insulated from these trends.

◇   ◇   ◇   ◇   ◇

While we speak of these trends taking place in England in the seventeenth and eighteenth centuries, it would be wrong to assume that only individuals in England were alienated from the old ways of doing things and hence attracted to the new culture to enhance their self-esteem or to achieve a new sense of identity — or that only individuals in England had opportunities to internalize the new culture (whose roots went back to the eleventh century). Individuals in France, Germany, and Poland were also becoming aware of the winds of culture change. Borders could not stop the diffusion of ideas about man, nature, and the universe from moving from one part of Europe to another, and spreading across the oceans to North America and to Japan. The British colonies were more influenced by these new ideas than the French or the Spanish. In Japan, a strong Shogun had united the country but inaugurated a repression of European ideas. Supported by the impoverished Daimyo, or Feudal Lords, an underground developed in the acquisition of knowledge by way of the Dutch trading post in Nagasaki.

Even in Eastern Europe the ideas of Spinoza, Leibnitz, Descartes, and Locke were penetrating the walls of the Orthodox Jewish Houses of Study, and young scholars were hiding their German grammars under their Talmudic commentaries. New currents of thought were spreading fast by way of the printed page. Although individuals in large areas of the world were insulated from these new ideas, the latter still made inroads from decade to decade. In China in the seventeenth century, Jesuits at the court in Peking were introducing the new mathematics, astronomy, and technology at the time that these new techniques were slowly seeping into the fabric of Japanese society. In India, the new technology was slowly percolating some levels of the Mogul court in Delhi, although the influences spread faster in the eighteenth century by way of the educated British clerks of the East Indies Company. In Russia, the small groups of foreigners living in isolation around Moscow served as the catalytic agents that influenced a young Peter during the end of the seventeenth century, and made him an agent of rapid and gigantic cultural and social change during the first quarter of the eighteenth century.

Although it might appear that iron-making and the textile industry spearheaded the spread of ideas in England that were termed the Industrial Revolution, these technological and management concepts were also dispersing through France, the Netherlands, Germany, and Sweden at the same time. In 1762, a pin factory in France was producing 62,000 pins per day by having a small group of six workers break down the components of the common pin, with each man specializing in making one small part. The Germans were concerned with improving the techniques of mining and the smelting of iron, while in Sweden a good deal of discussion dealt with the wealth lost by exporting raw iron rather than the finished products made from this pig iron. In the seventeenth and eighteenth centuries in the British Colonies of the New World, men were becoming more concerned with the new scientific spirit, with the need to manufacture items as well as to export raw materials, with the pressures to supply some of the local needs themselves rather than to import all their consumer goods from England.

Just as it was necessary for the ancient civilizations to organize men to serve the needs of the state, so the new technology and growing mass markets at home and abroad encouraged the development of a new type of factory management. In the beginning, the precedents were those of cottage industries as they developed in the Italian cities, the army, and the Church; but in the second half of the eighteenth century, new techniques of managing men, machines, technology, financing, and markets were developed out of the everyday practical decisions that had to be made by men who were treading new ground where precedents were few and in general ambiguous.

As a result of the spread of new techniques in agriculture and increased health measures which led to overpopulation, a supply of labor was available to man the new factories in the sprouting towns. If urbanization had not grown and if the colonies had not acted as magnets for the surplus of illiterate and unskilled men, famines would have become endemic in England — as they had in France in the seventeenth and eighteenth centuries and in Ireland in the nineteenth. The various Enclosure Acts passed by Parliament produced a supply of landless and illiterate peasants who saw that they had little choice between the crowded slums around the new factories and the slow starvation which was then occurring in the countryside. England needed a landless, poverty-stricken, illiterate, unskilled, mobile laboring class to take the new unattractive factory jobs. There were many Englishmen who preferred to work long hours per day and to have their wives and children toil for a pittance, accepting the harsh discipline of the eighteenth-century factory, than to be sent as indentured workers to the New World, to be impressed into the military services, or to be placed in the humiliating position of being refused shelter as they wandered down English roads looking for work.

The lower classes were treated harshly by the new industrial barons, and the new sciences were unconcerned about their living conditions, happiness, health, or goals. (Educated individuals of that day were also unconcerned about black slaves when they talked and wrote about such abstractions as liberty, freedom of conscience, and rights to life and happiness). The lower classes wanted only to survive, for survival meant an absence of starvation. And so, the new English factories of the eighteenth and nineteenth centuries were able to get a plentiful supply of cheap, hardworking, and docile labor — just as the Russians got theirs by using their serfs in the same centuries to do construction work, to man the machines, and to carry on the fighting. Asia also required cheap and docile labor, as did the New World. For most of the landless peasants in England in the late eighteenth and early nineteenth centuries, life in the factory towns was preferable to life as an unemployed landless peasant in the country — and this despite the insecurities involved in working as a factory hand, with the knowledge that he could easily be displaced by even cheaper and more docile labor.

The existence of the British Colonies in the New World added to the belief that wealth could be created. Men could get ahead in the New World by clearing lands, by growing two stalks where none or only one grew before, and by using their imaginations to think of new ways of acquiring wealth. Although men in Western

Europe at the end of the eighteenth century were thinking along similar lines, the American experience acted as a feedback to their ideas about an optimistic future in which boundless wealth could be attained by men using their ideas, labor, and imaginations. This buoyant expectation does not imply that the Old World was by any means finished, for it was not necessary for men to emigrate if they wanted more opportunity. What was required was a government more resilient to the desires and wishes of most of its population, one that did not stifle but encouraged initiative, and one that legislated as much freedom as could be absorbed so that men would follow their own inclinations, talents, and skills to create through their self-interest a richer and more expansive society.

◇   ◇   ◇   ◇   ◇

In England throughout the eighteenth century, there was a continuous feedback or interaction, between the merchants, the money lenders, the technicians, and the small but growing educated class, all stimulating one another with new ideas, information, awareness of markets, and goals of wealth and knowledge as being beneficial to a society seeking security and a higher sense of purpose. The need for greater amounts of thread so that the weavers could be kept at full employment led to the invention of the spinning jenny in 1764 (until then spinning was a parttime occupation engaged in by small farmers and their families during their spare time), which permitted one fulltime operator to take care of the equivalent of ten spinning wheels. The spinning jenny led to Arkwright's invention of the water frame, in which a more complex spinning machine was operated by one person, increasing the production of thread still more. Arkwright's success in utilizing the water frame (it is doubtful that he invented it, but more than likely took the idea from mechanics working on the concept even before his time) helped to create the factory system wherein operatives were employed to spin enough thread to keep fulltime weavers busy. It also encouraged many to try to improve upon his idea. An automatic weaving machine which could take the surplus of spun woolen thread and weave 10 to 50 times more cloth than was being woven by hand was invented in France.

In both England and France, the various academies of science encouraged research on practical problems by encouraging men to think about the theoretical possibilities involved in increasing output. The large number of small groups meeting together, eager to learn the latest in scientific and technological developments from the then known world, stimulated men to utilize the new ideas and to improve upon them. The early manufacturers were as eager to hear of new technological and scientific experiments that would benefit them as were the men who listened to the new lectures on physics, astronomy, or biology. Books incorporating the latest techniques and information were widely disseminated. Diderot used the research commissioned by the French Academy as an integral part of the text and illustrations of his famous *Encyclopedia*. In Japan, small manufacturers learned to make bricks according to European techniques, while scholars wrote texts for the benefit of the impoverished Daimyo, concerned with increased agricultural yields using the techniques that seeped into Japan from Western Europe via the Dutch trading post at Nagasaki.

Arkwright's rise to fame in the 1770's was a good example of the stimulating impact that new techniques had upon technology in a society receptive to anything that increased production, permitted sales that saturated new markets, and developed wealth not only for the individual but for the nation. Even child labor in late eighteenth and early nineteenth-century factories was also considered to redound to the advantage of society as a whole, for it kept the children out of poorhouses and on their own. Arkwright had millwrights and blacksmiths build machines according to his specifications and under his supervision. He then had these machines installed in large sheds built to house them. After this step, Arkwright recruited landless and poverty-stricken men and women who wanted and needed work and taught them to tend the machines, as if the latter were domesticated animals. And, because Arkwright had other activities that occupied him, he selected and trained supervisors who took over a good part of the production routine.

Despite his trained supervisors, however, Arkwright delegated little of his authority to them. He made almost all of the important decisions dealing with work and production, the repair of machines, or the purchase of new ones, including the design of improved spinning machines. Arkwright took his precedents from government and religion (plus the military) and functioned as the chief governing official within his plant. His word was law, and those who were insubordinate to him committed lese majesty and were therefore punished either through monetary fines or discharge. (In the seventeenth century, the few industrialists in England even put aside cells in the plant where they had unruly workers imprisoned for various periods of time.) The factory was looked upon by Arkwright (and by entrepreneurs who followed him) as a state within the state. It was highly centralized and authoritarian. Orders came from the top down, and little or no communication proceeded upward. The workers were paid at the lowest possible rate, just enough to let them keep body and soul together, were fined or severely reprimanded each time they got out of line or their work displeased the supervisors. They had no security within the plant; if they became ill or were injured, they were on their own (as wounded soldiers also were at that time). They were discharged when they could no longer keep up with their work, and what happened to them was of no concern to those who let them go. Those who became too old to work were either sent to poorhouses, where they remained until they died, or were supported by children who were barely able to make ends meet for themselves and their children. Those without family were pitied, but rarely were provisions made for them if they could not work. Workers in the eighteenth and early nineteenth centuries were given the freedom to leave if they did not like either the working conditions or the pay (so they could starve elsewhere). On the job they had to observe strict military discipline and be as passive as the machines themselves. They were expected to work long hours six days a week at wages that were little more than a pittance.

Arkwright knew that he could not bring his goods to the nearest cathedral town or county seat, for the local market was much too small to absorb his output. (The craftsmen worked chiefly for the local market, and continued to do so until mass produced goods put them permanently out of business by the early twentieth century.) The home market was much too small to absorb the ever-growing production of cotton and woolen goods. Arkwright had to travel to neighboring countries seeking merchants to buy his production and re-sell it to various retailers. Toward the end of the eighteenth century, even the craftsmen of India suffered from English competition, as the poorer Indians bought the cheaper Manchester-made textiles in preference to the finer quality but more expensive Indian cloth. English textiles were sold to the small but burgeoning mass markets in France, Germany, Russia, Spain, and Portugal plus the New World and Africa.

Arkwright, however, cannot be called England's first modern manufacturer. Others whose names are still unknown evidently pioneered in those techniques which enabled them to gather workers, train them to tend machines, and find markets for the products which they manufactured. In both France and England, there were modern manufacturers who did just this from the early part of the eighteenth century on: a contemporary of Arkwright's, Matthew Boulton, was one of the pioneers who set precedents in management which others followed in the nineteenth century. Although both Germany and Austria contained factories quite large in modern terms, Boulton was nevertheless a pioneer in developing markets and manufactures without any financing or direction from the state. In France, Prussia, Austria, and Russia, most of the plants that made goods for the Court, the government, and the army were run as part of the military establishment. Boulton had to operate as if he were his own king, government, and military domain.

Unlike many of his contemporaries who were chiefly merchants and traders giving contracts to others to manufacture on their own, Boulton had to be everything all at once: merchant, technician, financier, plant supervisor, and salesman extraordinary. Most of the early manufacturers referred to themselves as merchants. The role of manufacturer in the second half of the eighteenth century was seen primarily as corresponding to that of the seventeenth-century merchant: to know his markets, to know how to satisfy them, to finance manufacturing, and to organize workers to work. In Europe, the merchant had a long tradition of being the entrepreneur, the man who is able to bring together under his supervision a series of goods, finances, and people. His antecedents went back to the eleventh- and twelfth-century Italian cities, and to the fourteenth- and fifteenth-century Hanseatic League towns. Although the merchants of the Ancient World go back even further, we do not know whether the Phoenician, the Egyptian, the Cretan, or the Sumerian performed as many roles.

Matthew Boulton then could be called a modern manufacturer to distinguish him from his merchant predecessors. Between 1759 and 1764, he built a small metal-fabricating plant near Birmingham, England, with the assistance of a partner named Fothergill. Both specialized in their labors. Fothergill spent most of his time traveling on the European continent, seeking new markets for the metal buttons, watch chains, and steel buckles that the English plant made in increasing numbers. Fothergill knew what his European customers wanted, and from them he learned what new products to make and what patterns designed by others to imitate. Boulton stayed in the plant, carefully supervising the quality of his products, personally training his workers and supervisors, using his spare time improving both his machines and production techniques, attending to the correspondence with Fothergill and their European customers, and keeping the daily records of the plant. Within a few years, Boulton and Fothergill had gained a reputation as innovating metal fabricators: as early as 1765, Boulton had received tempting offers from Sweden and the continent to transfer his place of operations from England.

Boulton played the role of a manufacturer as well as a "culture maximizer" (to use the late Jules Henry's term for a cultural pioneer). In 1774, he offered a partnership to James Watt, who had improved Newcomen's steam engine (by inventing one that employed a condenser that used less heat but produced far more steam). Boulton believed that his plant could be used as a laboratory in producing improved steam engines. Watt spent 12 years experimenting with new manufacturing techniques and with making the boiler, condenser, and piston even more efficient. The resultant improved Watt steam engine could pump water out of deep mines three times faster than a Newcomen engine, while using less fuel.

As a result of Boulton's selling procedures, a steam engine was used experimentally to operate an air blower at the Wilkinson Iron Works, and succeeded in raising the temperature in the smelting process. Steam engines were also exported to France and Germany. In 1781, Watt developed the transmission of rotary power, an achievement which enabled the steam engine to become an important source of motive power in the new textile and other manufacturing plants. Potters began to use the new motive power as a source of energy, with Josiah Wedgwood of Staffordshire among the first to use it in his pottery plant. (Wedgwood was as much a pioneering manufacturer as Arkwright and Boulton. He had scoured Europe for ideas and markets, innovated new techniques and forms of pottery, lowered prices to get a mass market, and carefully supervised every aspect of the manufacturing process.) By the 1790's, the steam engine was being used to power spinning and weaving mills, sugar refineries, potteries, ironworks, and flour mills. (In the United States, John Fitch ran a steam-powered boat between Philadelphia and Wilmington in the late 1780's, while during the next two decades Oliver Evans of Philadelphia invented an automatic flour mill using steam power and an automatic dredge.)

Matthew Boulton had no precedents when he began to manufacture steam engines, although the ideas of mass production were no longer new. As early as 1701, the idea that a watch could be broken down into its component parts with each part being made by one individual doing nothing else had been suggested. Some experimentation with this technique had begun with the watchmakers of Nuremberg at the end of the seventeenth century and spread to France by the beginning of the next. By 1760, the common pin was being manufactured on a mass basis in France, increasing the output per worker from 20 pins a day to the thousands. By the 1780's, various Frenchmen were discussing the possibility of making muskets on a mass scale by breaking the musket down into its component parts and having each part made by a specialist using particular tools and metal forms to assist him. (Though the French discussed this idea in the late 1770's and early 1780's, according to Thomas Jefferson, then Ambassador to France, no financing was available to put it into production. The result was that the first manufacture of muskets on an interchangeable part basis was made in New Haven, Connecticut by Eli Whitney in 1797, using a contract from the War Department to obtain credit from local financiers.)

In many ways, Boulton had few precedents to guide him into becoming one of the first modern manufacturers: he had to create a new industry from scratch, with the social organization, division of labor, and subcultural norms that go with developing such a system. Unlike the peasant who worked long hours on his plot of land but who could nevertheless take time off to visit with neighbors or friends or even stop everything to attend to family matters, the worker in the factory had to learn strict military discipline (as a sentry does). He could not leave his job except with permission, and then only if someone came as a substitute to tend his machine. He could not come late to his job. He could not visit with friends or relatives while he was working (except to talk with workmates if the work permitted). He could not take the time to go to a fair, to celebrate a Church feast day, or to stay at home in bad weather. He was under strict military discipline while he was on the job, and he was required to show definite obligations to his employer (though his employer had few toward him: he could be discharged at whim, he could be released from his employment if he were ill, injured, too old to work properly, or if the employer did not have enough work for him).

In pioneering a new industry, Boulton had to train his workers to be painstakingly exact. Machine tools had to be improvised or even invented to make the various component parts of the steam engine. Unlike the textile mills at that time, the manufacture of steam engines required men of great muscular strength, good work habits, mechanical aptitudes, and expert hand dexterity. Locksmiths, tinsmiths, and millwrights had to be retrained to become boilermakers, skilled blacksmiths, and foundrymen. The cylinders of the new steam engines had to be made with geometrical accuracy, pistons had to fit exactly, the gears had to be milled as if they were being put into a large watch, and the boiler pieces had to be made with standardized diameters (unlike the manufacture of parts for the Newcomen engine which were generally crude, of differing measurements, and rarely fitted well).

◇   ◇   ◇   ◇   ◇

The experimentation of the seventeenth century made possible the beginning of an age of production in the eighteenth century: all parts of a machine were made exactly alike so that they could be interchangeable. This new system of production required precise measurements, with almost no variations permitted. Although the watchmakers of Nuremberg and Paris at the end of the seventeenth century were able to manufacture watches whose parts were machined to be interchangeable, most other production was on a rule-of-thumb basis: if it looked good to the eye, that was sufficient.

It is possible that the year 1785 marked the end of the rule-of-thumb period and the beginning of the Scientific Age with its exact measurements. While individual merchants were still inventing new machines without utilizing scientific research, their machines often could not be improved without recourse to a scientific theory which delineated the problem that needed to be resolved. A high pressure steam engine, for example, could not have been invented without a new theory of heat, new metallurgical processes had to wait for an expansion in the knowledge of chemistry, and engineering was restricted without further development in the science of physics.

In the early eighteenth century, the invention of the flying shuttle increased the production of woven cloth, thus creating the demand for mechanized spinners to keep up with the weavers. Almost as soon as the new spinning machines were put into operation, Englishmen and Frenchmen were working on an equivalent mechanical means of weaving. Although the first mechanical weaving machine was invented by an Englishman in 1784, its introduction was delayed because it was still not efficient enough for mass production; it remained too limited in the number of designs that it could weave on the cloth. Not until the invention of the Jacquard automatic loom in the first decade of the nineteenth century did the weaving industry become ready to enter the mass market by leaving the individual weaver behind. In 1805, a good English or French weaver working on a handloom could make about 172,000 weaving moves a week, working fulltime an average of 12 hours per day six days a week. By 1810, or five years later, one unskilled worker could look after two mechanical looms making 900,000 moves per week; but by 1850 one worker could operate four mechanical looms making more than two million moves per week. By the end of the nineteenth century, production that could be supervised by one worker had soared to more than ten million moves per week, to be increased even more fantastically by the middle of the twentieth century. Almost none of the profits derived from this mechanized form of production went to the worker watching the looms, but there were lower prices for woolen and cotton cloth on the mass market and larger profits for the entrepreneur and the new groups of middlemen who extended from the manufacturer to the consumer. As the new industrialization added to the wealth of England, individuals in the United States, France, Germany, Austria, Italy, and Russia sought to buy or steal plans for the machines and to copy English production and merchandising techniques. The competition from abroad kept English wages fairly low until the end of the nineteenth century, when some of the increased profits began to trickle down to the workers.

It is difficult to look upon the new industrialization as merely a continuation of the civilization and way of life that began with the Sumerian city-states in the fourth millenium B.C., any more than the latter can be seen as a continuation of the previous Neolithic Age. Something new was added in the seventeenth and eighteenth centuries. And that something new was a special way of looking upon man, his knowledge, and the world he lived in. The eighteenth century had entirely different explanations about the causes of natural phenomena than did the Sumerians, the Greeks, the Romans, or the Medieval inhabitants of Europe. Men now sought from nature itself new explanations to satisfy their curiosity about natural phenomena. Men were no longer content to shrug their shoulders and insist that everything was in the hands of God. They were pushed by their intellectual curiosity to search out the evidence in front of their eyes. A good deal of early scientific thinking was a matter of changing one's point of view as to what to look for and at. The nineteenth and twentieth centuries added new insights, new evidence, and new experiments; but basically the scientific point of view had been indicated roughly by the end of the eighteenth century — though it would be worked on, refined, and amplified tremendously. In the seventeenth century, men of science still carried around in their minds the cultural ideas of the pre-Scientific Age, as they would also in the eighteenth, nineteenth, and twentieth centuries. But slowly the scientific point of view of seeking evidence through hypotheses that could be challenged (but that would also lead to new insights) gradually became more prominent. (The scientific point of view would not be accepted completely even by the end of the twentieth century, although it would become a more important reference point for thinking.) The new age had less need for organized religion to give it explanations of natural phenomena, and bit by bit the old established religions either absorbed the knowledge of the secular world or withdrew from any visible confrontation with it — though some struggled against the new ideas of the secular age as heresies that needed to be stopped from spreading.

◇   ◇   ◇   ◇   ◇

While some men in the eighteenth century were convinced that all their problems could be solved by turning to "reason" rather than to "revelations," they did not always see "reason" as being critical of one's own hypotheses and self-fulfilling prophecies, but sometimes as a means to make these hypotheses "reasonably true." There were as many hypotheses based upon emotional revelations as upon experimental evidence, but men nonetheless for the first time in human history started to become critical of themselves, the societies that they inherited, and the responsibilities that they had to endure for the decisions which had been made for them. In the late eighteenth century, men began to look hard at themselves and the world which others had created for them. Although some philosophers saw the hand of a benign but still unknown Providence directing men's activities, there was also the bare beginning of an awareness that men to a large extent were what their ideas of themselves had made them.

And so, the heritage of the spirit of egalitarianism now added new features: the desire for individual achievement and growth; the right of an individual to participate in those decisions that spelled well-being, life, or death for him and his family; and the freedom of the individual to let his intellectual curiosity become his guide in exploring his social universe rather than past tradition or autocratic orders.

Because a few men in England for various personal reasons felt a need to amass wealth, and thus higher social status, for themselves — and in doing so utilized a rising awareness of mass markets, an available technology, skilled technicians, and merchant financing — England (as well as the rest of Europe) and the new United States became slowly transformed. With agriculture decreasing in prominence, and urbanization and industrialization increasing their positions, a new series of social classes arose composed of factory workers, maintenance workers, transportation workers, white-collar workers, and a small but rapidly growing technical middle class (which eventually turned out to be the most revolutionary force of all). The new civilization came out of the ideas which this small technical middle class created, transformed into reality, and spent its time improving. Not those who worked the forges, the looms, or the spindles, but the new managers, technicians, foremen, supervisors, the new professions of the engineer, physicist, chemist, and the academician (working in his laboratory or at his books) were the counterparts of the ancient scribes (who created and built the Primary civilization). They were the new scribes who created and built an urban civilization — a Secondary form of civilization, which brought a much higher percentage of the population into its milieu and which so completely dominated the lives of its citizens that they became unable to live independently of it.

XI   The Growth of Secondary Civilization

The new Secondary civilization spread quite slowly in the midst of the older civilization that gave it birth and nurture. From infancy, the technological side grew more rapidly than the culture that went with it. For example, the textile industry grew more than 15 times in the 30 years between 1770 and 1800, displacing the old putting-out or cottage system in England. Through cheap exports, it was able to destroy cotton handicrafts in India in a short period of time. The production of iron in England rose from 68,000 tons in 1788 to 250,000 tons in 1806 (but to more than six million tons a century later). Between 1790 and 1810, hundreds of cloth merchants with access to financing and with more than a passing acquaintance with the new manufacturing techniques opened factories for the production of textiles. Potteries increased rapidly from 1770 to 1800, lowering prices and exporting English china and earthenware to North America, Europe, Asia, and Latin America.

Still, England itself was not transformed overnight. The new civilization represented a slow process of cultural and social change in which the new lived side by side with the old for a long period of time. Although the factory system got its start in 1771, it was not until 1850 that most textiles in England were made inside factories by wage labor. It took another 50 years before most consumer goods were manufactured in factories rather than handmade by artisans in small workshops (the latter still dominated a good share of European production until after World War I).

Industrialization was a matter of ideas carried in men's minds and it took years, if not decades, for some of the important technical inventions to spread from one part of England to another; from England to France, Belgium, Germany, and Switzerland, to the United States, or to Russia. In the early part of the nineteenth century, an average of 25 years was required for a small factory to adjust itself to new inventions in mechanical production. It took more than 70 years for the flying shuttle, invented in 1733, to spread to the outlying areas of England, though its value in increasing the weaving of cloth was known by the 1750's. Handwoven cloth was still being made in England and Scotland by the end of the nineteenth century. In the twentieth century on islands off the Scottish coast, woolens for export are still woven on handlooms.

The ideas of industrialization reached the new United States before the American Revolution ended. By 1791, Moses Brown, a Providence, Rhode Island Quaker, induced an Englishman, who had worked on making textile machines for Richard Arkwright, to go into business with his son-in-law to spin and weave textiles for the American and foreign markets. Although in 1800 more than 95 percent of the American population lived on farms, the Industrial and Scientific Age within 70 years had made the new country a close industrial competitor of England.

Gradually the ideas of industrialization spread from England to the continent and, though England held its commanding lead for most of the next century, the wide gap existing in the early part of the nineteenth century narrowed with each decade. At the end of the Napoleonic Wars, industrialization moved into Belgium and France and in the 1820's into Germany. By the 1830's, it spread into Austria and northern Italy, and a few decades afterwards into Poland and Russia. In the meanwhile, industrialization in the United States had shifted to manufacturing for a much larger mass market than was the case in England. The Americans mass-produced clocks, paper for large dailies, guns, kitchen ware, ready-made clothing, and shoes — and after the 1850's, sewing machines and farm machinery.

The ideas of industrialization made possible mass production in agriculture (through new plows, threshing machines, rakes, and so on, along with scientific studies of soils, improved seeds, and better bred meat animals). These ideas and their symbolism spread quickly to Japan and after 1868 initiated the revolutionary Meiji Period (the roots of this industrialization in Japan also lay in the ideas brought there by the Portuguese in the sixteenth century and by the Dutch and English in the seventeenth and eighteenth centuries). These ideas temporarily bypassed India and China, but in the long run influenced these two nations profoundly. Industrialization and science also carried with them new ideas about the family, about the obligations of the individual to his society, about the relations between the sexes, about man's loyalties to the past, to tradition, to authority, and to how men should shape their lives.

The factory did not come alone to foreign shores. It brought in its wake the entire framework of a new world that was urban, non-traditional, and alienating to men as much as any previous period. It destroyed the old primary relationships that had kept families and villages together and that had made religion a source of knowledge. In their places it substituted the world of the stranger, the secular or political religion, and the emptiness of tedious factory work unbroken by church festivals or family and village reunions. In the beginning, the new civilization was perceived as a form of betrayal, in which the goals of a Heavenly City were secretly replaced by a polluted and enslaved Hell. Men frantically sought the primary relationships, the Golden Age, the Paradise of Adam and Eve, which they felt could have been theirs but which they believed had been snatched from their grasp. They searched for scapegoats to punish in the place of those whom they could not reach—but whom they felt had poisoned their hopes and betrayed their dreams of a better world and a friendlier human society.

The alienation of the landless peasant driven from the countryside where forces beyond his control condemned him to a life of starvation was similar to the bitter frustration of his urban cousin who had previously left the countryside to seek work in the new factories. Here he found that it was not his labor that was wanted but those of his wife and children (they were more docile to the military discipline of the workplace and more readily accepted lower wages than he). He was told over and over again by the economists of that period that there was little hope that he could move into a better life in his or his children's lifetimes, because wealth was limited and the supply of labor was greater than the demand. The new civilization thus went hand in hand with a deeply felt malaise that the Old World had died and a more insecure and frightful one had taken its place.

The landed aristocrats of England and France saw the new industrialization as a threat to their social and political status. But, while the French aristocrats turned themselves into a fixed caste and separated themselves from the rest of the population and from French history after 1789, the English aristocrats in the early part of the nineteenth century took a hard look at child labor in the factories and mines, and began to work on the religious conscience of England to impose restrictions on the rights of manufacturers to do whatever they considered they needed to do in order to make a profit. Lord Ashley was only one of many who found support among the aristocrats for legislation to bring reforms — but at the expense of the new manufacturers rather than of the aristocrats (who were being hurt in Parliament by the manufacturers' struggle for free importation of foreign wheat, which sold below the price which the aristocrats and large landowners wished to receive for theirs).

⋄   ⋄   ⋄   ⋄   ⋄

The technical changes brought about by industrialization were only a small part of the total picture, for technological innovations in the society brought far-reaching social, economic, and political changes in their wake. In England, the industrialists and their supporters organized themselves politically to pressure the government to support their social and economic efforts. In the new United States, the followers of the manufacturing and banking way of life supported efforts on the part of the Federalists to develop a centralized government that could use its power to enhance their new industrial goals. These important factions both supported science in the young United States. As early as 1817, the new industrialists were able to push through tariffs against foreign manufactures, to get government financing for much of their experimental efforts, for improving transportation (thus cutting down on the costs of retailing goods), and for creating a large government market for much of the manufactured products. In the second half of the nineteenth century, a good deal of the railroad network west of the Mississippi was made possible by the government contributing large amounts of land to the newly formed railroad companies to help defray the cost of constructing railroads (in most cases, the sale of the lands brought in more money than the amounts expended in building the lines).

In England, the manufacturers were the great defenders of free trade (especially the free trade in cereals, which they did not grow themselves but which were raised by the country gentry who saw the manufacturers as a threat). By cutting the tariffs on imported grains, the manufacturers continued their preeminent position in world trade by keeping the cost of English labor low (the advantage which many of the developing nations have at the present time). Since English manufacturers had little competition during the first part of the nineteenth century, they could afford to insist upon the principle of free trade everywhere — including the right to export goods to China and India, where local attempts to preserve the artisans from this unfair industrial competition were brutally pushed aside. To enforce the .concept of free trade, warships followed the trade routes, and in this respect the United States was not far behind.

◇   ◇   ◇   ◇   ◇

In terms of the expectations raised by the "Enlightenment" of the eighteenth century, industrialization in the early nineteenth century seemed to be creating and perpetuating new inequalities and injustices, and ignoring men's knowledge of the desirability to create a more egalitarian, democratic, and just society. The new industrialists were seen by those educated in the eighteenth century as merely replacing the old feudal lords and aristocrats. In the early years of the Industrial Revolution, the powers of the employers over

their workers was in many ways as absolute as the authority of
the Medieval lord of the manor over his serfs, with the important
difference that the latter had obligations toward his tenants, while
the industrialist had none either in law or in tradition toward his
workers. The feudal serf was tied to the manor and had rights which
the lord of the manor was legally expected to respect (though few
of them did). The manufacturer could discharge workers on whim,
when they were injured on the job, or when they were too old to
work. The worker who rebelled against this harsh one-sided obligation of loyalty to the factory was discharged without warning and
blacklisted from obtaining other work.

With very few exceptions most British, American, and French
manufacturers insisted upon their right to employ any form of discipline necessary to punish infractions of discipline on the part of
those working for them, except that of physical discipline, though
this was also used many times. Most believed that it was part of
"natural law" to pay the worker the lowest going wage, which in
the first 50 years of the factory system was generally barely above
subsistence. The manufacturers early organized themselves as a
lobby group to exert political pressure upon the government and
to fix prices. On the other hand, they also organized themselves
to exert pressure against the attempts of workers to organize themselves in labor unions. In the first half of the nineteenth century,
organization of any kind by workers was seen as "conspiracy" and
was severely punished by the courts. The workers first received
judicial approval for union activity in Massachusetts in 1842. From
the manufacturers' point of view, any attempt to restrict the supply
of labor was seen as a conspiracy against the state, which was thus
viewed as the protector of the market and its "laws."

◇   ◇   ◇   ◇   ◇

The earliest attempts to limit the power of the industrialists
over their workers were carried on by those social reformers whom
Karl Marx called "Utopian Socialists," and upon whom he vented
his contempt for their "naivete." The earliest of the "Utopians" (a
term which Marx used but which was never employed by those
who believed that a new society must be created, utilizing the power
of industrialization and science) was perhaps the Count de Saint-
Simon. Saint-Simon saw factory owners, workers, financiers,
artists, and scholars as belonging to a large productive class, as
against the aristocrats and large landholders whom he considered
to be "non-productive." Before Saint-Simon died in 1825, he offered
plans to reform the Industrial Revolution (which were not put into

operation until a century after his death). He supported the dignity and importance of labor, and he saw the creation of wealth as being necessary in building a better society, though he felt that the status of a scientist or a chief mechanic was as important to the greatness of France as a manufacturer or a financier, and he believed that their equal status deserved equal rewards. Saint-Simon insisted that men should have the right to a job, or to unemployment benefits if work was not to be had, just as they had rights to a minimum standard of living and a minimum pay scale, medical care, old-age pensions, free education for all, and the right to paid holidays. He also believed that the age of industrialization made it possible to unite the known world through better means of communication, and it was his followers who helped plan and create both the Suez and the first attempt to build a Panama Canal. Work was seen as a bond which united men and permitted them to make their proper contributions to human society. Creative work for the benefit of society (rather than of God) was extolled. At the same time, the world was ready for a new religion, a reform of Christianity, that would put into practice the teachings of Christ. Since the vast majority of man's neighbors were poor, the love that one was supposed to show towards them needed to take the form of helping them get out of their poverty by reorganizing the industrial state so that more wealth was created which would help everyone, employers as well as employees. Men needed to build a new Christian society so that they could enjoy the free development of their talents; men had a natural born right to utilize their aptitudes, and the society that guaranteed this free development of men would gain in the long run. Hierarchies, whether aristocratic or mercantile, tended to perpetuate inequalities, poverty, and the continuation of an imperfect status quo.

Charles Fourier, another of the early nineteenth-century "Utopian Socialists," was a self-educated businessman who believed that men could live cooperatively in voluntary "mini-societies," in which the machine would free man from the pain of work and the slavery of factory labor so that he could devote himself to reforming not only himself but his society. Fourier held that men must work because they want to, not because they are compelled to. Duty was a man-made word used by civilization to enslave man; a desire to be creative and to cooperate was, on the other hand, a gift of God. Men need the right to be themselves, to develop their own "passions," and to work voluntarily with other men in self-regulated communes or "phalansteries." Men, Fourier wrote, had the right to work on whatever interested them most and for which they had a natural aptitude. For this reason, Fourier believed that education which was free and individually oriented was necessary to help men find themselves. Men needed to learn to be themselves and not to be subject to obedience, to authority instituted from the outside.

Although the followers of Fourier attempted to establish their communes in France, England, and the United States, it was a Welsh textile manufacturer in Scotland, Robert Owen, who not only managed a large textile mill successfully, but also developed the idea of building "perfect communities" as models of the "perfect society." In these, the evils of the Industrial Age with its poverty, and its hierarchies of wealth and income could be replaced by communities in which all men would earn their living by using as a currency an hour of work.

After a career as a most efficient entrepreneur, Robert Owen traveled around Europe and North America attempting to organize his communities of "cooperative work." He sank a large part of his fortune in organizing a cooperative community in New Harmony, Indiana, in 1826, but this soon foundered because of faulty management and organization. After many years as a successful manufacturer, Owen ended his life as a most unsuccessful organizer and manager of men. The same aptitudes which enabled him to make a fortune as a textile manufacturer turned him into a bungling manager, unable to handle the day to day details of running a commune with men who were differently motivated to contribute their labor. Other reformers followed Saint-Simon, Fourier, and Owen, as they attempted to found new communities aimed at creating a new economic society — as one founds new religions, on the basis of revelations and untested hypotheses about human behavior and organization.

The nineteenth century expanded the breadth and depth of the new Industrial and Scientific civilization. There had been few large urban centers of over a million before 1850, but by the end of the century such cities had spread on all the continents. The century also saw the population of the world grow to more than a billion persons, as compared to a little less than half a billion three centuries before, and to a little over 250 million at the beginning of the Christian era. (By the year 2000, the population of the world will have increased some five to six times over what it was at the beginning of 1900.) Industrialization moved from isolated spots to encompass large areas of Great Britain, France, Germany, Austria-Hungary (though mainly the Czech lands and Austria), Scandinavia, Belgium, and across the Atlantic to even larger areas of the United States (and Canada), while moving slowly around Asia to find a home in Japan.

In the meanwhile, urbanization, scientific research, and the spread of the movement supporting greater literacy of the European and North American population (along with the Japanese) meant that the ideas born in the research laboratory, in the academic study, in legislative halls, and in political headquarters moved rapidly as the nineteenth century implemented Saint-Simon's ideas of tightening the bonds that keep people together. The mails, railroads, and ships made countries more aware of one another's ideas than they had ever been before. No longer did the countries of Asia remain exotic and hidden from view when thousands of travelers and explorers returned to describe what they had seen — and with more scientific detachment and more detail than Medieval travelers or the voyagers of the Ancient World. More books were written about the various countries of the world. By the end of the century, there were few areas that were not known to literate people who were able to use public libraries and the vast collections of books in the proliferating colleges and universities in those countries that had accepted industrialization and the scientific point of view.

XII   The Diffusion of Secondary Civilization

While men in the past had had some intellectual curiosity about themselves, their neighbors, and the world they lived in, there was little substantial accumulation of dependable information about man and his societies. Men were not seen as the cause of societal effects nor as the originators of their norms, values, and history, but as servants receiving their instructions, goals, and standards of behavior from the deities ruling them. History was the uncovering of the plans that fate or the deities had already written for man. Beginning with the seventeenth century, European thinkers discovered man as an autonomous being, affected by the Deity and given certain mental attributes by his Creator, but a being who was nevertheless on his own and who had to find out for himself the purposes for which he had been born. The eighteenth century made man even more autonomous, though endowed with natural rights given him by the Creator of the universe. But it was the nineteenth century that detached man from all affiliation with the Deity, that insisted that men made their own history through their conflicts and that, though no future history is inevitable on the basis of past trends, still men by their actions and their ideas determine the world that their children and their children's children will live in.

Some accumulation of knowledge about other peoples, other customs, and other religions took place in the Ancient World, although the best accounts were those written by men who lived in the culture they described (one example being that of Josephus writing of the Jews in the first century of the Christian era). Caesar and Tacitus were not as successful in giving us a description that could be used as a base. Perhaps the earliest of the modern records was that of the Spanish Friar De Sahagun in the early sixteenth century, who left us with a detailed account of the Aztec culture which had recently been overthrown by the Spanish Roman Catholic conquest of Central Mexico. The French Jesuits in the seventeenth century kept records of the particulars of Indian behavior in eastern North America, and a young Englishman working with the Hudson's Bay Company wrote an ethnographic description of life among the Cree and the Assiniboine Indians of the central part of North America at the end of the seventeenth and beginning of the eighteenth centuries. Italian Jesuits left us accounts of life in the Chinese Court at Peking in the same century. But it was not until the nineteenth century that men began to make systematic investigations of other cultures, other men, and other histories. In that century, men took long hard looks at themselves, their histories, behavior, and the physical and biological worlds in which they lived.

The nineteenth century was one of the large-scale organization of industry and politics, of the proliferation of institutions of higher learning, of the development and spread of new sciences from geology to biology, and of the transformation of philosophy into sociology and psychology. It was a century of great wealth: never before in human history had mankind increased so greatly its population, wealth, productivity, transportation networks, mass production of newspapers, and communication links that tied the world together through steamships, trains, telegraph, telephone, submarine cables, and wireless. It was the century that saw the birth of techniques that far surpassed anything of previous centuries. It also saw the transformation of England from a rural to an urban nation; of the United States from a rural nation of five million to an urban one of more than 75 million; of a poor and impoverished collection of German-speaking states into a powerful German empire; and of a feudal poverty-stricken, rural, isolated Japan into a mighty military and economic power that soon threatened European and American interests in Asia and the Pacific.

After 1815, industrialization spread to the continent from Great Britain, and the ideas of industrial organization mingled with those of eighteenth-century science to develop superordinate goals in which industrialization and science were viewed as twin benefits for mankind, but under new forms of social control. The nineteenth century saw a rapid shift from illiterate to a more literate urban Europe, from rural villages to urban cities, from pot-holed dirt roads to macademized ones and railroads. Without the technology of the nineteenth century, the world of man could not have become smaller and the process of world urbanization would not have occurred.

The spread of technology went hand in hand with controversies as to how these technical ideas should be used to benefit society. Although men in the first half of the nineteenth century were concerned with creating more satisfying human societies, those in the second half felt a need to know more about how human society began, developed, and where it was heading. Karl Marx began an analysis of his contemporary society in the mid-nineteenth century by attempting to uncover "laws" of human development (although the "laws" were not seen as "natural" ones given by a Creator, but trends put into operation by "human nature"). John Locke at the end of the eighteenth century had dealt with man making his own decisions but only within the "bounds of the laws of nature." Marx went one step further in suggesting that there were no laws of nature, but that there might be laws developed when men are made aware that they are being "exploited," or when they are unable to order their affairs in terms of their own self-interests. What Marx and Engels were saying was that men do not suffer unhappiness at the hands of other men easily; that sooner or later the under-class revolts against the tyranny of an over-class, and then creates a new social organization in its own image; that even government operates not (as Locke saw it) objectively but in the interests of those who control it.

The world of the nineteenth century gave men not only new points of view towards themselves and the physical and biological worlds they inhabited, but also suggested that options for knowledge and decision-making were endless and continuously epochal. Neither tradition nor precedent were necessary to let men's minds soar freely to new break-through hypotheses. If men's thoughts shattered past concepts, that should be considered normal, for the purpose of scientific thinking was not to preserve the thinking of the past but to prepare the ground for new ideas and concepts never before perceived. Men needed to be trained to accept revolutionary points of view, new knowledge that might completely contradict that which had gone before. Jean Jacques Rousseau in the eighteenth century had insisted that men cannot create new powers over those given them by nature, and that therefore they had to unite by social pacts to preserve those natural rights which they possessed.

In the nineteenth century, men went further in their insistence that they could be what they wanted to be. Here Auguste Comte in the early part and Karl Marx in the middle of that century took the leads — though there were many others, some unknown at the present time, who made their contributions. Comte believed that there were social laws which governed the actions of men; Marx believed that there were historical ones, though these operated through the social organizations that men created to let them earn their livings and to resolve their problems of production. Marx was followed by many social and economic philosophers and pioneer social scientists who either built on his hypotheses or carried on studies to refute them. The result was that mankind in the nineteenth century benefited by fresh viewpoints and a new accumulation of empirical studies that provided scholars with more insights in understanding men and the world they had been born into.

Charles Darwin had shaken the religious world of the nineteenth century (which was still in conflict with the free-thinking of the eighteenth) with his observations that life had continuously changed as it adapted to altered physical conditions. This concept suggested laws of biological development which had nothing in common with the "natural law" as enunciated by theologians, both Protestant and Roman Catholic. The idea of adaptation also appealed to men of science and of business, who saw evolutionary theory (re-translated by Herbert Spencer) as a compliment to their ability to survive because they were more able. During the nineteenth century, the English, French, and Germans were constantly told that they had come as far as they had because their national superiorities were based upon a selective process in which they became leaders in science, business, and industrialization largely because they were better able to adapt to changing world conditions than the backward, poverty-stricken nations of Southern and Eastern Europe, Asia, Africa, and South America.

⋄   ⋄   ⋄   ⋄   ⋄

At the same time, the North Americans considered themselves as world leaders because they had adapted better than the more effete nations of Europe. In Asia, however, Japan had been influenced by a fervent compensating nationalism which feared control by Europe and North America but which also spread the doctrine of a superior and adaptable people — a combination which let the country achieve industrialization and the complete acceptance of the new technology and science. (Also acceptable to the Japanese were the ideas of socialism, higher education, and new concepts of man, including that first voiced by Giambattista Vico in the early eighteenth century that man creates his own social world, an observation retranslated by Karl Marx and his disciples.) Toward the end of the century, the new social sciences and the attempts of Sigmund Freud to understand man through his unspoken emotional language brought about even newer and more revolutionary means of seeing man and the social systems he had created out of his ignorance, his confusions, and his need to live in a more predictable and secure world.

The world in 1850 was quite different from that of 1750 or 1800, just as the world of 1900 differed greatly from that of 1850 or from what would follow in 2000. The world of 1800 was still overwhelmingly rural with most goods made by artisans in small workshops or at home. Even the textile industry was not completely mechanized until after 1850. The world of 1800 operated with human energy or that created by streams of water pushing large wheels. Although a few steam engines powered some large textile mills, it remained a pre-steam age. In 1850, mules were slowly pulling heavily-laden barges on dirt paths alongside canals. By that year, the steamboat was tying settlements on America's rivers closer together and exchanging goods even more cheaply between the developing and developed nations. After 1830, railroads were introduced that cut down traveling time, encouraged men to travel less expensively than before, stimulated inner as well as outer migration, spread the influence of the written word through more books, newspapers, and magazines, and at the same time created an illusion which the nineteenth century fostered as being reality— that is, in spite of the technological revolution, human society was still stable, authority was still in control, and the best of all possible worlds would continue to remain that way. The belief was encouraged that men had reached a technological plateau from which they could climb higher, but that the social plateau had been attained and men could do no better.

◊   ◊   ◊   ◊   ◊

Although steamboats had been used on rivers from the first decade of the nineteenth century, ocean steamboats did not come into operation until the middle of the century. Until then, sail was still used: the wind energy derived from differences in air pressure still drove boats across the oceans, though they were better built, larger, and more efficient. The year 1850 was a watershed date separating the new industrial from the old artisanal way of life, the new urban from the old rural, and the steam-driven from the wind-driven. The year 1850 also inaugurated an age that kept better records of itself, that preserved itself in photographs, that communicated more easily by telegraph, by submarine cable, and within a quarter of a century by telephone. A man born in 1850 was able to enter new professions that were non-existent in 1800, possessed a standard of living that was quite different from that of his grandfather in 1800, was more aware of the world he lived in, was more urbanized, more dependent upon others for his necessities and services, and enjoyed better health because of advances in medical knowledge. One living or just starting life in 1850 had hopes of knowing and consuming more, of being aware of greater options and opportunities, of being more comfortable physically and more expectant that technology would evolve to higher levels. Wealth was now viewed as something one could create out of ideas that could either produce items more efficiently and cheaply, or contain possibilities for options that never existed before. Men were more optimistic in 1850 in believing that somehow conditions would get better and affluence would extend to a larger proportion of the population than it had previously.

The reasons for this greater sophistication in using machines, technology, management, and finance to achieve a more secure urbanized society are still clouded by ignorance of our society, of human motivations, and of the cultural accumulation of knowledge which began in the Ancient World and continues to the present (and will continue even further into the future than any of us can dimly perceive at the moment). Although much is made of the Protestant ethos of Max Weber, with its emphasis upon thrift, hard work, and moral behavior, and much of Martin Luther's reaction to the traditional concept of work as a curse or a byproduct of original sin, the fact remains that others in the world have worked just as hard as the middle-class British, have been just as thrifty and moral, but without inaugurating a new society and civilization. Mexican peasants have traditionally taken pride in their hard work, but have barely been able to rise about the subsistence level. European peasants have worked hard, been forced to consume little, and have followed the norms and values of their religious beliefs (as the Old Believers in Russia) without accumulating wealth or developing a modern industrial society. Hard work was the lot of black slaves in the early nineteenth century, as it was of the Chinese and Indian peasants also during that century. (Most poor in the world have been compelled to be thrifty primarily because they would have starved if they could not make-do with the little they had.) Man throughout history has had to work hard and live thriftily on what was available to him, so that hard work, thrift, and moral behavior are by no means satisfying explanations as to why Great Britain became industrialized, why the United States took the lead in industrialization after 1870, and why Japan was able to forge ahead so rapidly in industrial production in the century after 1868.

The answers evidently lie in the cultures that had been formed from the eleventh century to their rapid growth in the nineteenth and twentieth centuries. The accumulation of wealth by merchants and the productive increase in agriculture and crafts made financing available for the machines that could manufacture the goods demanded by a slowly rising standard of living among the majority of the population in England. Without this technological productivity, wealth would have gone down the drain, as in Spain and Portugal, where it was eaten up by greater military expenditures and a resulting inflation. With the development of better techniques to manufacture more goods or to gather more resources (plus the knowledge of what to do with these techniques), a surplus wealth was created, especially when the merchants and manufacturers held on to their original standard of living. (The vast majority of peasants, then the overwhelming number of inhabitants, could not increase their standard of consumption, but they could substitute the cheaper machine-made textiles, shoes, and household goods for the more expensive artisanal ones.) The increased amount of consumption among the peasants, the urban dwellers, workers, and the small but expanding middle classes made possible the further growth of factories that competed with one another upon entering the new mass markets. The growth of the mass market was at the expense of the artisans and parttime cottage industrial workers, who paid the price for this increase in wealth by being unemployed or by lowering their prices in order to compete with the new machine-made products.

The combination of technology with financing made industrialization possible in a society where labor, food, machines, and knowledge were available and for sale. In an underdeveloped country, hard work and thrift (as in nineteenth-century China) could do little to change a society from a rural pre-industrial one to an urban industrial one. The opportunities had to be available to those who wanted to take advantage of them. It was not possible for a poverty-stricken illiterate peasant to become a banker or an entrepreneurial manufacturer for the reason that he did not possess the knowledge or opportunities to do so. It was easier for bankers' and merchants' children to become merchants and bankers than for the children of illiterate unskilled laborers. Conversely in the ninth, fourteenth, or fifteenth centuries, a John Rockefeller or an Andrew Carnegie could not have done what either of them did. Preparation in developing levels of knowledge over many centuries was necessary to make possible a nineteenth-century entrepreneur or a twentieth-century billionaire. To say, as many of them did, that they made their fortunes by themselves and owed nothing to the past accumulation of knowledge and expansion of opportunities was to miss the cause-and-effect results that let them become what they were and are.

The long history of mining from Roman days on, the work on the iron forge, the blast furnace, and the experimentation that produced a cheaper and more effective metal all made possible the development of the Bessemer converter process in the late 1850's. The long line of men who worked over millenia to produce a more efficient means of transportation — from the first group of unknowns, who invented the wheel and then learned to harness animal energy to pull it, to those who later utilized wooden rails in mines for carts, who invented a steam engine, improved upon it, and turned it into a nineteenth-century form of rapid mass transportation — made possible the chain that led to the utilization of more efficient mining and smelting techniques ending with the building of a network of transcontinental railroads.

The development of chemistry from the alchemists of the Middle Ages, the work done on machines after the eleventh century, the invention of a four-stroke internal combustion engine in the nineteenth century in Germany and elsewhere, the development of a science of drilling for petroleum, the growth of a market for its byproducts, the further study of chemistry in nineteenth-century colleges and research laboratories, and the growth of urbanization, all these preliminaries made it possible for the oil found on Texas farms to make multimillionaires of their owners. Nor could the men who bought up oil leases have become later billionaires without the existence of these preceding conditions, plus the willingness of a government to subsidize the exploration for oil by oil depreciation tax allowances. Knowledge in the Industrial and Scientific civilization (as in the pre-industrial agricultural and administrative centers) meant power. And those who could command and use this culture were able to enrich themselves by utilizing facts built up painstakingly by thousands of individuals over countless generations. What had belonged to all men now became the monopoly of a few individuals in the United States and Western Europe, who utilized this accumulated knowledge by learning how to manipulate government to obtain the political assistance they needed in order to amass their fortunes.

◇   ◇   ◇   ◇   ◇

During the nineteenth century, probably more industrial fortunes were made in the United States than in any other industrialized country, though Western Europe was not far behind. These fortunes were made by men who took advantage of knowledge which they had but which was unknown to most others: a knowledge of whom to turn to for assistance, of where fortunes could be made, of access to sources where large loans could be obtained, and of where the markets were located that could be exploited with assistance from others. These fortunes were not made by men who devised new industrial techniques, who furthered the accumulation of knowledge, or who pioneered in making technical breakthroughs, but by a new class of men who perceived opportunities and who took advantage of them in an economy that had made knowledge indispensable to sensing the trends. If they had lived in the Ancient World and taken advantage of their opportunities, they would have been the men who financed and advised military conquerors, who directed the large public works, or who became the entrepreneurs of world religions. Such men obtained their power and fortunes by consolidating what had already taken place before.

In the period after the Civil War in the United States, industrialists made their fortunes by guessing right on future economic trends, by having advance knowledge of government expenditures, or by sensing that rapid urban and population growth increased the value of land held for investment. Although urbanization was a direct result of industrialization, rarely were the holders of real estate the industrialists. Many times holders of real estate who did little but sit tight with their land while the cities were burgeoning around them were able to make greater fortunes than those who actually did the manufacturing. The original manufacturers of clocks, sewing machines, or locomotives were not always the wealthiest of men, though many of the latter were speculators who had access to using other people's money.

In the second half of the nineteenth century, as industrialization made great strides with financial boosts from governments that were slowly becoming enormous markets themselves by being both customers and financiers, the fortunes were made through knowing governmental intentions or through having insiders obtain financing and contracts for the entrepreneurs. Many times fortunes were made not through innovation but through consolidation: consolidating a great many smaller and older industries in order to cut down on the probability of risk.

There is little doubt that the great entrepreneurs of the nineteenth century possessed a series of perceptive aptitudes which the contemporary industrial culture permitted them to utilize. (1) Without being inventors or technological innovators themselves, they had imagination enough to grasp the future significance of innovations. (2) They had the knowledge and cultural talents necessary for tapping available sources of capital for financing (they knew that those who had capital needed to loan it out if they were to profit from it). (3) They had the perception to recognize talents and skills in others, and the psychological know-how to motivate those having these skills to work for them. (4) They were open to new knowledge about marketing possibilities for the innovations in terms of buying and selling. (5) They had already become knowledgeable about production techniques and how to produce (with the aid of others) for the mass market. (6) They were imaginative about and receptive to new techniques of selling and distribution. (7) They knew how to employ and organize the specialized skills of others to manufacture or sell what others made, and at the same time to utilize these for training the large numbers of employees and supervisory personnel who had to be hired. All this presupposed a knowledge of how others had operated before them. In the middle of the nineteenth century, this knowledge could not be built up singlehandedly by a peasant living in an isolated area of the Andes Mountains or in Central Africa.

One cannot emphasize enough that knowledge is power and that managerial and entrepreneurial skills are learned from others; that no matter how high the "native" intelligence, these skills are not inborn but learned, and are easier to know if one has enough opportunities in his life to become exposed to them. It was possible to become an entrepreneurial individual either by serving an apprenticeship to another (or one's own father or close relative) or by utilizing these skills through possessing the finances to hire a staff knowledgeable in them. Hundreds of years of previous merchant and banking expertise went into the preparation of the nineteenth-century entrepreneur in merchandising, marketing, and financing. Knowledge of goods and markets was important to the merchant-financier from the days of the Phoenicians to the present. An eighteenth-century New England merchant had to be familiar with the names of the agents in every port in the world where his ship's captain could buy and sell, receive credit, and be kept informed about the state of every conceivable market in which he might be interested. Not only did he need to know with whom his ship captain could trade, but there had to be an understanding as to the other merchants' honesty, the importance of their word, and the extent of their knowledge.

The sixteenth-century family of the Fuggers in Bavaria could not have been successful in their various enterprises if they had not kept one another informed at all times by newsletters sent from the most important centers in the Western world which gave them advance information about possible loans, campaigns, and new sources of metals or goods. The Rothschild family had an enormous advantage over their competitors by having an intelligence network that supplied advance information which enabled them to buy or sell before others knew of such opportunities. In the second half of the nineteenth century, no entrepreneur or financier worth his salt could ignore the importance of having a personal network of informants to supply him with new information ahead of his competitors. The successful entrepreneur knew that knowledge was power, and this was why so many financed the seekers for more knowledge, whether they were professors at a college or the colleges or universities themselves. Education was important to the entrepreneur and he wanted more of it.

◇   ◇   ◇   ◇   ◇

The entrepreneur shared many skills with the warrior-organizer, but there was one important difference: unlike the warrior, he had early discovered that he needed the cooperation of others to get to the top; that it was often more to his advantage to cooperate with his competitors than to fight them. In the second half of the nineteenth century, the price wars in the United States were often the result of failures to get competitors to combine; if co-operation was not possible, then the competitors had to be forced out of business. The nineteenth-century entrepreneur even more than the eighteenth-century merchant had to take advantage of political opportunities to make economic gains. Many entrepreneurs in the United States profited from advance knowledge that one million Union soldiers had to have clothing, food, supplies, and guns in the period between 1861 and 1865, just as many speculators in the post-1865 period gained from being able to procure advance stock in the railroad construction companies before they received large grants of land from the United States Government (even before the first rail was laid on the lines running across the continent). Men needed a wide circle of political and financial friends (who could be sufficiently rewarded for their information and political influence) to enter the steel business that boomed as a result of the proliferation of railroads in the United States after 1865 and in Europe after 1870.

The entrepreneurial businessman "saw his opportunities and took them," but at the same time he had to be knowledgeable about the over-all state of the economy and the worlds of industrialization and finance in order to understand what his role within them could be. He needed special financial and technological knowledge to let him make perceptive judgments as to what would be profitable. Although he talked of risk-taking and looked upon his fortune as a reward for having done so, in actuality he could not afford to take risks. He had to bet on sure things or not at all. He needed to know as accurately as possible all the options that were open to him; this meant that he could not rely on his knowledge but on the information and judgment of others who were equally skilled. He was dependent upon the loyalty of those who could advise, assist, and help him to plan. He could be successful as long as there were others who would keep him informed, or who were well-trained enough to handle the myriad details of everyday production, financing, and marketing, but in doing so were willing to act as his loyal servants rather than as his equals. The nineteenth- and twentieth-century entrepreneur was seldom an egalitarian; he needed the esteem that came when those around him acknowledged his social and intellectual superiority.

Precedent based upon authority became extremely important for the loyal underlings, or servants of the company; too much freedom for them would have made it impossible for the entrepreneur to stamp his imprint and authority upon the plant or the business. On the other hand, enough leeway in making small minute innovations in the productive processes, in the techniques of marketing, and in financing had to be permitted, otherwise the plant or business would become moribund and non-competitive. Certain underlings had to be given the freedom which the eighteenth-century sea captain possessed, that of delegated authority which permitted them to make the day-to-day decisions necessary in running the plant, the business, the department, the government, or the university—without being restricted by precedents of the past or the authority of the entrepreneur. The carrot was in the form of the riches that success brought, but the stick was immediate dismissal for errors in judgment. The entrepreneur in the beginning could take minor risks, but once the organization had been built up, decisions were based upon as little risk as possible, and with the most precise knowledge attainable—even if it meant bribing or corrupting those with the knowledge which one needed to have.

The industrial side of the civilization (like the scientific one) had to be learned. Unless one had access to the knowledge which was required, it was virtually impossible to learn how to become an entrepreneur, no matter how hard-working, how Calvinist, or how thrifty one was. The poor, if they are able-bodied, are poor because they do not have the knowledge or training to become technically middle class. Unskilled laborers in a factory can work hard, and follow the strict discipline developed within the plant, but the chances of a poor unskilled laborer learning to become an entrepreneur are very slim, though not beyond the reach of possibility. There is an added ingredient which the entrepreneur possesses, but which is lacking in most workers, most peasants, and most clerks — and that is the enormous amount of self-confidence that is required to make a poor boy believe that he will be successful. Since there were so many more poor boys than middle class ones in the nineteenth century, a percentage of them were able to learn how to become entrepreneurs, although the vast majority remained what they started out to be: barely able to move from the social levels of poverty to the plateau immediately above. The entrepreneur had to feel self-confident of his knowledge, to be sure beyond doubt that he had the facts to succeed, and to trust his perception of where the opportunities lay in making money. The worldly entrepreneur rarely took long-shot chances, for success lay in minimizing risks as much as possible. One went into businesses that individuals one knew were also involved in, in order to learn the elements, rules, markets, and knowledge which were necessary to acquiring the self-confidence and contacts essential to letting one remain in business.

On the continent of Europe, in the New World, and in the under-developed colonies, the first of the entrepreneurs were those who as bankers or merchants had access to this new technical knowledge or who could finance those who did. The culture had to support, motivate, and encourage the innovator to push forward with his innovations. The modest shopkeeper needed to live in a stimulating business culture which encouraged the small merchant to branch out with relatives or friends, to form chain stores, or to use friends and relatives to assemble many small stores under one roof and develop a department store or a "galleria." Merchants became bankers to finance many of these new enterprises, though in general the financing came from the family or from close friends. The merchant-banker was more of a late nineteenth-century phenomenon, while the banker who financed "sure things" in business tended to be more of a twentieth-century development.

Because of their knowledge of where the ready financing lay, many bankers became industrialists or financed industries in which they had a large share of the capital. Many innovators beat a path to their doors hoping to obtain financial assistance. The men who became bankers had to know a good deal about the technological development that had taken place in their society; they had to know the soundness of the technological attempt to fulfill a demand for a market which was still in the making. In general, however, bankers like entrepreneurs were not pioneers; they preferred to have others assume the risks, and only got their own feet wet after others had waded in to test the depth of the water. The temper of the nineteenth century was to move cautiously after others had done the exploring: a good deal of money could be made in sure things without risking one's finances on the unsure ones.

The professional manager who took over from the individual entrepreneur was not allowed to hazard many chances with someone else's money, and no entrepreneur who was interested in conserving and building up his funds could permit an underling or a professional manager to take even the chances which he had taken. (Risk-taking has been very much exaggerated for the nineteenth-century entrepreneur. He became successful primarily because he bet on sure things. It was investors like Mark Twain who took the risks and lost. Bankers and entrepreneurs did not finance these risks, not if they could help it.)

The professional manager was primarily a nineteenth-century creation both in the United States and Great Britain. The mining and civil engineer had developed toward the end of the eighteenth century in England and on the continent, and the nineteenth century saw the creation of the professional mechanical and the railroad engineer, though in the beginning it was sometimes difficult to delineate the borders between the last three. Most entrepreneurs were self-taught and those they took into the business to help were usually sons and relatives who were trained to observe and emulate the behavior of the factory or millowners. Each factory in the eighteenth and early nineteenth centuries was unique, and the men who had been trained to work as production managers were often irreplaceable. The death of one could bring production almost to a halt: few factories were making the same items and the field of employment was fairly limited. A skilled mechanic who had worked in an early factory was worth his weight in gold, and could easily be financed to develop his own plant. As a result, England looked upon its embryonic factory managers as state secrets, and they were not permitted to emigrate to the United States, France, Germany, or Belgium. Even the making of a steam engine was a secret, and few foreigners were permitted to come anywhere near the foundry to observe how one was made for fear that the process might be stolen and repeated abroad, thus cutting down on the profit to be made by Englishmen. Any factory that went out of business became the meeting place of other factory owners seeking to employ its skilled workers and supervisors. Only the unskilled found their labor somewhat difficult to market. In general, until the second half of the nineteenth century most plants on the continent, in Great Britain, and in the United States operated under the control of the owner-manager. Plants were small, and few employed more than 500 operatives. The lesser supervisory force were easily promoted from the ranks, just as the superintendent of the plant had usually been a skilled foreman, but these supervisors had little authority to make important decisions: they could hire and fire, train, and make small adjustments to the manufacturing capacity of the plant, but beyond that they were unable to go. In general, the foremen were not looked upon as a part of management but as a category of skilled worker, for the work they did was seen as operative rather than as managing — and they were paid accordingly.

◇   ◇   ◇   ◇   ◇

In the early part of the nineteenth century, a small number of clerical workers helped the owner-manager; but by the twentieth century probably the greatest change that took place in the organization of the industrial process was the proliferation of clerks until they outnumbered the blue-collar workers. The need to collect and record information was not as important, say, around 1810 or 1820 as it became a century-and-a-half later, when most of the overhead in running a manufacturing plant went to the clerical, supervisory, and executive staffs rather than to the payment of the blue-collar workers. Productivity took place mainly in the manufacturing sheds of the large industries rather than in the board room, the executive offices, or the buildings that housed the proliferating clerical staffs. As products became more complex, as competition became keener, as sales became an important aspect of the firm, the number of individuals who advised the professional manager became much larger: when he had to supply more information to his board of directors, he increased the paperwork of his staff, which had to furnish the information he needed for decision-making. As the government became more important to the professional manager as important customer, as a needed financier, and as a partner in profit-making (through special interest tax loopholes), the more forms had to be filled out, the more files needed to be kept, the more letters had to be written, more contacts kept up, and more clerks and supervisory employees needed to keep track of what was written, what was received, and what the state of health of the plant was. The nineteenth-century factory had generally started as a one-man operation (or sometimes with two or three partners sharing various responsibilities) in which the myriad details of running the plant, knowing who the best customers were, and keeping track of supplies and suppliers, were generally in the mind of the man running the factory with the aid of a general factotum — who copied letters in a round legible hand, acted as bookkeeper, and supervised income and outgo. The factory hired more workers than foremen or supervisory employees, for a plant functioning with 100 workers (a fairly large operation in the middle of the nineteenth century) often had no more than two or three supervisory personnel which probably included a clerk to keep the records. While government and commerce used more clerical employees (though nothing like the number employed today), factories well past the middle of the last century seemed to operate and make money for their owners and partners with a very small staff.

The standard of living of both workers and supervisory personnel was fairly low until the end of the nineteenth century, certainly as compared to the one enjoyed today. It is difficult to compare the standards of living of skilled or unskilled workers in the same country over a period of a century, for there is little information as to what the pound or the dollar bought in 1800 in contrast to 1974. Keeping exact statistics and asking questions of this kind did not begin until after 1850. At that time, the British unskilled worker rarely had more than one or two rooms (with none of the facilities that one takes for granted in the 1970's). Food was mostly starchy with large amounts of bread and potatoes in the daily diet. Meat was a rarity with fish and shellfish only slightly less so. Meat was generally eaten as sausage, and the sanitary conditions under which it was made far from good. Necessities which workers take for granted in the 1970's were completely absent in the first decades of the nineteenth century. Gas may have been used for illumination in the houses of the urban wealthy, in large meeting halls, and on a few important street intersections, but neither miners nor mill workers had it in their houses. Kerosene lamps did not come into existence until after the middle of the century, and electricity not until the beginning of the twentieth century. Indoor plumbing including piped-in water for the kitchen was a late nineteenth or early twentieth-century luxury for the vast majority of workers in England, the continent, and North America.

It is accurate to say that real wages went up perceptibly only toward the end of the nineteenth century. A mill worker in 1830 and one in 1870 received roughly the same real wages, bought chiefly the same foods, wore the same sort of clothing, and lived in a similarly limited amount of space. The profits in the first half of that century went to making the owners and shareowners richer: the rule was that one paid workers the lowest possible wages without depriving oneself of their labor. The rise of the labor union with its pressure upon the employer to increase monetary wages caused a slow increase in the standard of living. In the United States, an awareness of the depth of the mass market encouraged manufacturers to look upon the workers of other manufacturers as consumers for their products, in addition to the limited market of merchants, government officials, supervisory employees, and professionals. The increase in productivity that occurred in the second half of the nineteenth century enlarged the wealth of the owning classes and their retainers to such an extent that some of it could be redistributed, usually as a result of political or union pressures, though often not until after a long and sometimes bloody strike. In the nineteenth century, the wealthy in all industrial countries wanted to hold on to their wealth, and had no desire to share it with the workers. The point of view toward labor was still that of Adam Smith: labor was a commodity that had to be bought as cheaply as possible, although the labor performed had to be sold to the consumer at as high a price as the market afforded. The struggle to obtain a share of the higher productivity created by better designed machines, more efficient work layout, energy-saving materials handling, and a greater volume of production at a small unit cost led to lengthy strikes in England, France, the United States, Germany, and Belgium — and also to new political movements that had as their goal the redistribution of wealth. In general, one can say that the large amount of wealth that accrued to the entrepreneurs was translated into more capital for the enterprises, into larger princely mansions, and into a series of trust funds that would make the descendants as wealthy as the original wealth-builders.

◇   ◇   ◇   ◇   ◇

The old aristocracies lost out to the new entrepreneurial middle class, and the traditions of inherited titles and privileges played second fiddle to the new heritage of wealth. Two or more generations of wealth when combined with university education guaranteed one a position in the upper class in almost all the new industrial countries, including the United States. In the latter country it was not the descendants of the eighteenth-century merchants who became members of the new upper-class elite, but descendants of the nineteenth-century financiers who had managed to hand on enough wealth to their descendants to permit them to live on their annual increments as seventeenth- and eighteenth-century aristocrats did in the luxury of their day.

After the middle of the nineteenth century, the United States quickly became a model of the industrialized nation. Growth based upon finance led the large cities to become headquarters for the big industrial corporations, the stock markets, and the industries supplying information to the industrialists and the country as a whole. By the 1870's, the United States had not only surpassed Great Britain as an industrial nation, but had also taken the lead in applying technological discoveries to mass production. France even more than England had been the pioneer in introducing the manufacture of interchangeable parts. (As I have already mentioned, the automated pin factory that Adam Smith described in 1776 in *The Wealth of Nations* had existed in France by 1762: Thomas Jefferson in a letter written in 1785 from Versailles described the operation of a musket plant run by a M. Le Blanc, which preceded the plant established by Eli Whitney in 1797 in New Haven, Connecticut, although the latter factory had better financing and a more reliable customer in the United States War Department.)

The factory throughout most of the nineteenth century was a paternalistic family domain in which the enterprise was considered an adjunct to the family rather than as an enterprise in its own right with its own goals and management. The modern corporation whose ideological roots lay in the religious and military organizations of the past is more a phenomenon of the twentieth century. In the nineteenth-century British, French, German, American, Italian, or Russian family firms (which is what most were at that time), the employees were considered as being in the same category as hired hands or servants. Their loyalty was to the head of the family firm, just as the servant had to be submissive and loyal to his master. Communication was one-sided, from top down, and attempts on the part of the hired hands to suggest any improvements for running the business would have been resented as "impertinence or insubordination," terms still applied in the twentieth century. Although the workers certainly knew their jobs better than the employer, few were able to participate in decisions which concerned them; the decisions were the prerogatives of entrepreneurs and the heads of the family firms. But one advantage which the family firm had was that the members of the family could criticize without being considered "insubordinate." The firm was the place where one placed one's sons, one's nephews, or even sons-in-law. The factory firm was also run by the family as a whole, and one cannot dismiss or discharge the family as one could a paid professional manager (as Henry Ford III did to a president whom he had hired from the outside). Since the profits of the factory went to pay for a daughter's dowry, or to expand the firm so that more relatives could be given employment, management had to be cautious and take few risks. All members of the family could participate in making important decisions, even though those within the firm had more knowledge and could communicate their views more efficiently. In many parts of Europe it was customary to trust only one's family, and so one rarely looked beyond the family for business partners or executives (though this was done often in the United States and Japan, where outsiders were many times considered to be more efficient and less argumentative).

An example of the family firm is that of the Boston Associates which brought together the savings of 15 merchant families and helped to create the first modern textile industry in the United States. Beginning in 1814, the group first hired individuals with technical skills who could build textile mills from scratch. These were considered chiefly as technical servants and were rarely promoted into the executive ranks. From the profits of their first textile mill, the Associates branched into other manufacturing activities connected with the cotton textile industry. As new industries were added to the Family Syndicate, individuals with technical skills were hired but never put into decision-making positions. From 1815 to 1825, the profits averaged about 20 percent per year. With their profits the families bought into newer and more diversified industries (but only after these had undergone their pioneering trial-and-error period) with each family supplying the top decision-making executives from within its ranks. By the middle of the century, the descendants of the 15 families owned more than one-third of all the cotton spindles in New England and had a top managing voice in all of the New England railroads, most of the Boston banks (which needed to invest the money derived from the large profits made by Salem and Boston merchants in the China, Philippine, and Sumatra trade from the 1780's through the 1840's), and most of the New England insurance companies (including the wealthy ones in Hartford that had grown because of the need of the early entrepreneurs to protect themselves from unforeseen risks caused by weather, death, or accident). As a result of the profits made by these enterprises the families descended from the original Associates were able to supply a large part of the capital needed to build railroads westward from Boston to Chicago, so that goods manufactured in New England could be traded for the raw materials which it did not have — grain, timber, coal, and livestock.

The first three generations of most of these entrepreneurial families generally worked hard at being the executives and over-all managers; later generations were dependent upon others to do the managing as they moved into differing activities, though they still controlled the hiring and firing of the professionals whose services they needed. While they no longer managed their financial interests directly, their influence was exercised indirectly, and they branched out to become decision-makers in the fields of education, politics, and public opinion. They themselves were better educated than their ancestors or the rest of the population, and their wealth and credentials (obtained in higher education) placed them in the new aristocracy of an American upper class, according to public opinion and the concensus of American sociologists. They ran for political office but were not as successful in competing for public affection as the children of the poor, who had moved into the lower middle class and with whom more Americans could identify emotionally. Although they did not manage directly, the new aristocracy had the finances to buy the media of information and to disseminate opinions much closer to their own. They had the wealth also to finance the candidates for political office who reflected their points of view, though the majority of voters were those who were attempting to take advantage of the Open Society that America claimed to be.

The descendants of the nineteenth-century entrepreneurs not only had the wealth for which others envied them, but the security and independence which went with the possession of this wealth. They were beholden to no man for their daily living, and were envied by the rest of the population who hoped that one day they too could be free of "bosses" and able to be their own master. Having a good deal of money implies to the rest of the population freedom to be oneself, to be able to tell superiors to "go to the Devil." The accumulation of money implied an enhancement of one's social status. When men were freed from money worries, they could apply themselves to doing what they had always wanted to do. Financial independence in the twentieth century became an important political goal, and parties competed with one another to add new provisions to Bismarck's welfare state so that the old could have more adequate financial protection, unemployment and sickness not lead a family to destitution, and financial instability would not lead to loss of faith in a nation's currency or economy. Conversely, financial security as an index of one's status was considered to be one of the most important "rights" which an individual could obtain.

XIII The Spread of Twentieth Century Technological Ideas

The Industrial and Scientific civilization with its high degree of urbanization and literacy, its complex organization of men, and its links through transportation and communication is more of a twentieth-century than a nineteenth-century phenomenon. The city with its satellite suburbs became a symbol of the new civilization during the first half of the twentieth century. At that time, even the most bypassed area felt the effect of the chemical and weapons technology of modern war. By the middle of the twentieth century, universities had proliferated everywhere, including the newly independent developing nations. Students throughout the world numbered in the millions. During the nineteenth century universities had been small with few subjects and few professors, and with students by the end of the century numbering a few hundred thousand. Until 1860, universities were mainly centers to prepare students for the ministry, law, or medicine. Few scientists came out of the universities and few courses were taught in the sciences primarily because the general physical and biological sciences were still in their pioneering stages, while the social sciences were limited to a few courses in economics or were combined with philosophy.

The impetus toward learning took place in the second half of the nineteenth century when professorial chairs were established in the new sciences. These were few and the professors holding them could have all attended a convention in a small hotel of that day without feeling crowded. Schools of science and engineering were separated from the military training of civil engineers, and were generally established in the second half of the nineteenth century. But it was the Land Grant or Morrill Act of 1862 that provided financing for the proliferation of new state-run universities in the United States to teach the practical and applied in the "mechanical and agricultural" aspects of human learning. In Europe, science had become respectable as part of university learning; in the United States, where each religious denomination had established colleges with faculties of fewer than ten instructors, or "professors" and with no more than 100 students, science was at the end of the nineteenth century still viewed as a secular heresy. These "colleges" had not been established to encourage the students and their teachers to explore together the new frontiers of the intellectual revolution, but rather to perpetuate denominational creeds. Education was still for the elites, and little formal training was necessary for the vast majority of farmers, workers, and small businessmen in the emerging industrial nations. Not until the middle of the twentieth century did most of the population in the latter have as much as an elementary school education. Japan and Germany, however, were among the newly emerging industrial nations that did achieve almost complete literacy of their populations at an elementary level, though the standard was low compared to what was required in the next century.

In the nineteenth century, as a result of a combination of factors including improved transportation, an extraordinary increase of trade, the invention of new and fast means of communication through the telegraph and later the telephone, cities in the industrialized areas of the world grew rapidly in numbers and beyond the capabilities existent in Primary civilization, when it took a large rural population to support cities of 20,000 to 100,000. In the eighteenth century, only national capitals were able to collect as many as 800,000 people (cities such as London, Paris, and Tokyo). The figures given for Medieval Chinese or Indian cities need to be taken with some doubt, for it is unlikely that any Indian or Chinese city before the beginning of the nineteenth century had as many as 150,000 to 200,000 inhabitants.

The development of the Erie Canal in New York State in the late 1820's increased the population of both New York and Buffalo, while it was the introduction of the railroad and lake steamships that made possible the growth of Chicago. In 1850, New York had only 700,000 inhabitants living within its metropolitan area, while Chicago had about 50,000. Philadelphia and its suburbs contained over 400,000, while Boston had a little more than 200,000. The American cities grew as immigrants swarmed in to take advantage of the need for unskilled labor in manning the factories. Little land was available to those who came to the United States after 1845, for the best land had already been sold by land companies and speculators to the older native stock as far west as Iowa and Louisiana. Poorer land was available for another three to four decades in Texas and states to the West. The buying and selling of land without hindrance from the state was considered one of the great human rights to be protected by the force of law and the power of the state.

The cities which acquired more than one million inhabitants during the second half of the nineteenth century expanded when new forms of municipal wealth permitted waterworks, sewage, gas lighting, and urban transportation. London experimented with running steam engines and passenger cars through shallow underground tubes, while New York built elevated railways above the streets. Cable tramways dotted many American and European cities, and the electric tram or trolley after the late 1880's united the various sections of the growing metropolis by a network of rails. The steamship also came into its own during the second half of the nineteenth century, for until 1850 steamships used their sails as much as their engines. Clipper ships without the aid of steam were operated in large numbers almost to the end of the nineteenth century.

The major cities served as financial and industrial centers, though most industries were established away from the large eighteenth-century port towns and national capitals — where they would have encountered interference from the artisan guilds who resented their competition. The factory areas were generally located near rural sources of labor. With the rising tide of immigration in the second half of the nineteenth century, however, they were established near sources of supply, convenient harbors, and railroad junctions. The industrialization of France and Germany resulted in industrial centers becoming important cities in their own right. In Paris, Berlin, and St. Petersburg, industrial rings developed as suburbs, encouraging the new workers to seek housing near the industrial plants (municipal transportation was used more by the new middle classes than by the poverty-stricken workers). In Japan, the cities of Tokyo, Osaka, Nagoya, and Kobe became industrial areas when production began to expand under the command economy of the Meiji period and as the peasants were able to increase their agricultural productivity — thus releasing their surplus workers to employment in the new factories, military services, and government bureaucracies.

Throughout the world, the effect of the new civilization was greatest upon the peoples who were subject to European rule. In India, merchants built small factories to supply the market created by the presence of the British. The British port cities of Calcutta, Madras, and Bombay attracted large numbers from the rural areas. In Africa areas around port cities were filled with tribesmen hoping to find ways to enhance their status and increase their standard of living. Large numbers of Chinese emigrated to the Philippines, Indonesia, Malaysia, and Vietnam to supply the growing markets and to find opportunities to work marginally for those who exported raw materials to Europe and imported goods from that continent. Soon the Chinese themselves began to participate as small middlemen between the natives and the Europeans. In China, sources of British, French, German, American, and Japanese capital introduced small enterprises in the port cities to take advantage of what was believed to be the immense Chinese market. Around the port cities and in the new extraterritorial areas of the urban conglomerations, the Chinese learned about phases of the new Industrial and Scientific civilization. Many trained themselves and their children to work with the knowledge which the Europeans,

Americans, and Japanese had brought to their shores, even though the Chinese felt humiliated that they had to learn from those who brought technical knowledge with their missionaries and warships.

In Russia and Eastern Europe, the new civilization spread with the railways, and through the need of the growing urban areas to import more food for their burgeoning populations. Though Eastern Europe and Russia remained overwhelmingly peasant throughout the nineteenth century, the increase in population resulting from better control of age-old epidemics sent many sons and daughters to the cities in search of work. The foreign settlements where the English, German, and French traders had been encouraged to remain also became the disseminating points for the new knowledge arriving from Western Europe. Peter the Great's feat in forcing the sons of Boyars to become receptive to the new learning also encouraged discontent among their descendants with the obscurantism and technical inefficiency of the Old Russia in contrast to Western Europe and America — thus producing even more receptivity to sweeping changes in the political, social, and economic framework of the aristocratic-peasant society. The slow increase in agricultural productivity, coupled with a rise in income, encouraged many of the middlemen and well-to-do peasants to keep their standard of living fairly constant while at the same time increasing their savings both in land and in money deposited in the new banks. The latter in turn helped finance railways, plants for the manufacture of railway equipment, and suppliers for the various governments whose expenditures for the military, police forces, and the expanding civil service grew enormously after the middle of the century. The new industrialization of Central and Eastern Europe resulted as much from the command economics inaugurated by their governments to enhance their military, and thus their international bargaining power, as it did from new entrepreneurs who took advantage of growing technical knowledge to help supply the expanding internal market. The Japanese Government used its powers of taxation, the export of silk (at a time when silk was at a premium because of a virus disease that had wiped out most of the silkworms in Italy and France), and increases in agricultural production to build up industrialization after 1868.

The new missionaries of industrialization were merchants, railroad builders, printers of books, and a few officials within the native governments themselves. As was perhaps true in the spread of agriculture thousands of years earlier, or in the diffusion of civilization, the original carriers were those who had been trained in its techniques. British and American engineers helped build Russian railroads in the early 1850's; British mechanics and engineers established textile mills in the United States, France, Germany, and Russia. Americans and Russians in large numbers studied in

German universities, bringing back the knowledge which they acquired in the lecture halls and from the books printed by the universities. Japanese and Chinese students studied in Great Britain, France, Germany, and the United States, learning to internalize the new intellectual culture of the universities. Even the missionaries sent out from Great Britain, the United States, Germany, and France brought the knowledge of the Industrial and Scientific civilization along with the creeds of their various churches. Most missionaries emphasized literacy in order that their religious messages could be read, but the indirect result was to open up for the student the mysteries of the printed page. The new ideas of socialism, technology, science, and democracy also came via the typescript.

◇   ◇   ◇   ◇   ◇

The British settled in India, Malaysia, and Africa; the French in Algeria, Southeast Asia, and West Africa; the Dutch in Indonesia; the Americans in China, Japan, and Latin America; all acting as models for the natives to emulate. Their standards of living, technology, and thoughts soon became known to a large percentage of the populations among whom they had settled. The elites in the underdeveloped areas sent their sons to acquire the techniques of Western knowledge, though often the sons brought back ideas of revolutionary change which caused them to react against their own cultural worlds.

In Eastern Europe, the influences emanating from France and Germany swept through the small Jewish settlements in the rural areas, encouraging many of the younger generation to move to the growing cities where they could be freer. The interaction between the two built up a reaction against the obscurantism of Orthodox Judaism and the stifling intellectual climate of the ghetto, thus supporting the more rebellious younger sons and daughters in their effort to identify with the new spirit of cultural and political change in order to be released from their traditional loyalties. Although at first they linked themselves with the new spirit of internationalism brought about by the concepts of the French Revolution, they were soon brought up sharp by the rising wave of petty nationalisms sweeping all of Europe at a time when men were searching for an identity in a century of rapid and terrifying changes. In the ghettos of Eastern Europe, socialism and a nostalgic messianism combined to form a secular Zionist nationalistic crusade in which the Jews sought their own ethnic identities.

Through the nineteenth century, nationalisms based upon shared goals, descent, and commonality of religion and speech rushed through Europe as both socialism — with its international superordinate goals — and the concepts of the French Revolution spread their ideas across borders in a quest for followers and organized strength. The aims of nationalism and socialism seemed to combine, as did the commonality of religion, language, and goals, with the ideas of self-realization and self-determination. Most of the European populations yearned for a brotherhood based upon discovering new relatives rather than upon a synthetic brotherhood based upon adjusting to aliens who were strangers. While some hoped for a Europe containing no borders, others wanted barriers erected to put a great social distance between themselves and those whom they considered as aliens. The growth of cities with their migrations of large numbers of peasant children also attracted foreigners from across national borders who sought the treasure that they hoped to find at the foot of the urban rainbow. While the peasants hoped to find the brotherhood and community that they had failed to find in the villages, the aliens were a reminder that the growth of cities encouraged an influx of strangers who disturbed their dream of finding common interests within the urban factories and workshops. The search for a sense of community, combined with the frustrations involved in adjusting to a world of strangers, encouraged narrow forms of nationalism wherein the strangers were made responsible for the daily frustrations which accompanied urban life. In France, Germany, Austria-Hungary, and Russia, the urban world became the center for new growths of linguistic nationalism through which men sought to recover the sense of community which they believed existed in the past before factories and wage labor had come to destroy it. The peasant village of the past was viewed as a lost but nostalgic childhood and became the basis for a new nationalism that united the descendants of those who had left it, giving them a sense of community, purpose, and social esteem. One no longer needed to adjust to a world of strangers, for one could fall back upon relatives, rediscovering them and bringing them back into a large extended family — wherein the latter became the ideal of the government itself.

Linguistic and religious nationalisms and the rising tide of ideological and messianic socialism with all of its manifold varieties were the answers provided by the nineteenth-century peasant and artisan world to the new civilization of industrialization, urbanization, and science. The latter's alienation, creation of new elites, perpetual insecurities, and economic depressions accompanied by unemployment, lockouts, inflation, and the impact of science, undermined traditional values with the force of nature-made crises. The need to find solace (or brother figures to comfort one) led not to superordinate goals that would unite a Europe that had been torn apart for centuries, but served instead to exacerbate the distinctiveness that had been born out of different linguistic, cultural, and historic conditions. The desire to escape centralized authority that brought punishment rather than gratification led to nineteenth-century ideologies and blue-prints for a twentieth-century future. But these turned out in this century to be more tyrannical, more alienating, and even less conducive to the growth of human freedom and personal achievement. The desire to reconstruct the lost extended family to one that embraced most of urban society only succeeded in making the state more repressive than even the father had been, with the new brothers and the rest of the reconstituted family enforcing the authoritarianism of the father rather than cooperating to replace it. The dreams of socialism before 1910 led in 1917 to a tyrannical authoritarianism under that label that did even less to enhance personal freedom and achievement than the nineteenth-century autocratic despots, though it was more efficiently organized and more thoroughly repressive. The ideology of nationalism, in which each individual had to submerge his personal desires so that he could work more enthusiastically for the higher status, liberty, and sense of community which only the state could possess, led to World Wars I and II, to Communism, Fascism, Nazism, the Co-Asian Prosperity Sphere, and the uneasy peace and proliferation of military dictators which followed all of these.

Despite the increase in standard of living that accompanied the Industrial and Scientific civilization and the rapid increase in literacy (the proliferation of printing presses put out enormous quantities of newspapers, magazines, and books), the new civilization seemed unable to formulate ideas designed to lessen tensions between men and the societies that they had created. Men still turned to the pre-scientific past for their values, norms, and hopes for the future. Although they saw the Industrial Age as expanding opportunities to develop their human potential, the frame of reference in developing industrial society remained that of traditional religion and the military. The hierarchies that had gone hand in hand in developing the religious, military, and civil bureaucracies of the Ancient World were also used in organizing the new industrial plant, government, educational systems, and media of communication. Men seemed continuously to turn to the past for their inspiration, even though that past had proven to be frustrating for those who looked to it for guidelines for future living. Men still seemed to view the world from the perspective of Hebrew nationalism in the second century B.C., or from the rising tide of exclusiveness and particularism that accompanied the development of Christian dogmas in the third and fourth centuries A.D. Even in the twentieth century, the new ideologies of nationalism and socialism went back to the eighteenth and nineteenth centuries to their ideological founding fathers for their standard operating procedures, precedents, and limitations.

The new civilization of industrialization and science swept through the developing nations and encouraged new nationalist movements that accented tribalism in order to separate their followers from those who were categorized as having another descent and another identity. The new nationalisms repeated the mistakes of the old: they urbanized and industrialized and established more schools and universities, but they used all these to enhance the power of the authoritarian state by employing industry and science to give more advantages to the military, and of the police to keep the strength of the state from falling into other hands. The organization of men went further than in the ancient Primary civilization. Although the latter could be overthrown because of its organizational weaknesses, both from within and from without, the various elites of the new civilization were able to gather enormous power into their hands to make certain that their hierarchical privileges would not be diluted, and the organization of the state affected by the discontent that might exist on the outside. The new civilization freed man from the mental tyrannies of the past, but at the price of placing new fetters on the freedom to disagree, dissent, or explore new intellectual horizons in the quest for options in decision-making.

The development of new social forms and of norms based upon fresh concepts, brought about by scholarly progress in human thought, moved slowly. At the same time, the frustrations of the urban world led to the centralization of authority and knowledge with more subtle forms of repressing that which contradicted official policy and thought. Men who govern usually possess little knowledge upon which to base their decisions. Although science proliferated its laboratories, much scientific thought was employed in developing better weapons systems, more efficient intelligence-gathering, and new technical concepts to help the thought-police in their surveillance of dissent.

◊   ◊   ◊   ◊   ◊

In the long history of cultural growth men tend to make necessary social changes too late. Problems multiply while the knowledge vital to dealing with them seems to stagnate. Although it is not possible to fault mankind for having waited until comparatively recent times to develop the social intelligence to make communal living more secure, efficient, and rewarding, it is nevertheless true that the greatest enemy to humankind has been procrastination cloaked in tradition. Only in the past two centuries have men begun to carry on research in order to seek new knowledge, but this research has had to be based upon a fundamental change in social thinking. One cannot carry on research on man, his universe, and the problems facing him within this universe unless one has accepted an agnostic point of view toward the concept of knowledge. If one assumes that knowledge is a matter of gnostic revelation emanating from a deity or deities, then one can only wait until the latter are willing to further human knowledge by providing the proper explanations through revelation. This assumption presupposes an unconfident, immature mankind that can no more gather information by itself than can a child. The analogy with the parent, or the adult teacher, becomes somewhat apparent when one places man in a child-like stance vis-a-vis a more paternal deity figure who in his own time will instruct the child-man in what he needs to know, with bits and pieces parceled out as the child masters the lessons already given him.

Although the ancient Greeks speculated about man and his universe, the thought was not based upon empirical evidence but more upon revelations or spiritual insights. Even the ancient Hebrew prophets obtained their insights through trances. Chinese and Indian thought was also based upon preconceived abstractions obtained through analogies with other traditional concepts. It was held that men could not control their destinies or the physical world about them, although the deities could — and so proper prayer and rituals had to be engaged in to get the deity or deities to assist man, though here the deity or deities could refuse such aid if they felt insulted in any way by man's indifference or rudeness to them. Men would survive only by doing what the deity had in mind for them; disobedience led to death, to unspecified punishment, to natural disturbances set in motion by the deities who control them.

From the seventeenth century on, man began to change the presuppositions of his thinking. Although in the past he had been willing to accept the creation of the universe by a deity, he now felt that it was necessary for him to discover what it was that the deity had wrought. The deity had given man intelligence with which to reason, and reason would unlock the secrets and mysteries of the universe which would in the long run help man to resolve his problems and tensions. The answers existed in nature, if men would only look for them. The key to the mysteries of nature lay in reason which would unlock nature's code. But rather than wait for the deity to signal whom he would use as his messenger, thinkers in the eighteenth century insisted that anyone could become the unraveller of the secrets of the universe if he were willing to use his mind to fathom them.

In England, on the other hand, men arose who insisted that pure reason was not enough, that men could observe only what existed in their daily experiences, and that it was far more essential that men learn to interrelate their observations if they were to draw the necessary conclusions. Both French and British scholars agreed that the world was rational, open to careful examination, and its operation capable of being analyzed logically. Both also agreed that man possessed the intellectual capacity to analyze how the universe functioned and what its laws of physical behavior were. Observation, replication, and the ability to form abstract generalizations of the observed interrelated facts were part of the thinking that made possible the eighteenth-century world of science.

This world of science was seventeenth- and eighteenth-century European in its formation. By the nineteenth century, it had developed a frame of reference based upon an indifference to first causes, although its scientific methodology employed observation, experiment, replication, and theoretical insights that derived from a study of observable facts. Scientific thought as it emerged in the nineteenth century, and was elaborated upon in the twentieth, was based upon models which could often be put only in mathematical terms and which were basically abstractions of concepts utilized as steppingstones to further investigation of phenomena requiring focus in order to be studied. This type of thinking was foreign to that of the Ancient World, and was even alien to that of the vast majority of Europeans and North Americans living during these two centuries. Scientific conclusions though abstract are tentative and subject continuously to verification based upon observation, a process of thought alien to most Europeans and North Americans (whose world of familiarity was and is often based upon data unverifiable on the basis of observation, but used instead to verify observations). Before the nineteenth century it had become traditional to start off with "laws" about the phenomena of nature and the organization of human behavior, and then attempt to force all new data into already-held patterns of thought.

Science and scientific thought went hand in hand with the thinking which lay behind the rise of industrialization. As early as the 1760's, the French Academy argued that research on nature had to be rational and useful. In England, the Royal Society was concerned that research increase the industrial as well as the agricultural wealth of the nation. The practical mechanic could only go so far in devising a new machine or new tool before it became necessary to develop abstract concepts combining the practical and theoretical with a new synthesis to enable the machine to become more efficient. A steam engine could only be improved upon by better theories of heat explaining in detail how energy derived from steam could be employed efficiently.

Although the Church had no objection to the improvement of steam engines, it opposed physical studies that led to an interpretation of the universe entirely different from that which it taught. The Church objected to studies indicating that the earth had developed independently from the theory taught as religious dogma by the authorities, and it reacted strenuously to the investigation of the biological nature of man indicating a close relationship between all forms of life plus cause-and-effect relationships at variance with those taught by tradition.

As science was difficult for the European or North American to grasp, because it went against all the familiar and traditional forms of thought, so was it difficult for the new Industrial and Scientific civilization to disseminate its culture and universalistic ways of thinking and behaving. The new science came into confrontation with the old traditions in Europe and North America, as it still does in the bypassed backwaters of both continents. The carriers of the new and those who had internalized the old thus looked upon one another as almost implacable enemies. The conflict became an either/or phenomenon: the individual must accept or reject one or the other.

The twentieth-century compromise was to put the concepts of both in separate and completely distinct worlds, though in reality the concepts of one gradually seeped into the world of ideas of the other. On both continents and in both centuries, there was a gradual move away from the traditional concepts about man and nature, and a greater sophistication of thought based upon the concepts derived from scientific observation and ideas that had been put under scholarly analysis. In the early nineteenth century, individuals who subjected the Bible to scholarly analysis were ostracised from academic society, but by the end of that century such objective study was slowly accepted. In the middle of the twentieth century, some nineteenth-century findings were incorporated into the thought of educated men, but they were still not quite accepted by the less educated followers of fundamentalist and orthodox religions.

The scientific world is still in its infancy. Although science has made great strides in opening up unknown worlds to the observing and practiced scholarly eye, it has not been able to translate its findings into concepts that have meaning for man in his everyday social life. Most decisions made by administrators, government officials, parents, teachers, and employers are not based upon scientific data, evidence, or thinking. The political decisions which affect the destiny of the people in the United States, the Soviet Union, Great Britain, or any other country have little to do with scientific experimentation, theorizing, findings, concepts, or even the research carried on by the subordinates to the political figures holding high office. Although science affects the technological and medical worlds, it seems to have little influence upon the everyday thinking of most of the populations or most of the executives in the highly developed nations of the world. (The facts of science, however, are slowly but surely infiltrating the thought processes of most people in Europe and North America.)

In interrelationships between nations, thought is still traditional — including the balance of power concept held by statesmen in the early part of the nineteenth century. There is still little identification in goals among the people of one nation and those of another. The problems faced by the population of a developing area elicit little interest from those fortunate enough to live in developed nations. The poor of any country are still viewed as social failures and there is little practical desire to help them raise their educational and economic levels.

If men do not see those outside their in-group in tribalistic fashion, they all too often tend to view them from a racist point of view as if they were a different species of men. The world as seen by physicists, biologists, or social scientists is not quite the same as that viewed by most inhabitants of the developed and the underdeveloped nations. Scientific thinking may perhaps be the frame of reference for individuals in the twenty-first or twenty-second centuries, but thus far in the developed and developing nations it does not appear to provide guidelines for either national or international thought.

Two bloody wars in the twentieth century have only led to a series of small ones. The gas chambers and the provincialism intrinsic in authoritarian nationalism have condemned to death or helplessness over a million Armenians, hundreds of thousands of Greeks, millions of Jews, millions of Chinese, tens of thousands of Biafrans, thousands of Hutis in Burundi, more than a million Moslems in India, hundreds of thousands of Bengalis in Bangladesh, hundreds of thousands of Hindus in Pakistan, millions of Vietnamese — and made helpless hundreds of thousands of those of Asian Indian descent in East Africa and tens of thousands of dissenters in the Communist countries. It was not a Nazi Germany that became "Judenrein," or free of Jews, but a Communist Poland in the 1960's. Past conflicts and their mythologies continue to haunt men's minds, and the unscientific belief that non-humans exist outside one's particular in-group is still with us today.

Although of no present use, it is nonetheless interesting to speculate on what would have happened in the twentieth century if Roger Bacon and John Wycliffe had inaugurated a trend wherein scientific thought and democratic egalitarianism had come into the world in the fifteenth rather than in the beginning of the seventeenth century. Supposing also that the movement for egalitarianism and democratic political representation had begun in Europe in the fifteenth or sixteenth centuries rather than in the late seventeenth and eighteenth centuries, it is more than likely that the problems facing Europe and North America at present could have been better resolved. Since it is not possible to go back to undo the errors and mistaken decisions made by generations in previous centuries, it is a tragedy for the billions of human beings living in the last decades of the twentieth century and for the tens of billions who will live during the next century that the Industrial and Scientific civilization did not have its beginnings 500, 1,000, or even 1,500 years ago so that the problems now facing the developing nations might have been resolved one or more centuries ago.

Since life is precious for all individuals (and since there are no second or third chances for men to undo the errors of their past and begin again, though with the wisdom which they had learned through the years), men who are not allowed to control their destinies to their satisfaction are doomed to lead useless, tragic, and senseless lives. For most of the world's population, men's lives from the beginning have been dependent upon the mistaken decisions and fateful judgments of those who knew little more than those who were their subordinates. The inability of men to assume complete responsibility for directing their own lives and those of others has led to the pursuit of self-interest and decision-making based upon tradition and precedent rather than upon the mathematical number of options theoretically available. On the assumption that knowledge was in existence if only men could find it, the seventeenth- and eighteenth-century intellectual explorers had sought out the unknown. But in the Medieval World men had assumed that everything that needed to be known was already available if one could only delve into the Wisdom of the Ancients to discover their sources of information. Age was associated with knowledge, which was seen as finite, already discovered, and chiefly available to the elderly sages, chieftains, priests, prophets, or ordinary philosophers. Succeeding generations were looked upon as children who lacked the keys to open this storehouse of wisdom.

Their diffidence toward the past caused men to spend their lives repeating the mythology of the Ancient World and the past theoretical understanding of the universe of man and nature which only the ancient sages had mastered, and this despite the fact that a technology — developed in the Medieval period — had pushed men in the twelfth through the fourteenth centuries much further into a more complex and sophisticated mechanical world. The Church suppressed men's attempts to explore the heavens above them, the earth under their feet, or the ideas which human beings had created around them. As in the case of later authoritarian regimes, the Church policed all attempts to detract from its legitimacy as the holder of all truths that men needed to live by. Later, the Counter-Reformation prevented the Industrial and Scientific Age from being disseminated through the Italian and Iberian Peninsulas, though the roots of this civilization had grown in the urban cultures of these two areas.

The Industrial and Scientific civilization needed a strong religious authority to struggle against, with support coming from those elites in the population who wanted to see the power of the Church reduced. It is difficult to pinpoint the causes of the industrial and scientific development in Europe after the seventeenth century as against their absence in China, India, Persia, or Turkey. Certainly the greater social prestige given in Europe than in Asia to merchants and guildmasters of wealth had much to do with it, along with the opportunities available for merchant-technicians to seek greater status for themselves in a somewhat unstable social and political world. There was also a receptivity among those in authority toward using the knowledge which had created the social wealth to reinforce their political power. But the growth of science required a new form of iconoclastic thinking (non-existent outside of Western Europe at that time) which assumed that rigid observations could lead to new insights not available before. The assumption motivating the Scientific Revolution was that man had grown wise and strong enough to pierce the mysteries of nature (without the intermediaries of priests and a church) and through his discoveries would produce knowledge that could contradict that held by the Church. The great religions without an authoritarian center were unable to follow up on secular observations: guilt that new discoveries might contravene or contradict the wisdom of the Ancients, and thus undermine traditional religion, repressed any of their possible innovations. In Western Europe, men were willing to take the chance of angering religious authority chiefly because they saw the Church as being composed of men similar to themselves — and thus they considered themselves as opposing secular rather than religious authority. The behavior of the priesthood, viewed as being corrupt, unable to live up to religious ideals, unimaginative in serving and in seeing the mysteries of God's handiwork in the world that He created, encouraged the heretical environment in Western Europe wherein science was able to flourish after the fifteenth century. Also present were the desires of secular authorities to weaken the competing authority of the various religious hierarchies within the Church. Although science evolved in the urban areas of northern Italy, France, the Netherlands, Germany, and England, its path to growth contained large pitfalls in the other countries of Europe.

It is difficult to specify why a mechanical age did not develop in Roman times, especially after the experimentation of Hero, Archimedes, Ctesbius, and others. If Rome had been interested in creating its own wealth through an improved agriculture, in manufacturing commodities that could have been used in other areas of the Ancient World, and in carrying on trade with those who lacked the goods which it held, the first steps to this new industrial civilization might have been taken more than a thousand years before. But Rome was uninterested in trade — unlike the Carthaginians, Etruscans, and Greeks — and saw wealth in terms of pillage from conquered areas and captured slaves who could be sold to the highest bidder so that Romans could live off the labor of others.

Considering the large number of glass makers at the turn of the Christian era who experimented with the making of glass in Galilee, Judea, Syria, Rome, and Alexandria, it is strange that no one thought of experimenting with the properties of glass in order to create the convex lens. This had to await the study of optics in the thirteenth century, which led in the seventeenth century to the discovery of the telescope and the microscope, both of which changed man's perspective about the world he inhabited. Could the science of optics have existed a thousand years before? If it could, then mankind might have gained by developing a more secure world for itself.

It is most unfortunate that generations have to pass on before discoveries are made or accepted that could have benefited them. The development of spectacles in the Roman period would have enabled scholarship to have continued over a longer time period in a scholar's life and might have led to further experimentation of the glass lens, perhaps even leading to the discovery of the telescope and microscope a thousand years earlier. If the Chinese blowpipe of the early Christian era could have been known in a Rome that was more receptive to new techniques and to more efficient ways of manufacturing common commodities, perhaps the bellows for a primitive blast furnace might have been discovered hundreds of years earlier than the Medieval period. The development of tools and machines that expanded man's physical skills enormously might have led to the discovery of techniques that were greater than the labor energy of human slaves or domesticated animals. This in turn might have led to the development of more extensive cottage industries utilizing machines and skilled labor to make as well as run them.

If the pioneering work carried on by Roman senators to increase their agricultural production had been taken up by others and furthered as part of a cultural movement, their example might have led to the development of higher economic levels that were not reached until centuries later. Unfortunately, however, the motivation for seeking out information that could have led to agricultural, industrial, and urban revolutions was lacking in the Roman world. Instead the Romans emphasized political and military authority over the large populations that they controlled. In China and India, these motivations were also lacking, and as in Rome the generations could only learn from past ones, repeating errors and operating on the same mistaken conceptions of themselves and the worlds they inhabited.

◇   ◇   ◇   ◇   ◇

At any rate, discoveries are made slowly and in terms of generations rather than in terms of human beings seeking to add to the fundamental accumulation of knowledge in their lifetimes. But if the slow accumulation of knowledge had been hastened by a fraction of a generation, it would certainly have led us to more sophisticated political, economic, and social systems than we possess today. An industrialization spread over the world in the fourteenth century would have encountered less difficulties than an industrialization that is taking place in the twentieth century when populations are over-extended and capital is in the hands of a few. An industrial civilization that could have been disseminated in the eighteenth rather than in the twentieth century would have been able to move into the cultural fabric of small populations rather than those that are over-spilling their limits. An India with 50 or even 150 million would have been in a better position to assimilate the new technical culture than one with 550 to 600 million. A China with 200 million would have been able to adjust itself better to the new forms than one with 800 million. Countries that could live adequately well with populations of no more than 100 to 200 million would have had more time to adjust their inhabitants to the skills, the spatial concepts, and the special thinking that accompanies the necessary development of a technical middle class to handle the management of an industrial civilization.

Further, if the Scientific Revolution had come a few centuries earlier, say in the fourteenth or fifteenth centuries, we might have progressed beyond our present irrational behavior of sinking huge national resources into the weapons of war and developing means of killing that are capable of completely destroying the civilization they are supposed to defend and protect. Perhaps we might also have been able to work out more intelligent means of resolving national and international tensions than by putting the weapons of death into the hands of teenagers charged with the mission of alleviating our political strains by destroying more of our opponents' teenagers than they do of ours. Although we have accepted the values of an industrial civilization, we still have not quite accepted the values leading to observing, experimenting, theorizing, and validating as bases for our daily opinions. Clearly this point of view does not yet apply to protecting the right of all individuals to live and to develop their human potential. For example, the sparse data that we have received from scientific studies have had little effect in inducing individuals to give up cigarettes, to eat balanced meals, and to walk or cycle instead of taking the family car to the corner supermarket to get a case of beer or soft drinks. We still ride to our deaths in complete ignorance of the guidelines for more healthful living. Decisions are still made on issues for which we have very little scientific evidence, for which we have few options, and to which we have given little thought. If the Scientific Age had come a few centuries earlier, perhaps we might have avoided having a Stalin, Hitler, Mussolini, or Franco in the twentieth century (though we naturally would not wish them off on previous centuries). The concentration camps that killed at least 20 to 25 million (if not more) in the Soviet Union and Nazi Germany might not have occurred in this century. Certainly modern man would not have believed the nonsense of "Nordic" intelligence or "Aryan" personality if adequate knowledge of what man is had existed in this century. We would not have had black slavery lasting until the last decades of the nineteenth century (or until the last decades of the twentieth in many of the bypassed Arab countries). The totalitarianism of present-day Communism with its emphasis upon tradition and a conservative political elite might have been avoided by a more successful attempt to deal with the inequalities of the modern-day age with its risks for those with set wages, its lack of democracy in the work place, and its organizational hierarchies of corporate and governmental bureaucracies. The information which we now need to make this a more secure world for the global mass of citizens might have been discovered in this century if we had started long ago to create the Industrial and Scientific civilization.

At any rate, there is little doubt that the present generation of world citizens is paying a higher price because those making the decisions which determine their degree of personal freedom make them on the basis of an abysmal lack of knowledge of alternatives available for decision-making purposes. The knowledge which our descendants will have 200 years hence is sorely needed today; yet generations will be born, live, and die without having the benefit of this knowledge. Its lack is due to the conservatism, the overwhelming absence of imagination, and the fossilized bureaucracies which have been governing mankind century after century, with the emphasis upon preserving traditional authority and seeing to it that fateful decisions are generally made by mediocrities (rather than by those more concerned to seek the best knowledge available for the decisions that would benefit the largest number of individuals in the world today).

Because of the unimaginative, mediocre, and traditional leadership that has cursed mankind for the last few centuries — including many today in the educational, industrial, governmental, and even scientific fields — hundreds of millions, if not billions, of men and women waste their human potential living dull, emotionally empty, boring, traditional lives. Instead of work that permits human creativity with each day being different from the one before, we have work that dulls the mind, that forces individuals to escape by turning to entertainment which makes them feel that they are momentarily living a different life. The media that entertain rather than inform, that serve as opiates rather than as stimulants, that are concerned with trivia rather than opportunities to expand human potential reflect this unimaginative world in which most lives are wasted, in which emotional emptiness is the rule rather than the exception, and in which entertainment in terms of sports, television, or the dreams of the movies become the only means whereby harassed and confused individuals can feel some hope for escaping the numbing lives that most are asked to lead.

Mankind today has lost the religious autonomy which Paleolithic men created with magic to control their lives and manipulate the forces of nature. As civilization began to develop, man was increasingly pushed into a role of dependency upon powerful deities who ruled through authoritarian chieftains, kings, and dictators. Only in the past few centuries did he begin to see that necessary ideas had to come from himself; that there were no deities waiting to advise him when the time was ripe. It was ideas that he himself developed that let him move forward to the goals which he himself decided upon. Only in the past few centuries have men seen that the legitimacy of authority derives from themselves and that they need to award this approval only to those actions that reflect their desires and chances for personal growth. Rather than accepting non sequiturs as answers to their wishes for more personal freedom, men need to be more specific about those rights which they give one another. This is necessary if they are to increase their sense of well-being, to promote their personal growth, and to stimulate their imaginations — all essential to articulating the problems which they have created for themselves plus those produced by their first priority of having to live in a physical world to which they must adapt.

The Secondary civilization of industrialization and science was thus an adaptation brought about by the need of European and North American man to struggle against traditional, hierarchical, and centralized authority. Out of this conflict between those who wanted more status and those who already had it (but who refused to give up so much as a fraction of authority), men began to work out new techniques for creating greater status and wealth than had existed in the past. If this conflict had developed hundreds of years before, it is probable that the quest for wealth would have still sent men searching for the unknown and uncharted areas of the world, as the Vikings in the tenth century sought out the new lands of Iceland, Greenland, and Vinland. Explorations to the outer regions might have taken place in the thirteenth century as Venetians, Genoans, and Portuguese sought new paths to the wealth and trade of the East. If the Chinese had been able to develop an interest in areas outside their country, perhaps their attempts to explore the Malayan areas and the coastal region of East Africa in the fourteenth century might also have led to the discovery of the Pacific regions of the New World during that and the next century. We know that the Phoenicians reached the Azores by the sixth century B.C., one-third of the way across the Atlantic. It is possible that some stray ships blown off course might have reached the New World at that date, or perhaps even earlier. None of these exploratory trips would have led to the ventures of the fifteenth and sixteenth centuries, however, primarily because the explorers came from areas of the world that were not wealthy enough to exploit these newly discovered lands for trading purposes. If the Industrial and Scientific Age had come on the scene hundreds of years earlier during the Classical World, Europe would have been in a better position to take advantage of its wealth by exploiting and colonizing the areas that it discovered. Even in the Ancient World, Phoenicians and Greeks planted colonies in the newly discovered regions of the ancient Mediterranean, regions away from the centers of Primary civilization at that time.

At any rate, we do not know what would have happened if men had hastened their puny efforts to create new forms of knowledge after the fall of Rome. If mankind in both Europe and Asia had been able to utilize the still unexploited brains of the hundreds of millions living in the Ancient World to resolve the problems facing an inefficient agricultural system and an equally inefficient operation of artisanal cottage industry, perhaps we would have been able to save the hundreds of millions who died of famine or disease, or who perished before they were able to live adequate and personally fulfilling lives. If we had the knowledge today that our descendants will have 200 years hence, we might feel less frustrated by life at present. We could build more comfortable cities to live in, and could know more about the range of possibilities available to us in developing a concensus about human rights. We might be in a more fortunate position to use the wealth now thrown away on war and defense establishments for more productive purposes.

We might also be more intelligent and wiser about trying to define the kinds of societies we would like to live in. We clearly could be more successful in helping those bypassed by the contemporary Industrial and Scientific civilization to rejoin their fellowmen in working out techniques for fulfilling their human potential. This is necessary if men everywhere are to contribute to forging future links to the chain that ties us from the one-celled animals of the past to the human beings who will be living on this planet hundreds if not thousands of years hence.

◇　◇　◇　◇　◇

Men learn slowly and falteringly, making great errors that need to be corrected after they are gone. Perhaps some day we may be able to create a society composed of modest, sage men, able to make their contributions without detracting from those made by others around them. Perhaps we may also be able to create a human society that can benefit all men by making them more aware of themselves, of the world they live in, and of their particular contribution in creating the imperfect societies that make men miss the opportunities which could be available. Men still turn away from seeking the knowledge that might help them make wiser decisions, and from building foundations which would permit future generations to waste less time in resolving their problems — as they shift their goals to experimenting with social techniques that would enrich their lives, and thus their estimation of themselves.

XIV Industrialization in the Developing Areas

Men in every generation re-create their goals to explain the purpose for living. Hence we are precluded from returning to any intrinsic human nature to explain the diffusion of culture or the birth, growth, and spread of the Industrial and Scientific civilization to other countries and areas of the world. There is no doubt that the greatest appeal of industrialization lay in its creation of new forms of wealth and the encouragement it gave men to seek more expanded opportunities for providing purpose, goals, and reasons for existence. Industrialization also helped many men to achieve higher social status, and thus to still their self-doubts and confirm their desires for greater self-enhancement.

The Industrial and Scientific civilization had much in its favor as it proclaimed its superiority over the previous Primary civilization. From any objective point of view, the Industrial and Scientific civilization was able to solve many of the problems which had plagued the inhabitants of past civilization. Primary civilization could do little about the periodic famines and epidemics which swept one part of the inhabited world to the other, wiping out large parts of the population. It could do little to enrich the lives of the majority of its citizens, who lived in complete ignorance of their human potential. It could do little to assure that babies could survive birth or the first five years of life, let alone the possibility of living to an old age. The chances of any individual taken at random living more than 30 to 40 years was rather poor. Most inhabitants of Primary civilization finished their lives not too far from where they were born, unless they were captured by invading armies and sold into slavery. They knew little of themselves and their neighbors, and even less of those who lived 500 or 1000 miles away, who were chiefly legendary or mythical non-persons. Most of the world's inhabitants who lived under any Primary civilization were illiterate. As late as the eighteenth century in England, the American colonies, or Japan, more than half could not write their names, read the classics of their culture, or own a written or printed book. In the urban areas of England and Japan, 40 percent of the males could write their names, read simple sentences, and perform arithmetic problems that would be on the fourth grade level in a modern elementary school. But the vast majority of the population lived in rural areas and few were literate. The women, including the wives of landlords, were generally unable to read and write, and the few who could usually taught themselves by observing the instruction given to their brothers.

Today, most of the world's population is still illiterate; most still go to bed hungry; most never receive any modern medical or dental care; most do not have enough clothes to protect themselves from cold if they live in a temperate climate. Most of the world's population have no one to turn to in case of need except close relatives, and if these are also in need, they can only passively accept starvation or the destruction of their villages by natural calamities as part of their fate. Most have little or no protection against the diseases caused by polluted water or infested earth. Most turn humbly to their religion, hoping that in some way a deity — whether Christian or Moslem — or the deities, if Buddhist, Hindu, or Pantheistic — can help them avert catastrophies. If prayer, sacrifices, and rites do not help, then the villager or urban dweller must accept what appears to be an inflexible fate.

In most of the world, generation follows generation with little change for the better in terms of food, clothing, or shelter. The wealth accumulated in those parts of the world bypassed by the Industrial and Scientific civilization is small in amount and in the hands of a very few, rarely more than 5 percent of the population. Political regimes are fairly unstable in the non-Communist, non-developed areas, where military dictatorships tend to be the most common form of government — in which men, untrained in solving the problems resulting from a Primary civilization, attempt to keep conflicts from arising between those who have and those who have not. In the Communist world, development takes place at a slightly faster pace as the Communist dictatorships use the Industrial and Scientific civilization not to achieve higher standards of living for the population but to further and support the police and military in preventing conflicts from developing which would threaten the stability of the regime from either the outside or the inside.

◇   ◇   ◇   ◇   ◇

Men in the past lived lives of dependency upon other men, permitting them little scope for personal growth. But the majority of men living in our contemporary world are still unable to follow guidelines for living that are otherwise than they were for their parents and grandparents. Most individuals are still unable to participate in the important decisions that concern them, or to determine whether they are to go hungry, be unemployed, or possess the personal and economic security that would make their lives less frustrating. Most have not been able to achieve a sense of personal fulfillment and the feeling that their lives have been well spent. Most are unable to develop new options out of the extraordinary array of possibilities that will be open to our descendants hundreds of years hence. Most men are governed by unimaginative, uneducated decision-makers who are attempting to acquire a sense of self-esteem at the expense of others whom they look upon as politically, economically, or socially inferior to themselves. The hierarchical bureaucracies of the past that tried to put each person in his allotted place are still with us today, whether they exist in Communist, so-called capitalist, or developing areas of the world. In the United States, Western Europe, Japan, and other developed nations, men with little imagination still make the important decisions for their fellow human beings, as they do in the Communist and the developing areas.

The Industrial and Scientific civilization is viewed by men of power as one that benefits them personally through preserving their hierarchical position; as one that permits their nations, which are looked upon chiefly as personal extensions of themselves, to be militarily strong vis-a-vis neighboring nations; as one that permits an underdeveloped nation to achieve higher social status for itself in the family of nations and of men; and as one that rewards those loyal to men in power with sufficient wealth and privileges to let them escape the risks of everyday life in the poor countries.

Secondary civilization is spreading rapidly around the world, much faster than its predecessor moved in the Old and New Worlds. What took thousands of years in the past is now a matter of less than 100 years, for only in this century has the Secondary civilization come of age. Urbanization has now become a way of life for the vast majority of the world's poor, who can leave the grinding frustrations of rural life only by escaping to the new urban areas where they live in shacks and nondescript housing at no higher standards than they left behind, but with a glimmer of hope that somewhere at some time jobs may open up that will permit them to raise their aspirations. For even the poverty-stricken in the developing areas need to believe that their children, if not they, will be able to expect life to be good, and that it is not necessary to die in order to change one's lot.

Men in both the developed and developing areas are still struggling to make some sense out of their lives, to have greater self-respect, to hold values of worth, and to feel it possible to move toward definite goals. While the inhabitants of the developed areas want more out of life than the possession of a color television set, electricity in their houses, or meat on the table, those in the developing areas would be happy to have one good meal a day to allay the pangs of hunger, to have a comfortable bed to sleep in, to have adequate shelter against the cold, to wear a pair of shoes, and to own those things that make them feel that they are no longer inferior to the rich with their independence, social worth, and freedom from fear of an unknown future. The developing and Communist nations are now struggling to create an Industrial and Scientific civilization in their lands so that their inhabitants can also share the daily satisfactions enjoyed by those living in such a civilization.

XV   Latin America and Its Problems

The countries south of the Rio Grande River, extending to the Straits of Magellan and eastward to the Caribbean and the Atlantic Ocean, encompassing the Spanish-speaking, the Portuguese-speaking, and the small areas speaking English, French, and Dutch are all developing nations. All are struggling to adapt themselves to the world of industry being imported from the developed nations, though they are fairly indifferent to the complementary world of science that accompanies it. Despite the enormous amount of industrialization and the dotted growth of cities containing millions of inhabitants, the vast majority on this continent and its nearby islands are still peasants, tilling small family plots of land, bypassed by the rising tide of industrialization in the cities and gaining little from the increase in wealth produced by roads, factories, railroads, technical schools, and universities. Although more than 200 million speak Spanish and over 100 million speak Portuguese, Latin America is by no means a unified continent. Neighbors are viewed more often as being enemies than friends. Railroads and roads link the hinterland with the port cities to provide trade to North America and Western Europe rather than to neighboring countries.

Latin America is a continent whose people are divided rather than united by languages. In a fraction of the continent on the northeast, French, English, and Dutch are spoken; and from the Rio Grande to the Straits of Magellan, Spanish is used. Although there may be slight differences in pronunciation and slightly different uses of common words, a Mexican can read a Chilean or Argentinian newspaper or magazine, and vice versa. (It is more than likely, however, that an educated Mexican will prefer to read a North American magazine rather than a Chilean one, and an educated Argentinian will choose a French journal to a Mexican one.) Although Brazilian Portuguese and South American Spanish with slight variations are interchangeable and can easily be read by one another, still the educated inhabitant of Rio de Janeiro or Sao Paolo is more interested in what is happening in Western Europe or the United States than in Mexico or the Argentine. The educated man in Montevideo is more likely to be concerned with what is going on in Great Britain or Germany than in adjoining Paraguay; his colleague in Buenos Aires is less interested in what is new in Asuncion or even Montevideo than in Paris, London, or Rome.

In the past, the Indians in the Americas south of the Rio Grande numbered in the millions from the Mexican Valley to the highlands of Peru, but today the Indian, still the symbol of oppression, plays an almost imperceptible part in the cultures and growing nationalisms in South America. At an early period in the Argentine, Chile, and Uruguay (whose present populations are almost exclusively of European origins from Spain, Italy, France, and Germany), the Indian was almost exterminated. In Brazil, the Indian was either pushed into the Amazon Basin or almost wiped out when the early settlers with their Negro slaves moved into the interior from the coastal regions. Brazil is black, mixed Indian-white, and white with the latter concentrated in the southern regions of the country. White is seen as middle class, black as of low social rank. The term "Indian" is also viewed as a cultural phenomenon rather than as a racial one. One's brothers can be Indian even if one is not, the differences being culturally based upon non-Indian social behavior and way of life. The majority in Peru, Ecuador, Bolivia, and Paraguay still have a way of life that is seen as being chiefly "Indian." The differences between "black," "white," "mestizo," and "Indian" are considered to be cultural rather than based upon skin pigmentation or physical features.

In most of South America the Indian is segregated, illiterate, and socialized as an "Indian." The middle and upper classes are chiefly white with a small intermixture with blacks and Indians (although this mixture may be more than is generally supposed). Throughout South America, one can see the social division of the cities in upper-class mansions, middle-class apartments or small private housing, lower-class slums and shanty-towns. Middle-class areas with paved streets, sewage, electricity, and water are often only a few minutes away from shanty-towns with unpaved streets, no running water, no sewage or electricity. Although Spanish and Portuguese-speaking America may not be as racially-conscious as South African Boers or North American whites, they are certainly as class-conscious. And though South America may be divided into separate social classes that have profoundly different ways of life, most people are united by a polite respect for the individual human being and an awareness that individuals do not become more lovable when humiliated by those with the power to do so. The dependency upon the great man, the *Caudillo*, is also offset by the scepticism of most of the continent's inhabitants about the innate "greatness" of the man with political, economic, or social power. There is always a conscious effort to cut the "great" man down to size.

Despite an almost common Iberian background (the acculturated South Americans of Indian descent are culturally closer to their non-Indian fellow citizens than they are to their ancestors who inhabited the continent before the arrival of the Europeans), little neighborliness and little acceptance of common superordinate goals exist to help unite them all. Brazil sees itself as the chief power south of the Rio Grande, with a population that is now over 100 million and that may increase to almost 200 million by the end of the century, with the greatest industrial potential on the continent in her two large cities of Sao Paolo and Rio de Janeiro. Although Argentina with more than 30 million inhabitants saw its future as that of a great industrial nation in the days after World War II when General Peron was spending the country's surplus to purchase both industrialization and a welfare state, the Argentine today is neither as wealthy in per capita income as oil-rich Venezuela, as industrialized as the southern portion of Brazil, nor as much the intellectual leader and receptacle for foreign investments as Mexico. Yet, beneath the surface of Mexico and Argentina there is a great indifference to one another as Mexico looks northward to the United States — and Argentina, conscious of its Italian and Spanish roots, looks to Europe.

◇   ◇   ◇   ◇   ◇

Although South America had less than 100 million inhabitants at the turn of the century, it has more than 300 million today. It will have a little over 600 million by the end of the twentieth century, making it second to Asia as a populous continent. Like Asia, it is overcrowded where the soil is fertile (and the burgeoning cities act as a magnet for the landless peasants) and underpopulated in the large stretches of poor soil (including the huge area of the Amazon River Valley with its endless forests, high rainfall but very thin topsoil). During this century, the populations throughout the continent have virtually exploded. Brazil has grown from 34 million in 1900 to over 100 million today. Mexico on the eve of its Revolution in 1911 had around 11 million; today it has more than 55 million, and may reach the 100 million mark during the next 25 years. Intense poverty stretches from one part of South America to the other, including those countries that have an almost exclusively "white" complexion, such as Chile, Argentina, and Uruguay. Even little "white" Costa Rica has one of the highest birthrates in the world, one that is certain to double its population during the next 20 years.

The cities are huge. Mexico City has more than five million, as do Buenos Aires, Rio de Janeiro, and Sao Paolo. Like many of the urban areas in the nineteenth-century Europe, national life tends to be centralized in these cities with the smaller ones playing little of a role in the industrial, financial, governmental, or cultural life of the nation. There are many cities of more than one million.

Any nation having more than 10 million has a capital city with a metropolitan area encompassing more than a million, whether one is concerned with Santiago and Valparaiso in Chile, Montevideo in Uruguay, Bogota in Colombia, or Caracas in Venezuela.

Yet, despite subways in the large cities, the mass production of automobiles, the presence of large industrial plants in urban centers, literary journals, universities, and anthropological museums, the area south of the United States, including the Caribbean, is a vast underdeveloped poorhouse. The gap between rich and poor is wider than in any other area of the world, and the disparity between the technical middle class and the illiterate, poverty-stricken peasant is extensive. The Industrial and Scientific civilization has been diffused in Latin America by carriers from North America and Europe. But the civilization has thus far bypassed the vast majority of the inhabitants who are not members of the technical middle class. Though these are modest consumers for the products of the Secondary civilization of industry and science (few of the world's inhabitants do not consume at least some of its manufactured products, or are not affected to some degree by its medical and scientific research), they have little to do directly with this civilization. Many of them may produce the agricultural goods which are exported in order to import the industrial plants, but few are brought into the thinking of this civilization. They are passive spectators to an extensive social change that moves around them without affecting them directly.

Only two countries south of the United States have per capita Gross National Product indices of more than $1,000: these are Venezuela with its oil wealth, and Argentina with its diversity of agriculture for export, its manufacturing plants, and its high level of literacy. The "Indian" countries — Bolivia, Paraguay, Peru, and Ecuador in South America and Guatemala in Central America — are the poorest (except for black Haiti, which is the most poverty-stricken and on an even lower economic level than any other country in the Caribbean or South America). But in Mexico, Brazil, Colombia, and Chile, there is a vast difference in standard of living between the "rich" industrial pockets in the large cities and the "poor" illiterate rural areas away from paved roads, modern conveniences, and schools. Although Latin America and most of the Caribbean stand above Africa (except for South Africa) and Asia (again, except for Japan on one end and Israel on the other) in per capita income or in per capita GNP, they stand far below the incomes of both Western and Eastern Europe, or of the United States and Canada.

Despite the instability of political regimes in this area of the world, revolutionary governments seem to end up becoming conservative ones, and little appears to get accomplished in terms of developing innovative societies or economies. The overthrow of Porfirio Diaz in Mexico in 1910 led to a revolutionary time during which the chief activity dealt with the institutionalization of the Mexican Revolution, wherein those who had been rural landlords were supplanted by urban men of wealth who later became landlords on the side. Although the Indian became a symbol of exploitation and subjection, little was done to make him the new carrier of the Industrial and Scientific civilization. In the continent of South America, in Central America, and in the Caribbean, the middle classes, the educated elite, the government officials, the new industrialists, and even the revolutionaries were whites of European background. The poverty-stricken part of Mexico is Indian, with whites concentrated in the industrial and financial areas. The wealthiest section of Brazil is found in the three southernmost provinces, where the whites are concentrated: the most poverty-stricken area is the northeast and Amazonia, whose populations are composed of blacks, black-white, and Indian-white mixtures. Although Spanish and Portuguese America may pride themselves on their tolerance, still it is probably more difficult for a black or an Indian to rise to high social acceptance than it would be in the United States. The whites are wealthy and educated, the blacks and the Indians are poor and illiterate. In Brazil, for example, the top 20 percent of the population, all white, get more than 75 percent of the total national income; the blacks, the mixtures, and the poor whites get the rest — though 60 percent of Brazil is still classified as white. One can also say that more than three-quarters of the wealth in all of Spanish- and Portuguese-speaking America is owned by a little more than one percent of the population. (In Cuba, less than one percent of the population make the important decisions concerning the wealth of that country.)

Illiteracy of blacks, Indians, and poor whites is the rule. Although each country gives lip service to the needs for universal quality education, in actuality the educational system from primary level to the higher universities is poorly funded and dominated by whoever controls political power. While Cuba is probably making the greatest effort to increase the literacy of its population, education is seen chiefly as a form of docility to domination by the government. In no country of Central and South America can one say that academic freedom is guaranteed, or that the universities and higher schools are marketplaces for ideas. Despite the revolutionary regimes and despite the late experiment of a democratically-elected Socialist in Chile, it is difficult to see these countries making the effort to use scientific techniques either in tackling their social problems or in adjusting their populations as smoothly as possible to the oncoming Industrial and Scientific civilization. Tradition, conservatism, and cautiousness in governing are more typical than

revolutionary activity. Not even Cuba has inaugurated a revolutionary system of society but has attempted to emulate the so-called
"socialist" countries of Europe. South America and Mexico have
also attempted to emulate the revolutionary experiences of others
in the eighteenth century, but without themselves inaugurating
any important changes. Military dictatorship and censorship,
whether in Cuba, Brazil, or Argentina, are the rule. From Mexico
to the Argentine, intellectual life, while giving lip service to past
revolutionary ideals, tends to be sterile and cautious about creating
difficulties with authoritarian regimes. Alienation, economic frustration, and inability to articulate innovative national aims seem
to be as true of Haiti, as of Cuba, Colombia, Chile, Paraguay, and
Bolivia.

South America is still a continent that has been bypassed by
the European Industrial and Scientific civilization. In Brazil, more
than half of the adults are illiterate and another one-quarter are
functionally illiterate. More than 70 percent of the wage-earning
heads of families receive less than $35 per month; more than 75
percent of the peasants are landless with a little more than one
and a half percent of the Brazilian population owning more than
half of all land. In the northeast of Brazil, the poorhouse of the
country, life expectancy is less than 30 years, and a majority of
the population goes to bed hungry, rarely sees a doctor, owns few
if any shoes, and only a small number of their children ever see the
inside of a classroom.

In both the Caribbean and Spanish- and Portuguese-speaking
America, the Industrial and Scientific civilization is defined as a
variant of "capitalism" — and therefore suspect. Industrialization
is viewed as helping the rich become richer and the foreign capitalist to take even more wealth from the poor, thus further enriching
himself and his own country. Industrialization is seen as being of
little benefit in modernizing a backward peasant country, for it
is postulated as a way to permit the top 5 percent of the country's
population to amass more riches through industry than they could
through exploiting the peasant. "Capitalism" is also interrelated
with "industrialization" and has a pejorative meaning among the
students, the employed middle class in general, and among most
literates — including the landed gentry.

On the other hand, "socialism" is associated with modernism
and modernity. Even the clergy find that "socialism" is a more
acceptable term in articulating the nation's goals, though it is seen
entirely as nationalization of the means of production rather than
as a new cooperative society. "Capitalism" means the sale of the
nation's resources to the rich from North America, Western Europe,
or Japan. "Socialism" and nationalism go hand in hand as future
goals when more than two-thirds of the continent's population find

themselves shut out of the mainstream of the "modern" economy, either subsisting on small plots of land utilizing a great deal of hand labor and few tools, or moving into the slums and shanty-towns around the great metropolises and joining the large percentage of unemployed squatters there. In the booming and burgeoning city of Sao Paolo in 1971, the Brazilian government estimated that almost half of the adult population was unemployed.

The wealthy see themselves as representatives of the "modern" section of the population, while the poor view their lot as a never-ending struggle containing little hope for moving ahead economically in their lifetimes. But since the foreign capital which the government wants is considered to be regressive while "socialism" (or the nationalization of all the resources for the good of the population) is seen as a means of modernizing the economy, the conflict implies that free elections might lead to the socialization of the economy — and thus frighten foreign investors and those who would expect to gain therefrom. The end result has been that the military, who see themselves as "nationalists" rather than as "capitalists" or "socialists," have taken over the reins of power and tried to attract foreign investment while hoping that various "socialist" welfare measures will reform the national society. A smart ambitious young man sees a brighter future for himself in the burgeoning bureaucracy of the military than in the smaller, weaker commercial or governmental bureaucracies.

◇   ◇   ◇   ◇   ◇

The Church is ineffective and powerless throughout Spanish- and Portuguese-speaking America, and the middle class (especially the male members) tend to be anti-clerical and even agnostic in sentiment. The result is that the lower clergy, better educated than the rest of the population, identify their own powerlessness with that of the poor peasants and slum dwellers. Their reaction against the Church and military hierarchies encourages them to see themselves as spokesmen for a new revolutionary form of society that will unite the selflessness and vows of poverty of the monastic orders with the organization of a society that will be egalitarian, "socialist," and "Christian."

In this vast continent, it is the military who are attempting to introduce a pseudo-modernity by building more roads, railroads, and schools, though virtually ignoring the intellectual activity that goes hand in hand with industrialization and science. Those who are outside the money economy, which includes most, are also isolated from the thought that goes with that economy. They lack the self-confidence, knowledge, and hope for the future which propel individuals to adapt themselves to a world that is based upon continually changing thought. The Indians who were conquered by the Spaniards were crushed in spirit, for previous Indian conquests had extracted complete passivity as a price for survival. In Brazil and the southern "white countries" of Argentina, Chile, and Uruguay, disease exterminated as many Indians as the European gun. Unlike those further to the North, the Indians in these areas were less numerous and less adaptable to spending a life of serfdom to Spanish or Portuguese soldier-adventurers. Brazil imported millions of blacks who were not freed from slavery until the 1880's. Even after they could no longer be bought or sold in the marketplace, they were not trained to earn their own living, but continued to work as poorly paid unskilled farm hands doing basically what they had done as slaves on the "fazendas," and still dependent upon the master for their daily necessities.

As in most of the underdeveloped areas of the world, development is quite uneven with industrialization located in the large capital cities where it caters almost entirely to a local market. Spanish- and Portuguese-speaking America tend to export agricultural products and import manufactured and consumer goods. But in recent years the South American countries have faced a good deal of competition from the newly independent countries of Africa, who are attempting to supply the developed countries with coffee, cocoa, rubber, vanilla, and sugar. Ghana, for example, grows more than one-third of the world's production of cocoa, compared with less than one-fifth in Brazil. East Africa grows almost one-third as much coffee as Brazil. The latter also faces competition from the production of its neighbors. As the price of coffee goes down on the world market, each producing country tries to plant more in order to earn larger returns, which means that there is continuous pressure to depress the agricultural prices of the developing countries.

Each country is suspicious of its competitors, and is thus unable to organize to keep prices high for cocoa and coffee (the tea-producing countries of Taiwan, Assam, India, and Ceylon also face competition from the developing countries of East Africa). Cuba, despite its hopes for diversifying and manufacturing more goods, has discovered how dependent it still is upon a sugarcane economy. The need to be free from dependence upon a few crops has encouraged much of the revolutionary activity in Spanish- and Portuguese-speaking America; the reaction is as much against the foreigner who buys their products and invests in their lands as against the rich landlord and the merchant-exporter. The powerlessness of the educated South and Central American is identified with the lack of economic power of his country. His inability to regulate his life and to achieve his modest goals are identified with the difficulties of his country in attaining its aims and regulating its national life. Revolutionary activities are often based upon the need of the educated Latin American for an orderly, predictable, secure existence for himself. What makes these revolutionary activities so interesting is that they are not directed toward the creation of a new or counter-society, but rather toward taking over political power. They are willing to act as a shadow state while using violence in order to become the real state. The urban guerrillas of Uruguay, Argentina, and Colombia, as was true of the past national revolutionaries, were recruited on university campuses as were many in Bolivia, Peru, Ecuador, Venezuela, and Guatemala.

⋄   ⋄   ⋄   ⋄   ⋄

None of the countries south of the United States has successfully internalized the Industrial and Scientific civilization. Segments have embraced parts of this civilization, while the rural areas have continued to live chiefly in the past. Mexico and Peru have experienced relatively successful agricultural revolutions, though these are still unfinished. The changes in Cuba have pushed it no closer to becoming part of the new civilization than it was in 1959. Despite the spread of urban industrialization, Latin America is barely able to satisfy local markets. Exports as in the past are still raw ores, coffee, oil, cattle, wheat, corn, and cotton. The continent as a whole has a per capita GNP that is one-tenth the American, and the educational standard is still below one-fifth. Its few universities are politicized, under military control, and produce fewer scientists and professional managers than lawyers, physicians, and humanities graduates. Although attempts have been made to create the legend that North and South America share the same goals and a similar democratic culture, American foreign policy in fact sees the area as far less important to the interests of the United States than Canada, Europe, or Japan. American investments tend to be concentrated more in the wealthier areas of Australia, Canada, and Europe than in Latin America. The latter is a continent where the upper classes are quite indifferent to the living conditions of the lower ones, where most educated individuals have no clear conception of what "modernization" implies, where "socialism" is largely viewed as the state playing the role of the bountiful capitalist, and where industrialization is considered as being far too important to put into the hands of private capitalists. A growing middle class, mainly of European origins, has an almost total monopoly of the technical knowledge which is required to supply the local market and to handle the export and import trade.

The greatest problem in Spanish- and Portuguese-speaking America is the short amount of time still available for modernizing economies and cultures. The population is increasing much too rapidly for the resources which have been set in motion to supply each individual with minimum amounts of food, clothing, shelter, and medical care. Although industrialization is spreading in the larger cities, too many unskilled peasants flock to them seeking work, and few have the skills which are needed in today's industrialization process. One hundred years ago industrialization required a good deal of hand labor for tasks which could be easily learned in a short period of time. Today industrialization is often a matter of putting up a petrochemical plant that needs very little hand labor, or an automobile assembly plant that is slowly becoming more and more automated. The skills which can be employed require the use of entrepreneurs who are able to interrelate the low-cost labor of the continent with the markets which exist elsewhere. Unfortunately these entrepreneurial skills are still in short supply even in the large cities.

The greatest resource open to any developing area is available labor which could be employed at competitive rates, which means that Spanish- and Portuguese-speaking America need to make only those things for export that can utilize large amounts of labor at a lower cost than is possible for industry in developed areas. But unlike Japan, which got its industrial start before World War II as a workshop for the developed areas by using low-cost labor (as do the contemporary areas of Singapore, Taiwan, and Hong Kong), few sections of South or Central America and the Caribbean are able to assume this task at the present time. Manufacturing firms are permitted to enter the country to compete in supplying the local markets, but they utilize more machinery than manpower. National status also plays a part; it is more important to the national ego to know that its growing core of industries includes a large steel mill, a huge refinery, or an automated automobile body plant than it is for the country to be recognized for its cheaply produced clothing, inexpensive household consumer goods, or labor-intensive electronic industries. The national image is thus more important to its leaders than raising living standards or developing entrepreneurial self-confidence.

Further, the leadership on the continent is generally unaware of what industrialization is or what stimulates scientific discovery. In the Americas south of the United States, countries are ruled either by an oligarchic bureaucratic one-party system or by military dictatorships. Neither lawyers nor generals are the most knowledgeable of men when it comes to an awareness of the priorities necessary in turning a peasant non-money economy into an urban middle-class industrial one. Their concepts of leadership are directed toward exerting power, preserving their authority, and developing a command economy that will build up the military or governmental bureaucracies and indirectly add to their own financial security. In most of South America, if one cannot get into the military on an officer's level, the next best thing is to train oneself for the professional managerial positions that are open on the staffs of the foreign corporations that bring in their own finances, technical knowledge, and much of the industrial expertise necessary to take advantage of the local consumer market. If these options are closed to one, then the next possibility is to identify oneself with the revolutionary nationalist leadership in the hope that new positions will open up once the foreigners are divested of their monopolistic economic power within the national economy.

With the exception of Cuba (where the poor have been helped both socially and economically by the Castro government), there appears to be little belief or conviction on the part of the poor elsewhere in the southern hemisphere that they live in open societies where mobility toward higher social and economic status is possible. The assumption is widespread that top positions in the military, in foreign firms, and in revolutionary nationalist organizations are all reserved for those who are white, educated, and possess enough family connections to assure confidence in getting ahead through proper influence. Being poor in almost all of South America is to be Indian or black. Skin color is correlated with lower social rank and hence with unskilled work. Just as there is man's and woman's work, so there is labor for those who are lower-class Indians and lower-class blacks. The middle classes give their sons social advantages through formal education and political influence so that the sons encounter less competition for the few good jobs which are available. In the eighteenth century, the relatives of the French or British kings, no matter how poor, enjoyed preference when applying for governmental positions. As the children, grandchildren, and great-grandchildren of a king proliferated (though they were moved further and further away from the center of royal power and authority), they still retained the specific right to call upon their royal relative in power for assistance in procuring available governmental, military, or religious positions.

The poor everywhere are continuously disadvantaged by being denied the opportunity to get that first job which leads to social and economic advancement. In Latin America, the poor do not have the self-confidence to insist that they have the right to obtain the knowledge and skills that go hand in hand with working in an industrial environment or with learning to manipulate its interlocking and interdependent parts as a bureaucratic administrator. The Industrial and Scientific civilization can in fact be compared to an enormous machine with intricate interchangeable parts, each component of which can be driven or moved by those with the specific knowledge and training to do so.

The Secondary civilization which began to emerge as a specific culture in the eighteenth century rapidly disseminated its component ideas throughout the world in the nineteenth and twentieth centuries. It moved rapidly in Latin America after 1920, and especially after 1945, disseminating its machines, roads, railways, airplanes, interconnected urban areas, consumer products, utilities, and even entertainment. Unlike the peasant world to which one learned to adapt through the socialization process within the bosom of the family, the new culture could not be learned from the family or from relatives or neighbors, but only from strangers, through the classroom, and through the medium of the printed word. The contemporary world of industrialization and science is chiefly a world composed almost entirely of strangers: strangers with whom one works, who do the instructing, and who disseminate their particular technological and managerial knowledge. Taxes are collected by strangers, and one is ruled by strangers who also make important decisions that will affect the way one lives and works. Strangers determine whether or not one will be able to achieve one's goals and to obtain a sense of moderate personal security.

◇ ◇ ◇ ◇ ◇

The world of industrialization and science is one containing an infinite division of labor. It operates by organizing millions of men with each one doing somewhat specialized work, having a slightly different body of experiences and knowledge, and working as autonomously as possible. Almost no top executive, academic president, top governmental official, or military leader can know what all of his underlings know, or even understand what they are doing, or how they are doing their work at any given time. The system is based upon faith and operates upon faith, faith that the man on the bottom will be able to interrelate his work with that of the man either above him or working alongside him, and faith that the enormous amount of knowledge which is available can be divided into component parts, understood by those who are in charge of each part, and result in a total cohesive system in good operating order. No military planner can lay out a battle in complete detail, but must operate on the assumption that the overall plan will be carried out by each man performing a small part of it; the details and interpretation must be left to each individual man. No large-scale industry could operate if all details for running the plant were spelled out in advance from the top to the bottom echelon of men. No governmental plan, no matter how brilliant or well-devised, could be put into operation without the cooperation of the men who will be expected to carry it out. It could be sabotaged on any level once it leaves the executive's office, since its execution depends upon the cooperation of a series of planes and a large number of men, each having complete confidence in one another to bring the policy, plan, or manufactured item to a successful conclusion.

The Industrial and Scientific civilization is thus based upon the successful cooperation of millions of men, each disciplined to carry out his work as efficiently and quickly as possible. Although military discipline can enforce peacetime regulations, the actual carrying out of a successful military operation will require more autonomy for the men and their leaders than is the case in a barracks situation. The efficient diffusion of the Industrial and Scientific civilization also requires a good deal of democratic freedoms, the freedom to visualize one's work as effectively as possible without being restricted to the point of view of one's hierarchical superiors. There must be freedom to stand up against what one considers mistakes in judgment by one's immediate or top superiors, and freedom to explore new ways of working and of seeking new information. One must be permitted to explore new intellectual horizons to understand the problems faced, along with the shortcomings of the industrial machine.

Against this background and perspective, it is possible to see the problems which developing nations face in attempting to adapt their rural economies, their passive uneducated populations, and men functioning in bureaucratic hierarchies to the new culture of industrialization and science. The requirement is for autonomous individuals, for self-confident optimistic men who are able to take charge of units in this regulated societal system and operate them with imagination, intelligence, and efficiency. Developing nations do not have too many individuals with these skills. The latter must be trained in the home, in the school, and through experience and success on the job.

An efficient Industrial and Scientific civilization needs carriers who have authority to make the daily decisions necessary to seeing that the social machinery moves as smoothly as possible. Although leadership is required to set the goals and guidelines, to supply the financing, and to put the organization into motion, the actual running of the cumbersome machinery, the working out of the standard operating procedures, and the daily decisions which eventually become an integral part of policy are all developed by middle management (the straw bosses, the staff sergeants, and the chief clerks). But for the latter to operate there must be common agreement that superiors will not interfere with what they do, that the reward for efficiency is the freedom to be left alone and to make the small daily decisions (that eventually turn into the larger policies, and company or governmental decision) as long as one does them well. Making the wrong decisions means denial of promotion or even tenure on the job. Freedom thus becomes a reward. What is meant by morale is the opportunity for men to work together congenially, to cooperate as important equals, to be rewarded for the improvements in productivity they suggest, and to experience the satisfaction that comes in knowing one's job better than the straw boss or the man on top.

◇ ◇ ◇ ◇ ◇

Although there is no reason why industrialization cannot occur without the intervention of foreigners (who bring in capital in the form of machines, technology, and market knowledge), the alternative should not be political men in command positions who have no knowledge of how to motivate men to create new forms of energy, ideas, and material substitutes. Latin America like all developing nations needs a grassroots revolution concurrently with a corporate one, but both need to be coordinated with a good deal of trust and responsibility. At the moment, any overall planning seems to be very much in the distant future. If industrialization is to take place, as it undoubtedly will, its spread will be in bits and pieces done by isolated individuals, each attempting to fill a narrow vacuum in the total market, all doing their jobs very much as Adam Smith assumed they would 200 years ago (except that the benign role of the government is more needed at the end of the twentieth century than it was at the end of the eighteenth). There are no groups of financiers who can collect capital for a developing nation as rapidly as the governments of the developed nations. Within the developing nation, no bank or banks can raise as much capital, put into motion the construction of heavy industry, or pay for the social overhead of roads, railroads, telephones, radio, schools, and municipal services as even the poorest of national governments.

While government can play a dominant part in the diffusion of industrial and scientific ideas, it cannot operate all the myriad pieces of a complex social organization without a good deal of help from a large number of men and women who are the virtual carriers of this complex series of forms and ideas that we call the Industrial and Scientific civilization. It is most unfortunate that, in order to use the government both as financier and as customer, enormous sums of capital go into the construction of a complex bureaucracy to police the government's funds and the clients' receipt of those funds. The more important the role of government becomes in developing this process, the greater the social overhead and the larger the number of individuals employed to service and police legislative efforts. Taxes are extracted from the population; and as their totals rise, as various interest groups maneuver to obtain special concessions for themselves, and as others attempt to pay as little as possible, the greater becomes the compulsion to employ more individuals to collect and police the taxes, and the more difficult it becomes to obtain fair shares for taking care of necessary social needs.

While industry and science try to become more productive with less expenditure of energy, government as it is constituted in both the developing and the developed nations becomes even more topheavy, employing more and more bureaucrats at greater costs but no savings of energy. In the military dictatorships of the world, including most of the Latin American countries, the need to protect governmental legitimacy means a greater expenditure of tax funds to organize more effective military and police establishments. The generals in power prefer to see the expansion of industry and science slowed down if it means cutting into the armed forces which support their power. As a result, only a small percentage of tax funds are used to spread the Industrial and Scientific civilization within any individual country. Rather, most funds are used to protect the legitimacy of the government in power or to create a social overhead more concerned with keeping a population under control than in educating new carriers of the Secondary civilization (thus creating educated elements who might become sympathetic to the overthrow of government authority).

The unfortunate aspect of the contemporary Industrial and Scientific civilization is that its priorities are set by men who are neither industrialists nor scientists, but who may be either financiers behind the political leaders, interested chiefly in short-term financial gains, or military men who see technology only as a means of preserving their legitimacy. The thought processes of these men might well be categorized as pre-industrial and pre-scientific, which means that the technological aspects of the new civilization are far ahead of the thought processes of the men who make the important decisions for their diffusion. What is termed alienation does not derive from the broken promises of this civilization, but refers to the separation of the men who direct it from the thought processes and logic implied in technology, in management concepts, and in the goals of industrialization and science (in their efforts to understand the world of man and the universe surrounding him).

Building factories does not create a culture of industrialization and technology any more than the sudden creation of universities develops environments in which science is stimulated to grow.

Individual motivation and encouragement are important ingredients, along with a self-confidence created by past successes. Laboratories do not make chemists, but intellectual curiosity (that finds no barriers erected against it) can assist. There must be rewards for innovation, for imaginative entrepreneurial qualities and intellectual curiosity, along with opportunities which the culture and governing bodies encourage to permit these skills to come into play. An Industrial and Scientific civilization requires not only the freedom to innovate, but also the freedom to know and to make certain that the resulting knowledge is available to those who seek it. The role of government is to set guidelines that will encourage the new culture to grow and to continue growing. Once this culture has been accepted by public opinion, it will grow of its own accord. The culture cannot come out of governmental offices, for its birthplace is the academic classroom and its midwife is the media. This means that its progenitors are not illiterate peasants and workers, but men and women who can take raw ideas and translate them into concrete reality.

Workers and peasants do not have enough confidence in their ability to be innovators of ideas, whether these are technical, financial, or scientific. The new technical middle classes, offspring of the merchant, clerical, and artisan classes of the past, are the carriers of this revolution. In its beginnings, workers are needed who can perform heavy labor and be disciplined enough to react automatically to their work in a military fashion. It is not rigid discipline, however, that encourages resourcefulness, but rather an autonomy that is born out of freedom and self-confidence. Workers trained to be dependent upon a leadership other than their own become lost when that leadership fails them. Armies that win battles are those in which the men are encouraged to develop their own resourcefulness at the spur of the moment as the battle scene shifts, but this requires a motivation which no military system can develop or devise: the motivation of the soldier who is identified with a goal higher than just surviving or getting along with as little difficulty as possible. The intent can be that of not letting his comrades down, if there is an esprit de corps that encourages each man to think of the survival of the group, or it can be that of not letting down the army, the country, the community, or others. Men need to feel that they have an important stake in the outcome and that their efforts make a difference in achieving it.

The fatalism of the peasant — that there is little he can do to control his destiny — is an obstacle to the effective operation of a series of interchangeable parts that make up the total social machine, wherein each individual manning his particular station needs to feel that the effective running of the whole depends to a great extent upon him. While peasants can become efficient unskilled laborers, whose sense of duty makes them feel that they must do a day's work for a day's pay, they still need to be directed by others. Not being innovators and entrepreneurs, peasants can tend looms, they cannot invent them; they can shovel coal into furnaces, they cannot invent more efficient boilers; they can become effective trackworkers and trackwalkers, but they cannot develop a more efficient track for trains. Their training is important, but their goals do not include developing new industries, forms of communication, means of transportation, marketing techniques, workflows, or more efficient materials handling. But they do encompass having and holding a job that will permit them to live on or above a subsistence level. The job is important because the individual's assessment of himself comes from the job he holds. The motivation to develop a more efficient means of utilizing man's energies, however, is certainly not a part of his reason for working eight hours a day, five days a week, twelve months a year, year after year, decade after decade. Those who become the new executives, the chief engineers, chief accountants, production and sales managers are motivated by attitudes far more complicated than merely holding down jobs, for their self-esteem is measured through intricate personal plans.

The contemporary peasant may not get stomach ulcers as often as the executive who works under greater pressures, but he is still aware of his deprivation, his low social status, his sense of unease in not knowing very clearly what the purposes of his life tend to be, and his conviction that he is not the son with equal opportunities—but the stepchild who is bypassed by the hated stepmother (or middle-class society) in favor of her children who are more advantaged. Although the peasant may have been happy at some time in the distant past, it is doubtful that the peasantry of Latin America, Africa, India, or the Arab world feel a deep sense of satisfaction with their lives and with what they have been able to accomplish through the opportunities available to them. The main motivation for the development of the Industrial and Scientific civilization in the Third World exists chiefly because the world's peasants are locked into a malaise produced by their conviction that conditions for themselves and their children are not turning out very well.

The motivation to push Latin America in the direction that Japan has taken during the past century presupposes a belief among each individual that he has an obligation to devote his energies to making certain that his country can be free of dependence upon another. In Japan, the motivation was that of a compensating nationalism, as it may have been in England in the seventeenth and eighteenth centuries and as it was not in France until the twentieth century. In Latin America, nationalism has been somewhat submerged; the upper classes are identified with outside forces generally in the United States and Western Europe, while the peasant is almost completely out of the mainstream of daily life. The workers are divided on the basis of way of life, of color, and of a subdivision among the literate skilled and the illiterate unskilled workers. Only a few students feel the need to react against the United States by developing a revolutionary nationalist counter-pressure, although the reaction is equally strong against their own upper classes who are viewed as agents and allies of the American "imperialists."

In Cuba, a revolution has taken place on nationalist grounds to eliminate the "out-group," the "imperialists," and the upper classes who are allied with them. But the Marxist concept of a class conflict seems to be out of place in Latin America for, although the gap between rich and poor is wide, the poor are still lacking confidence and a consciousness of what they could one day be — and are thus unable to become revolutionaries in any Marxist sense. The lower classes are conservative and traditional, and are by no means the shock troops of any future social revolution. The desire for revolutionary change is largely absent throughout the continent, and there is little support even for the mild revolutionary changes created by the introduction of technology and science, except among a few in the large metropolitan cities.

The steadiest employment in all countries is as a public servant and in Latin America millions are employed as *empleados publicos*. These include the police, soldiers, custom officials, bureaucrats, and teachers. In Argentina and Chile, more than half of the adult population is composed of white-collar workers, petty bureaucrats, police, military officers, teachers, storekeepers, and their employees. All subscribe to the need for technological or industrial development for the continent, but few are trained to act as initiators. The Industrial and Scientific Age is seen as a messianic movement that will automatically resolve the problems resulting from underdevelopment: poverty, lack of social mobility, illiteracy or functional illiteracy, disease, and the frustrations of daily living. Yet there are few in the literate classes who can develop guidelines on how this civilization should be incorporated into the social fabric, and even fewer who are aware of the social problems that will be introduced into the society in its wake. All seek short cuts to a higher standard of living, which means that the state is seen as the initiator, as the impartial arbiter, as the good father taking care of dependent children — with the father taking the initiative and making the proposals, and the children listening and obeying.

◇   ◇   ◇   ◇   ◇

Although strides have been made in economic development, the overall judgment is that the continent has failed in incorporating the new civilization into its traditional social and economic fabric. Agriculture and the extraction of oil and minerals still produce most of the wealth; the populations remain insufficiently stimulated to want to become the carriers of the millions of ideas that in their total effect become the Industrial and Scientific civilization. The middle classes, though large, are still a bureaucratically-oriented section of the population, mentally stagnant, and unable to stimulate the rest of the citizenry. The non-middle classes are passive and dependent upon the classes above them for guidance and self-esteem.

Psychologically and culturally there is a mixture of freedom for the non-ideological individual personality but a good deal of authoritarianism which insists that figures of authority be accorded loyalty and submission. While a Castro and a Peron give their followers a sense of human dignity, they at the same time place them in Mafia-like straitjackets. Elementary school pupils are expected to be docile and passive, but university students are given more freedom to judge administration and faculty than would be true for American or Western European students. For those who are poor and humble, the military dictatorships provide a measure of dignity which was lacking in their past. This enhanced status makes revolutionary movements against these dictatorships almost impossible.

Latin America is a continent of deprived peasants and urban poor led by a growing military class, which has taken over most of the power as well as the wealth, allied with a small entrepreneurial middle class. A wide gap thus exists between those of European and those of Indian and black backgrounds. Large numbers see the government as the only supplier of steady employment. The various governments have thus far failed to meet their growing problems, and at present one can see little to support feelings of optimism about the future. They have failed to learn from the United States and Western Europe, or even Japan, and the path to the future promises more wreckage from revolutionary nationalist movements, all accomplishing something but still ending in failure. The Americas south of the United States consequently face enormous obstacles in their goal of bringing greater satisfaction to the lives of their numerous inhabitants.

XVI Transitional Phases In Africa

Africa both north and south of the Sahara Desert is a largely underdeveloped area containing exploding populations, illiterate adults, and not nearly enough educational or economic facilities to bring the continent into the Industrial and Scientific Age. The Union of South Africa is the exception, but even this is a country divided and segregated, representing insecure frightened competitive middle-class whites against Asians, "coloreds," and blacks. Africa has become acquainted with Europe only in the past 100 years, though North Africa's introduction occurred a little earlier as a result of Napoleon's conquest of Egypt in the first decade of the nineteenth century and the French acquisition of Algeria in the 1830's. Morocco and Tunis came under French influence in the latter part of the nineteenth century: Libya did not have its confrontation with Italy until the beginning of the second decade of the twentieth century. In the European scramble for colonies, both East and West Africa were not grabbed until the last two decades of the nineteenth century. Missionary activities, which changed Africa south of the Sahara beyond ancestral recognition, did not begin until the end of the nineteenth and the early part of the twentieth centuries. The Ibo of southeast Nigeria, those "go-getting" entrepreneurial people, did not become aware of how much they wanted to get ahead in the world, "to raise the village up," until Roman Catholic missionaries from Ireland brought schools with them at the turn of the century. (Since then, the Ibo have never been the same. Ibo students today are found in almost every large American university, or even small college, seeking the education that will enable them and their kinsmen to "get up" in the world.)

Africa is a continent of illiterates, whether whites in the North or blacks south of the Sahara, emerging from tribal and village isolation to be confronted by a Technological and Scientific civilization symbolized more by its canned meats and fish, motorcycles, bicycles, automobiles, electricity, and modern armies than by any scientific thought. In the North, Islam is still the majority orthodox belief, as it is along the East African coast, the areas surrounding the southern edges of the Sahara Desert, and the lower Nile River. Despite a myth of Pan-Africanism, Islam has still not created a transcontinental spirit. Railroads and roads connect the African nations with seaports whose links are with Europe and North America, not with one another. Despite the Pan-African Congresses that meet, any common bonds of unity are feeble, including the hatred for white Rhodesia and white South Africa. There is also a common conviction that as long as Europeans and Asians dominate commercial life, the Africans are less likely to acquire the self-confidence necessary for industrializing the continent.

Africa is also divided into a Muslim area that is Arab in sentiment, and a Black area that sees itself as a buffer between the Muslims in the North and the whites in the South. Although the continent has been involved in the process of nation-building since 1959, it is sharply divided by hundreds of tribes and languages. Tribal ties are important, just as they remain so among the various ethnic groups within the European family of nations. African nations are still divided by a large number of tribes, each speaking a different language, following separate religious traditions, and having no ancestors or rites in common. In Nigeria, General Gowon, a member of a small Christian tribe, has the almost impossible task of bringing together millions of Yorubas (with their urban and hierarchical traditions), an equal number of Ibo (with their autonomous villages), the large populations of Hausa and Fulani (with authoritarian Muslim traditions going back hundreds of years), plus dozens of smaller tribes reacting against the domination of the larger tribes around them. In Uganda, a former Prime Minister, Milton Obote, operated only by destroying the power of the largest tribe, the Baganda, and their king, or Kabaka, and by giving military power to the smaller tribes who were oppressed in the past by the larger kingdoms of the Baganda, the Ankole, and the Toro. In Ghana, the Ashanti had to be cut down in autonomy to prevent their greater loyalty to their kingdom from subverting the allegiance of the new citizen to the Ghanaian state. In Zaire, the former Belgian Congo, military pressure was used by Premier Mobutu to keep the various isolated regions from separating themselves from the new national state. In Kenya, a new nationalism had to be built up by bringing together tribes, who had nothing in common and distrusted one another, and by turning their inter-tribal jealousies against Asians and Europeans.

North Africa also suffers from divisiveness, but here the superficial ties that bring people together of differing backgrounds, goals, and interests are the beliefs that they share an Arab kinship, have a common religion in Islam, and a common enemy in Zionism. But even with these links, there is little that makes a Tunisian look upon Algerians as being blood brothers, or makes revolutionary nationalist Algerians view the Moroccans as fellow Arabs. Tunis and Morocco are so distant from Egypt that they are more influenced by currents emanating from France than those coming from Cairo. Both see Algeria and Libya as revolutionary threats to their political stability and legitimacy.

Africa south of the Sahara was greatly influenced by the Colonial powers that governed this territory from the end of the nineteenth century through the 1950's. Those formerly controlled by Great Britain use the language they acquired from the British as a common speech that cuts across tribal and linguistic borders. The former colonies under French or Belgian control continue not only their Colonial linguistic heritage, but also the educational and judicial systems. The areas seized by France, Great Britain, and Germany in the last quarter of the nineteenth century followed no natural, tribal, or linguistic borders. Only in the North alongside the Mediterranean coast from Morocco to Egypt was there a common religion and a common language (containing dialectic differences), but not a common culture. Although Tunis, Morocco, and Algeria are divided by different historic backgrounds, they all share the common tradition of having been governed by France until the 1950's and of being influenced by French culture. On an overall basis and to differentiate themselves from the Egyptians and the Arab-speaking residents of Southwest Asia, the Northwest Africans see themselves as part of a distinct cultural area.

Although the population of the North is mixed with an ancient underlayer of Bushman blended with more recent Caucasoid and small amounts of Negro genes that came in with the slave trade for over a thousand years, it still feels a tie with the Islamic and Arabic areas to the East. There is no sense of kinship, however, with the desert tribes in the Sahara or with the blacks living to the South. While the countries may call themselves Arab, there are still large numbers of separate Berber tribes, each owing primary loyalty to its chieftains and still seeing itself as somewhat culturally separate from fellow Arabized townsmen. In the past the Berber tribes served as middlemen between the coastal Arabized population and the blacks living along the southern edge of the Sahara Dessert.

While the northern third of Africa belongs in the Islamized civilization introduced by the invading Muslims during the seventh century of our era, the largest part of Africa — south of the Islamic borders along the southern edges of the Sahara Desert, stretching from the highlands of East Africa to the coastline of West Africa — had been much affected by the spread of agriculture, blacksmithing, and husbandry that diffused from the Sudan and Ethiopia after the beginning of the Christian calendar. Africa was not physically isolated from cultural currents from the Mediterranean, Southwest Asia, and India, but it was impossible for outsiders to penetrate the area until the end of the nineteenth century because the African tribes and petty kingdoms were too well organized as fighting forces. In terms of political organization, judicial systems, and complex social institutions, Africa south of the Sahara at the beginning of

European penetration a century ago possessed the same cultural levels as the copper-age proto-cultures of Sumer and Elam before the arrival of writing — though Africa had the techniques of iron-making, which arrived in the early Christian era from the north-east. Only the pagan areas in Africa were receptive to the new education brought in by Christian missionaries at the beginning of this century.

The continent of Africa remains poor and underdeveloped despite the great strides that have been made in the past 75 years. The gap between Africa and Europe is still wide, however, and will probably not narrow in this century. In contrast to Latin America, Africa's population is poorer and possesses fewer technical skills; but in comparison to India, the poorest Africans live slightly better than the poverty-stricken landless peasants of India or Bangladesh. In many ways, most residents of Ghana and the Ivory Coast have a somewhat higher standard of living than the majority living in Egypt, Algeria, or Morocco (though not Tunis and Libya). The inhabitants of the various cities of Nigeria, including the northern cities of Jos and Kano, may have a somewhat higher standard of living than do those who live in the slums of Calcutta or Dacca.

Africa both north and south of the Sahara is still living in the shadow of Primary civilization. Although the continent contains more than one-fifth of the land area of the world, its population is smaller than that of Asia or Europe, though larger than that of North or South America. Its population of over 360 million is about one-tenth of the world total. It carries on less than 4 percent of the world's trade, has less than 2 percent of the world's Gross National Production, and has an illiteracy rate of more than 84 percent (in contrast to India's 70 percent and the world's rate of 48 percent). Its health is below world standards, with life expectancy at birth for an African male of 35 years, as compared to a world average of 48 years, and a Western European and a North American expectancy of 70 years. While the rest of the world averages 54.3 physicians per 100,000 population, Africa has to make do with a little over 5.3. The poorest of the African countries are not those that have been under French, British, Belgian, or Italian domination, but those such as Ethiopia and Liberia that were never under foreign control for any length of time.

Africa as a continent has never been isolated from currents emanating from great cultural changes elsewhere. Until about 5,000 B.C., the Sahara Desert was fairly well-watered and by no means the arid area it is today. Blacks occupied the southern as well as the middle sections. Trade between the blacks of the Sahara and the Caucasoid Berbers to the north was well established even at that time. The Phoenicians established their colonies along the North African coast in the first millenium B.C. to take advantage of this trans-Saharan trade. Over a period of thousands of years, agriculture from the Middle East and North Africa permeated areas to the south of the Sahara. Cattle from Egypt and subsequently from India came early to East Africa. Goats and sheep were introduced into East and Central Africa by the first millenium B.C., though most changes in agriculture and husbandry were not diffused until just before the beginning of the Christian era. Metal working, especially in iron, spread rather rapidly over most of Africa, including West Africa, during the first millenium of the same era.

Africa south of the Sahara and the Red Sea has few natural harbors and no river that is navigable from its mouth into the interior. The rivers are full of dangerous rapids, as they flow from the highlands down to lower plateaux, and thence rush rapidly toward the sea. As a result, the first traders to move into the interior of Africa from the north were the blacks themselves; East Africans acted as middlemen for the tribes and kingdoms located in the interior of the continent. Although Phoenicians may have circumnavigated Africa by the sixth century B.C., it is doubtful that any succeeded in traveling into the interior. Whatever trade they, the later Middle Easterners, the south Arabians, the Indians, or the Chinese engaged in was mostly concentrated in a few port towns along the East African coast. Even the west coast was not penetrated by the early Portuguese or any of the later Europeans until the end of the nineteenth century. The slave trade was managed chiefly by Africans themselves, who sold their catches to European traders at various forts along the coast. The east coast slave trade was taken over by Arabs from Yemen, who from the seventh century on, used Zanzibar as their center. The first kingdoms of black Africa in the north were established in the early centuries of the Christian era, as a result of influences arriving through cultural centers in the Sudan and Ethiopia. Although these centers were early examples of Primary civilization, the kingdoms established later in Uganda, Zaire, among the Yoruba and Ashanti were somewhat in a pre-civilization mold, since there were no records, no writing, and no group of administrative scribes who acted as civil servants for the kings and nobles.

Although the African blacks in Zimbabwe (Rhodesia) in the eighth and ninth centuries of the Christian era used stonework as a result of influences from the north, none of the kingdoms in the interior or on the west coast used stone in building their administrative centers. The kings and paramount chiefs possessed larger compounds and larger huts, but there were no administrative centers anywhere in Africa similar to those erected by the Sumerians, the early Egyptians, or the Harappans. The African kingdoms, though their subjects numbered in the millions, never quite reached the levels of the early Sumerian or the Elamite city-states in the fourth millenium B.C. On the other hand, aspects of a later metal technology diffused slowly from the northeast and east coasts to the interior of Africa and its west coast. Agriculture, while using plants emanating from the Middle East through Egypt, never quite left the hoe to turn to the plow. Most of Africa continued in a late Neolithic framework of culture until the twentieth century. The civilization of the early Christian era, much as the kingdoms of Bornu, Songhai, Ghana, or Mali, were chiefly kingdoms of the Central African variety rather than of the Egyptian-Phoenician-Greek-Roman urban administrative centers.

Africa south of the Sahara would have been able to achieve the levels possessed by ancient civilizations if it had been conquered by the Egyptians, Phoenicians, Carthaginians, Greeks, Romans, or even by the later Arabs. The administrative levels of Ethiopia and the Sudan were established from the outside, as south Arabs brought their language, culture, and religions to these areas. Although conquests bring a good deal of misery and suffering, they also act as diffusers of new ideas both in technology and government. While Ethiopia was able to achieve administrative centers before the rest of Africa, the latter had to await nineteenth- and twentieth-century conquest before it was able to achieve higher educational, technological, and urban levels. Conquest by a more advanced technological power acts as a spur to the acceptance of the latter's more efficient ideas, if there is to be any sharing of the power base.

Conquests by the Islamized Moroccans brought new political organizations, writing, legal codes, advanced technology in metal-working, and religious concepts to the black kingdoms south of the Sahara from the twelfth century on — though all these concepts were retranslated and reinterpreted by the receivers. During the first half of the twentieth century, the British, French, and Belgians left a wide legacy of commerce, legal codes, judicial systems, and bureaucratic organization, along with schools, universities, and research institutes (plus the use of English and French as important international languages) to the peoples that they had governed briefly. It is easier to enter the Secondary civilization if that civilization has already been introduced by conquerors than it is to create schools and universities that never existed before, or to build new roads created from scratch by natives out of books which they had learned to read by themselves.

On the other hand, it is easier for the Ivory Coast or Nigeria, say, to enter Secondary civilization if the expense of creating new schools and of supplying teachers was first borne by the French or British, or if the social overhead involved in inaugurating universities, research institutes, or banks with their own trained personnel was originally paid for by the occupying power. The national problem arises when the occupying power makes no attempt to train natives for the executive positions, but tries to keep its own personnel as a caste in top positions as long as possible. Without the European powers bringing in their own ideas, capital, and personnel, however, it would have been virtually impossible for any of the African tribes to organize a nation-state through their own initiative.

The concept of freedom for the colony, leading to the formation of the nation-state, came from the European occupying powers who also brought their ideas of individual as well as national freedoms. France had a tradition from the French Revolution which its Colonial executives, even though they might have paid scant attention to the goals of the Revolution, brought in with their schools. The English officials, despite their caste-like behavior, used English newspapers and books in the schools they established to train minor civil servants from among the sons of chiefs and paramount chiefs. Through the printed page, the French, British, and Belgians brought in extensive ideas from the outside. The sons of native chiefs were thus trained to become French, British, or Belgian civil servants, as if they were Frenchmen, Britons, or Belgians themselves. It became a matter of high social status for tribes to send their most adept pupils to Europe or North America for an education in Secondary civilization, so that the sons upon returning would serve as its carriers.

◇   ◇   ◇   ◇   ◇

It is also difficult to overstate the important role played by the Christian missionaries as they moved into Africa after the sixteenth century, and brought European civilization with them. European and American missionaries whether Protestant or Roman Catholic also brought European and American technology, scientific points of view, conceptions of the importance of the individual, plus various political philosophies concerned with the processes of governing people. African students who went to European universities returned with conceptions of the millenarian Heavenly City, while those returning home from American universities brought ideas of a historical covenant wherein Africa was considered to have a historical mission to perform.

Even North Africa was influenced by the French and British Colonial administrators: Algeria, Morocco, and Tunis by the French, and Egypt by the British. Before the modern period, North Africa had been affected by the Arab conquest in the seventh century and by the social currents which swept through that area from Islamic Spain, Baghdad, and Cairo. Culturally, Egypt belongs with the Middle East, while Morocco and Tunis belong to the Berber world, though their people long ago adopted Arabic as a language and Islam as a religion. North Africa sees itself as "Arab," but the number of Arabs who came into the region with the Moslem conquest was exceedingly small and it is doubtful that the mixture of a Berber majority with a small Arab minority changed the genetic structure very much. Although numbers of Arabs from South Arabia moved into Egypt after the seventh century, it may be questioned whether they ever formed a majority. The Arab population of North Africa is "Arab" only in an honorary sense; like other areas in the Mediterranean world, it is mixed with different strains that arrived through the continuous migrations of peoples. The Phoenicians were not the first to found colonies on the North African coast, just as the Arabs were not the last.

While both North and South Africa have not been too isolated from the currents of European civilization, the motivation for one to become a carrier of this civilization requires an educational background which is not available in most geographical areas to most of the continent's population (just as it is lacking in southern Italy, Syria, Greece, or the poorer areas of Appalachia). Both North and Central Africa remain chiefly peasant areas, in which most of the inhabitants practice subsistence horticulture. The illiteracy rate is still high, and tradition plays a greater part in daily life than ideas disseminated by the schools or the various media of information. While Africa has made great strides toward becoming self-governing and autonomous, the continent has not been able to narrow the gap that exists between itself and Europe. Africa is still a developing continent whose promise lies very much in the future. The Scientific and Industrial civilization is more than a cultural accumulation of technology and concepts; it is also a way of life that exists in the minds of individuals who have been trained or socialized to be receptive to it. Africa's problem is that neither its leadership or most of its population are very stirred by this civilization. The role of schools is to make students into carriers, but the amount of schooling required extends from a minimum of 10 years (for the skilled mechanics who can translate the ideas of the managers, technologists, and scientists into manufactured or service products) to 16 or more years (for the entrepreneurs, the disseminators, the engineers, the skilled administrators, and the trained teachers who are needed to turn out skilled generations for the future). At the same time, the ideas of the civilization must exist within the country either in the form of books and periodicals or in the minds of individuals who are either imported for this purpose or trained to disseminate these ideas.

Until this century, Africa was self-sufficient and traditional; this included all the regions with the possible exception of the small European enclaves existing in East and South Africa. Missionaries coming from Europe and North America served as important catalysts, but the Moslem world was more resistant to their influences than were ancestral and nativist religions and cults. Although European culture first came into Africa under the guise of organized religion, the Africans have changed this religion to fit their own cultural needs.

◊   ◊   ◊   ◊   ◊

While the story of Africa until about 12,000 years ago paralleled that of the other continents, it was influenced by the agricultural and pastoral revolutions of Asia at a much later date than were Europe and the American continent — only Australia was more isolated. Although agriculture and the pastoral economy came into the Nile River region some 6,000 years ago, it evidently did not spread to the other regions of Africa until thousands of years after that. Most of the diffusion appears to have taken place in the first millenium of the Christian era, when new plants and animals from Southeast Asia seem to have been spread by the Malayan settlers of Madagascar and by continuous contacts with Indians from the subcontinent along the East African coastal region.

The migrations of the Bantu-speaking peoples to Central and East Africa may have taken place as a result of their increase in population, brought about by the introduction to them of the new Asian forms of horticulture, such as the banana and the yam, in the first millenium of the Christian era. The early Caucasoid pastoralists in the highlands of East Africa could have been the initiators of the Iron Age and the diffusers of the pastoral economy from the upper Nile River Valley, Ethiopia, and the cultural currents that came across the Red Sea to East Africa. Later on, they merged with the blacks when they were unable to stem the inroads of the more numerous Bantu hunters and fishermen who expanded from north of the equatorial forest region of Central Africa to the regions south, east, and west.

The history of Africa from the first millenium of the Christian era to the beginning of the European scramble for African territory in the second half of the nineteenth century is not too well known. Most of Africa around 1,000 A.D. was chiefly composed of folk cultures, in which agriculture was on a subsistence level. The tribes and even the petty kingdoms were organized on a kinship basis, but all possessed a highly complex social organization. One can say that the Africans south of the Sahara at this time were on the same social level as the various Celtic tribes in Central and Western Europe before the Roman Conquest.

While we cannot speak of the various highly organized tribes and the kingdoms they produced as being "civilizations" (since they did not have an administrative bureaucracy nor records, as did the Sumerians, Egyptians, and Harappans), we are in need of a term that will separate the stage of folk culture from that of organized civilization. It is difficult to use the Greek term "barbaric" for this transitional stage. The term carries a pejorative implication of a lack of "civilized" behavior, which would certainly not be true of the organized African kingdoms, in which justice and judicial forms played important parts and in which the norms and values of the cultures were carried by complex oral traditions of proverbs and folk tales. Perhaps the term "proto-civilization" may come closest to describing this transitional phase that ends with the arrival of Primary civilization with its organization of men and resources, its keeping of records, and the development of a bureaucracy that through a series of hierarchical levels attempted to carry out the decisions of the kings who headed them.

On the other hand, both North and South Africans, like peoples elsewhere, were concerned primarily with their immediate families, and by extension with those to whom they claimed ties of kinship. Slavery was as much an African institution as a Greek and Roman one. Most of the slaves sent to the New World were kidnapped or captured in war by nearby African tribes (and either transported by the latter to the coasts for export or sold to Arab slavers or Europeans), who handled the details of sale themselves — as if the human beings they sold were fat cattle, sheep, or goats ready for market. As in the rest of the world, there was a good deal of cruelty between those who governed and those who were governed. There was intense competition for social status endorsed by public opinion and tradition, and a general cultural inability to put oneself in the place of anyone who was not related by kinship, who did not subscribe to common goals, who did not speak one's language or share one's common culture. But, at the same time, there was public approval for those individuals who were peaceable, hospitable, generous, respectful of the old, and who went out of their way to care for the sick, the crippled, or those who were considered to be demented.

In both North and South Africa, Islam is a strong and conservative force. There are more Muslims than Christians or Nativists. Islam does not shatter but reinforces the traditional cultures south of the Sahara. It permits polygamy which is universally accepted. It is a simple religion which is not wedded to technology or education (as are the various forms of Christianity), and it makes no demands that native cultures must first be destroyed before conversion can take place. Islam lives side by side with native witchcraft, as Christianity cannot; it ignores the ancestral cults, which are part of traditional African culture in both North and South (though in the North the ancestral spirits take on the characteristics of saints), and it can be indifferent to all movements that exist outside the daily round of Islamic rites, norms, and values. Under Islam, one accepts things as they are; with Christianity the need for getting ahead affects the converts and their children, since missionaries bring their middle-class values along with their religious teachings.

◇   ◇   ◇   ◇   ◇

Modern Africa is a continent much affected by twentieth-century urbanism. Although there were peasant villages that were extensive and even densely populated, as among the Yoruba of western Nigeria, towns of the kind found among the ancient civilizations in Southwest Asia, India, China, or even the New World were entirely absent. The contemporary African city with its hundreds of thousands of inhabitants, its municipal organization and services, its magnetic attraction to the young from the villages, its schools, universities and governmental offices, its commercial as well as industrial districts, is a twentieth-century innovation brought into being by the Europeans who took over the supratribal administration. Many of these new cities, especially in populated Nigeria, have a population of more than a million. Cities grew from seaports that exported slaves and raw materials, from important trade confluences along the rivers, and from around the extensive mining areas of the center and the south. Today they represent the contact points where Secondary civilization meets Primary civilization and the traditional folk cultures. It is in the cities that Africans are made more conscious every day of the gap that separates them from their ancestors and from their fellow tribesmen in the villages of the hinterland.

Having the same skin color does not make the African south of the Sahara feel a kinship with those who are similarly tinted, any more than Caucasoids elsewhere see skin color as a unifying and supranational force. African tribes look upon the outside tribesman as potentially hostile and as a permanent stranger. Those living in Ibadan, Lagos, Entebbe, or Nairobi do not see their urban houses as their roots, but as temporary abodes away from their tribal territory. Tribesmen can relax in their village settings, but in the cities they become aware of the different social roles they must play, and the pressing need to make continuous compromises in their daily behavior and beliefs. Although vague attempts are made to develop a Pan-African spirit with a sense of kinship to blacks everywhere, the tribe retains the first loyalty of most Africans. The Hausa of northern Nigeria, who are Muslims, massacred the Ibo of southeast Nigeria living in their cities, who are Christians, with the same fanaticism as the Crusaders against the Jews in the Middle Ages, the Turks toward the Armenians in their midst in 1915, or the Hindus and Muslims in their communal riots in the cities of India in the 1940's. Although the concept of the nation-state with loyalty to the nation in the form of nationalism is slowly taking root, it is still far from having displaced the primary loyalty of an African to his tribe and his kinfolk.

The Europeans who came to black Africa (south of the Sahara) after the second half of the nineteenth century not only brought their technological, religious, and scientific cultures, but they also brought their ethnocentrism and neo-Darwinism, which assumed the genetic superiority of whites over those with a black skin. There was a belief that the cultures the Europeans brought with them were inherently physiological, which meant that, though the African could try to imitate the European, he could never genetically become his intellectual equal. In the twentieth century, the Africans themselves reversed this ethnocentrism by insisting that the African was biologically different from the European. He was more concerned with color, rhythm, and using his senses in general than the European. Although the latter might attempt to understand the sensuousness of the black African, he could neither understand nor be like him. Both points of view negate the concept of culture, for what the European and the African learned through the socialization process, through peers, and through the marketplace of ideas had less to do with physiology than with their receptivity to learning.

There are Africans and Africans, and even among the same new nation-states there are differences in cultural behavior between tribes, between those who live in cities and those in villages, between those who have been to school and those who have not, between those who are members of new African religions and those who adhere to European forms of Roman Catholicism and Protestantism, and between those who are Muslims and those who belong to ancestral forms of religious beliefs. It is even more difficult for Africa to develop a new supranationalism of Pan-Africanism than for Europe to develop a political and cultural community that embraces the entire continent in this or the next century. Africa is no more ready to develop a new supranationalism based upon skin color than Europe is to create an overall identity based upon a lack of pigmentation in the skin.

On the other hand, there is no doubt that in the long-range future, Africa like Europe might develop a less nationalistic and a more cosmopolitan point of view, wherein men will be able to see their similarities first rather than their differences. But at the present time Africa is more divided by the latter than united by the former. Black Africa is divided from white Africa, both Arab in the north and European in the south — and its divisions will remain. Even North Africa is divided. The Arab conquest of North Africa lasted only a few centuries, then Muslims from the Kabyle Berber tribes of Algeria and Libya conquered Egypt, to be conquered in turn by the Moroccan tribes of the Almoravides and the Almohades. The latter two tribes not only conquered all of North Africa, but also destroyed the Muslim-inspired civilizations to the south of the Sahara.

In East Africa, Arabs from the Arabian Peninsula and Egypt carried on centuries of commercial activities in their cities of Mombasa, Zanzibar, and Mogidishu, with slavery as the most important trade followed by that in spices, copper, gold, and silver. North Africans engaged in extensive trade across the Sahara, bringing Islam with their goods. Most of the regions to the south bordering on the Sahara Desert are still Islamic in religion and in judicial outlook. In the past, Islam was the religion of kings and their retainers, but in the twentieth century it has increasingly become the religion of the masses. As Islam becomes more widespread in black Africa, it also develops schisms and disunities when it becomes colored by the new nationalisms of Africa south of the Sahara, and as the North Africans compete with one another to determine who should lead the new "Arab" drive for Islamic unity. None of the North African or the "Arab" nations can permit any other than themselves to be known as the "center of Arabism."

◇   ◇   ◇   ◇   ◇

Africa south of the Sahara is changing even more rapidly as the tribes compete with one another to build the new nation-states. It is usually the smaller tribes who have combined to offset the power of the larger ones, and thus resist their assimilation into the latters' power base. Military dictatorships, often controlled by men from the smaller groupings, have taken over the largest part of West and East Africa (excepting only the Senegal, the Ivory Coast, Liberia, Kenya, and Tanzania), using the new power of the state to offer positions and security to those from the smaller tribes who help them remain in power.

Living in the urban communities has caused the African to become more receptive to the technology and commerce of the European. Although African towns are not to be compared to European or North American ones, there is a trend wherein the dwellers want to emulate the Europeans in the size of their houses, furnishings, and the number of appliances that they can buy. Although tribalism is the first loyalty of the urban African and the Tribal Union the second, there are enough inter-tribal marriages and friendships to break down the stereotype that the tribal African associates only with those of his tribe. In general, however, it is the fellow tribesmen who obtain employment for the newcomer, who offer him room and board until he can find work, and who then exert pressure upon him to join the local Tribal Union (which acts as community center, savings and loan credit bank, and enforcer of the communal image which the members try to project upon the outside community). The Tribal Union handles the lawsuits that arise between members, encourages its members to bring pride to the Union through their accomplishments, and stimulates its members to get ahead in the town by utilizing schools, credit associations, technology, and government employment.

Although there are other tribes that are equally receptive to the learning brought into Africa by the European and North American, the Ibo of southeast Nigeria stand out more than the others by their democratic village organization (as contrasted to the more authoritarian hierarchic rule of the Yoruba to the west, or the Muslim Fulani and Hausa Emirates to the north). At the turn of this century, the Ibos, who differed from the other tribes to the west and north in language and culture, numbered about five million, living in more than 200 independent villages or territorial groups, with each village or territorial group having its own government independent of the others. Unlike the Hausa to the north or the Yoruba to the west, there were no large political groupings, and few petty states or kingdoms. The Ibos were affected by the slavery that existed from the seventeenth through the nineteenth centuries, both as slaves and as slavers. (An interesting eighteenth-century document was that of an Ibo slave in England who bought his freedom, learned to be literate, and then spent the rest of his life trying to eradicate the institution of slavery in England.)[1] The Ibo were chiefly organized in extended patrilineal families ruled by councils of elders. Although chiefs were sometimes elected by the councils, the former had little actual power. Unlike the other areas of Nigeria, there was no traditional centralized authority that could be reinforced by the British, with the result

---

[1]DeGraft-Johnson, J.C., *African Glory* (New York, Walker and Company, 1954), p. 159.

that the educated younger Ibo stepped into the power vacuum which was created when the chiefs and councils were unable to agree or develop a concensus. Fortunately for the Ibo, the British never maintained large administrative staffs in Nigeria, especially in the areas occupied by the Ibo (the British relied upon indirect rule to get their decisions accepted). Unlike East Africa, there were never any temperate highlands for European settlers to organize into homesteads, so that the Europeans could not act as a middle group between British rule and the mass of the Nigerian population. The Ibo were thus able to fill the openings then available for native artisans, clerks, and minor administrative officials. Unlike the Kikuyu of Kenya, who shared a roughly similar tribal organization to that of the Ibo, the latter had less competition from Europeans and Indians.

The Ibos started off with a sort of Protestant work ethic, so dear to contemporary middle-class Americans, wherein each individual had to make his own way in the world. Ibo society has always been an "open" one in which any individual through thrift, efficiency, and education was able to "get ahead" by gaining and enhancing his prestige. In the past, one got ahead by acquiring the necessary capital to buy one's way into the various "title" societies where one could increase one's social status. Each individual had to be able to acquire "capital" by obtaining loans from relatives, friends, and those with whom he was associated in various organizations. The need to acquire social prestige and authority was transferred from the pre-British village organization to the contemporary urban scene. As a result, when the first missionaries arrived at the turn of the century, the Ibos wanted the former's schools and educational curriculum more than their Roman Catholicism or Anglicanism. The Ibos saw education as the magic door through which one could enter to take over the authority and social prestige of the British administrators, and no people in Africa have looked upon education as being an important value more than the Ibo. Others may have come close to their point of view, but none has gone beyond it. Although the Yorubas to the west started educating their sons to become lawyers and physicians decades before the Ibos, the latter made higher education available for their more able sons through a community tax. Villages began to compete with one another to build their own schools and employ their own teachers. Though universal coeducation has existed among the Ibos since 1953, it still needs more implementation. When compared, however, to the Muslims in the north of Nigeria or in North Africa (including Egypt), there is little doubt that the Ibos have fewer illiterates.

The Ibos stress both individual and group achievement. Each village community has as its chief goal the need to "get up," which means that each village competes with all the nearby villages for the most schools, churches, village halls, clubs, associations, and health clinics. Each individual has the obligation to "get up" in the world, indicating that he must strive to become part of an elite— and once in a leadership position has the duty to help his relatives also to "get up" in the world. According to Victor Uchendu, an Ibo himself, "A man who 'helps others to get up' commands much prestige. He is the 'big man,' the popular man, who deserves much respect and obedience . . .

"The Ibo world is not only a world in which people strive for equality; it is one in which change is constantly expected. Its contractual character makes it a constantly changing world . . . If you ask the Ibo why he believes that the world should be manipulated, he will reply, 'The world is a marketplace and it is subject to bargain.' "[2]

The competition between villages and extended families for higher social status implies that each individual has an obligation to educate himself to provide necessary leadership for his kin and village. Western education early became important, and various Improvement Unions and Credit Associations were formed to help each Ibo get the money he needed to go on to the university, to open up a business, to buy real estate, or to organize a small factory for making goods for the local consumer market. The Ibos after 1962 took over many of the jobs that were open to Nigerians in the British Administration and in the Nigerian Government. Ibos became officers in the army, civil servants, engineers, and technicians.

The fear that the Ibos, and to a lesser extent the Yorubas, were becoming wealthy at the expense of the northerners led to the slaughter of some 40,000 Ibos in the city of Kano in 1966. The saying that the Ibos would do anything to earn money, plus their sense of thriftiness and obligation to their relatives, encouraged an intense fear of competing with them. The massacre in 1966 led the Ibos to withdraw to their homes in southeast Nigeria, and there to set up the independent nation of Biafra. After three years of bloody civil war between Biafra and the rest of Nigeria, the former surrendered in 1970. Most of the Great Powers sent military aid to the Federal Government of Nigeria; only France and Portugal assisted the Biafrans. The Ibos have slowly forged a new tie since 1970 to a federated Nigeria. Though the Nigerian Government provided them with little technical assistance to rebuild their shattered cities and towns, all outside observers report that the Ibos have been able to reconstruct their war-ravaged areas by themselves in

---

[2]Uchendu, Victor, *The Igbo of Southeast Nigeria* (New York, Holt Rinehart and Winston, 1965), pp 12-15.

a short period of time. Economic assistance has come from "sons" abroad or various Ibo Improvement Unions in the non-Ibo cities of Nigeria to which many of the Ibos returned at the end of the civil war. The Federal Government of Nigeria promised that there would be no reprisals against the Ibos, and there have been virtually none. The Ibos are back in the universities, in commercial establishments, in factories, and in trade and transportation, though they are not yet permitted to return to their former positions in the Nigerian Federal Civil Service. Village and town dwellers are still sending their sons to universities abroad, since there are only 11,000 places in the universities of Nigeria, and there are more than 11 million Ibos. There are few universities in Europe, North America, or Israel that do not have their proportion of Ibo students.

The cultural motivations for the Industrial and Scientific civilization are thus more prevalent among the Ibos than among the other large tribes of Nigeria. The competitiveness of the Ibos and their need to compensate for their defeat in the Civil War encouraged them to embrace even more skills, create new industries, and take advantage of the opportunities open to them in a Nigeria of more than 60 million inhabitants. The latter is for the first time on the way to creating a nation-state, even though it is still divided by tribalisms, backwardness, corruption, and uneven levels of development among the tribes themselves. The Christian southerners will continue to be more literate and skillful than the Muslim northerners, with the Ibos competing with the Yoruba, the Ijaw, the Tiv, the Hausa, and the Fulani for the opportunities to "get up" that will be present in the expanding economy of Nigeria — perhaps with the Ibos pursuing their opportunities more than the others. Whether competitiveness between the tribes will lead to new superordinate goals wherein the need to do something for Nigeria rather than the tribe will become more pressing remains to be seen. A Nigeria that can utilize the cooperation and competitiveness of its tribes for nation-building can become an important counterweight to other influences in Africa.

While "socialism" of a sort will be promulgated by both the East and West African new states, one can assume that a Nigerian "socialism" is very much in the future. Such an ideology could unite many of the competing tribes under the umbrella of a new Nigerian nationalism, competing with other African nations, Europe, and North America. Although most of the population is still rural and peasant, with a per capita income of little more than $150, Nigerian cities such as Lagos and Ibadan are becoming important industrial centers with populations of more than a million. Even the Ibo urban areas are rapidly increasing their influence with at least six cities containing more than 150,000 inhabitants. The trend is toward urbanization, higher levels of education, the establishment of more universities, and more local entrepreneurs learning to produce what is now imported in order to take advantage of the local markets.

In the rest of Africa, tensions between tribes are still present. Nation-building is still going on under the aegis of military dictatorships, with some tribes being receptive to the new Secondary civilization and others resisting its changes. The competitiveness between the tribes for the goods which the new civilization has made available to them suggests that along with the new nationalism there is also an increase of scapegoating of those designated as "outsiders" or "out groups." One can assume that neither the Indians nor the Europeans are safe from this nationalistic reaction. Foreign merchants, traders, and industrialists will be increasingly viewed as "enemies" who subvert the new national feelings, or who hold nationals in contempt. While the French continue to play an important economic role in their former colonies in West Africa, it is difficult to see them holding on to their power as more and more African nationals become educated and come to believe that the competition with outsiders is unfair and one-sided, that the Africans are not permitted to have the capital, skills, nor social status possessed by "outsiders."

◇   ◇   ◇   ◇   ◇

Africa as a continent is not going to lead the world to shortcuts to the "New Society," for there are no such paths. Its problems are as intense and perhaps as insoluble today as those of Latin America, North America, Europe, or Asia. It has no sense of overall social purpose in mind as it modernizes, except perhaps that of benefiting those who modernize quickly at the expense of those who move slowly. Africa is as "racist" as Europe or Asia and as "revolutionary" as the other continents, though her revolutions await future generations to complete.

Like Latin America, the continent of Africa unfortunately cannot narrow the gap that exists technologically and scientifically between itself and Europe, Japan, and North America. As a continent Africa lies between Latin America and India, but possesses neither the technical facilities nor the trained manpower of these two, though it equals them in the peasant populations that have been bypassed by the Industrial and Scientific civilization. Africa has no "free competitive enterprise" economies growing or likely to grow in the future; the number of individuals who can create this type of economy in a vacuum are too few and far between. Governments will be expected to become the entrepreneurs, revolutionaries, technicians, and scientists. They will be expected to find and supply the capital, educate the populations, display leadership (which traditionally governments rarely do), and set the directions in which Africans are expected to move in the future. Because those in power, and especially those who come out of the military, do not have the knowledge which they need to direct these functions, their followers will experience intense frustration when the promises are not implemented, when the citizenry recognizes that it is too dependent upon the government to do things by itself, and when little is done to make the lives of the citizens fuller or their sense of purpose in life more meaningful. This can easily lead to persistent attempts to make the government more revolutionary, more rigid in trying to define its governing purposes, and at the same time more of a failure in trying to do something which it is unequipped to do.

Perhaps the Village Improvement Associations of the Ibo offer more hope that grassroots democratic organizations can develop their own sense of purpose than can synthetic plans developed by governmental leadership aided by bureaucracies primarily concerned with keeping their special positions within impoverished economies. Cooperative village organizations and credit societies on the urban level, working together with other regional associations, could provide a good deal of the education, technologies, and capital which Africa desperately needs. Sooner or later, Africans will have to learn how to blaze new pathways instead of following in the footsteps of others. Africa possesses too great an expanding population and too little time in which to cope with its mounting frustrations to permit it to turn to others for guidelines.

Africa needs to export finished products rather than raw agricultural or mineral resources, but this requires a technology and a culture which the continent still does not have. Too much of its small amounts of capital go into supporting massive armies and police forces, leading more and more to the formation of authoritarian if not totalitarian governments. Its small elites, like those in Latin America, are more concerned with the security of guaranteed government employment than in cutting down their consumption through higher taxes in order to provide more capital aid to agriculture or to the masses of illiterate poor. This suggests continuing growth in revolutionary nationalisms as the poor attempt to get out of their hopelessly low socio-economic status. To keep their power, the traditionally conservative governments will need to project plans that cannot be carried out, thus aggravating the continuous political as well as economic instability and creating more systems of "African" (or Arab) socialism, wherein government offsets the advantages held by the Asians, Lebanese,

Syrians, Europeans, or Americans by increasingly handicapping them as much as it is forced to by growing public opinion.

It is difficult to see future trends clearly in Africa. The wealthy Arab nations will certainly increase their flow of technical and military aid to exacerbate the nationalist need for the Africans to differentiate themselves from European, Israeli, and North American "outsiders." The Arab nations will also try to step into the breech left by departing Asians by training Africans to take their places, and to provide capital and technicians to displace the remaining European and American firms. Libya, Kuwait, and Saudi Arabia may use their billions to displace France and Britain from their former colonies. But instead of training technicians who can improve the level of life in the Arab countries, the wealthy Arab nations may fritter away their funds by supporting and exporting prejudices, which in time could also turn against the Arab nations themselves as being interfering "outsiders."

In the process of building new nations and new identities, it seems now as if Africa is doomed to repeat the political mistakes of Europe in the nineteenth and twentieth centuries, when nationalism was developed through defining members of the "out-groups" as "national" enemies. The concept of the "nation" suggested that decisions had to be clear as to who could be a member of the "nation" and who could not. Loyalty to the "nation" also meant submissiveness to the leader, who was seen as an incarnation of the nation as well as a reflection of what the followers saw in themselves.

Further, Africa is divided into urban versus rural areas; between former rulers and those ruled, as in Burundi and Ruanda; between the older and wealthier families along the urban West Coast and the newcomers; between "Africans" and "non-Africans;" between the educated and uneducated; between the budding middle classes and burgeoning proletarians and "lumpen-proletarians;" and between "socialists" and "conservatives;" modernists and traditionalists; Muslims and Christians; as well as between the Christians themselves. Africa both north and south of the Sahara is still polycentric, polyethnic, and polycultural. It is a mixture of Secondary civilization gently nudging Primary; it is in the process of growing as well as exploding, and of trying to achieve something new without knowing what or how. What will develop out of these frustrated personal, tribal, and "national" goals is anyone's guess, but conflict appears very much in the picture of Africa's future as the continent attempts to compete with the more developed areas of the globe for national status and indirectly for individual prestige.

The "elites" still insist upon adding to their "Western" type accommodations, appliances, cars, and food, while the lesser administrative employees, artisans, and shopkeepers try to emulate the standard of consumption of the senior civil servants, the wealthy older families, and the educated professionals. Africa is thus in the process of economic change, which could slow down but will not stop. The revolution in expectations will go on, affecting laborers, peasants, and the unskilled in general — adding to the "crime in the streets," "get rich" schemes, plans for industrializing whole regions with little capital and even fewer administrative skills. At the same time, however, it will encourage more young people to see that education is the door to higher civil service positions, military rank, and the entrepreneurial administrative levels.

The Technological and Scientific civilization will sweep Africa from one end to the other, causing immense problems that the Africans will not be able to solve by themselves. Urbanization as well as nation-building may continue at the expense of discovering new "out-groups." The government, the educated elites, and the media will flounder as they all try to articulate just what it is that they are attempting to achieve, what the social purposes of industrialization and urbanization are, and exactly what prices men are willing to pay for "progress."

XVII The Industrial and Scientific Age in Asia

Asia is the largest, the most populous, and the most culturally diverse of the continents. Out of its mass have come events that have already influenced human history or will affect it in the future. It has from earliest days sent innumerable invasions into the New World and the other continents; Europe is only a peninsula of it and migrations from north of China to the English Channel have been effected in the past without geographical obstacles barring the way.

Asia is the home of most of man's early innovations. Agriculture, the domestication of animals, the first permanently settled town, the development of irrigation, the growth of city-states, the first civilization, the first forms of writing, the first use of metals obtained from smelting ores — all of these and more were developed here and then diffused elsewhere. The first kingdoms and empires, the earliest use of brick, of architectural innovations (including the arch and dome) — all came from this area. It was also the region in which the great traditional religions of the world developed and grew: Hinduism, Buddhism, Judaism, Zorastorianism, Christianity, Islam, Confucianism, and Taoism. While Europe gave birth to scientific knowledge, the continent of Asia and its marginal regions stressed revealed religion as a source of wisdom.

Although Primary civilization developed and diffused from here, most of Asia's problems have resulted from its conservatism. While China, India, and Japan developed their Primary civilizations even before the beginning of the Christian era, their growth and development were within the confines of a peasant world ruled by a small elite. Illiteracy was rife, poverty was endemic, and generation succeeded generation with little economic or social change. The world was fixed, and men needed only to rear their children as they themselves had been reared through time-worn traditions. Men were expected to live within the traditional mold of a static human nature, a rigid form of traditional civilization, and a circumscribed social way of life that had been worked out in the past and was assumed to be valid for all time. Within all these forms there was contentment, though the search for happiness was not an important goal for mankind in Asia: one was born to do one's duty to one's family, kin, and social group as ordained by the past. The division of labor was fixed and men were expected to play their alloted roles in terms of what was customary for one's social class and social identity. Until the twentieth century, there was an almost complete absence of alternatives or options in the individual's life.

While India carried on an extensive trade with East Africa, Southeast Asia, Indonesia, the Philippines, China, and areas to the west, the amount of trade was accumulatively so small that its retroactive effect upon Indian culture and civilization could be said to have been almost nil. Although China also diffused her civilization to Korea and Japan, carried on an extensive trade with Southeast Asia, the Philippines, East Africa, and perhaps the islands of the Pacific or the New World, still its commerce did not have the effect upon the mainland or hinterland that Europe had experienced through trading with the East or that the United States and Western Europe in the eighteenth century had undergone in opening business relations with China. Asia also did not have the caliber of intellectuals of seventeenth- or eighteenth-century Europe, who were influenced by the ideas of the New World that had been discovered.

If Indian, Chinese, or Japanese sailors had visited the New World in the past, they have left no record of their trips. There was not enough intellectual curiosity among the literate officials at that time to be concerned with the customs, technology, or thinking that went on among those in foreign areas not related to them by culture. Men were satisfied with what their ancestors had left them, and though they were often frustrated in their daily lives, they saw few alternatives except within the frame of their culture — a choice between being of service to the elites, or through insurrection removing them and taking their places.

Lower castes in India could try to emulate the religious behavior of the upper ones (thereby hoping to raise their caste status one step at a time), but this was a slow process and the individual was dependent upon the cooperative behavior of the entire group. Men were concerned with the future only to the extent that they were preoccupied with death, the probability of famine, and the fear of a crippling disease. They did not have the confidence to change what had been predetermined by destiny, by fate, and by gods and spirits. Men had to do the best they could, hoping for rewards in a vague later life.

Existence in Asia, as in Europe until the seventeenth century, was a round of doing what one's ancestors did. One lived one's life as fully as one could, circumscribed by the past, by tradition, by the expectations of one's village, kinship group, and fellows. There was little in the past cultures of the vast continent of Asia that would have encouraged the individual to seek changes in the social structure, in agriculture, or in the restructuring and reorganization of the economy. There was little motivation in India, China, or the islands of Indonesia to develop a Heavenly Society on Earth. Men were not concerned with understanding how the world had been put together, nor did they feel that the Creator of the world had given man reason so that he could learn to make his own decisions on the basis of what he had discovered. Asia was chiefly concerned with what had happened in the past and not with what could take place in the future, irrespective of any thrust in that direction. The civilizations of Asia, and especially those of India and China, operated on the assumption that they were eternal, that they would continue as long as there were men to carry their cultures. And until the seventeenth century, they did go on unchanged despite various invasions from the north, east, and west. Dynasties were toppled, but the new rulers did not affect the way of life of the overwhelming mass of their subjects.

◊   ◊   ◊   ◊   ◊

Changes came about in Asia through abrupt and immediate contact with the Europeans, who brought their revolutionary culture with their ships, trade, Bibles, and guns. The new conquerors brought better means of meeting epidemics, improved means of hygiene, and better links of communication. Although abject poverty was the lot of most Asians, the population increased enormously after their arrival. From about 250 million at the end of the seventeenth century, its inhabitants doubled in number by the end of the eighteenth and nineteenth centuries, and then doubled still again by the middle of the twentieth century — to double again by the end of this century. From about 50 million in the middle of the seventeenth century, the subcontinent of India, including modern Pakistan and Bangladesh, has now reached over 700 million. China grew from about 140 million to more than 800 million today. The Indian subcontinent may well reach a population level of more than one billion by the end of this century, and China may not be too far behind (though it is trying to control its growth at the present time). Japan has also increased its population five times during the same interval, although it is perhaps the only country on the entire continent that has been able voluntarily to slow its growth.

Japan, the Philippines, and Indonesia came into the most contact with the European powers by the early part of the seventeenth century. By 1609, the Japanese Shogun had already begun to persecute the 300,000 Japanese who had been converted to Roman Catholicism (which was originally seen as a variant of the Pure Land Buddhism — a religion of salvation with which they were most familiar). The Shogun or military dictator viewed Christianity as a Trojan Horse employed by the Portuguese and the Spanish. Christianity was later repressed and the country put off-limits to foreigners, but the Dutch were permitted to have a small trading post at Nagasaki as their monopoly. The latter were consequently in a better position to introduce the technology and science of Europe than the Spaniards or the Portuguese. The effect of Spanish culture upon the Philippines first took place in the sixteenth century in religion, music, and literature. Although the Spanish conquerors brought their technology, they encouraged no further innovations. Indonesia came under the influence of the Dutch in the seventeenth century, following earlier invasions by the Hindus and Moslems from India and Malaya.

India and China traded extensively with Europe after the seventeenth century, but their populations were too isolated from both the traders and European ideas. The British in India made little effort to disseminate their culture to the Indians until after the middle of the nineteenth century. During the eighteenth century, England and France were more influenced by the cultures of India and China than the latter were affected by European technology or science. Only Japan, behind the wall erected by the Tokugawa Shogunate after 1610, was slowly being stimulated by the growth of scientific knowledge in Europe, including research on increasing agricultural yields and military technology, which had seeped in by way of the Dutch trading post at Nagasaki. Large numbers of Japanese scholars learned to read Dutch so that the latter's treatises on science and technology could be translated. The Daimyo, repressed by the new power of the Shogunate, encouraged the scholars at their various courts to seek out technical and military knowledge that would enable the lords to meet the extensive power of the Shogunate. Since the latter through tax levies kept the former poor, they had a strong motivation to increase their wealth through improved agricultural production and artisanal techniques. A revolutionary change took place after 1868 with the resignation of the Shogun and the subsequent growth of a nationalist movement. The new superordinate goals of protecting the Emperor and Japan from foreign conquest became the bases for support for an agricultural revolution along with an industrial and scientific one. Japan became receptive to European technology through the scholarly underground that developed after 1750 when scholars and merchants were encouraged to accept the European learning that was channeled to them via the Dutch.

China

China was another story. Although there was contact between the Jesuit priests and the emperors of the Ming Dynasty, the Jesuits were not the conduits for the industrial and scientific spirit as was the case with later Western European and American missionaries. The overwhelming majority of Chinese scholars were isolated from European and American currents of thought, for, unlike the Japanese, Chinese Mandarins did not need the new European knowledge to help them resolve their social problems. Even after the coming of the Manchus in the middle of the seventeenth century, there was still no desire on the part of the scholars to overthrow the Emperor, to substitute their high status for something else, or to change themselves — since there was nothing to be gained by doing so. It was more in the interests of the Mandarin-scholars of China to prevent change from taking place within the country through the introduction of European ideas than to encourage it by playing the role that the Japanese Samurai-scholars had engaged in during the eighteenth and nineteenth centuries. The Chinese Mandarins were less scholars than priests, more concerned with preserving tradition and ensuring their own special high status within Chinese society.

Even the merchants in Canton, the only port permitted to receive foreign traders during the eighteenth and early nineteenth centuries, were by no means agents of change. Their social status vis-a-vis the Mandarins, the court officials, and the large landlords was low. Unlike the Japanese merchants who had enough wealth and social influence to create a special culture around Osaka from the seventeenth century on, the merchants in Canton were chiefly limited to that area, and their influence upon the rest of the country was almost non-existent. The real agents of change in China were the Protestant evangelists who came in large numbers after the Opium War of 1842, when China was forced to accept European and American merchants and missionaries.

The great Taiping Rebellion in the 1850's owes as much to the ideas brought in by the missionaries as to the past traditions of peasant revolts. The leader of the Rebellion, in which as many as 20 million may have lost their lives, was a middle-aged man who had studied with Christian missionaries in the 1840's and who was convinced that he had to convert the Chinese to a new form of Christianity with God the Father, Jesus the Elder Brother, and he, Hung Hsiu-ch'uan, as the Younger Brother. He was highly successful in attracting alienated and discontented younger peasants, with whom he was able to conquer large areas of China. His program advocated land reform, the removal of the Emperor, and a new form of Christianity. The movement endured 15 years before it was crushed with the aid of British, American, and mercenary soldiers (who were also Christian). But its after-effect was to give underground approval to the destruction of the Imperial Way of life and to encourage the peasant to become somewhat receptive to any new moves that guaranteed him his land and family stability that would permit him to rear sons to help him work it as well as support him in his old age (and honor him after death when he joined the ancestors in protecting his descendants from other baleful spiritual influences). The Taiping Rebellion gave sanction to the premise that the peasants themselves had to safeguard their security on earth with the assistance of their ancestors in their spirit world.

The peasant world of nineteenth-century China was based upon extremely hard work, long hours of drudgery, and a round of activities that went on in the same fashion year after year, generation after generation. Growing rice in China was far more arduous than growing wheat in Europe or North America. The rice is first planted in small seed beds. Then, when the conditions and weather are ripe and after the ground has been properly irrigated, each stalk of rice grain is planted by hand in the wet fields. To understand what this means, it would be necessary for a European or an American to imagine planting an acre of wheat stalk by individual stalk while standing in muddy water up to one's knees in temperatures ranging far above 100 degrees in the sun or above 90 degrees in the shade — if there were shade. No Protestant work ethic required its followers to work harder, to bear the worst sort of drudgery more patiently, or to live more thriftily. Despite their adherence to hard work and thrift, the more than 300 million Chinese peasants in the mid-nineteenth century lived along the margin of abject poverty, little better off than their ancestors of 4,000 B.C., when agriculture first came to China. Millions died periodically from famines that swept the country from one end to the other, and millions more died of disease that found ready victims among the continuously malnourished children and adults in the countryside.

The peasants could not expect much from their lives of intense poverty. Dependent as they were upon an unknown spirit world that controlled the vagaries of weather and upon individuals far removed who could and did tax away the tiny bit of surplus that they were able to save for the hard times ahead, they also had to cope with the threat of bandits who swooped down upon their villages at harvest time to remove the rice that could enable them to last through the harsh winter weather; and to face the danger that their sons, their only comfort and hope, would be snatched away by government soldiery, wealthy landlords, or bandit gangs.

As was true elsewhere, insecurity was the mark of being a peasant in China. The Indian peasant was comforted by the fact that his contemporary behavior determined the course of his future life, but the Chinese was conditioned to believe that life was based upon unpredictable random forces that affected one's ability to survive. Man alone could do little to decide his own fate; all he could hope for was to unite with his kin to obtain the little bit of support that would make the difference between survival and death. The family was everything, for the peasant could not appeal to the Mandarins or administrators above him for justice, since he knew that each administrator was primarily concerned with looking after his own family. Nepotism was a way of life. One could expect nothing but hostility or at best indifference from those who were strangers. There was a competitive struggle between all men for the few treasures that existed upon earth, and those who won were those with the more powerful relatives. The individual by himself was helpless to ward off ill-fortune, for if worse turned to worst, he had no one but himself to fall back upon — which meant complete disaster. On the other hand, if there was a closely-knit family, or relatives nearby whom one could call upon, then in case of ill-fortune one could seek assistance, and then return the obligation to those who had helped him.

In the nineteenth century, no over-all spirit of Chinese nationalism existed with superordinate goals to provide a motivation for men to be thrifty and give their savings to the state so that it could strengthen itself against outside hostile forces. Nationalism played an important part in motivating the Japanese to accept the Industrial and Scientific civilization from Europe and North America. The vast majority of the population in China, however, were insulated from these currents until war, famine, and mass destruction in the twentieth century encouraged the growth of a new nationalism geared to the security of the state so that the individual could survive. The Industrial and Scientific civilization was brought to China through conquest by the Japanese, the French, the British, the Germans, and the Americans. The missionary activities of the latter led to the establishment of American-type colleges, medical schools, and scientific institutes supported by religious and American philanthropic institutions. The new civilization did not merely beat on the gates, as in Japan before 1868, but knocked them down and entered unannounced.

The Mandarins in China could not play the same role as the Samurai-scholars in Japan by becoming the new agents of change. Their training had made them traditionalists, with no loyalty except to the past and to the institutions that gave them high social prestige. Unlike the Medieval scholars in Europe who laid the intellectual foundations for the later humanists and scientists and who helped bring about much social change from the seventeenth through the twentieth centuries by their interpretations of the social order, the Chinese Mandarins were too much of an elite to support ideas that they knew would topple them from their high social pedestal. It was not the Chinese scholar, but the scholar trained by the European institutions and transferred to that country bodily who brought about the changes that shifted China's view from the traditional past to the resilient future, from an agricultural past to a new combination of the industrial urban with the scientific agricultural revolution.

The wars of the twentieth century also played their parts by helping to destroy the fabric of Chinese traditional society, and thus making most of the inhabitants receptive to a complete social overhaul. The changes are still taking place today, as the cities become more industrialized, as the rural areas are affected by the new agricultural cooperatives or communes, and as education (more widespread than ever before) is used to bring modern technology and science to help the peasant grow more food (without the machines, the fertilizers, or the chemical insecticides and herbicides to be found, however, in Western European countries and North America).

Though Communism took over China in 1949, it is difficult to say what the long-range effects of Chinese Communism will be. Mao's fear that it is normal for human societies to become bureaucratized and family-oriented has made him carry on a series of upheavals within China to make certain that no permanent elite will be in a position to control that country. Mao Tse-tung sees himself as a modern-day Confucius, laying down a new ethical and moral code for the future governing of China. While the new leadership is trying to industrialize the country and to give indigenous science a big push forward, China still remains a peasant country, with more than 75 percent of its population living in some 600,000 villages (now organized into communes). Its per capita GNP is still low, a little over $100, indicating that China is still a developing nation and that the gap between itself and Japan is still quite wide with little possibility that it will narrow for many decades to come.

Compared to Taiwan, Hong Kong, Singapore, and South Korea, which are on the way to becoming modern industrialized and scientific nations with an average per capita GNP of about $600 to $800, China still has a long way to go before it can amass the technical skills, the social overhead, the schools, and the trained individuals who can take the Industrial and Scientific civilization and carry it forward. China is by definition still an underdeveloped country, even though it has been made an "honorary" superpower through its possession of a seat on the five-nation Council of the United Nations. It is still not as well developed as many of the smaller nations around it nor likely to close the gap separating it from the Russians to the north or the Japanese to the east. There is little likelihood that it can catch up to the Americans in this century or in most of the next.

China's problem is that it needs to industrialize the nation with peasant power, for its population is huge, more than 800 million, and it cannot get sufficient financial or technical aid from any other power. The honeymoon with the Soviet Union ended by 1960, when the split between these two Communist nations developed over whose ideas would determine the future course of the world Communist Revolution. Mao had attempted to carry through a revolution in a most un-Marxist fashion by using the peasants rather than permitting the industrial workers to lead the vanguard. Mao was also convinced that the Chinese Communist Revolution had to be carried through by looking to the peasant revolts in the past as lessons. He was strongly opposed to the development of any bureaucratic, intellectual, or "Party" elites; therefore the peasants had to be educated to give no sanction to any authority except to the exacting one of Mao. Mao was unable to forget the lessons of Yenan in the 1930's, when, driven from Central China by the superior forces of the Kuomintang or the Nationalist armies led by Chiang Kai-shek, the Communists lost more than three-fourths of their effectives. They escaped the traps placed for them by marching 6,000 miles over almost impossible terrain, ending in Yenan where they created the base that led to their military take-over of China in 1949. At Yenan, men learned to make-do with what they had. They learned to be self-sufficient in almost all supplies. The survivors at Yenan had an esprit de corps which made them willing to sacrifice, themselves if necessary, for the common good. Despite the poverty of the Yenan period, the experience inspired a heroic effort on the part of all, wherein everyone cooperated to help solve the overwhelming problems faced by this tiny force, which through its own efforts provided the nucleus of armed forces that defeated the Nationalist armies and became the core of the later ruling Communist bureaucracy.

◇   ◇   ◇   ◇   ◇

China has been composed of hundreds of thousands of almost self-sufficient villages, each manufacturing most of what was needed and growing the food that the villagers consumed. Mao is now trying to keep the peasant and the self-sufficient village as the base for future Chinese industrialization, though this may be difficult to attain. Self-sufficiency on the national level is the goal; emphasis is placed upon everything that the nation needs being made within the country. As far as possible, light industry is located in rural areas to utilize the huge resources of labor they possess. Although the cities are growing in both industry and population, the emphasis remains upon greater industrial growth in the countryside, where mechanization is still in a primitive state and hand labor all-important. While science has been accepted and is growing in university laboratories, China has a long way to go before its science becomes as sophisticated or as widely supported as in Japan, South Korea, Taiwan, Hong Kong, or Singapore.

In the middle 1970's, China is still a poverty-stricken country despite its considerable progress. By the end of 1972, it produced more than 25 million tons of steel, 30 million metric tons of oil, and 150 billion kilowatt hours of electricity. On a per capita basis, the United States produced more than 20 times as much steel, 60 times more oil, and 200 times more electricity. China is on the way to becoming an industrial nation, but relying on its own efforts means that its progress will be slow. The nation has made great strides since 1949, but it has also made great mistakes which wasted much of the country's substance.

Before 1945, Japan invested large amounts of capital in Manchuria, but during the short Russian occupation of that province at the end of World War II, much of the machinery, locomotives, and rolling stock were removed. While Shanghai possessed extensive factories which had been established by the Japanese, British, French, and Chinese, these provided only a small base for the eventual industrialization of a country of 800 million. China still needs to increase its industrial production at least 20 times per capita to equal that of the Japanese.

During the honeymoon existing between China and the Soviet Union from 1950 to 1960, the latter supplied China with a good deal of its industrial base — even though the Soviet Union at that time was also a developing country and had barely been able to get over the devastating effects of World War II and the destruction of most of its industrial capacity in European Russia. By the time of the split between China and the Soviet Union, help from the latter had been extensive. The USSR turned over to China 24,000 sets of scientific and technical documents worth hundreds of millions of dollars, including blueprints and complete detailed descriptions for 1,400 large enterprises. By 1960, 51 percent of the railroad rolling stock, 85 percent of the trucks and tractors, 40 percent of the electric power, 55 percent of the steam and hydraulic turbines, 19 percent of the generators, 25 percent of the aluminum, and 100 percent of the synthetic rubber were all produced from enterprises built by the Soviet Union. With Soviet help the Chinese were able to triple the amount of roads and rail lines within the country in a little over 10 years. During the First Five-Year Plan, China made 55 percent of the machinery and materials she needed. In the Second and Third Five-Year Plans, the amount of self-sufficienty increased to more than 95 percent. But after the split with the Soviet Union, the Chinese wasted their manpower and resources in attempting to get a higher steel production through inefficient backyard furnaces and by rushing through a system of communes in agriculture when the leadership was not ready to organize them in an efficient fashion.

China near the end of the eighth decade of the twentieth century is ready to take its place as one of the world's industrial and scientific nations. Although its production is still low, its per capita income places it with the poor developing nations, and its education and technical levels are still below those of Japan or Europe, including the latter's Communist areas. A good deal of the national substance has been spent trying to compete with the USSR, Western Europe, and the United States in technical aid to the developing nations of Europe, Latin America, Africa, and Asia, in order to increase its political influence. While China can build roads and railways in East Africa, it would have been far better if it had built more roads and railways in China proper to extend its communications network.

The index of an industrial nation lies not in its number of urban centers with their electric power plants, factories, department stores, and paved roads, but in its amounts of electric power, industry, and paved roads in the rural areas. China's influence as a genuine world power would increase materially if it had the per capita wealth of Taiwan or Singapore. As it is, Taiwan and South Korea have already bypassed Mainland China in per capita production, education, and wealth, while Hong Kong and Singapore are at levels that China may not reach for another 50 to 60 years. It is difficult to say whether the attempt by Mao to develop grassroots autonomy for the villages, intellectual participation in the process of industrialization, and the combining of factory and school will succeed in hastening modernization. Thus far, China unlike Japan is not a twentieth-century success story, though there is little doubt that it is stronger than ever before, more stable politically, and wealthier economically. For the very poor, China has turned out to be a miracle. For the small educated middle class, the time is still too early for it to count its blessings.

India

India has made great progress since its independence in 1947, but has also increased its population to almost unbearable levels. Compared to China, its yearly progress has been somewhat less in spite of its possessing greater advantages. India inherited a larger transportation system, a better organized governmental bureaucracy, a more extensive educational system than China, plus closer contacts with the technical and scientific knowledge of the West European and North American worlds. India has also been governed by a true parliamentary democracy where the rights of free speech and a free press are guaranteed and have been practiced, especially if contrasted with the non-existence of such rights in totalitarian Communist China.

But unlike China, India is divided by caste, religion, language, and geographic region. Indian managers may have more access to technical know-how, but most studies seem to indicate that their achievement level and professional competence appear lower than those of their colleagues in China, who may lack the breadth of Indian technical competence but who make up for it by a drive encouraged by Chinese culture. Poverty in India today is more intense than in China, and this despite the severe winter climate in northern China, which requires that houses be substantially built, that large quantities of fuel be used for heating, and that clothes be warmer and thus more expensive. China does not have the hundreds of thousands of poverty-stricken sidewalk dwellers one sees in India who are born and die homeless. Although the poverty in China today is widespread, the extremes of pauperism and relative lack of deprivation appear to be less than in India, where thousands of dollars can be spent by a government bureaucrat, a manufacturer, or a professional on the wedding of a daughter.

India is divided by language as China never was. Although Mandarin cannot be understood by someone speaking Cantonese, still the common ideograms do unite the literate in the entire country. But an educated professional in Madras, speaking Tamil or Telegu, has no common bond with the professional in Delhi speaking Hindi, or the one in Calcutta who uses Bengali in his professional and daily life. The one language that unites all the educated is English, but this is seen as a carry-over of the British Colonial period. India is trying to make Hindi, now spoken by 40 percent of the population, as the single official and national language. At present, it seems more than likely that this transitional period may last for many decades to come. It seems improbable that any language can replace English as the tie that connects India with the rest of the world.

India is a very poor country with a population of more than 600 million, more than three-quarters of whom live in the 550,000 villages of that subcontinent. More than half of the population is illiterate, though great strides have been made in getting a majority of the children from ages six to eleven into elementary schools. While the caste system generally continues in the more conservative and traditional villages where each caste plays a part in supplying some needed service to the villagers, it is slowly breaking down in the cities in government offices, factories, and schools. The top three castes, who form less than one-fifth of the country's population, have more motivation for learning than do the Sudras (the servant or peasant class), who number over 300 million, the 100 million Harijans or Untouchables, the 60 million or more Muslims, or the 40 million or more members of the various tribal groups.

While there is a strong motivation for the lower castes to raise their social status, the chief means of doing so is still through traditional religion — by attempting to emulate the ritual behavior of the top three castes (the Brahmins, Kshatriyas, and Vaisyas or the so-called "reborn" castes). Despite the spread of education over the past 25 years, there is still no universal free education through secondary school for the vast majority of the children in all parts of India. Most engineers, managers, professionals, scientists, and technicians come from the top three castes, and from the Bombay and Madras areas rather than from Calcutta or Kerala. For many decades, the skilled and the professionals will continue to come from a tiny stratum of the population, the more affluent, intellectually-inclined castes and subcastes that were concerned in the past with learning, administration, and priestly activities. Despite the quotas set by the government for the Harijans, or Untouchables, in the civil service and in the universities, the motivation for a lower-caste child to go to school, to spend years studying, even under scholarships, is still low. The desire for education and the belief that one can be successful in learning is not part of the socialization of the vast majority of the population of India.

At the present time, the 100 million Harijans, or Untouchables, and the 300 million or more Sudras, or peasant caste, represent the most poverty-stricken elements in the population. The government of India in November, 1972, estimated that most of these live below the Indian minimum standard of living, which it placed at less than $5 per person per month. There are still more than 40 million members of various tribes who live outside the caste system in subsistence farming and herding, and extend their food supply by hunting where possible. There are also 60 million Muslims and more than 10 million Christians who are outside the caste system, which in India is the community to which one belongs. There is still no national secular entity with which all those born in India can identify. One is still known by his caste or subcaste, by his education, his income, his region, and the language which he speaks: being a Sikh, a Muslim, a Christian, or even a Buddhist puts one outside the Hindu community. Religion is the community for the overwhelming majority of Indians who live in the villages and in the cities. A smoldering hatred between Hindus and Muslims still burns beneath the surface of the various communities who form the basis for the populations of the large cities. The frustrations for the poor are still great. The government frankly admits that it may take another 30 to 50 years for the vast majority of Indians, who are poor, to reach minimum consumption standards.

There are differences in economic development between a Bombay and a Calcutta. A Bombay is able to develop industries that can meet outside competition; a Calcutta is dependent upon outside forces for the specialized knowledge which it does not possess to run industries efficiently. Calcutta remains an example of urbanism that is more a nightmare to those running it than a promise for the future. Its population is swollen by refugees, pushed off lands which they did not own by new agricultural techniques and over-population. The new "Green Revolution" in new species of dwarf wheat and rice have increased production to the point where India can almost feed itself, but the price has been very high: large numbers of surplus peasants, along with the new productive crops, becoming concentrated in the hands of non-peasants with the capital and knowledge to experiment in growing more grain for local markets. The small peasant cannot risk his subsistence by experimentation even with successfully-grown new species of grains.

In India as in the United States, the agricultural revolution goes hand in hand with declaring large numbers of individuals surplus and sending them off to the cities, which lack the facilities, manufacturing resources, and finances to absorb them. The rural problems are thus dumped into the laps of the cities which are not equipped to handle the enormous influx of unskilled and illiterate peasants. The cities need funds for sewage, water supplies, municipal housing, health clinics, schools, and other forms of social overhead which they cannot get either through their own sources of taxation, from the provinces, or from the Federal Government. India's problems are vast and the country has not begun to solve them even partially.

How is it possible to carry on an agricultural revolution that requires enormous amounts of capital, technical know-how, and locally-produced machinery, chemicals, and selected seeds with a traditional, apathetic, fatalistic, illiterate peasantry that is willing to mortgage its future to pay for a wedding or a funeral (the peasant fears losing face vis-a-vis his extended family and the members of his caste or subcaste in the village)? How can one stop an enormous population explosion where there is no social security to take care of the old, the sick or the injured; where children are seen as assets rather than as liabilities; and where one would be afraid to cut down on one's offspring without some assurance that at least two to three children will survive? Despite the optimistic forecasts emanating from India of the number of Indian males who are willing to accept vasectomy to limit their progeny, or the number of women who are willing to use the "loop," there is little likelihood that India can stabilize its population much below that of a billion and a quarter human beings, a number that it cannot handle even with the industry, education, and science that it will undoubtedly have at the beginning of the twenty-first century.

India has at least 40 to 50 million permanently unemployed individuals and at least 200 million or more underemployed in its villages, towns, and cities. It is moving into the Industrial and Scientific civilization at a time when machines are doing more work and automation requires upgraded skills rather than unskilled or semi-skilled workers. Even with the increases in consumer and food production that will undoubtedly take place during the next 20 to 30 years, hundreds of millions of Indians are doomed to an abject poverty that cannot be ameliorated very much. As more people move into the cities seeking work that does not exist, social problems will become more acute and almost insoluble, leading to frustrations which can produce greater apathy and fatalism or violence that can put in the shade past acts of organized revolutionaries or religious fanatics. The past violence of Maoist students in the Calcutta or Kerala areas could lead to widespread senseless burning and killing, as more individuals seek a means to lead them out of their present entrapment. The standard of living in India for the few affluent — though very low when compared to that in Japan, Western Europe, Israel, or North America — is still high enough to have an effect upon the personal goals of the mass of the population who benefit from almost none of it. Even the new countries of West Africa give more affluence to their professional and technical classes than the latter possess in India — let alone Bangladesh, which is still poorer, less industrialized, over-populated, frustrated, and more under-capitalized. Men no longer are willing to tolerate misfortunes, if they believe that there are ways to avoid them. Mao's China may turn out to be the torch that could set India's countryside on fire.

It is difficult to see India continuing on its present path of permitting both private enterprise and public industry. It will be pushed more and more toward the revolutionary and authoritarian Left as it attempts to persuade the affluent to cut down on their standard of living so that more capital can be saved for the government as entrepreneur and banker. Nor can the paths taken by the Soviet Union or China satisfy the growing needs of the Indian population, for the hardships endured by these two countries in industrializing could easily tip the balance toward widespread violence in India, where poverty and frustrations are greater. Industrialization and modernization require motivation and enthusiasm in the beginning, but later there are no substitutes for technical knowledge or expertise, plus the freedom to innovate, seek, and coordinate. As Professor Barry Richman[1] of the University of California

---

[1]Richman, Barry M., *Industrial Society in Communist China* (New York, Random House, 1969), p. 821.

at Los Angeles phrased it, "It is not too difficult to achieve substantial industrial progress in an industrially backward country even with sloppy management if people have the basic drive, motivation, and resourcefulness to improve their economic performance and productivity. At a certain point along the development spectrum, however, managerial talent and knowledgeableness become just as important as motivation and attitudes. If such motivation and attitudes lose some of their effectiveness, managerial know-how will become more important that much sooner."

Although motivation, achievement, and attitudes are more positive in Communist China than in India, the latter has one special advantage which it needs to utilize more efficiently in the future: that is, its managers have more access to the technical know-how which is required for an advanced industrial society than China does. The unfortunate aspect of modernization in India is that its new carriers are so few compared to the rest of the population. The overwhelming number of Indians are still outside the Industrial and Scientific civilization. Even the students are in no position to hasten the process of industrialization and scientific problem-solving; thus the burdens of modernization are put into the hands of only a few whose decisions will affect almost all the inhabitants and all the regions of the country. The few in India who are put in charge of modernization are not the most knowledgeable or the most imaginative, nor do they best know how to absorb and utilize the knowledge of the developed world for Indian purposes.

While it is clear that the peasants need to be brought closer to the knowledge of modernization, it is certainly easier to do so for children reared in middle-class families — where learning is prized — than it is in peasant families — where tradition, conservatism, and authoritarianism are all-important. The chief problem facing the underdeveloped world, including India, is how to get the vast majority of the population, rather than merely a small stratum of the educated middle class, into the mainstream of modernization. This is the problem that not even the United States, Great Britain, or France can solve successfully, let alone Japan, the Soviet Union, or Israel. The Secondary civilization has come on the scene too soon and spread around the world too rapidly to have enough time for building up a special knowledge as to how one changes an individual reared in the mentality of a Primary civilization into one who is able to adapt, adjust, and participate in the techniques carried by the Industrial and Scientific civilization. Since this basic knowledge is lacking in most of India, those frustrated by the slowness of modernization may turn to totalitarian shortcuts that bring modernization no sooner, though they may appear to bring pseudo-answers.

◇   ◇   ◇   ◇   ◇

India is in a very confused position as it attempts to develop priorities in investments for the next two to three decades. While the Community Development Program will have some lasting effect in bringing more knowledge to the villagers, still the effort has been minor rather than major, for little or nothing has been done by the government, by the universities, or by segments of private industry to deal with the rural problems that lie ahead. An agricultural revolution is badly needed, but there is still not enough land for those who want to continue to cultivate it as it has been in the past. An exploding village population means that it is more important to increase enormously the food production per hectare than to put into cultivation all the land that lies fallow. Much of the latter is of poor quality, and the vagaries of the weather make its cultivation a gamble by men who cannot afford to take risks, who are very much undercapitalized, and who are suspicious of all those not of their caste or subcaste. The entire Community Development Program has been predicated upon bringing in individuals from the outside who would serve as the Servant of the Village (Gram Sevak); but, since these individuals are strangers who are sent in by the government and who occupy a superior economic and social status, it is to be expected that their influence will be minimal until the villagers themselves become agents of change (which has not happened thus far). The ones who have gained most from the Community Development Program, from the "Green Revolution," and from the knowledge of the Industrial and Scientific civilization as diffused into India, have been the more educated members of the upper three castes. As the richer upper castes, retired military officers, and businessmen who have invested in land mechanize their farming to take advantage of the enormous local market, more and more inefficient and uneducated peasants are pushed off the land and move to the cities where they are unwanted. The priorities require that enormous sums of money, which India does not have, be invested to keep the peasants in their villages but with a diversified local industry and more self-sufficiency. Cheap rural labor needs to be used in manufacturing processes that require a small capital investment. The rural areas must also have a far better transportation network than the countryside possesses at present.

The Industrial and Scientific civilization spreads in waves. In a developing nation such as India, it comes first into the areas that were formerly the administrative and supply centers of the British occupiers. These towns attracted population from the surrounding area, and in turn were affected by the work, technology, and ideas of the occupiers. The early industrialists were suppliers to the British, and often came from the new commercial centers such as Bombay, Madras, and Calcutta — none of which existed before the eighteenth century. They often came from groups considered "outsiders" by the Brahmins — the Parsis (or Zoroastrians), Muslim trading groups, and the Vaisyas (or trading caste). At times, groups who wished to raise themselves socially tried to become suppliers to the British in order to advance through wealth and bureaucratic privilege rather than through emulating the top Brahmin subcastes. The children who were sent to the "English" schools when they opened in the nineteenth century became the adults who advanced by way of the economic and political social systems which the British organized to manage the Indian population more easily and efficiently. Through these schools, the ideas of the Secondary civilization circulated throughout the Indian subcontinent.

As urbanization increased and as the number of schools, newspapers, journals, and books grew geometrically, the influences of the new civilization spread with them. Missionaries also helped to bring in the new ideas. At the same time, the British Raj (or administration) attempted to suppress those Hindu and Muslim ideas of the past which could counter the incoming concepts of efficiency, good management, a scientific point of view, and the eighteenth-century humanist image of the individual. India was more influenced by the British Raj than it cares to admit at the present time. The Christian missionaries also stimulated the Hindu priestly subcastes subtly to change many of their attitudes toward those beneath them in the caste hierarchy. The two catalytic agents, the British Raj and the Christian missionaries, both affected India greatly without being influenced themselves. The coming of Independence in 1947 returned many to England who had lived their entire lives in India, though they remained British in culture rather than Indian. Many a missionary returned home after spending a decade or more in India, but with his fundamentalist Christianity unaffected by Hinduism, Islam, Buddhism, or even the pantheistic point of view found among the hill tribes. Although India has attempted to resist incoming cultural knowledge by reforming the images it had of its past, the changes taking place today are making that past legendary as new cultural forces lead the country into a world of industrialization, an all-encompassing scientific point of view, and a need to visualize the nation's future more clearly.

◊   ◊   ◊   ◊   ◊

The problems of India as it moves into the last two decades of the twentieth century are vast, for no other country, not even China, can equal them. Unhappily, it lacks the research facilities to resolve these problems, and no other country can help with their solution for no other country labors with social handicaps of such extent. It is most unfortunate that the Industrial and Scientific Revolution could not have come to India two or three centuries earlier, for India might have resolved its problems with a population of no more than 100 million easier than it can with one of 600 million that is increasing at a rate of two-and-a-half percent per year. An Industrial and Scientific civilization introduced among a small population could have carried on an agricultural revolution and displaced millions to the areas of industrialization without becoming catastrophic. Industrializing a huge population at a time when automation is growing, when agricultural production has been revolutionized by new industries in chemicals and agricultural machinery, and when cities are unable to meet incoming tens of millions displaced from the land, means that India is in a poor position to take these changes in stride. With the rising levels of elementary and secondary education, plus the proliferation of universities (India cannot stop this flood of new educational facilities even if it wanted to, and it does not), the need to employ graduates at wages above the abject poverty levels of the villages will pressure the national government into devising means of increasing the nation's wealth fast and efficiently. Time, though, is not on India's side.

The greatest task facing India is how to increase opportunities for opening up access to the knowledge which is embodied in industrialization, management, transportation, distribution, and a government that interlocks the villages, towns, districts, regions, and urban metropolitan areas into an overall organizational plan. For India to take advantage of the technological and organizational knowledge required to give 600 million people an above-subsistence standard of living suggests the ability to train at least 10 percent of the population, or over 60 million, as skilled mechanics and machinists (to translate blueprints into activity), technicians, skilled clerical workers able to work with sophisticated computer information processing, educated and trained supervisors of all kinds, highly skilled management personnel, scientists, research assistants and associates, accountants, financial experts, merchandising managers, skilled personnel for distribution points, communication workers, teachers of all kinds — including those who can funnel new knowledge into the villages, factories, schools, government offices, and so on — plus more and more individuals trained to coordinate all these activities so that the whole complex can work more efficiently.

Starting in 1960, the Indian Government began an educational program in Hyderabad for training small entrepreneurs. The courses, lasting some three months, were designed to help men manage small businesses. But even if all the small entrepreneurs could afford to be away from their one to two-man businesses for three months, there are only 100,000 of these small industrial units in all of India, and at least ten times more than this number is required. The level of education among these men may not be enough to help them carry on the businesses that management consultants and advisors doing the teaching seem to have in mind, and there is little likelihood that any large number of small managers will be trained by such institutes in the next decade or two. Although institutes and programs of this sort increase the opportunities for Indians to learn more about the culture of industrialization, which includes modern management, still these opportunities are fairly limited compared to what a country like India must have to push it through the next few decades.

India needs to undergo a breakthrough in opening up more opportunities, in saturating the urban as well as village areas, in making the culture of modernization as much an everyday affair as a special body of knowledge which can only be assimilated through schools and books. How to do this is still an unsolved problem. Even the developed countries have not found solutions to upgrading the skills of the unskilled and to making greater opportunities available for the underemployed, the unemployed, and the underutilized in general. The body of knowledge embraced in modernization needs to be brought to the people rather than restricted to institutes, schools, and special classes for a few in community centers. It is also quite likely that the culture embodied in modernization may not be sufficiently understood to be taught in schools. A good deal of its knowledge is unspoken, its judgments based upon precedents, and its details of operation passed on orally rather than through the printed word. Research in understanding this complex culture has still not been undertaken to boil down the mass of its norms, values, behavior patterns, and interpersonal relations into material that can be codified, summarized, and articulated. Although the technological aspects of this culture have been written down and abstracted in definite divisions of study disciplines, it is doubtful that the behavior that creates the innovator, the skilled manager, or the successful entrepreneur has ever been summarized and organized into a discipline of its own.

The pioneers in industrialization and modernization in the developing areas obtain as much information from their business-oriented families as from formal instruction, books, or journals. The background in acquiring the knowledge on how to become an entrepreneur is absorbed chiefly in daily contact. It is also a conditioned series of conscious options or responses to particular behavioral stimuli. The motivation for modernization is thus to be found more among the trading and commercial classes within the peasant populations than among the peasants themselves. Unfortunately, modernization is also a means of enriching those merchant-capitalists who are already wealthy, thus creating large well-financed industries (as in nineteenth-century Russia and Germany) rather than small-scale entrepreneurs trying to amass capital for further expansion. If in the beginning profit margins are extremely high and if government is willing to erect high tariffs to keep out foreign competition, then industrialization as modernization can take place, but it also involves a partnership with government — which implies corruption and enriching those politicians with the favors to give. It is most unfortunate that in the underdeveloped areas science and scientific thinking do not have the stimulation of profit to get them started; the inability to view science as a means of enriching the perspective of the community-at-large rather than as a medium for building up the military and police powers of the government tends to restrict its growth.

◇   ◇   ◇   ◇   ◇

Modernization as now practiced assumes that the rich will become richer. As Gustav F. Papanek put it in a recent publication, "Governments who want to promote a rapid industrial development without relying on direct foreign investment need not be discouraged if their country does not possess an experienced industrial class, a well-educated population, or trained technicians and managers. It need not rely on a slow process of expanding the number of indigenous retailers or processors. If it has a small group of profit-seeking merchants who either possess the capital needed or have access to it, government policies to force a number of them out of their usual occupation and into industry, and to give them the high profits required for further capital accumulation, should do the trick.

"Once the industrialization is well-started, however, the country may have to cope with a high concentration of control in industry. An industrial class protected by high tariffs and other favorable regulations, possibly inclined toward nepotism and gaining in political influence, may become strongly entrenched and fail to maintain a drive toward efficiency. For political and other reasons some alternative pattern may be preferred; but a more decentralized industrial growth is likely to be less rapid in the early stages. Opening the economy to import competition at a later stage, however, can mitigate some of the potentially unfortunate aspects of concentration."[2]

---

[2]Papanek, Gustav F., *Economic Develoment Report No. 128,* Harvard University, 1969, p. 32.

The modernization process as practiced in a non-Communist country suggests that certain groups of men with access to capital will continue to become wealthier than the rest of the population and that this gap will widen rather than narrow. This process inevitably brings about political conflicts in countries with large populations, as many of the more ambitious members of the new middle classes see others being enriched and raising their social status while their own standards and levels remain stationary.

It takes a long time within any developing economy before the wealth created by modernization can filter down to those on the bottom, and in the meanwhile those who are supplying the capital for modernization are seen as reaping most of the benefits. This implies that developing countries are pushed to develop strong centralized governments who can encourage modernization through offering high rewards but also regulate and tax the new industrialists in order to siphon away a part of the wealth gained — a process necessary in order to raise the technical and educational levels of the rest of the population. Government is used both by the new industrialists, who wish to keep much of their wealth from being drained away, and by the new technical middle classes, who wish to make sure that enough wealth is equalized to give them a larger share of the benefits. Government itself is thus placed in the position of becoming an entrepreneur, with enormous power in the hands of the bureaucracy formulating the regulations and priorities for government spending of the capital derived from taxes.

The developing countries do not have any well thought-out plans for the organization of modernization but possess instead a patched-up piecemeal pragmatic series of political decisions made on the spur of the moment for the sake of day-to-day governmental expediency. This is the area in which greater research is needed so that governments and the educated part of their populations can have better knowledge of what the alternatives or options tend to be for themselves. In an era of industrialization and science, science is poorly prepared to offer the world a science of human development. Too little is known and not enough research has been financed to provide such a science with a basic foundation. Many times the social and developmental sciences turn out studies that do not touch the basics necessary to create a science of human and social development.

Japan

Japan is an example of a nation that has successfully passed through the transitional phase of modernization and is now contributing to the knowledge of this new stage in civilization. In industrialization and scientific research, Japan ranks among the top three nations of the world. In per capita production of steel, ship-building, electronics, and machine tools, the United States surpasses it only in machine tools. Japan is ahead in steel production and shipbuilding, and only slightly behind in the field of computers and electronics. In overall industrialization, it is ahead of the Soviet Union, though in some fields of the sciences — especially those that have military application — it is likely that the Soviet Union may have more research laboratories and scientists employed in weapons development, space research, and the investigation of atomic energy. Japan is at present a capital-rich nation, with a standard of living approaching that of Western Europe (its per capita income was $2,300 in 1973). Its educational institutions are on a par with those of North America, Western Europe, and the Soviet Union, and far superior to those of India, China, South America, and Africa. The Japanese Government is stable as is the economy, though few modern nations have such a high percentage of "leftist" Socialists and Communists in their electorate. A majority of students in Japan are convinced that capitalism is doomed despite the special kind of state capitalism (wherein Big Business and Big Government cooperate closely in setting priorities to benefit the nation) that has been in existence in Japan for more than a century and has succeeded even beyond the wildest expectations of the original planners of the Meiji Period.

Japan has been in close touch with Western knowledge for more than four centuries, as a result of the arrival of Spanish mis-sionaries in the early part of the sixteenth century. Even though the missionaries were driven out less than a century later and Christians forced openly to recant, this contact with the West con-tinued through the Dutch trading post at Nagasaki, already refer-red to, from the early part of the seventeenth century until Japan unlocked her gates to Western influences after the middle of the nineteenth century. Although her merchants were given low status by the Samurai from the fifteenth century on, by the eighteenth century a commercial revolution had taken place in both Osaka and Edo that raised the income and capital levels of the merchants and created a market receptive to banking, chain store operations, and large-scale cottage industry. By 1700, Edo (present-day Tokyo), the seat of the Shogun (the military generalissimo) and his large bureaucratic staff, had about 800,000 (a population equivalent to that of Paris or London at that time) and thus itself a large market. Osaka, the commercial center of eighteenth-century Japan, had more than 400,000. Kyoto, the home of the Emperor, also had a population close to 400,000, while there were many cities containing 40,000 to 100,000. By the early part of the eighteenth century, 10 percent of the Japanese population lived in cities of over 10,000, a figure that was roughly equal to the urban percentage of Western Europe at that time.

This urban expansion and the existence of a large consumer market encouraged the growth of wholesaling enterprise and a large-scale rural cottage industry, utilizing the parttime labor of peasant families. There was also a development of artisanal enterprises in the cities which catered to the Shogun and his court, the bureaucrats, the Lords (who were compelled to station their families in Edo), the Samurai (who were supported by the Daimyo, or the Lords), and large numbers of Ronin (masterless Samurai, who turned to mercantile pursuits of various kinds to make money, even though wealthy merchants earned the anger of powerful Daimyo who often confiscated their wealth on the grounds that they were too ostentatious).

A paper currency came into existence at the end of the seventeenth century, and by the early part of the eighteenth century the creation of a money economy, displacing the use of rice as a currency, required that banks be established. Many of the large-scale department stores found in Japan today had their start in the chain retail stores established during the early part of the eighteenth century by merchants in Osaka, Kyoto, and Edo to cater to the urban market while at the same time employing close and trusted relatives to manage them. The wealthy merchants of Osaka and Edo were able to develop an entertainment market, including a new form of theater, the Kabuki, a new literature, and a music which was different from court or rural music.

At the same time, Christians who had gone underground during the repressions of the Shogun in the early part of the seventeenth century proved receptive to Western influences that emanated from the Dutch trading post at Nagasaki. Schools were also encouraged at this time by the Hans, or clans, as many of the Daimyo encouraged historical scholarship to dilute the power wielded by the Shogun (who held a balance of power between the Emperor and his court at Kyoto and the various clan Daimyo, or chieftains). Technical knowledge also provided a means with which to offset the high rate of confiscatory taxation against them by the Shogun. The Lord of Mito, for example, used historical scholarship to emphasize that the Shogun ruled illegally, for he had usurped the military power of the Emperor.

The merchants, or the Chonin (many of whom were descended from disgraced Samurai or masterless Samurai or Ronin) were during the seventeenth century placed in a caste-like social category from which it was difficult to escape. They could not move into the Samurai world, nor use wealth to enter the category of nobles. As a result, the Chonin or merchants began to concentrate their energies upon business success and to create the economic climate in eighteenth-century Japan that led to its rapid modernization in the nineteenth century.

The need for literacy by the Shogun and his bureaucracy and by the merchants, all of whom had to keep records, encouraged the growth of a variety of schools — schools supported by the Bakufu (the Shogun bureaucracy), schools financed by the various clan chieftains or lords, temple schools, and small private ones (these alone numbered more than 10,000 by the early part of the nineteenth century). The result was that Japan, though isolated from the rest of the world, had a rate of literacy similar to that of Western Europe and much higher than that of China or India. By the early part of the nineteenth century, Japanese males were 40 to 50 percent literate and females 15 percent. All the Samurai were literate, along with most merchants, rural entrepreneurs, headmen, and many of the well-to-do farmers — although literacy was largely a matter of reading Confucian-based Japanese classics. A good deal of intellectualism was also encouraged among the Samurai, who combined military training with intellectual pursuits in order to better serve the Daimyo or clan lords and the Emperor.

Loyalty to the concept of the nation came early to the Samurai. Many supported commercial growth in the early nineteenth century as a means of increasing the wealth of the country, citing Holland as an example. The Daimyo encouraged increased agricultural productivity to offset the penurious condition in which many found themselves as a result of the Shogun's attempts to keep them from revolting. Japanese officials connected with the Dutch trading post at Nagasaki in 1700 urged the Shogun to lift the ban on importing foreign books, insisting that there was much that Japan could learn from Western science; and the ban was removed in 1715. Dutch was encouraged as a language of study and large numbers of Dutch books were translated into Japanese. These dealt with agriculture, astronomy, anatomy, biology, fortifications, geography, navigation, technology, and related subjects. A small group of Samurai scholars supported both by the Shogun and the various Daimyo translated into Japanese in the eighteenth century all books that were considered to have practical value in strengthening the Japanese economy, military efforts, and technology. Once sanction was given to this scholarship, greater status accrued to those studying Western subjects than to those devoted to traditional studies. Although Western books were briefly banned after 1715, the flood of Western information dealing with science and technology continued to be funneled into Japan from the Dutch trading post at Nagasaki.

There was no censorship of Western ideas, for receptivity was encouraged by the political authorities; nor was there any reaction to these ideas from the various religious orders, Buddhist as well as Shintoist, since the latter saw no conflict between the new foreign ideas and their traditional ones. Unlike Europe or the Muslim world, there were no outcries of heresy against the new knowledge. At no time did the small number of Samurai scholars break the regulations defining their work as set down by the Shogunate, nor did any of them use their studies to attack Confucianist concepts of loyalty to those in authority. As a result, Japan was able to assimilate even larger amounts of Western knowledge after 1850.

Acquiring knowledge of the new world of science and technology was stimulated in the 1850's, as the intellectual elite of Samurai saw how weak Japan was as compared to the United States, Russia, Great Britain, or France. Japanese awareness of the Chinese experience with the military force of the British during the Opium War of the 1840's motivated a search for all technical knowledge that would make Japan stronger militarily and economically. The arrival of Commodore Perry in 1853 also acted as a spur. At the same time, the equivalent of the European millenarian movements swept the various sects in Japan in the first half of the nineteenth century, promising their followers a millenarian existence, wherein there would be few or no frustrations, disease would be cured, and men would live in peace with one another as brothers. These attractions appealed to large numbers of peasants who were suffering from perennial underemployment, endemic famines, and a rising inflation caused by the continuous debasing of the rice-connected currency. The younger Samurai were also buffeted about by a sense of uselessness caused by the inability of the Daimyo to support them with any funds. These were now pushed into a movement of reform to change the feudal patterning of mid-nineteenth-century Japan into a national state in which men would be able to work for the national good rather than for any particular feudal authority, and with the Emperor as the chief symbol. The new national state required a high degree of receptivity to Western technology and military science. This motivation encouraged the Japanese elites to compete with one another for more knowledge in order to do the most for the nation. The personal need for achievement was evidently present in Japanese culture even before the nineteenth century, but it took the various crises of that century to bring up this subsurface prerequisite for competitive achievement and to place it in the service of the nation, with social recognition as the chief reward.

Within seven years after a group of Samurai scholars had climbed over Commodore Perry's ships in 1853 (examining each detail of construction, analyzing the parts and horsepower of the ship's engines, and noting the ship's armaments), the Japanese were able to sail their own French-made warship across the Pacific, arriving in San Francisco two weeks earlier than the American warship sent to bring the first Japanese diplomatic mission to the United

States. While the ship was being built in France, the blueprints used in its construction were studied as minutely by the new Japanese naval officers as the navigation of the ship itself. By 1868, a new period had begun in which conscious modernization for the good of the nation was encouraged by the Daimyo of the four largest clans. The reforms themselves were carried out by younger men from the poorer Samurai, with the aid of a large number of Chonin, or merchants from Osaka, Kyoto, and Edo (now Tokyo).

Japan in 1868 was the predecessor of the Japan of the 1970's, but the differences were great. The population was a little over 30 million. The nation was poor and militarily weak. The feudal lords of Satsuma, Chochu, Mito, and Tosa encouraged the impetus that put an end to the Tokugawa Shogunate, ended the rule of 250 semi-autonomous feudal baronies, and pushed Japan onto the path of becoming one of the great examples of an industrial and scientific nation 100 years later. The motivations for modernization were present within the culture. A great deal of freedom was given to the various literary and debating societies to deal with the question of how modernization was to take place — not *whether* it would take place, but *how* it would be put into operation. In the 1860's, scholars debated what were the best means for incorporating Western culture into traditional Japanese institutions: whether it might be better to assimilate completely to Western civilization or to take large areas selectively; whether Christianity was part of Western civilization, and if it might be best to assimilate Western forms of Christianity together with Western technology and science. In the end, it was decided that technology and science could easily be taken over without upsetting the traditional balance of Japanese social beliefs and behavior.

◇   ◇   ◇   ◇   ◇

The Government of Japan in the period after 1868 was put into the hands of young intellectuals, who had studied in the West (at a time when students were forbidden to leave the country), and who thereupon inaugurated reforms with the approval of their elders. At no time during the nineteenth century was authority within the clans challenged by the young men who were refashioning the nation. Whatever they did was done with the approval of the clans and in the name of the Emperor, even though the Emperor possessed almost no secular power. Over and over again in the documents of the Government at this period appears the phrase "to avoid shame and win respect," for Japan was embarking on the path to modernization with the full approval of the national leaders to avoid being shamed, as China had been, and to win respect in the eyes of the Western nations. Basically, this strong need to do something positive for the nation, rather than to engage in negative acts of nationalism, helped push the majority of Japanese into the position that they had obligations to make their country modern, wealthy, and militarily strong.

Groups of students were sent to the various Western nations to learn about modernization. One of the Japanese chroniclers of this period wrote in 1873, after a trip to study industrialization in Europe, "If you compare the Europe of today with the Europe of 40 years ago, you can imagine how great the changes are; then there were no trains, no steamers, no telegraph; small boats were pulled along the roads . . . " In other words, Japan was not too far behind Europe and could soon catch up.[3]

The Government also took the step of forcing the entire rural population into a money economy by doing away with the agricultural tax in kind and insisting that it be paid in cash, thus commercializing subsistence farming and forcing the rural population to increase production more in order to exchange it into money with which to pay taxes. The agricultural surplus, and especially the rural production of tea and silk, were exported in order to purchase the machines that were needed for industrialization. Fortunately, Japan was able to take advantage of a worldwide shortage of silk then caused by the viral destruction of the silkworm in France and Italy, plus the chaos in China brought about by the Taiping Rebellion. The need of the rural populations to meet the increasing burden of taxes placed upon them by the Meiji Government meant that more of the peasant's family were used as labor by the rural entrepreneurs in their efforts to fill the markets of the cities as well as abroad. A good many of the products exported before 1900 were made by the parttime labor of millions of peasant families.

From 1868 on, the Government supplied the capital to build those enterprises that it considered important in shoring up its military power. It staffed plants with foreign technicians and managers who were required to train Japanese to take their places, or were later supplanted by Japanese trained abroad in engineering and management. When a plant was running smoothly after a few years, the Government sold it at a low subsidized price to the newly trained industrialists who came from the merchant, Samurai, and Daimyo classes.

Government officials, military officers, and entrepreneurs represented all segments of the population, for the emphasis was upon ability rather than upon nepotism. The largest number of new officials came from the Samurai class primarily because it (even before

---

[3]Jansen, Marius B., "Japan Looks Back," *Foreign Affairs,* October 1968, p. 41.

the nineteenth century) more than any other emphasized training and intellectual discipline. Two-thirds of all government officials in the early Meiji Period, 83 percent of the army and navy officers, 44 percent of the entrepreneurs and corporate executives, and over 30 percent of the financiers were sons of Samurai. The wealthy peasant and merchant classes supplied the remainder.

Within 26 years after the decisions of the powerful feudal clans to make Japan into a modern state, the new navy was able to defeat the weak Chinese fleet in a short war and to annex Formosa (Taiwan). By the end of the century, Japan had become a completely literate (though not educated) nation. By the beginning of the twentieth century, it was able to challenge Russia in Korea, and within a few years defeat Russian military forces in Manchuria and a large part of the Czarist navy in an engagement off the west coast of Japan. After 1905 and 1918, Japan annexed the southern Manchurian ports, which had been developed by the Russians, and southern Sakhalin (the Russians took it back in 1945 and occupied islands off the northern coast of Japan which had never been in their possession). Japan occupied Korea and the German concession of Shantung in China, plus important island groups in the South Pacific which had been German until World War I. During the latter war, Japan became an important supplier of industrial and military goods to the United States and Great Britain.

After World War I, authoritarianism of the Left as well as of the Right increased steadily among the frustrated members of the lower classes. Universal male suffrage in 1925 encouraged an anti-aristocratic and anti-intellectual vote among the artisans, small-town merchants, and peasants, which led a large segment of the population to support authoritarian nationalist groups. The growth of nationalism among the younger military officers from the lower-middle classes in the rural and urban areas was also a reaction against the authority of the elders, or the Establishment, who were viewed as being too "liberal," "intellectual," and commercially-oriented. This steady growth in authoritarianism among the young led to a national politics of expansion which inevitably produced a conflict with the United States and embroiled Japan in World War II. Efficiency and population increases in the rural areas displaced millions of young people, most of whom flocked to the cities seeking secure employment. This was to be found, however, only among the large corporations who employed less than 10 percent of the working population. The new assertions of the militarists and nationalists that it was now necessary to create a new "co-prosperity sphere" in Eastern Asia found a receptive ear among the frustrated young in both rural and urban areas. Assassinations, terror, and mystical appeals to uphold the cult of the Emperor helped bring the new authoritarians to power.

During the closing months of the Pacific War, American incendiary bombs burned most Japanese cities to a fine ash, excepting the ancient capital of Kyoto (which was spared by American bombers because of its irreplaceable architectural treasures), Nara, and Nikko. Two atomic bombs turned Hiroshima and Nagasaki into holocausts. In Tokyo, Osaka, Nagoya, Kobe, and other industrial and commercial cities, the blackened, roofless shells of ferro-concrete buildings stood like rigid corpses in the destroyed business sections; surrounding them were empty spaces stretching for miles in all directions, where the flimsily built houses of millions of Japanese had originally stood.

◇   ◇   ◇   ◇   ◇

The reforms effected by the American Military Occupation (which fitted into the patterning of the seventeenth-century Tokugawa Shogunate, General MacArthur being seen merely as the new Shogun) became part of Japan's postwar political culture. Education was opened to all. University enrollment increased to more than 20 times its prewar figures. The Socialists and Communists, representing more than 30 percent of the electorate, are still the main opposition parties to the conservative Liberal Democrats in power. The Right is, however, small in numbers and influence. Academic freedom is widespread, and along with freedom of the press and speech, the right to join a labor union (which had been forbidden in the prewar period), the right of women to vote, and religious freedom are all guaranteed by the Japanese Constitution (which is not a piece of paper as is the famous Stalin Constitution of 1936, but is enforced by an independent judiciary system). With all of its faults (the chief one being that of cultural arrogance), the authoritarian American Military Occupation did succeed in bringing Japan back to its prewar path of liberalism and parliamentarianism.

◇   ◇   ◇   ◇   ◇

Japan has grown rich since 1945 largely because the Korean and Vietnamese Wars were close to Japan and it was possible to furnish the American military with large amounts of supplies it needed. Japan's economic structure is more than 20 times as strong as it was when the country first began its adventures in China in 1937. If Japan had then been as powerful economically as it is today, the United States would have found it almost impossible to defeat it. Never in Japanese history have its people been as prosperous, educated, and democratically-inclined as they are today. Agriculture has been revolutionalized, and considering the small amount of land available for tillage, the Japanese do better with their small plots of land than the Americans with their large farms. The small Japanese farmer using less than an acre of land grows more rice, using more fertilizers and pesticides than the American, though he also puts in more hours of work. Farmers in Japan operating less than one-half of an acre sell almost 40 percent of their produce. Farmers owning one to two-and-a-half acres of land market almost two-thirds of their crops. Japanese farmers have been producing for the market from the Tokugawa days on. Despite intensive modernization, utilizing machines that are inexpensive and in use continuously, Japan has twice as many small farms as are to be found in all of America, but no surplus farmers and no landless laborers. The average farm sells produce worth more than $5,000 annually. Unlike India, where there is little social incentive for a small landowner to increase the productivity of his acreage, the Japanese farmer feels compelled to work harder to push his production per plot of land ever higher. Despite the urbanization of Japan, the average small farmer makes enough money from his small plot of land and the parttime labors of his family and himself to provide a standard of living roughly equivalent to that of a semi-skilled worker in the cities.

Japan is continuing on its path to greater industrialization, though its modernization is somewhat uneven. At present, it is one of the top three of industrial nations, although on a per capita basis it has left the Soviet Union far behind and is drawing closer to the production and living standards of Sweden, Germany, Switzerland, France, and the United States. Its universities are on a par with those of the United States or the Soviet Union. Though there is not quite as much research carried on in Japan as in the United States, the Japanese perform on the same level as France, Great Britain, and Germany. Because so much social and cultural change will take place in the next two to three decades, it is difficult at present to deal with Japanese trends. There is no doubt that the country is a success story that will continue into the next century. Its standard of living will rise, as will its industrialization, and there is little doubt that as far as super-economic powers go, Japan is a very important member of that club. It may well be followed in Asia by South Korea, Taiwan, Singapore, and South Vietnam. But the economic gap between Japan and its neighbors will continue to be wide, for it has a headstart of many decades. Although Japan is lacking in raw materials, there are enough supplies within the coastal regions of both sides of the Pacific to enable it to be able to go even further in industrialization. There are enormous resources still uncovered nearby that Japanese capital and technical skills can bring into production. Too, the world is moving rapidly toward discovering new and still unknown sources of energy, plus new synthetics from common materials. In these fields, Japan has a strong incentive to be one of the few pioneers in exploring technical frontiers. Men thus far have attempted to investigate the limited supplies of metals, fuels, and energy. During coming centuries, the inexhaustible ones will need to be uncovered.

Because Japan is faced with the same research needs as the United States, it will be propelled into the next civilization, the Tertiary, just as swiftly as the latter. Japan needs to learn to industrialize without making cities unlivable; to communicate without making the media a new opiate; to educate without repeating the irrationalities of the past; to create more knowledge without ignoring the ideas that have already been brought into being; to utilize all the new knowledge without restricting usage to those ideas that are seen as having practical importance only for the moment; to develop new freedoms without losing the sense of obligation that the Japanese have always had to the society as a whole; and to encourage a series of new guidelines to bring into being the large number of varied aptitudes and talents which exist in the population.

◇   ◇   ◇   ◇   ◇

Like the United States, Japan needs to learn not to waste its economic substance in military adventures. With one-fifth of its postadolescents in colleges and universities, it needs to use its trained minds to help it avoid making decisions which are not viable, and to assist it to open up new intellectual horizons which will enable it to work closely with its neighbors without giving them the impression that it is out to dominate them. Japan also needs to use its enormous capital and intellectual resources to help its neighbors resolve their seemingly insoluble problems, for Japan is obligated to play the leading part in Asia's future history mainly because of its enormous resources which none of its neighbors possess.

The Soviet Union will be unable to build up Siberia to equal the wealth of Japan during the next few decades. Certainly China, in this century at least, will come nowhere near to Japan's per capita GNP, and neither will India, Indonesia, Pakistan, Bangladesh, or the Philippines. Eastern and Southern Asia are on the path to development, and there is little doubt that the next century on that continent will see revolutionary changes taking place. But in that time no Asian nation, including the Siberian portion of the Soviet Union, is likely to catch up or surpass the development of Japan. A few of the smaller nations may progress rapidly, but none of the larger and more populated countries can possibly move up to Japan's continuing lead in this race of nations to assimilate themselves to the new ideas of industrialization, urbanization, and science — while at the same time bringing most of their populations along with them.

As an editor of one of the largest journals in Japan phrased it more than a decade ago, Japan is still in a transitional phase from which there is no turning back: "We stand today half and half between Asia and America. Historically and geographically we are part of Asia, and this explains our yearning to be close to China, but industrially and culturally we have become an inseparable part of the Western world . . .

"On one side is still the world that is traditionally Japanese: our religious sentiments, our family feelings, our attitudes toward our children, our social personalities, our ideas toward work and achievement, and so on. No matter how modern our young people may be, they still have their marriages arranged for them by their families, though this is slowly changing among the educated ones. Our homes are slowly being Westernized, but they are still one of the last physical links which we have to the pre-Meiji Japanese past . . .

"On the other side is the modern world of Western-type skyscrapers, apartment houses, superhighways, superspeed railroads, department stores, supermarkets, television sets, and books and journals from the entire world that threaten to flood us in Japan. We need time to assimilate them all, for they have poured into our country at a fantastic rate. More and more we are becoming part of the West . . .

"You can't take in industrialization and the spirit of science and technology without taking in at the same time the thought that goes with them . . .

"We are now in the middle of our transitional period, as we move out into an entirely new world. We do not know what sort of future is in store for us. We do know that we are more confused today than ever before as to what our purpose and our goals need to be . . . We know that our defense efforts will not influence the course of history, which is why there is so little enthusiasm for rebuilding the military forces in Japan. We have lived through the horror of war and we know that military might never solves problems, but merely covers them up for future generations to resolve.

"Urbanization is now part of the fabric of Japan. We are becoming detached from our families, from the extended group that gave us a sense of security in the past . . . We need a purpose, a sense of idealism, a working for society as a whole, as well as a higher standard of living. We shall get the latter, but we hope that we shall get the former in cooperation with other nations so that together we can build a world in which there is freedom, peace, and a sense of security for the common man and his children. This is what we would like to see in a Japan of the future, a good friend and neighbor to all and an enemy to none."[4]

[4]Excerpt from a personal communication.

XVIII   Return of the Industrial and Scientific Age to Europe

Europe is the home of the Industrial and Scientific civilization, but the forms it developed for that civilization are now returning after having been changed again by their stay in North America and other parts of the world. Although its birth took place in the western parts of Europe in small isolated areas, it has now returned to sweep most of the population in the remaining localities into its vast informational receptacle.

Europe is still an important area with a population of over half a billion; only Asia has a larger population. While Europe is overshadowed by the greater prosperity and economic strength of North America, the gap between it and the United States is narrowing rather than widening. The former is a continent that believes in "progress," though the means used to implement it differ from region to region and from nation to nation. Europe is small, overcrowded, and highly urbanized. Even in ancient times it was a peninsula of Asia, and there were no geographical obstacles to prevent migrations from the Lake Baikal area of Siberia, or from Outer Mongolia, from moving all the way to the English Channel, nor in reverse to Eastern Asia. Asia Minor, or Southwest Asia, has always been in touch with Europe even before the growth of civilizations as the connecting link between it and Southeast Asia, Central Asia, and Africa. Europe was also in direct contact with Africa tens of thousands of years ago. After the rise of the Mediterranean Sea following the last Glacial Age and the desiccation of the Sahara area, there were still ideological currents moving from Europe to Africa and vice versa. North Africa has been fairly close culturally to Europe and Southwest Asia during the past 15,000 years.

Although Europe was a marginal area during the early growth of urban civilization, a few thousand years ago it moved quickly to become one of the centers of urbanization with the further organization of men and the keeping of records. Six hundred years ago, Europe became the chief center of both Primary civilization and the new Secondary civilization. While China was the center of technology and the growth of knowledge from the eighth to the eleventh centuries, it ceased to be so after the fourteenth century. After 1300, Europe became less isolated from the cultural currents of other continents than the latter were themselves. Despite various plagues in the fourteenth century which reduced the population by more than one-third, Europe in the 300 years after 1650 grew from 90 million to over 550 million.

Europe is divided by language, by nation-states, by tribalisms that emphasize common descent, and by totalitarian and authoritarian religions. It has also been unable to share political panaceas to implement the concept of "progress" which is as European as the English Revolution of 1688, the French Revolution of 1789, or the Russian Revolution of 1917 — the three revolutions that were exported to the rest of the world.

Europe has not only emphasized the concept that men through reason can make their own world, but it has also engaged in some of the bloodiest wars and massacres that the globe has ever witnessed. The Secondary civilization owes a good deal of its growth to the various European kings and emperors who sent army after army across the borders of their neighboring enemies, burning, pillaging, and killing on a mass scale. The Renaissance period is known for its great artistic creativeness, but it also needs to be remembered for its wars, its insecurities, its destruction of imaginative innovation, its famines, and its slaughter of large numbers of innocents. Crime in the streets was rampant in the towns and villages, and doors and windows had to be bolted and fastened against the ever-present criminal invader — often the soldiers of outside armies, but more often the unemployed, the desperate, and the unpaid and hungry ex-soldiers. The seventeenth century may have been the century which saw the spread of science, but it was also the period of the Thirty Years' War which devastated large parts of Europe and brought on wide-spread famine. It was a century of scientific progress, but it was also a time in which the common man did not see the conditions of his life improved to any extent. It was an era that witnessed religious intolerance, the repressions of both Catholicism and Protestantism, vast peasant poverty, high levels of illiteracy, wide-spread famine, but also strivings for egalitarianism, the insistence of men that they possessed the right to seek new intellectual horizons, and the growth of scepticism about the efficacy of contemporary government.

◇   ◇   ◇   ◇   ◇

The Industrial and Scientific civilization is primarily a late nineteenth- and twentieth-century phenomenon — for most Europeans were illiterate and inefficient peasants throughout most of the earlier century. It was only toward the end and the beginning of the latter that the peasants became a minority in the population. Only during the past 100 years have cities grown to more than one million; none had this many in 1800 or even 1850. The communications that now bind the continents together and that spread the ideas of man from one country to another are again more a phenomenon of the end of the nineteenth than of previous centuries. In fact, most consumer goods were artisanal or made in cottage industries until less than a century ago; it was not until after 1945 that the majority of consumer goods were produced in large-scale plants rather than in small family-operated units. Even universal education and the mass distribution of daily newspapers and magazines intended not for the highly literate but for the semiliterate belongs more to the twentieth than to the nineteenth century. One of the features of the Industrial and Scientific civilization is the enormous market that the commercial media create to cater to the mass consumer audience. Although the scientific side of this civilization started as an elite reaction to the obscurantism that existed in previous intellectual endeavors of the Church, the industrial side of this civilization began as a mass market in textiles, then in guns, clocks, sewing machines, shoes, and assorted consumer goods. The ideas of "progress" in human society and concepts of freedom in the eighteenth and nineteenth centuries were appeals to the newly literate mass markets. Although the roots of civilization go back to the eleventh century and its growth began in the eighteenth and nineteenth centuries, its spread has chiefly taken place during the last 100 years. It is still seeking out isolated villages in the various nooks and crannies of Europe in order to add them to its following.

Europe is a series of contradictions. Although it is a continent of men striving for equality, it has nevertheless produced as much social inequality as Asia, Africa, or Latin America. The middle classes were able to cut down the social barriers that existed between themselves and the aristocrats through the English Revolution of 1688 — eliminating the functions of the aristocracy and the age-old concept of the divine right of kings to rule. Yet the desires among the non-commissioned officers in Cromwell's Republican Army for equality with the large land-owning merchant middle-class families were frustrated by this revolution, just as the lower-middle class was disappointed by the French Revolution of 1789. These yearnings for equality had much to do with the development of the nineteenth-century reaction against capitalism, which also saw the transfer of the former aristocratic privileges to the new property-owning middle classes. The latter then proceeded to ignore the need for achievement among the vast segment of the population that stood below them in the social hierarchy, and to develop even more social distinctions than had existed previously.

The Communist Revolution of 1917 attempted to satisfy some of these yearnings, but it ended up completely frustrating those who had dreamed of a new society composed of brothers whose behavior expressed their belief in social equality and social justice.

The building of railroads after the 1840's accelerated the further expansion of the ideas of the new civilization. As the villages were increasingly linked by rail, many villagers moved to the nearby growing industrial centers where they took employment in the factories. The existence of the railroads with their steam locomotives, passenger and freight cars, stirred the imaginations of the young to dream of the places that were connected by these rails and of the steamships that were links to far-away and exotic countries.

Unlike the steamship, the ancient sailing ship was unable to provide the feeling of closeness of one part of the world to another. The railways and steamships opened up large areas of Europe to outside influences, but these railways also transported military forces. Concurrently, European Colonialism used steamships to humiliate China, carve up Africa, and increase its dominant hold on India, Southeast Asia, and Indonesia.

Europe was also the home of primitive tribalism, racism, fanatic self-centered revolutionary nationalism, and police states that attempted to solve the problems of egalitarianism and social justice by repressing all moves in those directions and making dissent lese majesty subject to prison terms — if not execution.

European contradictions continued in the daily conflicts between the old mentality of Primary civilization and the new one of Secondary civilization. Ethnocentrism at the tribal stage was raised to a national level, and even to an imaginary "racial" one, utilizing modern means of communication, organization, and transportation in order to accomplish reactionary political aims. The wars which devastated Europe in the twentieth century, which caused damages extending to trillions of dollars, which killed, maimed, and injured at least 100 million people were again born in the Primary civilization mentality of generals, kings, and emperors who knew nothing of technology and science, but who were in a position to use the techniques of this civilization to mobilize tens of millions of men, manufacture mountains of munitions, and utilize the railways to bring both of these to the borders of the countries they were fighting. Adolescent concepts of masculine honor were voiced by grown men in positions of inordinate power to utilize the new civilization to destroy as many as possible of those who were defined as "enemies." Men with mentalities that went back to the Sumerians wrote books pointing out that war and its destruction represented the highest form of national diplomacy in realizing the goals of a national will. Too many statesmen believed that the simplest solution to the problems existing between nations was to mobilize as many young soldiers as possible to kill the young soldiers on the other side, so that the side which lost the most adolescents had to sue for peace on the victor's terms.

Europe was the home of the concept of the "Nordic super race," the area of "Christian" crusades, and the center of the dogma that altruistic Europeans were carrying the "white man's burden" (as semi-educated civil servants made the natives under their rule aware of their position of utter dependency on and racial inferiority to themselves). The British in India and Africa; the French in North Africa, Africa south of the Sahara, and Southeast Asia; the Dutch in Indonesia; the Germans in their pre-World War I occupation of East Africa and World War II occupation of Europe; all felt it their duty to let those occupied know of their "racial" as well as "cultural" inferiority to the occupiers.

◇   ◇   ◇   ◇   ◇

The eighteenth century developed philosophers who spoke of mankind as a unit. Though this trend continued in the nineteenth century, it was offset to a large extent by the rising tide of ethnic nationalism, which exacerbated regional prejudices and provincialisms of all kinds. Men who looked around and saw the advantages they had gained from the greater knowledge of the Industrial and Scientific civilization asked the back-patting question of why all this had accrued to them alone, and the answers they gave themselves were all variants of the theme, "We accomplished all this because we are a remarkable people."

The latter part of the nineteenth century saw another variant of this ethnocentrism in the pseudo-Darwinian concept of "the survival of the fittest," developed by the English philosopher, Herbert Spencer, which told the wealthy, the industrialists, and the British especially that they were all deserving of their affluence because they represented the "fittest who survived." The ideas of Fascism and Nazism were already born in the authoritarian attitudes of Europeans who reacted against the new tolerance of the scientific and historic mentality of Secondary civilization with the ignorance, violence, and vestiges of the tribalism of Primary civilization.

A few men in Great Britain, France, Germany, Scandinavia, Austria-Hungary, Italy, and Czarist Russia voiced the ideas of man's need for autonomy, for the right of dissent, for freedom to explore new intellectual horizons, and for the obligation to point out where the majorities and the elites were harming the future. Although socialism as a broad movement, along with its variants of anarcho-syndicalism, philosophical anarchism, and Christian socialism emphasized the importance of modesty, humbleness, and the strong links that connected Europeans to the rest of mankind, these movements also broke up into national units with strong authoritarian and dogmatic trends within their respective organizations.

Socialism grew in the nineteenth century because modernization was seen as rewarding only a few entrepreneurs possessing resources of capital, while the workers, who formed the basis of the Industrial Revolution, were treated as beasts of burden to be fed only enough to let them carry on their work. Instead of a humanist society that operated on the basis of equality, the Industrial Revolution came to be viewed as substituting a crude and vulgar aristocracy based upon money in place of a useless one based upon ownership of land. Modernization was not seen as benefiting the vast majority but only the select few, who had access to the new technical knowledge, bank financing, and paid political favors. Socialism and anarcho-syndicalism were seen as egalitarian blueprints that permitted the nation to be run by its population, wherein the industrial and scientific knowledge could be disseminated to the widest segments of the citizenry, who then learn to become self-governing and innovators. The new capitalist societies were viewed as elitist, anti-democratic, anti-humanitarian, and selfish. Industrialization and science were considered as important means to build the new society, but capitalism was seen as an anomaly belonging neither in Primary nor Secondary civilization. It possessed the mentality of the old in the way the rewards of society were distributed. It used industrialization and science not for the good of society but for amassing private wealth, and it utilized both for supporting past traditions of militarism and war.

In the main, European democratic socialism has been the cornerstone for later egalitarianism. It has supported all moves for broadening educational opportunities for the vast majority of the population, and in this sense it has been anti-elitist. It has been less nationalist in its appeals to the population than the more conservative political parties, and it has had the optimistic hope that national borders could be torn down by greater educational understanding. It has aided scientific research for creating a healthier human society and it has been opposed to the utilization of science in weapons research. Although many of the socialist parties were nationalist in their appeals for votes, few of them ever attempted to play up to ethnocentrism or European tribalisms. While a good many of the authoritarian political parties of the Right needed dependency upon strong disciplinarians who could be elder brother or father-figures (a carry-over from European formal Christian movements), the socialist parties emphasized instead the autonomy of man, his need to stand on his own feet and to learn to make his own decisions. Only the authoritarian leftwing socialists who became Communists after 1918 turned to an all-powerful political organization to act as the messianic vehicle that would lead the people to socialism. A large part of the membership, however, became disillusioned with its rigidities when inter-party conflicts within the Soviet Union were projected onto the other European Communist Parties and when the despotic tyranny of Stalin became more apparent.

Capitalism in most of the nineteenth century was seen primarily not as a new but as an old economic movement. Nor was capitalism considered the motor that moved Europe to modernization; socialism was viewed in that role. Throughout a large part of that century, most articulate spokesmen for an improved society were convinced that capitalism held industrialization and science back rather than pushed them forward. Most educated critics were convinced that, if one's goals were those of a society moving on to new and higher aims, then socialism as a way of life had to be the soul of that new civilization rather than the elitist forms of capitalism. Socialism was seen as the chief carrier of Europe's dreams of egalitarianism, democracy, and individualism. The French Revolution was considered to have carried the English Revolution of 1688 one step forward, while the socialist revolution was viewed as the means that would bring the French Revolution to completion. Under socialism, there would be a new mentality based upon the findings of science. Formal religion was viewed by most socialist parties and their members as an opiate that resolved no problems but only lulled individuals into accepting passively an unsatisfactory society based on the thesis that the present world was of no importance but that the next world (where one spent eternity) was. Socialism in this sense followed the millenarian traditions that had been underground during most of the past 1,000 years. When Jesus did not return to earth as expected, men thought that through their behavior they could create their own Earthly Paradise.

Intense nationalism and European community, capitalism and socialism, authoritarianism and democracy, altruism as a social ideal versus self-centeredness elevated into patriotism, urbanization versus traditional conservative villages, intellectualism versus anti-intellectualism, agnosticism versus fundamentalism — all these were part of the European scene during the past 100 years as the new ideas of the Industrial and Scientific civilization began to spread from a small group of scholars to the wider population, as science that came from the educated middle class began to upset traditional values that were derived from the past and reinforced by both Roman Catholicism and Protestantism. Primary civilization was virtually peasant-based. It was an elitist-run social system that was hierarchical, traditional, and assumed an unchanging world in which each individual had to know his place and could strive for a better social position only in the next world. Against this static civilization arose one that was more optimistic, that insisted that man himself had created the social world that frustrated him. While past centuries instructed man that he was dependent upon the will and whim of the supernatural deities for most of his happiness or unhappiness, men in recent time slowly began to assume that, though God is in His Heaven, He is quite uninterested in the affairs of men; that men could make a Heaven or a Hell out of their earthly lives, depending upon their own desires; and that men were born good but corrupted by the societies in which they lived. In the nineteenth century, men were told for the first time that they were alone, and that their thoughts would affect their lives and those of their descendants; that society as well as the content of culture were human inventions. The twentieth century has carried this further by stressing that man must know himself and the societies that he has created so that in the future he can do a better job of fashioning a way of life that will provide the least amount of frustration.

◇   ◇   ◇   ◇   ◇

Although Europe is unified by a common overall culture that stresses industrialization, urbanization, ethnocentrism, tribalism, and conservative beliefs, the continent is even more divided by linguistic nationalism than is India, and almost as much as Africa. Little Belgium with its population of 11 million has been divided for the past 2,000 years by a linguistic border that separates a Germanic-speaking Flemish area from a French-speaking Walloon area to the south. Yugoslavia is divided by alphabets (Cyrillic versus Latin), by religion (Roman Catholic versus Serbian Orthodox), by education (Slovenia versus Serbia), and by language (Slovenian, Croatian, Serbian, Macedonian, and their dialects). A Hitler was able to promise unity to Germany in 1933 primarily because there was so little in common between a Bavarian, a Hessian, a Saxon, or a Pomeranian, or between a Roman Catholic and a Lutheran, or between the educated urban middle class and the less educated lower-middle and peasant classes. Czechoslovakia was divided by Czechs and Slovaks, who shared neither a common cultural past nor the same attitudes toward authoritarianism or religion.

A pre-World War II Polish Government carried on warfare against Ukrainian and Lithuanian villages and even conquered Vilna, the ancient capital of Lithuania, which had been before 1919 more Yiddish- than Polish-speaking. Great Britain is still divided by England, Wales, Scotland, and Ulster, although its strong social class barriers of the past have somewhat loosened. France still has its Breton minority with nationalist overtones; Alsace and Normandy still represent subcultures, as do the Provençal and Nord areas. Italy is composed of two separate countries with the city of Rome separating the two. Northern Italy shares a cultural need for achievement with France and Germany; the area of the Mezzogiorno, or the south, still lives encased in the mentality and social violence of Primary civilization. In Norway, the sense of being Norwegian is divided by three languages in which the population can express its lack of unity: Riksmal, Landsmal, and Ny Norsk. Although Russian cultural imperialism has been disguised by internationalist Communism, the greatest problem faced by the leaders of the Soviet Union (which is neither Soviet, nor a Union of equal partners) is the growing nationalism among most of the large number of minorities within its borders in reaction against the Russification which denies them identities of their own.

Despite the divisions resulting from historical and political backgrounds, democracy as a way of life is now an integral part of Western Europe, excepting the peripheral areas of Yugoslavia, Albania, Greece, southern Italy, Spain, and Portugal. During the nineteenth century and the first part of the twentieth, only the Czechs, the Scandinavians, the British, and briefly the French had democratic traditions that were accepted by most of their populations. France voted to become a Republic in the last quarter of the nineteenth century because the Chamber of Deputies by a narrow vote decided to take over the rule of the country, which implied that a President was needed to serve as the symbolic Chief of State. In France, authoritarianism was as much a part of the country's background as it has been in Austria, Germany, or Italy. Most Frenchmen have always voted authoritarian by large majorities, whether the vote was for a DeGaulle, for Communism, or for the Conservative Right (which to describe its identity often used political terms which were at variance with its actual point of view). Even the terms Right and Left are French in origin, since they referred to where the various parties sat in the Chamber of Deputies.

Yet Western Europe, divided by historical backgrounds, cultural differences, languages, religions, and differing views of democratic and authoritarian politics, is slowly becoming unified by an economic union (though a political and cultural union is still decades, if not a century away), primarily because of the weaknesses brought about by two world wars in which the balance of political power shifted from Great Britain, France, and Germany to the United States and the Soviet Union. Although there is little in common between the various countries of Western Europe, the one thing they all share is their relative military weakness vis-a-vis these two superpowers. Their fear of the unpredictable Communists more than of the Americans has encouraged the organization of a customs union, the European Economic Community. But, unlike the German customs union of the 1830's, the European one may wait until industrialization, science, and the social democratic parties have developed a wider area of commonality.

Although both industrialization and science have their roots in Western Europe, a good part of the nineteenth- and twentieth-century industrialization represents a rediffusion from the United States. What has been termed the Americanization of Europe is only the redeployment of industrial patterns of organization and urbanization from the United States to Europe, especially in the period after 1945 or after World War II. In the decades following 1860, the United States began to build the culture of industrialization whose root ideas it had received from Europe. Between 1880 and 1920, America began to diverge from European models by emphasizing the role of the consumer market and by developing the mass manufacture of interchangeable parts. The rise of new American cities in the period after 1860 encouraged a type of architecture unknown in Europe, the skyscraper, which is more efficient in lowering the costs of housing per square meter and in making more efficient use of very expensive land. Although the skyscraper was almost exclusively an American type of building until World War II, it has since spread throughout the world, including almost all European countries. Even the Communists have learned to adapt the skyscraper to the creation of monumental public memorials, much as the ancient Romans used the Babylonian arch to create a sense of grandeur in such prosaic systems as piping water into urban areas. Europe has still not become "Americanized," despite the diffusion of American ideas concerning the organization and efficient utilization of the cultures of industrialization and of scientific thought.

Although Karl Marx emphasized the role of class conflict in trying to explain how culture change came about (and there is undoubtedly a good deal of validity to this overall and generalized social phenomenon), still the "exploitation" of classes was most often articulated by those not directly affected by the clash of exploiters and exploited: the educated intellectuals who, though competing with the rich for social status, are by no means "exploited" by them. It took Disraeli to articulate the existence of two "nations" in England during the early decades of the nineteenth century, just as Lord Ashley ferreted out the facts of child labor in the coal mines, or well-to-do Friedrich Engels described in the 1840's the living conditions of industrial workers in the Midlands. Karl Marx himself, son of a moderately well-to-do lawyer and son-in-law of a Prussian civil official, Baron von Westphalen, was one of the chief "defenders" of the "exploited," teaching that a new society could only come when the capitalist expropriators of labor were also expropriated. Then the workers would be able to manage the new industrialized society themselves, since it was they who performed the labor that made profits possible.

While Karl Marx gave recognition to the fact that the nineteenth-century capitalists had revolutionized production, turning out mountains of goods where previous ages had made only small piles, still he believed that this utilization of improved technology and the fruits of science were secondary to their primary goal of profit-making, which in the long run only impoverished industrial society. What the capitalists did in production could easily be handled by the salaried manager, technician, or engineer. Although capital was recognized as being essential in the beginning of an industrialized society, along with the amassing of profits, still a period arrived in which more efficient planning, research, and management techniques became of greater importance. Marx believed it should be possible for society to encourage the growth of scientific and technological knowledge which could easily displace the profit-seeking capitalists with groups of educated technicians, engineers, and scientists working for the enrichment of all.

In fact, what happened in the last half of the nineteenth century and the first eight decades of the twentieth seem to have indirectly borne out Karl Marx. The real revolutionary element was not that of the class-conscious urban working class but the new technical middle class composed of the educated carriers of technological and scientific ideas. It was they who learned to manage as professionals the large industries that were created after 1870, who worked out the new techniques for increasing the productivity of workers, who developed the scientific theories that helped the technicians understand what sorts of problems they were trying to solve. It is not the workers (or the peasants, whom Marx intensely disliked) who became the revolutionary carriers of the new civilization, but the educated and trained brain-workers who articulated its culture and who developed and diffused it to other areas of the world.

Although Karl Marx saw socialism as the new society created by the workers educated to take over and improve the society managed by the capitalists, it was not the industrial workers that he really had in mind but the new technical middle class of technicians, engineers, managers, and scientists. It was the scientific intellectual who was the revolutionary, and it was he who saw a conflict between himself and the capitalists, whom he viewed as being anti-intellectual, asocial, and short-sighted — criticisms which the twentieth-century intellectual still voices against those with more money than education. Karl Marx and Friedrich Engels were eighteenth-

century humanist intellectuals reacting against the development
of a non-democratic society in which they felt alienated and frustrated. While they attempted to organize the industrial workers as
a political or a revolutionary movement to bring into being a new
industrial society, neither Marx nor Engels believed that the workers by themselves could create this new society without being educated to the levels of a technical middle class.

The role of the socialists was to further this education, to make
certain that it was open to the worker and his sons so that they
could amass the knowledge needed for leadership. Without this
technical and scientific knowledge, the workers would degenerate
into "Lumpen-proletariat," violent, anomic, and authoritarian. The
peasants, on the other hand, according to Marx and Engels, were
self-centered petty capitalists who were only concerned with making
more money at the expense of their neighbors. They were not capable of being reeducated to act as the carriers of this new knowledge
by transforming themselves into a new class of educated farm intellectuals — as socialism would slowly transform the workers into
industrial intellectuals.

◇   ◇   ◇   ◇   ◇

The workers in mid-nineteenth-century Europe were generally
first-generation unskilled laborers off the farm. While the second
generation wanted their children educated so that they could occupy
the vacuum then being created between the unskilled workers and
the entrepreneurs, most of the first were more concerned with survival than with the concept of social mobility — which was implied
in Marx's analysis of class conflict. The English industrial workers
revolted half-heartedly against the industrial machines that displaced them by trying to destroy these machines, but most
nineteenth-century workers were concerned with adapting themselves passively to an industrial world they never made. The
Parisian artisans, on the other hand, were more concerned with
authoritarian revolt against the aristocratic world of both titles and
money. The replacement of that world by one that was based upon
an aristocracy of talent (the eighteenth-century dream) was, however, not in their fantasies. The German workers who were
attracted to the socialist movement were most often the skilled
workers and artisans who saw in its ideals not an equalization of
themselves with the semi-skilled and unskilled, but rather opportunities for rising to the level of the middle classes. There was greater opportunity because the process of socialization within the family fitted the sons of socialist fathers to achieve higher levels of

education than it did the children of non-socialists. In Scandinavia, Germany, Austria, and Great Britain, the Social Democratic Labor Parties emphasized the need for greater educational opportunities for the children of workers. Socialist parties in general have always been favorable to raising standards of education, plus legislation granted more money for scientific research to insure better health, social security, housing, and education for the vast majority of the nation's population. At the same time, they have been anti-militarist, anti-imperialist, and anti-religious, since most of them viewed the Establishment churches as supporting the status quo. The Social Democratic and Labor Parties have also emphasized the need for achievement on the part of the population, for most of them have had the vague ideal of creating a future society that would encourage the fulfillment of individual potentialities. Articulate writers, artists, social scientists, and theoretical physical scientists were encouraged by the Socialist Party press and journals to deal with social problems. The role of the physician in healing the ills of men became transmuted into the image of educated technicians and scientists curing the social illnesses of society.

The continental socialist ideal of a state that stands above classes, that operates in a neutral fashion for the good of the population, and that can be manipulated by the popular will, is basically an Hegelian concept going back to the eighteenth-century ideal of the Prussian state, in which the officials served the state loyally, even blindly, were incorruptible, efficient, and just — so that whoever took over the power of the state also employed its loyal civil service. The state could serve the capitalists, but its officials could also serve the socialist society, for bureaucracy was viewed only as an efficient means of organizing men and the work they did: a bureaucracy was neutral, though the officials would carry out the policies laid down by those who controlled the state. The German Social Democrats, the Austrian Socialists, the Scandinavian Social Democrats and Laborites, and certainly the British Labor Party saw the state as something that could be captured and made to carry out the popular will.

In France, Spain, and Italy, the Social Democratic movements were small and ineffective. In all three, the future socialist society was seen by anarcho-syndicalists as stemming from the individual's resistance to and separation from the state, as was the case among the Utopian Socialists of the first half of the nineteenth century. The state was seen as evil, and its bureaucrats as venal and corruptible. Both had to be completely destroyed so that a cooperative society could come into being wherein freedom for the individual from domination by centralized institutions was most important. They believed that once men were organized into political parties, those who held the reins of power in the party would dominate and rule the members who elected them to office. Rather, they held, the socialist state had to be developed by individuals who worked in cooperation with one another, who elected trustees to represent them on higher councils, but who could never be trusted with power through which they could enrich themselves or enhance their social position vis-a-vis those who elected them. The Communist movement which stemmed from the anarchist and anarcho-syndicalist traditions in these three countries tends to carry out this negative view of the contemporary state. Parliamentary representation in the past was seen as being ineffective, and the vote where it existed was seen as being meaningless — since the capitalist class was viewed as too ensconced, too powerful, and too all-controlling to give up its special privileges without a fight. The struggle had to be revolutionary rather than parliamentary or revisionist. It was possible to discipline the German Social Democrats from above to believe that they could take over the state peacefully, even going so far as to pay for their platform tickets as they took over the railroad stations (as humorously described by Lenin), but the only way in which the state could be used was to destroy it first and then create a new form of government.

The Communists believed that it could be created out of the Party (which was seen as voluntary, democratic, and non-bureaucratic), since it acted as the vanguard of the workers and was subject to their opinions and vetoes. The anarchists and the anarcho-syndicalists, on the other hand, were sceptical of displacing one authoritarian government with another based upon an authoritarian party, for they wanted only a voluntary, non-coercive cooperative group of equals to act as a substitute for the state. But the concept of the state itself was seen as evil, for any state, including a socialist one, was viewed as being coercive unless the opposition had the protection that is provided by a legal base. Voluntary cooperation, anchored upon a strong belief in the importance of the individual and his right to dissent, to be heard, and to participate in all decisions that concern him, was viewed by the anarchists as the only means of erecting a socialist society.

In France, Italy, and Spain, where centralization was a way of life for the monarchy and the Church, the Communists with their mystic belief in the Party as the substitute messianic state gradually supplanted the anarchists and the anarcho-syndicalists with the slogan that, since the destruction of capitalism and the capitalist class would take place as soon as the revolution was effected, the state was only temporary: it was not based upon class exploitation and therefore it would soon "wither away" (using Lenin's term). In all three countries, the repressed struggle for individual rights has had some effect upon the organization of the Communist Party, though the Italian Party is a trifle more experimental than the

French (despite the latter's flirting with the Socialists in an electoral alliance in 1973). In both France and Italy, the Party is still conservative and traditional, and by no means gives encouragement to intellectualism. In both, Party organization attempts to act as the rallier of past traditional revolutions rather than as a tocsin for the new. And in both, the financial support for their large bureaucratic staffs still comes largely from the Soviet Union.

From the beginning of this century, Europe as a continent has gradually been moving into Secondary civilization. Industrialization and scientific thinking have slowly spread from the large metropolises and universities to the smaller towns and villages. The carriers of this knowledge have multiplied from a few individuals to numerous surrogates — from the merchant, or master artisan turned entrepreneur, to the enormous number of technological bureaucrats, skilled technicians, scientists, their supporting staffs, and the proliferating research and administrative offices with their journals, monographs, and mimeographed papers and memos. The civilization is carried by an educated class with new values, a nontraditional way of life, and strong emphasis upon socializing its sons and daughters to have greater expectations and to accomplish more in their lives.

The new technical middle classes subscribed to future-oriented activities, other-directedness, and tendencies toward autonomy. They displayed greater egalitarianianism toward their wives and children and yearned to identify themselves with others, for they wished to escape the narrow parochialism of their elders, villages, and small towns. They identified themselves with an optimistic view of a future which the Utopian Socialists, the "Scientific Socialists (Marx and Engels)," and the anarchists (Proudhon and Bakunin), believed would be born out of the frustrations of the first half of the nineteenth century. To these men, the clash between eighteenth-century Enlightenment, nineteenth-century greed, and short-sighted goals led to a desire to substitute a new moral code for capitalism.

Class differences in behavior had always existed in preindustrial Europe. These became increasingly differentiated, however, as the first generation of educated technicians, managers, teachers, and scientists began to shift from the previous culture in which they had been socialized to one that came out of the newly printed page. They felt a need to become more aware of outside social and cultural forces and to keep abreast of new ideas so that they could cope with this changing world. They believed that future status would go to those who knew what the avant-garde were trying to achieve rather than to those who looked backward for guidelines as to how to meet new heresies that seemed to come from "outgroups."

As the nineteenth century galloped to a close to usher in an even more challenging and upsetting century, those socialized by the past sought an "in-group" to which they could turn for moral support, one in which they would not feel threatened by a changing world which they were not educated to understand. The new nationalist politics appealed to those who had been bypassed and alienated by the ideas of this new civilization which had been accumulating strength, vitality, and support after the 1860's. While many twentieth-century individuals may complain about the confusing world in which they live and which they cannot understand, a more pronounced culture shock hit the traditional peasants, landowners, artisans, and urban middle class during the second half of the nineteenth century. Most European populations in that century had been reared by traditional parents who in turn had been born and socialized by parents who were pre-industrial and pre-scientific in their mentalities, who looked backward for guidelines rather than ahead. For most of Europe's peasants, workers, and traditional middle classes, the past offered greater wisdom than the present; and, though one could perhaps gain from the new means of transportation and communication, still they had little to do with the eternal truths which had been laid down in the dim past.

The new knowledge which swept Europe in the nineteenth century had its origins in the universities, in the small research bureaus connected with them or with governmental bureaucracies, and in the top levels of the military where the blueprints of the new command economy were drawn. Although the middle classes after 1860 were growing in France, Germany, Austria-Hungary, and even in Russia and the Balkans, the stimulus to the growth of industrialization and science came from the need of the military to have bigger and better armies, along with industries to service them and railways to move them. While capitalism played its part in the nineteenth century, government encouragement and financing were perhaps even more important factors. Some of the more significant metallurgical discoveries of the nineteenth century were stimulated by the pressing need to have more and better metal for the railways that were put into operation in Europe (though not in Great Britain or the United States) as potential means of military transportation to reach one's neighbors and to defend one's borders.

With government financing and orders for business, heavy industry developed in many areas of Central and Eastern Europe. Military mechanization was almost entirely a post-World War I phenomenon. The armies of the nineteenth century had been larger, required more armament, and used up far more taxes than previous military forces, including the armies directed by Napoleon in the early pre-industrial part of the nineteenth century. Heavier cannons in greater quantity were part of military rearmament after 1860, along with more railways to transport the armament, the soldiers, and their supplies.

Since the nineteenth-century army could not forage for itself in the countryside in which it was stationed, men were encouraged to research the problem of developing foods that were nonperishable and suitable to be used by soldiers in the field. This development in turn had the indirect effect of encouraging the creation of a consumer food industry for the use of the growing urban areas. The organization of food supplies for cities of half a million or more gave new employment to more specialized segments of the growing middle classes. For most of the nineteenth century, the greatest application of new ideas on distribution of goods for the new consumer mass market took place chiefly in the United States and in Paris (rather than in France). Although the Europeans were ahead of the United States in the sciences, all of which were developed in Europe, the Americans after the 1860's led Europe in both industrialization and the application of science. Various Western European countries specialized in producing certain items: Great Britain still led in building steamships and boilers; Germany specialized in chemicals of all kinds; and France went after the luxury markets, producing finer textiles, perfumes, jewelry, soaps, and furs.

The spread of technology and science encouraged European leaders to use them as a means of enhancing their national status at the expense of neighbors of territories in other continents. The nineteenth century thus became one of European imperialism, as smaller states were absorbed by larger ones — as keeping the balance of power became the imperative which encouraged the weaker nations to become stronger by building overseas empires to which they brought their "civilizing" influence. The rise of Swedish, German, Austrian-Hungarian, Russian, French, and Italian nationalisms also encouraged the rise of Norwegian, Flemish, Czech, Slovak, Polish, Lithuanian, Latvian, Finnish, Rumanian, Bulgarian, Serbian, Croatian, Slovenian, Montenegrin, and Albanian nationalisms. The actions of the larger countries made the smaller ones suspect that they were doomed to be absorbed by the former because they were inferior, weak, and not as productive.

Yet, despite the absorption of Bavarians by a German Empire based upon Prussian hegemony, or the theoretically legal equality of the Hungarians with the Austrians within an Austro-Hungarian Empire, the Bavarians with their particularism did not want to enter a Prussian melting pot any more than the Hungarians cared to be an ingredient in the Austrian-German stew. Slovaks and Croats were given to understand that economic success within the

Hungarian sphere meant emulation of the Hungarians, though a Slovak or a Croat could never completely become a Hungarian anymore than a Pole could become a German, a Czech an Austrian, or a Bessarabian a Russian. Each large nation in Europe felt that it had a special mission to "civilize" or raise to its own cultural levels the minorities that it was able to absorb, but at the same time to increase the nationalist in-group feelings of its own core of citizens.

By the beginning of World War I, Europe had become a continent in which each man's hand was raised against his neighbor. It was easy to assess the hatreds piled up by the jingoism encouraged by the new nationalism and militarism, but it was difficult to enumerate the sympathies of one country for its neighbors. The French did not like the Germans, the Spaniards, or the Italians — let alone the British. The Germans did not like the Poles, the French, or any of their other neighbors. The Austrians, though part of a multi-national empire, encouraged the growth of a German nationalism that made possible the eventual emergence of an Adolf Hitler, in which the Germans became a "chosen people" of a mythical Teutonic history. The Slavs saw a pressing need to unite to preserve their own special "soul" from being destroyed by the materialism of the Germans, though there was little love lost among the Slavs for one another at a time when the Germans were moderating their own linguistic imperialism.

Poles and Czechs traditionally had little in common, while Czechs and Slovaks were divided by almost 1,000 years of separate rule. The Slovaks had come under the Magyars in the tenth century and did not manage to separate themselves until 1918. Poles have traditionally considered both the Prussians and the Russians as hereditary enemies, with the Austrians only slightly less so. Lithuanians have considered both the Poles and Russians as enemies of their national and linguistic heritage. The Ukrainians have seen these two as conquerors who denied them the right to be themselves culturally as well as linguistically. Flemings and Walloons have viewed each other as anything but brothers, and the English have seen all Europeans as lesser breeds (though the Welsh, Scots, and Irish have traditionally resisted being transformed into Englishmen). All the European countries, however, had one thing in common: the one "out-group" that could be used most conveniently as a scapegoat were the Jews. But even the Jews in the 1890's, because few were permitted entrance to any of the other European nationalist movements, had to develop their own nationalism in the form of Zionism.

◊   ◊   ◊   ◊   ◊

Although the ideas of the French Revolution swept through Europe as a tidal wave, they were still seen as "French." The French Revolution and the Bonapartist wars left a residue of fear of ideological subversion through conspiracies among the more nationalist groups in Europe. The Revolution was not looked upon as bringing to fruition the goals of Medieval Europeans for liberty, equality, and fraternity, but rather as a form of French imperialism using revolutionary slogans to subvert others. The fear of the eighteenth-century conspiratorial Jacobins became an undercurrent in all reactions to the nineteenth-century ideas of the European Social Democrats, just as it formed the basis for the authoritarian and totalitarian reactions to the Russian Revolution of 1917, which was seen not as a liberating movement but as an enslaving one. Conservative Europeans in the nineteenth and twentieth centuries viewed any political movement whose ideas crossed their borders as being conspiratorial with hidden motives and leadership. Since violence was seen as the end result of any movement, aggression toward its initial growth was deemed as being justified. Both capitalism and democracy were at various times considered conspiratorial movements brought in by Jews, socialists (in the pay of Jews), Communists, or American capitalists. The forgeries of the *Protocols of the Elders of Zion* found a receptive market among large numbers of insecure Europeans (just as it did among Americans in the 1920's or Arabs in the 1950's), for the Jews were merely the latest to be placed among the other imaginary conspirators — the Bavarian Illuminati, the French Masons, and the hidden Republicans in the monarchist countries.

The disorganized conditions of Western Europe after World War II submerged the attempts to build new imaginary conspiratorial enemies, although the weakness of the Russian Communists did not stop them from re-creating new conspiracies of Jews and other counter-revolutionaries in the pay of the Americans, of "rootless cosmopolitans," of "creeping capitalists," of "social fascists," and "revisionists." Those who disguised themselves as anti-Stalinists, from the official Russian point of view, were in reality Nazis, or in the pay of Israel, or of "world-wide Zionism," of "agents of capitalism," of "the C.I.A.," of the "Pentagon," of "Trotskyites," or were paid by the new betrayers of the unity of the working class, the followers of Mao Tse-tung. The Russians enjoyed a field day of success in reviving not only one but a whole series of interconnected conspirators and conspiracies attempting to overthrow the Soviet Union with help from various nefarious outsiders. Even the rising tide of intra-Soviet nationalism was seen as counter-revolutionary and directed from either the Pentagon or Peking.

While Western Europe has been sharply divided by language, class, and cultural background, Eastern or Communist Europe is even more fragmented. Since 1945, Western Europe has made an attempt to develop superordinate goals that would unite the various nations that had previously been hostile and divided. Communist Europe has actually exacerbated the divisions that formerly existed. Where there had been little hostility against the Russians, or at least the Pan-Slavic ideal, the leaders of the Soviet Union through their totalitarian political decisions have created much negativism, resentment, and hostility.

The new European Community, though still an economic ideal, was brought into being primarily because of fear of the Soviet Union and the spread of Russian-induced Communism. It was helped by the United States, who saw the need to have a powerful buffer state between itself and the Soviet Union, and by the Germans, who saw their defeat in 1945 as an end to one type of nationalism and the beginning of a new era in which it was possible for them to be identified with an even greater political force. The fear of being dependent upon the United States and the threat of being swallowed by the Soviet Union have pushed the nine countries of Western Europe into some form of economic community, though the possibility of political union remains far in the future.

Yet, a Europe united even by a customs union is a formidable economic power even when its political pressures remain weak. The nine members of the European Community have a population greater than that of the Soviet Union or the United States. Its wealth is second only to that of the United States, though it spans a range of uneven economic development from southern Italy to Scotland and Northern Ireland. But Europe since 1945 is in the process or throes of ongoing economic growth, which is still not finished. Some of the areas, as in Germany and Denmark, are wealthy compared to the poorer countries of the Balkans and Eastern Europe, but the gap between one section of a country and another is still fairly wide. Paris is the wealthiest area in France, as are Hamburg and Bremen in Germany. Copenhagen is the center of wealth and education in Denmark. London and the Midlands are wealthier than Wales, Scotland, or the North Country area. The regions around Brussels and Antwerp are more developed than the coal and iron areas of Wallonia. The rural and small town regions away from industrial areas have only recently come into the Industrial and Scientific civilization, and the latter's growth represents less than a century of effort.

◇   ◇   ◇   ◇   ◇

Taken as a whole, Europe runs the gamut from the under-developed areas which were bypassed by the educational revolution of the nineteenth century — such as Albania, Greece, Bulgaria, Portugal, Spain (although Spain is pushing itself forward industrially at a rather rapid rate with its per capita GNP reaching the equivalent of $1,000 in 1972), and southern Italy — to such wealthy ones as Sweden, Switzerland, Germany (both East and West), Denmark, Norway, Belgium, the Netherlands, France, Great Britain, and northern Italy. The Communist nations are still under-developed, even though the Czech lands before 1939 were centers of large-scale industry and rural development, including such huge areas as the Karvina, Cesky-Tesin, Plzen, Prague, Brno, and Hradec Kralove regions where Czech capital and entrepreneurial talent had created large machine-building industries in the years between the two world wars. Poland is still a developing nation with a per capita production far below that of West Germany, France, or Great Britain, let alone Sweden and Switzerland. Rumania and Bulgaria are underdeveloped, as are Hungary and Yugoslavia, which until fairly recently were almost entirely rural in production and employment. The Soviet Union, despite its enormous military expenditures, is far below the nations of Western Europe in production on a per capita basis or income. East Germany, or the German Democratic Republic, is ahead of the other Communist nations, largely because of its special links with the German Federal Republic, and also because of its own development after 1945. But in standard of living it is still far behind West Germany, Great Britain, France, Belgium, the Netherlands, Austria, Switzerland, Sweden, and the other Scandinavian countries including Finland.

The levels of European education are still below those of the United States, Japan, or the Soviet Union. Fewer administrators are trained in the universities, smaller numbers of scientists are employed in research and development, and less money goes into the training of men for research-oriented industrial positions. Only since 1960 has full employment been reached in the Federal Republic of Germany, Switzerland, Sweden, Denmark, and France. The demand arose for unskilled laborers from the outside as their own citizenry were upgraded when the formerly unskilled and semi-skilled workers became skilled operatives. Women began to enter the proliferating clerical fields, thus creating a demand for labor to take their places. A new migration of laborers from under-developed Yugoslavia, Greece, Spain, southern Italy, and Turkey (along with unskilled laborers from Tunisia and Algeria) spread into the more developed countries. At the present time, the new migration of unskilled workers is in no position to demand high rates of hourly pay, and so mechanization is not seen as an alternative. But as wages become higher and as the new migratory laborers become absorbed into the population, Western Europe will need to seek relief from its labor shortages by greater mechanization and automation.

In many ways, the Industrial and Scientific civilization seems to be coming to Western Europe from its more advanced position of strength in North America. There appears to be a gap of about 20 years in knowledge and management techniques between Western Europe and the United States, and even a chasm between Japan and Western Europe in terms of assimilating the available knowledge disseminated by the new civilization. The gap today in GNP between the various developed countries is more a matter of utilizing and advancing the amount of information available to manufacture, transport, manage, and distribute, as well as to carry on research and teaching. The differences between Stockholm, Hamburg, Frankfurt, and Naples lie precisely in the number of individuals employed in utilizing or spreading this knowledge. Despite the wide diffusion of knowledge to the developing countries, a developed country such as the Federal Republic of Germany possesses 50 times more engineers, technicians, skilled craftsmen, management personnel, and university students per 1,000 population than a country such as Nigeria with roughly the same inhabitants. There are more skilled craftsmen in the Hamburg area than in the Naples or Palermo regions; more skilled farmers in Hesse than in the Abruzzi; more educated entrepreneurs in the Oslo area than around Athens.

Though there has been an increase in industrialization and the growth of universities and universal education in the Communist bloc of nations, the gap between Western Europe and the Communist nations is growing rather than narrowing, primarily because of the large number of individuals in Western Europe working to increase both agricultural and industrial production. Not only are management and management techniques more efficient in Western Europe, but productivity per worker is higher, transportation and distribution better organized, automation more widespread, and larger amounts of capital available for farm machinery, transportation, communication, and the dissemination of knowledge. In the Communist countries, there is neither formal training for management executives nor sufficient rewards to motivate the latter to achieve more efficient production. While Western Europe and the United States (as well as Japan) are moving rapidly into the Tertiary section of production — with more employed in servicing the production industries through information as to what the various plants are doing, the Communist nations are still in the throes of being unable to increase consumer goods. The need for large armies, expensive weapons of war, huge and unwieldy police forces, plus governmental and industrial bureaucracies puts a greater premium upon traditional than upon innovative behavior. While the Communist nations use the concepts of "democracy" and "democratic centralism," they are employed in an entirely different sense than in Western Europe or North America. Democracy in the Communist nations means adhering to authoritarian ideology, or to the lines of action and behavioral norms laid down by those who theoretically represent the vast majority of the population (though never elected by them) and who are to lead the citizens to a new society in which autonomous science and scientific thought will play the greatest part in fashioning human concepts and behavior.

It is difficult to know where to put the transitional phases of Communism in the never-ending story of mankind, for it seems to be a mixture of new ideals and old practices, the mentality of Primary civilization directing the establishment of Secondary, and of conservative leaders being asked to bring about reforming trends. Though Karl Marx believed that the new society would arise out of the ashes of the old capitalist order and that the socialist state would first develop in the more advanced industrial nations, the Soviet Union and its satellites (with the exception of the Czech lands) have been almost entirely developing countries, with standards of living and levels of industrial production far below those of Western Europe. Communism and the Communist Party have been means used to industrialize these underdeveloped nations, to bring them up to the levels of the modernized capitalist countries. While industrialization is taking place at a rapid tempo, with the state acting as entrepreneur, financier, and manager, there is little scientific freedom within the Communist nations which can encourage new scientific paths or lead to developments which will outpace those in the capitalist nations. It is difficult to put one's finger on what is wrong with the tempo of both industrial and scientific growth within these Communist nations. Part of the problem may lie in the enormously centralized control of all industries, scientific institutes, and universities. An economic and social system such as Communism as practiced in the Soviet Union, which eliminates or systematically hampers the initiative of the large number of individual undertakings within the country, tends at the same time to remove an important source of innovation. Although a good deal of innovation appears to exist in certain phases of the massive industrial areas in the Soviet Union, it seems to run in spurts, depending upon the decrees of the Communist Party Presidium at the moment. While there have been interesting developments in surgical tools, oil drilling machinery, and even in machines, the Soviet Union is still dependent upon the non-Communist world for many of its industrial necessities. Japan does not need to invite outside industrial concerns to set up passenger car and truck manufacturing plants, but the Soviet Union still does.

Although there are important scientific research institutes in the Soviet Union which have made many discoveries, most of the research is done for the military. As in industrialization, there is a good deal of unevenness in the scientific production of the country. While millions have been educated as technicians and hundreds of thousands as research scientists, the problems that they work on and the support which they have received thus far are dependent upon the particular military priorities of the moment. The sciences that have little to do with industrialization or the defense posture of the nation receive the least of governmental funds. As in the case of the industrial undertakings within the Soviet Union, local initiatives are discouraged by the economic system in which they operate. Priorities for the sciences are set by a political body, whose leaders are the top officials in government, industry, and military forces, most of whom may not be the best informed either in the mentality of the sciences or in what scholarship can contribute to the priorities for the nation. From 1917 on, the Soviet Union has lived and continues to live as a garrison state. There is little doubt that it has destroyed private capitalism within the confines of the Communist bloc. What is not apparent is whether a socialist economy has been constructed in its place. Since 1917, the Soviet Union has been experiencing an industrial and scientific revolution but under conservative control. The country is a more powerful state today than it was in 1921 when the Civil War ended. Whether the Soviet Union has been able to inaugurate a "socialist" society remains very much in doubt, though it may approach becoming one during the next 100 years.

Part of the confusion which the Soviet Union faces in developing a socialist society is that it uses the term "socialism" in much the same restricted way as fundamentalist Christians use the term "Christian." Karl Marx never described in detail what he meant by class behavior — let alone "class conflict" — any more than he was able to identify the type of society that would be termed "socialist." He had assumed that the "bourgeoisie" would be replaced by a more able, better educated, and more pioneering social class, though he never quite stated it in such terms. Although the Soviet population is far better educated today than it was in 1917, it has clearly not become the model of the new socialist man for the rest of society. It is better educated, yes, but still not educated enough. Its vision is narrow. It possesses all the prejudices, maladjustments, and inability to identify with those not of its immediate group that all Europeans are heir to whether of the "Right" or "Left."

The Soviet Union has become highly industrialized and has left the old Czarist Russia far behind (though it is difficult to say whether a Russia that had industrialized without the Communist

Revolution or without World War II, which it indirectly caused, might not be further ahead industrially than the Soviet Union is today, or at least as far ahead). It is also clear that the Russian people have paid a very high price for industrialization. Just as English textile factories in the early stages largely employed small children and women at starvation wages, so the Russian Five-Year Plans were carried out through the slave labor of tens of millions who were paid only a bare subsistence. From 1929 until 1953, tens of millions were arrested and placed in concentration camps under Stalin's regime. Millions died as a result of their incarceration or were executed as "counter-revolutionaries." More millions died in both World Wars I and II, in the Civil War between 1918 and 1920, in the famines which followed, and in the wake of starvation which existed in the Ukraine and elsewhere when Kulaks (well-to-do and middle peasants) destroyed their herds of cattle, horses, and pigs, grain and buildings in pique at the forced collectivization of their farms after 1930. They were then either killed or sent to concentration camps to work as slave laborers building canals, railroads, or cutting timber and mining coal.

The men who created the Russian Revolution were mostly dead or in exile by the time the reins of the Party, and thus of the Government, passed firmly into the hands of Josef Stalin as Party Secretary. Although the names of Karl Marx and Friedrich Engels are called upon to witness the growth of the "socialist" society, little has developed in the Soviet Union since 1917 to recall the dreams that men had before then of a society that would have more freedoms, more opportunities for personal growth, more decentralization, and more decision-making on the part of the average citizen. The new society in which men work selflessly and innovatively for the good of mankind has still not been created in the Soviet Union. A society composed of citizen-intellectuals, spending their spare time learning and trying to build a more moral, ethical, and empathetic world has not evolved from the ashes of the Czarist regime. Instead, an equally authoritarian, equally unstable, and equally provincial empire has arisen that repeats the mistakes and inefficiencies of the past.

The complex system necessary to industrialization requires an enormous division of labor, which means that those outside the system are not in a position to be knowledgeable about it or to set its priorities. In the Soviet Union, the priorities have been made by political conservatives working closely with military bureaucrats and technocrats to create a command economy wherein the growing wealth goes chiefly to build up the military and police forces. The Communists have assumed that the socialist society cannot be built up until the industrial infrastructure and superstructure are completed. Men, they assumed, would not sacrifice themselves for social ideals until they had been socialized in an educational system that trained them (or conditioned them) to live in such a society. In the meanwhile, until that generation could be reared (a process requiring at least two to three generations), some rewards had to be given to the population so that it would continue to work for the national priorities. These assumed that their "socialist state" had to be protected from all attempts to overthrow it while it was in the process of developing the new socialist world: the society would be so revolutionary, and hence threatened, that it would not be able to co-exist in peace with the capitalist areas. At the same time, the problems involved in industrialization were so complex that those inhabitants who deviated had to be threatened with punishment. The rewards in terms of a high standard of living could not come into existence for many decades. In the beginning, the Communist Party hoped that the Socialist Revolution would spread to the more industrialized nations, who in time would aid the weaker and underdeveloped countries (Russia being in that category). Without a highly industrialized society, Party leaders believed, "socialism" would be difficult to implement.

The Soviet Union still suffers from backwardness in technology and science vis-a-vis the more advanced countries of Western Europe, North America, and Japan. The standard of living for most of the population is still low, even though costs and wages have been kept down. The centralization of priorities means that those making the national plans have little understanding of what could be accomplished with autonomy on the lower levels, since there is little meaningful feedback from the latter to the planning boards and thence to the Party leadership. The emphasis in all plans is upon obeying orders and achieving production quotas that can be met quantitatively rather than qualitatively. Local managers must meet their quotas, even though they need to go outside the system to do so. As a result, a complex infrastructure of a barter system developed within Soviet industry to supply the government with its manufactured priorities. Individuals were employed sub rosa to locate raw materials, and a system of exchanges developed between the supplier and the supplied that had no legitimacy within the volumes of plans and hundreds of thousands of pages of printed paper that went to all the industries within the Soviet Union.

In the industrial plant, loyalty is one-sided, from bottom to top — though commands come down in reverse order. The trade unions, the Communist Party, the levels of management, all operate to make certain that the manager's quota is met no matter how, since the important thing is to make production statistics look good on paper. No one represents the worker within the plant, no one asks him how he sees a more efficient production schedule, how to improve his job, or how the informal information which he gathers for himself can be used by the manager in making the plant run better. Since the market does not exist in the Communist economic society of the Soviet Union, no one consults the consumers about what they need and how they can best be supplied with their daily products. The autocratic centralization that brought about the death knell of Czarism became the totalitarian use of terror that Stalin employed between 1929 and 1953 to force the entire population of the Soviet Union and the satellite states to do his bidding.

The greatest problem confronting the Soviet Union and the other Communist states is not how to socialize every means of production, but how to make the economic system work more efficiently and with the least amount of frustration for the populations who are required to carry it on. As the Czech economists discovered in the middle 1960's, Communism cannot compete with the mixed economies of Western Europe, the United States, or Japan without becoming more decentralized, democratic, and less repressive. The ideology of Communism has never been defined except as complete submission and obedience to the dictates of the Party leadership, who see the system as a series of dogmas more concerned with an ideology of totalitarianism than with democratic freedoms or behavior.

With the exception of the strong priority still given to building up heavy industry for military purposes and the statements attributed to Lenin and Marx about "socialism" (neither of whom said very much about the forms of the future socialist society), the present regime is content to state that it is in a transitional stage between capitalism and communism, which it chooses to term "socialism." In the future, everything will theoretically be so organized that each individual will receive whatever he needs while devoting his talents to serving society. With the present regime continuing to operate only in a classic money economy, however, such a society still remains far in the future.

Although industrialization has been rapid, it is doubtful that the process has led to any great degree of efficiency or innovation, or to new products. While the extremes between great poverty and great wealth are absent in the Soviet Union, and while the poor have been given a floor beneath which they cannot drop, this record has been achieved by an egalitarianism wherein the technical middle class, including teachers and professionals, has fallen far below the middle-class standards of other developed nations. Despite the enormous proliferation of schools and technical institutes, including university and research institutes, the Soviet Union still needs outside technical knowledge, management information, and other tools required to run an industrialized society. In the next 100 years, the Soviet Union will be a highly industrialized and educated nation, but one can also say the same for the countries of Western

Europe, for North America, and Japan. It is obvious that in the next 100 years industrialization and science will embrace increasing numbers of the world's population and that there will be far greater internalization of this culture by political leaders and industrial policy makers than exists today.

In terms of what the Soviet Union has accomplished since 1917, its blunders, its mediocre leadership from Stalin on, the enormous losses during World War II resulting from Stalin's policy mistakes, and the millions who have died since the arrival of Communism (with its enormous repressions and inability to create a more efficient, democratic, and humanly satisfying form of social organization), one can only say that at the moment the system has been a striking failure.

Communism is reactionary in tone, going back to the Czarist regime for its police methods and repressions. It is not an innovative system in the arts, sciences, or technology. It is unable to persuade the inhabitants of its satellites, let alone its own minorities, to believe that there are superordinate goals that they could all work toward which would make life freer and pleasanter for them. Although Communism is based upon the social dream of an international brotherhood of brain workers as well as hand workers — all united to create a new society for mankind — in actuality it has created as its base a Great Russian jingoistic nationalism. Its repressions have exacerbated the nationalisms, linguistic and otherwise, among its own minorities (who now form half the population), and the various linguistic and cultural groups that make up the populations in those areas occupied by the Red Army after World War II, or brought into the Communist net by the blunders of a non-Communist coalition in Czechoslovakia in February 1948. The Soviet Union is a military force that can defend its frontiers today easier than the Czarist or the Stalinist regimes. It is a world military superpower, though not an economic or cultural one.

Yet, one has the feeling that there will be massive changes within the Soviet Union during the next few decades primarily because the regime is unable to provide its populations with any timetable for the fulfillment of the "socialist" dream, or to let them know the next steps to the Communist one. The new "socialist" man, made up of a merger of the scientific intellectual, efficient manager, and perceptive worker is still far in the future, but this unrealized ideal will require massive steps to bring about its evolution. Too many young people are being educated within the Soviet schools to desire an improved society, even though that society is vaguely described, and they want "socialism" within their lifetimes.

◊   ◊   ◊   ◊   ◊

One can speculate that, if Communism had not come on the scene in 1917, Russia might have become the first fascist state in Europe (with its generals, Czarist bureaucrats, large landowners, and wealthy industrialists, who were all fearful of continuing revolutionary changes brought about by Russia's exhaustion in World War I). The totalitarianism that has marked Russian transformation into a highly centralized Soviet police state could well have continued by creating the same industrial priorities for a post-World War I Russia that marked past planning within the Soviet Union. It is possible that under a fascist state, millions might also have perished in a postwar Russia. The Soviet concentration camps that Hitler emulated could also have come into existence, for there was little or no humanitarianism among the military mediocrities of the White Army leadership in Czarist Russia who would have formed the basis of any postwar regime, either supporting a Czarist dynasty or ruling without a Czar.

The Russian Revolution of 1917 remains an unfinished one, just as the French Revolution of 1789 was an incomplete one. The trends in European culture toward egalitarianism, democracy, and the protection of individualism will continue, for the currents run deep and the need for men to believe that there is a purpose to life above simple subsistence will almost guarantee its continuance. Within the Communist nations themselves, too many in the population have now been educated to believe that egalitarianism, democracy, and individualism are intrinsic goals, and this drive will not be submerged in the future.

Throughout Europe men are being educated. And hence they are acquiring an optimistic belief in the future, in the possibility of creating the Heavenly City, of assuring their social importance while they are still living, and of assuming that the brotherhood of all men is a realizable dream. Industrialization and science have also become ingrained in the education of most young Europeans, who sense that it is possible to use the techniques that have eradicated hunger, disease, illiteracy, and slavery to create the new society that can achieve old goals and develop new ones.

In Europe as a whole, and this includes all the Communist nations, men no longer accept the premise that state agencies running state-owned industries and distribution centers in an authoritarian economic system automatically create "socialism." Or that state capitalism which takes over the ownership of the means of production does not automatically transform human society into one wherein egalitarianism and democracy create a cooperative brotherhood. State ownership of the means of production encourages hierarchy and authoritarian centralization as does the private control of industry and crafts. The Communist state has so far not been able to develop an anti-authoritarian society in which all men are permitted to explore new intellectual horizons, to disagree with and to veto the priorities and policies set by those who govern them, or to build the foundations of a society where they can decide what they want it to do for them.

XIX   The World
of Tomorrow

From the beginning of man's awareness of himself and the world around him, there have been weak explorations, experimentations, and testing of the new, plus occasionally feeble attempts to peer into the almost invisible future. Although only a few individuals have ever done the experimenting, the innovating, and the sighting of the future, they have nonetheless managed to drag the rest of their fellow human beings along new and untrodden paths — despite the fact that most of the latter have spent their time looking backward trying to see where they had started rather than ahead to where they might be going.

Many of the paths taken have been blind alleys from which it has been exceedingly difficult to extricate mankind, but there has been a narrow though continuous path leading from the days of the Neolithic agricultural and pastoral revolutions through the development of Primary civilization into the urbanized Industrial and Scientific civilization of our time. Men have covered the entire earth with their settlements. Their numbers have grown geometrically until there is a danger that they may have overpopulated available space. Despite the relative poverty of the underdeveloped areas of the world (which have been bypassed by the technical middle-class Industrial and Scientific civilization), men are better fed today than in any other period of human society, are better clothed, have better housing, and enjoy better health. Even in the poverty-stricken areas of the unskilled peasant cultures, men live longer than in previous centuries.

Men may still be provincial, but few in the world today remain unaware of the cultural varieties that exist in human societies. No matter how technologically underdeveloped an area may be, there is still a knowledge of the existence of the automobile, radio, airplane, modern medicine, schools, writing, books, pictures, photographs, and other aspects of our contemporary Industrial and Scientific civilization. Men are closer together than ever before in terms of communication, of awareness of what is happening elsewhere, and of understanding a world-wide culture that utilizes the innovations, scientific discoveries, and products of the more affluent modern societies. Although it may temporarily appear to be otherwise, men are in greater contact with one another than ever before, are more aware of one another's strengths and problems, and are more conscious of the differences that separate men as well as the similarities that bring them together.

The strong desire of all developing nations to join the main-stream of modernization means that the spreading Industrial and Scientific civilization of this century will include most of the world's population during the next 100 years. The poorer nations of the world are primarily motivated to want "socialism" because they would like to possess the strengths of the industrial nations without the weaknesses of glaring income inequalities, competitiveness, and tendencies to develop monopolies of the special skills that create wealth, industrial achievement, and affluence. Capitalism is seen as one means to industrialization and modernization, but its price is considered high: that is, ignoring the vast majority of the unskill-ed and uneducated. It is seen as operating for the benefit of the few rather than for all of society. Bringing in foreign sources of capital and technical skill is looked upon as keeping the local popu-lation inferior, non-competitive, and submissive. "Socialism" is viewed as developing native skills and utilizing local capital to create the entrepreneurs from among the indigenous population. It is believed that the latter do not have the opportunity to learn skills under the caste-like conditions developed by foreigners who build industries but only by "exploiting" cheap local labor, which makes it worthwhile for them to come in. "Socialism" to the under-developed world has the connotation of developing and furthering local talent, of working together to build up capital so that society as a whole will benefit from the building of railroads, industries, power plants, and the mining of minerals and fuels. One can expect "socialism" as a defining term for modernization to become more and more used during succeeding decades as the underdeveloped countries attempt to compensate for their low levels of achievement.

◇   ◇   ◇   ◇   ◇

It is difficult to see how the developing nations will be able to assimilate most of the technical and managerial knowledge of the Industrial and Scientific civilization during the next 25 to 50 years. The number of university students, trained technicians, pro-fessionals, and entrepreneurial personnel in the developing world have increased enormously during the past 25 years, but their total numbers still represent a small fraction of the populations. Nigeria with 60 million has only 11,000 students in all of its universities, with most studying law or humanities and few in engineering, technical, scientific, or business management courses. Compared to the Federal Republic of Germany with an equal population of 60 million, Nigeria has less than 1/25th the number of university students, and perhaps only 1/100th of the engineering, scientific, or agronomy students capable of managing the country's growing technical base.

The vast majority of the populations in the developing nations are still made up of inefficient, illiterate peasants who are marginal participants in the economy. China and India have few carriers of the Secondary civilization, and their impact upon the economy is still weak. The developing nations have only begun to grow, and are moving into the Secondary civilization 100 to 200 years too late. Instead of being in a position to utilize their greatest resource of unskilled and docile cheap labor (whom they could have used profitably 100 years ago), they are trying to move into the Industrial Age at a time when new skills are needed and machines are cheaper to use than unskilled labor.

As we move further into the age of industrial and agricultural automation, larger numbers of individuals will be bypassed by the employment possibilities that will open up. Young people need to be trained for jobs that do not yet exist, especially in the developing countries. Industrialization using modern machines produces more goods at a lower cost. Mechanized agriculture on large farms grows more food per acre than can be cultivated by hand. The developing countries, however, need not only to industrialize and to grow more food, but they especially need to utilize their surplus hundreds of millions of peoples, who in many ways represent their most important resource.

Human beings have been considered as figures in censuses, in planning, and in taxing. In both the developing and developed countries, the present need is to see the human as an important resource to be discovered and properly utilized. By default, human beings appear to be of secondary importance to the primary one of exploiting fossil fuels or minerals. Developing nations today are more concerned with planning on how to feed their growing numbers of citizens than to uncover their talents to help in solving the country's problems. The development of human beings takes enormous resources which even the developed nations do not have.

The development of human resources leads to a greater utilization of the physical resources that exist within each nation, and these are unlimited even in those countries that are theoretically assumed to be resource-poor. Hydrogen and oxygen in water are plentiful resources, and so are the enormous amounts of energy that come each day from sunshine, the winds, and the still unusable forces of gravitation. All these, plus others still unknown, may turn out to be more important sources of the future requirements of an industrialized society than the acquisition of coal deposits, iron ore, or large sources of gas and oil.

In terms of the amount of time that stretches on to the ever-extending future, mankind has barely begun to utilize its enormous brain power. The potential for further growth is limitless. There will be civilizations without number following one another in rapid succession, and where any of these may lead none of us can guess at the moment. The only conclusion we can make about the future is that we are still in a fairly primitive state of development. We are moving rapidly to another stage in civilization which we can call the Tertiary, since it will be based less upon production and more upon new services. It will be more oriented toward problem-solving than our present civilization. And, though consumption levels may continue to be high, perhaps the emphasis will be more upon raising the quality of life than upon the quantity of our possessions.

The new civilization will not be one in which leisure is guaranteed to most individuals. There appears to be a trend indicating that the civilizations of the future will demand more obligations from its citizens: that they become better informed, that they participate more in helping to determine guidelines for the future, that they be active carriers of the new civilization, and that they spend more of their time learning so that they can become innovators as well as disseminators. Future civilizations may not permit their citizens to be dependent upon the determining judgments of a few. At the moment, we seem to be continuing past trends whereby father-figures rule and make the important decisions for us — since the cultural image makes us into adult children, dependent upon political and economic figures to give us our daily bread, tell us what we can and cannot do, discipline us to work, and give leadership to the norms and values which we are unable to articulate for ourselves. The world of tomorrow may well demand a cooperation and a participation from all of us that few are equipped to provide at the moment.

Civilizations thus far have been expanding the demands which they place upon their citizens. In the low participation of the latter in Primary civilization, 99 percent shared in no innovating, no decision-making, and no actual development of that civilization. Secondary civilization also started off with a very high percentage of nonparticipants, but as it moved into the twentieth century the percentage of its carriers and participants slowly increased. Tertiary civilization will require more educated, better informed individuals, and the percentage of its participants and carriers will exceed those in Secondary. Other stages of civilization will follow which will be based upon the new ideas and contributions of men and women to be born in decades hundreds and thousands of years hence.

◇   ◇   ◇   ◇   ◇

The world of tomorrow is still invisible to all of us. Its directions will be based upon techniques and knowledge that may not become apparent to any of us in our lifetimes. It will be motivated by systems of ideas and concepts that have not been thought about; its way of life does not yet exist even as a blueprint. To deal with something that is not in existence takes us into the realm of speculation, yet the trends present in Secondary civilization and the generalizations concerning how we reached our present levels of technology and society suggest the continuation of certain types of thinking that man makes about the world he lives in.

Certain trends in man's thinking over the past 1,000 years suggest that they may continue into the dim future. Man's reluctance to live with inefficiencies, with wastages of energy and human resources, implies that the trends toward mechanization will become more pronounced as decades and centuries pass. The world of automation, which started before the discovery of the printing press and which is now making quite a dent in the work formerly done by hand labor, will clearly be improved upon. But what we wish to emphasize here is that the future is not composed entirely of new technological forms, though they will certainly exist. What we hope we made explicit in previous pages is that technology, which is a part of human culture, is in many ways passive. The automobile did not change American civilization after 1910, but the need for freedom in which to use the car affected changing mores, relationships between the sexes, and projections of the social image of the owner. The world of automation will be influenced by the way men think about their economic and political institutions. Tools and machines have no goals within themselves; they are means designed by men in terms of what they want out of life. Because we are in no position to know how men will see themselves 50 or 100 years hence, it is not possible to view the future clearly. Will men 100 years from now continue to believe that the possession of a large automobile enhances their social status with neighbors and friends? Will they still be willing to accept inequalities in health care, housing, educational opportunities, recreation, consumption levels, and individual well-being? Will they make the same assumptions about social and religious activities? Will their social, economic, and political goals have anything in common with those that most of us have today?

Yet, certain trends that began in Europe in the eleventh century accelerated and from the eighteenth century on led to the development of the Industrial and Scientific civilization. The millenarian movements following the eleventh century had much to do with the growth of egalitarian tendencies in Europe after the fourteenth century. The cultural underground that apparently surfaced briefly during the late Medieval Period played an important part in the growth of the political movements that mirrored folk frustrations and ended in the destruction of the aristocracy and the termination of a monarchic control that had been legitimated by the divine right of kings to rule. The modern world has evolved from a past which produced a middle-class revolution when the growing needs of men led them through their own achievements to believe that they had earned freedom from parental repression and domination.

The trends which exist today may not necessarily continue very far into the future. Those soon to become obsolete concern the creation of more leisure for individuals who work for a living at dull jobs on assembly lines and hence must be kept dependent upon father-figures on the job or in government. The next century may bring about revolutionary changes in what will be considered the natural rights of man — among them being the right to an interesting, challenging, and educating job. Life may well be considered too short and important to waste the most valuable of all resources, the human being, in performing work which the machine can do easier and better. As time goes on, there is no doubt that more efficient machines will be devised, better energy sources discovered, and more efficacious work methods developed. The story of man's quest for autonomy thus far has been an account of man's gradually freeing himself from drudgery so that he can devote his time to doing that which no other animal can do (and that no machine devised by man can perform) — and that is to think.

◇   ◇   ◇   ◇   ◇

Mankind has come a long way from the days of *Homo erectus*. Men have learned a great deal, though there is much more for them to learn. Their tools, or the extension of their arms and bodies, have become more complex. New forms of energy have been harnessed: in the first stage of man's development, power came from man's own arms; in the second stage, man learned to harness the strength of animals; in the third stage, he devised tools or machines that ran with energy derived from water or air; in the fourth stage, he discovered the explosion produced when water was heated to the expansionist point and transformed into steam. (Steam permitted man to engage in activities that were impossible to do in the past. By harnessing it, loads could be pulled that were beyond the capacity of horses, and at speeds that no animals could equal, continuing mile after mile and hour after hour. With steam, man was able to conquer the oceans in a way impossible for sailing ships.) In the fifth stage, man learned to use the energy derived from friction, or electricity; and from here he moved rapidly to a sixth stage which utilized fossil fuels. Man harnessed these more efficiently to pull longer and heavier loads, to fly in the skies at speeds no bird could equal, to create a substitute for the horse that went everywhere (though smooth and paved roads were needed) at speeds equalling those of steam, and which could be put into the hands of individual owners. Although it was restricted to roads or trails, the car gave man an independence which he had not known previously. The airplane appeared and went even faster into areas where there were no roads or trails, though it was restricted by its requirements of landing places and storage of fuel.

One can expect that man will invent other forms of energy to free him from drudgery, that he will use it to create even higher standards of living and endless opportunities to rebuild if not to re-create his environment. At this stage of human development, it is difficult to see what new forms of energy future generations will use, though there is little doubt that more effective ways will be found to utilize the enormous amounts of energy coming from the sun, from changing weather, tides, or gravitation. Man's dependency upon fossil fuels is short-lived, for they create problems which he has been unable to resolve. These involve not only problems of pollution, but wastage in transporting them long distances inefficiently. (Although ships have become larger, more automated, and faster, they represent a danger from over-spills with their disastrous effects upon the ocean itself. Each large ship transporting oil is potentially the equivalent of an atom bomb that men cannot control, for its damage can easily be as extensive. With tens of thousands of trips per year on the oceans of the world, accidents could become catastrophic.)

The resource of oil, for example, cannot be replenished once it is used, and its disappearance will leave a void requiring men to research the next stage of energy development. The use of hydrogen, sunshine, or gravitation, however, would apparently provide an endless source of energy. All countries could participate rather than, as at present, those underdeveloped countries that are oil-rich but that do not use the proceeds derived from petroleum sales to develop themselves. As the demands for oil consumption increase, the need grows for more efficient and cheaper sources of energy, and for more imaginative means of transportation. The world cannot easily afford the wasteful extravagance of permitting the United States to use up a disproportionate share of the rare metals and fuels of the earth. During the next 50 years, a world-wide tripling of industrialization will bring enormous shortages unless research to discover more efficient substitutes is accelerated — and soon. The poorer countries as they push into the future cannot afford the path taken by the extravagant United States in wasting resources. Their mechanization, educational levels, political and economic thinking will need to be founded upon bases that are completely unknown to them today. The developing countries must devote far more of their scarce resources to planning ahead for greater manpower utilization, all within new forms of industrialization in factory and farm, and with new techniques to induce greater innovation and cooperation among their populations than the developed nations have been able to generate among theirs.

Although it is difficult to see the forms of society hundreds of years hence, we can be assured that the trend for greater individual growth and autonomy will continue. As each succeeding generation meets the basics of human subsistence — food, clothing, shelter, and protection of health — its new goals will turn toward making the individual feel more important through utilizing his potential intelligence, through believing that society is better off because he has lived in it, and through opportunities to make a contribution as a cooperative member and carrier of his civilization.

The unfolding future during the next infinite period may insist upon the upgrading of all skills if it hopes to resolve its problems or seek means whereby men can live useful rather than useless lives. Goals could rise with each generation. Although it is difficult today for us to imagine a society in which our contemporary goals will have been achieved, nevertheless the inhabitants of such a future state of bliss (from our point of view) may be pushed toward new aspirations. What these will be, say, a thousand or more years from now, none of us can imagine today.

There are trends present now that may continue into the indefinite future. The first of these is the partial mechanization of man's work. During the past 200 years, a good deal of work which men once painstakingly performed is now done by machines. Women no longer spin thread by hand; men no longer weave cloth slowly line by line, woof versus warp. Men no longer pull or carry large burdens; nor do they craft shoes or clothes by hand. The machine has become the maker, substituting its greater energy for that of man and performing a given item of work cheaper, more efficiently, and in much larger quantities than handwork could do. In the modern industrialized world, the machine is cheaper as a unit of energy than the human being. Anything that can be done by man routinely can be taught to machines. The latter can bore and drill and start and stop. Any item of work that can be broken down into component parts could easily be done by machine, and in the future machines will be invented to perform tasks they cannot do now. With the costs of labor becoming increasingly expensive in each generation, much work done by the present labor force may be mechanized out of existence during the next 20 or 30 years. Any skill requiring a coordination of hand and eye can be managed by a punched tape that runs a machine or a series of machines. The output of skilled mechanics or machinists can be erased by building them into machines that are manufactured and sold. Such machines could easily be programmed to do anything that can be taught to any skilled worker. The developing nations instead of training individuals to run machines need to acquire or manufacture tools which run themselves. Railroads can be automated, as they are not today, to transport long trains without making human errors and without using men to direct them. Airplanes can be made to fly easily with more mechanical and automated controls than at present. Machines can be automated to diagnose repairs — what is wrong and what requires replacing. Machines can be manufactured which automatically repair themselves by redesigning sections that remove themselves when they diagnose themselves to be in need of substitute parts.

◊ ◊ ◊ ◊ ◊

Society has always been involved in the process of change. The history of modern industrialization goes back to the first tools which men fashioned and the energy they added to the use of tools to manufacture goods required in daily living. Man's society along with the means involved in industrialization have undergone constant change, one that through the accelerating processes of automation will continue into the indefinite future. Society no longer needs slaves to do its work, or the unskilled to collect its garbage. The machine is easier, cheaper, and more efficient.

Society has entered a continuous process of mechanizing the functions of daily living in growing food, manufacturing goods, transporting men and materials, collecting information, and so on. Information daily collected can be correlated later for other purposes, which means that the feeding of facts into large storage electronic devices will continue to become even more complex in the distant future. Undoubtedly the information of large libraries will be computed with instant retrieval on the part of the library user. Most of the accumulated information possessed by the highly developed nations in the technologies, sciences, mathematics, and decision-making processes can be purchased by the developing nations to go hand in hand with their future industrialization.

It appears pointless to train mechanics and machinists to repeat what others do; it would seem more efficient to purchase machines and tapes that can manufacture for a developing nation what is being made in a developed one. What the poorer nations need are individuals who can use the information retrieved from the developed nations to create higher technical and scientific levels within their own countries. This means that the ability to translate this information into immediate action is one to which the developing nations need to give top priority. Rather than duplicating the mechanization already developed, their emphasis needs to be upon utilizing for special national purposes the mountains of information already available. If this were done, the under-industrialized developing nations could then devote themselves to a type of priority research that may not be as important at the moment to the more developed nations. The problem of the former is how to translate the information from the developed nations into providing solutions as to what to do with their own uneducated, unskilled populations. How to utilize people in efficient and humane ways represents the most important task the developing nations face during the next century.

The present and the past have not been too concerned about problem-solving. Past attitudes believed in ignoring problems in the hope that they would go away. At present, the feeling about conflicts which sociologists and economists would call "problems" depends upon the amount of time allotted them by the media, upon the emotionalism of the presentation, and upon the amount of time the "problems" remain in public view — which is generally not very long.

We are moving slowly but inevitably in another direction wherein the emphasis is upon each individual assuming responsibility for the course that his society takes. This implies the future obligation among citizens that they be well-informed, that they take their democracy seriously, and that they be held responsible for the workings of their society. The concept that we are moving into a future wherein most men will spend their time playing, wherein leisure will be a paramount value, wherein retirement from work will come at a comparatively early age, seems to be more of a wish projection of contemporary commercial interests that are concerned with selling leisure, play, and retirement.

The world of the future will not be concerned with retiring large numbers of individuals at an early age, but rather with putting more and more to work. Automation is a fact of life whose future is now unfolding, and the trend is for most manufacturing, agriculture, mining, smelting, and transportation to be run by highly automated machine systems supervised and regulated by even more complicated computers than we possess at the present time. The automated world of the future will require fewer and fewer man-hours to produce a ton of steel, a bushel of potatoes, an automobile, a house, a telephone, or a sophisticated receiver of media signals — but more and more man-hours spent by the citizen in informing himself.

Industrialization should not be seen chiefly as a means of assuring employment to a large number of individuals possessing various skills. It is not a means to ensure greater employment, but it is a medium whereby human labor can be saved and shifted over to more important priorities that machines cannot do. The story of the Industrial Age has been an increase in labor productivity that has risen geometrically decade by decade from the middle of the eighteenth century on. It has increased the wealth of society enormously. It employs fewer and fewer individuals to turn out the basic necessities of life, leaving more and more time for them to do things that could not be done previously. Industrialization in the United States has permitted smaller numbers to be used in producing our food. In 1800, 95 percent of Americans grew their own: in the 1970's, this has been cut down to less than 3 percent, and the number will go down even more during the next quarter of a century. We employ fewer individuals to produce a ton of steel (the Japanese have cut the labor hours down to two), to mine more coal, to make larger numbers of cars, refrigerators, air-conditioners, television sets, and airplanes. Compared to those living in 1875, men in the developed countries live in insulated houses that are warmer in winter, cooler in summer, contain more space, are better lit by electricity, have more comfortable furnishings, are easier to keep clean, and have more efficient plumbing fixtures. Men have better dental and medical care, live longer, and are more aware of the causes of illness. Their food is better processed (though this still leaves much to be desired), they eat a greater variety, especially of fruits and vegetables, and compared to their total income, all of it is cheaper.

In the 1970's, men in both the developed and developing nations are better educated than ever before. The level of education in the United States is more than secondary school with some 30 percent of those of college age attending an institution of higher learning. Compared to 1875, men read, see, and travel more. They have a greater awareness and knowledge of other men and other nations, and though ethnocentrism is still with us, it is doubtful that the next two generations will put up with Hitlerism, Stalinism, or apartheid. There is perhaps greater toleration of other religions, cultures, and physical appearance than existed in the past. Although there was a good deal of awareness of the irrationalities of human culture in the 1870's, there is perhaps even more consciousness of human vagaries in the 1970's.

Industrialization has enabled the more developed nations to have a greater variety of food, housing, and consumer goods, with fewer men employed in producing them. As a result, there have been both rational and irrational priorities set by industry and government in deciding where the surpluses are to be employed. Each generation must decide anew what it wants its manpower to do and what its priorities are to be. The economic depression after 1929 indicated that there were too many employed in growing food, building shelter, and making consumer goods. The government took up the slack with the New Deal, but it was only the arrival of World War II with its enormous expenditure of capital, employment of men, and destruction of property that enabled the highly developed American society to attain full employment. In the post-war period, it took an expanded peacetime military budget, a rapid proliferation of municipal, state and federal employment, extensive subsidies to farmers, farm manufacturers, real estate men, builders, shipbuilders, oil processors, and large sums to schools and colleges (through the Veterans' Bills, plus direct educational subsidies) to provide enough work to employ its growing adult population.

◇   ◇   ◇   ◇   ◇

Today, more individuals are working in service positions than in actual manufacturing or extracting, whether food, coal, or oil. More are employed in white-collar positions collecting and collating information than in the manufacturing processes. There are more schoolteachers than farmers; more in the military than in coal mining; more in the professions than in the construction industry; and more in research than in the past (though most of the research is still military-oriented). There are more employed in civil service at all levels than are used in the entire transportation industry from trucking to airplanes. Yet, despite the trend away from workers in actual production, the wealth of the United States, Western Europe, and Japan is greater than ever before, although most of it appears to be siphoned off into non-productive areas such as entertainment, sports, the military, the tobacco and alcohol industries, restaurants, hamburger stands, the leisure-oriented manufacturing industry, real estate, and the massing of large sums for retirement whether through private or public pension plans. If society wants to set these priorities, it has the privilege of doing so, though it is difficult to measure labor productivity in selling real estate, insurance policies, or in most brokerage activities. We still do not know how productive our civil service on all levels tends to be, or our schools, medical facilities, or nursing homes. How productive is the entertainment industry (here we must include radio and television as well as newspapers, especially in the United States), or professional sports teams?

Although supermarkets are more productive than the retail stores of the 1870's, they can be made even more efficient, using less labor. And so can department stores that seem to be an anomaly in the latter part of the twentieth century, operating as nineteenth-century grocery stores and no longer serving as efficient retail establishments. The large number of middlemen, processing businesses, auto repairmen, the services to homes and apartments, the maintenance men of our cities, states, and federal governments, all can be made more productive by redesigning the machines and appliances that they service and by building into the appliances or machines small audio devices that signal a need for replacement. The latter can even be made automatically by computer and tape in large-scale machinery complexes, perhaps in smaller units. But in all these service industries, one can expect in the future a greater degree of labor productivity requiring fewer manpower hours. In the next century, the automatic retail center, appliances that service themselves, plus the fully automated farm, factory, and office may become realities. Trends point in this direction as yearly labor costs go up, and as machines and the complex computers that run them become increasingly cheaper than unionized workers. The next 100 years may see a greater displacement of manpower, as it becomes more expensive and less productive, than has taken place during the past century. The year 2075 will undoubtedly produce a more automated society even in areas not thought of at the present time.

◇   ◇   ◇   ◇   ◇

On the other hand, most people would agree that one cannot separate large numbers of blue-collar and white-collar workers from their livelihoods without supplying them with other work. But the kinds of work that exist are based upon what society has decided it wants most from its members. The priorities change as men shift their aims. The one that may undoubtedly rank high in the next 30 to 50 years may be that of supplying more meaningful, interesting, and productive work to those displaced by greater mechanization and automation in future American industrial society. In the past, as industry displaced blue-collar workers, it hired more white-collar workers, specialized junior executives, assistants to the president, vice-presidents, and other staff officials. When these become displaced in the somewhat distant future, new positions may open up in the changing bureaucratic systems by utilizing individuals in special research tasks, either on-going or temporary. And perhaps the greatest of all research tasks facing the social sciences is how to use profitably the large number of individuals who are either under-utilized today or working far below their potential skills. The study of human resources could well turn out to be one of the greatest breakthroughs in all the social sciences.

Part of the difficulty in setting priorities at the present time lies in the fact that we do not know enough of the needs which America will have, say, by the year 2000. The needs will be based upon future research on the then contemporary society whose results we do not have at the moment. But at the same time we are not posing the questions at present which we need to answer during the next 10 to 20 years. We have developed research techniques, but have not decided how to use them. As a result, we have not been able to delineate the areas or define the problems that we think will be important during the next one to two decades. Considering that we live in a Secondary civilization that is slowly being transformed into a Tertiary one, wherein the technical middle classes will become increasingly important politically, economically, and sociologically, we still have not focused on planning ahead for the future that we know is definitely coming. Those born today will spend their lives in that future, as will the majority of the population living today. The entire technical middle class ethos is based upon planning for the future and being oriented in that direction, yet politically as well as economically our civilization operates on a year to year basis. We may do some planning by providing for shifts in spending of government and corporation budgets, but this is mostly based upon the spending of previous years or activities of the recent past. There has been little understanding in either government or corporations of the trends leading to the world of the next few decades.

Those living in the world of tomorrow will be better educated and better informed than those living today, just as we are better educated and more informed than those in the world of yesterday. But in terms of the knowledge needed now for the momentous decisions that are being made every day in governments and industries, we are neither educated or well-informed enough. The trends that are leading to a better educated society, in which more of the population spends a larger part of its life span in schools, seem to be irreversible. Future society will certainly demand more of its citizens than is the case today (when little is required).

The increasingly mechanized and automated society we are moving toward will not encourage or reward early retirement. Although leisure is stressed by those who sell leisure-time activities — whether they are a second home in a resort or the countryside, a boat, extra cars, sports equipment, television sets, and so on — the trends I believe do not appear to move in that direction. Too many leisure time activities seem to be forms of escapism wherein individuals either drop out of responsibility to society or engage in time-consuming sports that are irrelevant to the needs of themselves, their families, or the nation. Leisure is viewed as a means to escape from boring, repetitive work which adds little or nothing to a sense of accomplishment, creativity, or self-fulfillment. This area appears to promise the greatest change in priorities. Future generations may insist that it is a natural human right to expect to have work that is fun, interesting, creative, of service, and at the same time self-fulfilling.

The productivity following the cut in man-hours of work required to produce the goods, foods, and services which mankind needs has been increasing at a geometrical rate over the past 200 years. The chances are good that this increase in societal efficiency will grow at an even faster pace during the next 50 to 100 years. Certainly one can expect new forms of appliances impossible to imagine at the moment, but it is to be hoped that the conditioning of future generations will not make them believe that they cannot live comfortably without them. The standard of living during the next 100 years will be different from the one that many of us enjoy today, with the increase in real wages taking place not so much in the goods, services, and foods which we now utilize, but in nonexistent items which will have high priority during the next century.

Who among those living in gaslit middle-class urban homes in the early 1870's (when half of the country's population lived on unlit farms and another third in unlit villages, small towns, and rural areas — but not as farmers) could visualize the way urban and small-town citizens would live and spend their money in the 1970's? How could one in the 1870's imagine electric lights in the home, an electric refrigerator, a dishwasher, a washing machine, an air-conditioner? If one had never seen or heard of an internal combustion engine, how could one possibly imagine more than 100 million automobiles riding on interstate highways, when even the paving of roads was unknown in the 1870's? And how could one in the 1870's have visualized the use of telephones, data retrieval computers, diesel engines, jet airplanes, space ships, supermarkets, and so on, even if one had heard of the ideas that lay behind their operation?

◇   ◇   ◇   ◇   ◇

During the past 100 years in all the advanced industrial nations, food habits have shifted to include more fruits, vegetables, and protein in the daily diet. Food prices have not gone up as rapidly as wages, with the result that the average worker's family can afford a greater abundance and variety of food (at lower relative cost) than was possible in the 1870's or was available only at certain times of the year. Men then ate more carbohydrates, more bread, potatoes, cakes, and pies. Perhaps the food in many areas might have been fresher, since there were few facilities for preserving it except through canning, smoking, and drying. But sanitary conditions in handling provisions were not always good. There is no way of knowing how many children died through diseases transmitted by unpasteurized milk sold with a high bacterial count — or for that matter, how many adults. It was difficult to send fish inland from the seaports, for there were few ways of keeping it fresh, though railroads in the 1870's were experimenting with refrigerated cars and ice in small quantities was made artificially in the cities. The handling of food, both in processing and retailing, must have transmitted many kinds of bacterial and virus diseases of which physicians in the 1870's were quite unaware. Louis Pasteur in France was doing pioneering research in these areas, but he never saw a virus and did not know what it did within the human cell. The chances of receiving adequate medical care in the 1870's either at the hands of a physician or in a hospital were poor indeed, with most physicians knowing little outside of splinting a fracture, lancing a boil, and perhaps delivering a baby at home. Although surgery goes back thousands of years, in the 1870's diagnosis and operations were underdeveloped as compared to today — and primitive indeed in contrast to what physicians and surgeons will know 100 years from now.

Prices have skyrocketed since the 1870's (increased productivity does not always keep prices down). Technology today has let men buy more things, though food, housing, clothing, and services are from five to ten times more expensive in monetary terms than they were then. It has also permitted men to live in better insulated and lighted houses with modern bathrooms and kitchens — plus access to the electronic media. There is more variety to life now than in 1870. Levels of education are higher for almost everyone, though still not enough.

Perhaps we can project these trends and accomplishments onto the future when men will expand their horizons in ways that few of us can imagine at present. They will have new labor-saving appliances that have not yet been invented. Their housing will surely be more efficient than ours, for the building of houses in the 1970's is still a cottage rather than a mechanized industry. Our cities in adapting to the automobile have expanded immeasurably since the 1870's. Our suburbs resulted primarily from the inauguration of mass transit after the turn of the century, of the automobile and the paved highway after 1910, and through the later adaptation of the automobile as a form of mass transportation. Our urban areas will doubtless change even more drastically as we move toward the end of this century and into the next.

Perhaps we are beginning to see the faint glimmers of a trend toward rebellion against commercialism in television which will not accelerate until the twenty-first century. In the United States at the present time, for example, many items advertised on television are in the same dubious category as the patent medicines sold in carnival fashion in the 1870's, wherein medicines (mostly alcohol with large lacings of opium) were praised as cure-alls for everything from fallen arches to cancer. As these patent medicines receded when new laws were passed in the first decade of the twentieth century, so one can assume that equivalent items and even the commercials themselves may gradually disappear from the media as they develop further in the next century. The present-day captive audiences may become enfranchised during the next 50 years, and perhaps we may acquire more autonomy when the media evolve into ones through which citizens can in actuality become better informed. The price for this freedom will be the willingness of users to pay for both sophisticated entertainment and information. The corporations for producing and operating the new media may well be other forms of old cooperative associations. It can be expected that the universities and the non-profit dramatic and musical associations may use new forms of cable television to increase their audiences (through the sale of annual memberships to support their products and concerts). Clearly contemporary book publishing, newspapers, magazines, radio, and television will not survive far into the next century, let alone into the last decade of this one, primarily because they are inefficient, expensive, and mind-wasting in emphasizing escapist entertainment rather than helping to provide the age-old goal of enriched human experience. What forms these new media will take must be left to those to come who will have far more information and precedents to aid them in planning the future than we do at present. It is therefore difficult to guess whether the theater as such will be eliminated, with all new plays, movies, and concerts taking place in the livingroom or den, or whether they will survive with the act of attendance becoming a form of entertainment in itself.

We need new criteria for collecting and disseminating information, plus new definitions of what should be considered "news" as against "events." At the present time, much desperately needed information is narrowly disseminated or not at all. To the average reader of book reviews in the more important newspapers and magazines (or television), those receiving the most notice are ones that appeal to fairly low levels of intellectual curiosity. Sex still appears to be an important ingredient in best-sellers, and any book that attempts to deal with it from almost any angle is certain to do well.

Future society needs to stress new ways of disseminating knowledge as well as using it. Learning is a human undertaking, and intellectualism is perhaps the most human way of using our thought and our senses. Although few persons are concerned at present with stretching their minds to the utmost, future centuries will more and more try to develop the potential for creative thinking which exists in most individuals. This may become a top priority that will be subsidized increasingly as generations to come shift their goals to those they believe will enrich and develop society. The next century will certainly see more men concerned with the development of the greatest of all resources, the human mind.

Too many universities are today inefficient, authoritarian, and traditional in subject matter. Most faculty, courses, and administrators tend to be duplicates of those that exist elsewhere. There is little emphasis upon creativity, and the classroom is by no means a marketplace of ideas whether in the United States, Western Europe, or Japan. New techniques are needed to make faculty, students, and administrators more efficient and creative — a challenge that can easily become a research project that will keep social scientists busy for centuries to come. Good students need good faculty members, while good faculty need good students and good administrators. At the present time, mediocrity and ineptitude in all three areas is the norm rather than the exception. More understanding is needed of how to keep men learning from their earliest years to the moment that death comes, for the greatest memorial to one's life is what one has left behind for others to add to their learning.

We need to know more about the interactions of parents and children. Though we speak much about the role of socialization within the family system, in fact we know very little about the process. We need to know more about how socialization works, how it interacts with what we do not know about the growth of human personality to produce not only the deviant individual, the psychotic, the neurotic, the psychopath, the sociopath, the drop-out, but also the manager, the vocational engineer, and so on. Although in making decisions we fall back upon a mythological "human nature" and the bits of learning about mankind which the social sciences have been able to give us, we actually know little about human motivations, norms, and deviances compared to what men in the next century will know.

Yet, we must operate on the assumption that we know what we are talking about else we become paralyzed by the contradictions, ineffectiveness, and emptiness of a good deal of what we call knowledge. It is necessary to have premises and hypotheses as long as we recognize them as such. Although we have not been able to get adequate validation for a good deal of our academic thinking about man, still we must push ahead on the theory that assumptions are necessary even when we may not have all the proof we need — if they lead to further inquiry. In contrast to thinking in the past, we do have more observations, more empirical data, more sophisticated reasoning, more awareness of where the gaps lie, and more knowledge as to what was faulty in much of the thinking engaged in by statesmen, scholars, and common men a century ago. Speculation, premises, hypotheses must all be seen as leading us further toward the conceptualization and categorization of our data, just as theory must be viewed as directing us to assumptions concerning the meaning of the data we collect. Although the theories may be invalidated, along with the premises and hypotheses, they become so only with the development of more sophisticated explanations based upon more insights and the wider use of new data.

◊   ◊   ◊   ◊   ◊

Men in the future are also going to become more concerned with human rights, but instead of viewing them narrowly as today, they may see new combinations and new varieties that escape the observations of men living in the last decades of the twentieth century. The rights of freedom of speech, press, thought, and religion are eighteenth century in scope, but the twentieth century has also seen how important it is that men not be subject to the authority of others who are less equipped to make decisions aout their lives than they themselves. This century has also seen the rise of the need to define anew the rights of those who are born poor, of uneducated parents, in the "wrong" countries, of the "wrong" color, sex, or religion. Only in this century have we become aware of how few are able to fulfill their life goals, how few have interesting work, or a sense of satisfaction in work well done. We have become more aware than ever before of the need for men and women to be of service to others and to be able to live satisfactorily with themselves in terms of what they have been able to accomplish with their lives. Men and women need to learn to govern themselves better than they have been governed by others in the past, and this requires a new bill of rights for the industrial worker, the clerk, the civil servant, the teacher, and the citizen in general. So far we have done little to bring such a bill of rights into existence, and yet it will be needed if men and women are to transform the twenty-first century into the twenty-second. Men and women must have the right to make suggestions, to innovate, to be critical, and even in the case of ineptitude to be able to fire the inefficient boss — a right that is sorely lacking in the world today, organized as it is on the basis of the "divine right" of hierarchies. And, though elected officials can be refused reappointment, the ability to discharge them while they are on the job is still in the future. It is now impossible for workers to discharge an inept foreman or shop superintendent, for teachers to get rid of an inefficient principal, or for citizens to replace a government official. The trend is toward the creation of new political mechanisms to arise during the next century to remedy some of this built-in authoritarianism.

The trend in the future is thus for more democracy, not less; for more "rights," not fewer; for more citizen participation in government rather than for a continuation of bureaucratic authority. Employees need more rights within their work places — even though the future factory may be automated with only a few skilled workers in charge of various controls. Men need protection against feeling helpless, powerless, and useless. Perhaps in the future they will find such protection in new forms of education, laws, and levels of public opinion which will directly influence political decisions. Men will hopefully move in the direction of trying through concensus to establish the greater width and depth of what may be called the "rights of mankind." One gets the feeling that the next century may well see an accelerated growth in new dimensions of the concept of democracy. It has now become quite evident that rigid authoritarianism presents insuperable difficulties in managing a complex Industrial and Scientific civilization. Any attempt to have solutions come from the top ranks of non-supermen executives becomes self-defeating, for a feedback from those below is necessary in order to expose all aspects of a problem. One must be able to locate decisions made by the executives above one if they are part of the causes of inefficiency. When the man above in the bureaucratic hierarchy controls one's increase in pay and promotion, innovation and imagination are strongly inhibited as one learns to do basically only that which the man above wants and needs. As we move on into the dim and unknown future, the chances are good that men will have obligations to come up with their thinking on the enormous number of options that are open to make society more efficient, better-adjusted, and secure. Thus far, the growth of democracy in all of its phases has been on a primitive level.

Men still do not know how to get along with one another: the mass warfare of the twentieth century has been proof of that. No century has seen the mass destruction of men and property as much as this one. Few countries have been fortunate enough to have escaped mass murders and wanton destruction. It has been the age in which lack of freedom and the imprisonment of large numbers of men have been elevated into national ideologies both by the Communists and the Nazis — though other authoritarian regimes have not been far behind. While we have grown enormously in the accumulation of knowledge, in an awareness of the unity of mankind, in the greater extension of human rights to women and national minorities, still the mentality that brought about the concentration camp and the ideological tribal nation-state is still with us, and there are few countries that cannot look inward and not say, "Mea culpa. . ." Psychopathic and sociopathic killers are encouraged to some degree everywhere, even in high office. And not all the decisions made by national executives have been humanist in intent. The United States has carried on its share of bombing innocent civilians and destroying other people's property, just as it has practiced putting individuals whom it did not trust into concentration camps (for example, that of the Japanese-Americans removed from their homes on the West Coast in 1943 and put in internment camps).

Although the path to humanitarianism has been rocky and pitted, we now have on average a bit more than existed in the past. The trends are not toward a world ruled by self-centered gangsters, political psychopathic personalties, military adventurers, new Hitlers or Stalins (though these may still appear in some form during the next 100 years), but rather toward the development of new constitutions and governments that may make totalitarianism and authoritarianism in government less likely. We are moving toward a greater understanding of the enormous variety of human needs. It is difficult to correlate this greater understanding of peoples and cultures with the mentality of Primary civilization which produced the concentration camp, the secret police, and the atomic bomb as a weapon of war. In time, we can expect far more documentation on the effects of authoritarianism on the maladjustment of the human personality than we have uncovered thus far. Over the next few hundred years, if mankind can survive the mediocrities whom it has put and will continue to put into decision-making positions — and if we can be spared an atomic holocaust — we may be inching our way slowly but surely to a more egalitarian, democratic, and individualistic civilization.

◇　　◇　　◇　　◇　　◇

Children have a right to a useful life, one in which they can find opportunities to fulfill their human potential. In the future, men will be concerned with a bill of rights which guarantees to each child the right not to be reared as a psychopath, a psychotic, or a neurotic. Each child has the right to grow up healthy, both physically and socially. But the implementation is difficult at the present time, as our poor and those reared in slums have discovered.

Just as children need a new bill of rights, so do husbands and wives. Marriage is an indispensable institution for mankind for which there is no substitute, whether the contract that cements it be civil, religious, or common-law. Within that institution, the roles of both husbands and wives have changed during the past century, and will certainly change even more in the future. But no matter what the external form or the changing roles within, the institution is still indispensable and one of the most useful we have in our society. Marriage will become more of an equal partnership than it is today. And, though it will continue to rear succeeding generations, the emphasis will be more upon the man and woman living together as the primary relationship. Parents will make fewer attempts to keep up a faltering connection with children as the cementing force, but a greater emphasis than today will be placed upon the equality of husband and wife, with both sharing the burdens, responsibilities, and one another's interests. At present, the wife is dependent upon and subordinate to the husband, but in the future a wife's career may be as important to her as the husband's is to him. There is no reason why the husband cannot be the housekeeper and "mother" to the children if the concept of "masculinity" is removed from the marital structure. Today, the married woman is dependent upon her husband not only for support but also for status fulfillment. On the other hand, a married woman can plunge into poverty upon the death of her husband, for women's skills are not as easily marketable or as well paid as those of men. Although social security payments and pensions act as insurance against abject poverty, a young widow with two or three children is often forced to lower her standard of living. All this may change during the next century as men and women become more equal in the eyes of society. There is no relationship between two people that offers potentially so much as marriage in terms of friendship, companionship, emotional support, and sexuality.

The intense frustration that mankind feels about the present dearth of knowledge for resolving problems is pushing us inexorably toward the Tertiary or Third civilization. As men come increasingly to reject their sense of helplessness, hopelessness, and worthlessness, pressures will mount to do something about them. While in the past men had no choice but to accept a fatalistic attitude toward the forces which buffeted them about and which they could not control, today men are becoming less willing to accept frustrations when they believe that something can be done to resolve them. Men will increasingly spread this point of view everywhere during coming decades. Though we still do not know how to carry on organized research, though the state is no longer seen as a benefactor, though too many universities are often boondoggling institutions in which tradition and conformity are given high priorities, still there is a vague but pervasive belief that something somewhere must be done to produce a more satisfying urban and modern world, a culture that is not inimical to the desires of most of its citizens, and a society that does not punish accidents of birth but encourages instead the self-fulfillment of the largest number of its members.

It is quite difficult to see future political trends, for men in the next five to ten decades will develop their political beliefs out of their contemporary frustrations and aspirations. But one thing seems possible, and that is that the types of "socialism" practiced in the Communist and Third World countries will have a fairly short life, since thus far they have led to blind alleys. For example, it is difficult to imagine the populations in the Communist countries with their higher levels of education in the year 2025 remaining willing to accept restrictions on the accumulation of knowledge or unnecessary totalitarianism with its enthronement of mediocrity. Communism cannot work without a huge infusion of democracy and a conviction on the part of most of the adult population that innovation, education, and even life itself must be rewarding — and that working for the good of society should be perhaps the greatest reward of all. But at present there is little to gain in any Communist country from working harder than the other members of one's work team, from offering suggestions to top management on how to make work more efficient, or from exploring new intellectual horizons without permission from one's superiors. One cannot offer suggestions on how the Communist society might be made to work as a "socialist" one. Communist society, as it has developed on the basis of the Russian model, does not fulfill the dreams of the nineteenth-century utopian, Marxist, or even anarchist socialist thinkers. These had hoped that a new cooperative world would emerge out of a better-educated human society, one that would insist upon each individual having a sense of personal responsibility for the direction of his social, economic, and political worlds. The nationalization of the means of production, as many followers of Russian Communism early discovered, does not lead to a "socialist" society but rather to a more centralized and bureaucratic one. The organization of the Communist Party, as Lenin hoped, did not lead to the creation of a group of thinkers to advise the rest of the population on how to achieve the "socialist society," but instead (as Robert Michels warned in 1911, and as Rosa Luxemburg and even Leon Trotsky pointed out before World War I) to a rigid bureaucracy completely controlled by those who captured its machinery, its sources of information, and its police and military powers to engage in coercion of the membership. Men who have enormous amounts of power will not give it up easily as Marx, Engels, and Lenin reiterated over and over again. But the monster that they saw in the "capitalist" world has emerged in even more hideous form in the Communist one.

The Czechs and Slovaks discovered, along with the Poles, Hungarians, and East Germans, that infusing democracy into the

Communist organization leads to the gradual destruction of the powers held by that Party, and the latter will not easily give permission for others to plot its demise. Yet, as time goes on, the need to reform Communism in order to make it work will emphasize anew the importance of democracy and democratic behavior if any large complex system of organization is to function. Without research into the reasons why Communist industry, agriculture, distribution, and retailing perform so poorly, little can be done to work toward resolving their problems. But permission for the research will not be given if it leads to loss of status by the Party, the governmental organization controlled by the latter, and the men in charge of developing priorities and making final decisions. The Soviet Union faces a dilemma which it cannot resolve without being pushed into the problem-solving Tertiary civilization.

Too many young people in the Communist part of the world are educated to live in a future "socialist" society without being able to do so at present. Communications are narrowing the gaps in the world of man; it becomes more and more difficult for students, professionals, and educated laymen to accept censorship of information, or be deprived of access to what others are thinking, doing, and writing. Although the contemporary Communist Party leadership may see this drive for intellectual freedom as "revisionist," "counter-revolutionary," and even as "creeping capitalism," public pressures against the police state that is today's Communist society will mount rather than diminish.

Whether the Communist Party will voluntarily share its power with its subjects is also a question. A good deal of the brief liberalization that took place in the Soviet Union after 1956 was brought about through the relative permissiveness set in motion by Nikita Khrushchev. Sooner or later, the need to reform Communism in order to make it work may be a chief factor in injecting a large dose of democracy into the Communist system — leading to decentralization, feedbacks of various kinds, freedom to see problems and solutions without the intervention of the party, and thus to greater intellectual innovation. Unfortunately, the intellectual freedom to deal with pressing social problems is one that is rarely encouraged even in the so-called "free" countries.

In any balance sheet, it must be admitted that the Communist countries have carried on a good deal of industrialization, encouraged and supported most of the physical, geological, and biological sciences (despite the removal of support from genetics by Stalin because he believed that it was sapping the authority of the Communist Party to change the world), and brought about a universal educational system in which millions have been trained in higher schools as scientists, engineers, technicians, and administrators. Although the population has been made literate, academic freedom as such does not exist in the Soviet Union. Any social science or physical science that runs counter to the official Party line is not allowed to be disseminated. Censorship exists in the classroom, with selected students often acting as police agents. Publication is at the sole convenience of the Party, which permits the publication only of those ideas which it supports. Censorship of the printed word is the rule, not the exception.

Poverty of the abject sort has indeed been abolished in all Communist countries, although this has been accomplished by bringing the technical middle classes down to an egalitarian level in which most share a low standard of living. One can say that there are no beggars under Communism, and the strict morality of the regime permits few deviates. Prostitution has been legally abolished and, if it does exist, operates chiefly underground. Juvenile delinquency has not been eradicated and neither has violent crime. Social problems under Communism are roughly of the same order and within similar dimensions as in the non-Communist countries. Alcoholism in the Soviet Union is as much of a problem as it was in Czarist days. Though we know little about the extent of the drug problem, it seems evident that the same dependency need that encourages the use of drugs in a non-Communist country also exists in a Communist one.

Communism has developed no new sciences or pioneering industries, including those in retailing and distribution. Its educational systems provide no models for others in the developed world to emulate. Although it has done yeoman work in developing modern industrial techniques in building module apartment houses, the improvements have minor importance. Few middle class individuals in Western Europe would care to occupy a modern flat in the Soviet Union.

If "socialism" is to develop into a system of society more efficient and satisfying than that which exists in the non-Communist world, then the emphasis needs to be placed upon the future growth of democracy. Without democracy there can be no "socialism" — as that term was used by nineteenth-century social pioneers. Communism, with its nationalization of the means of production, has merely concentrated all ownership in the hands of the Communist Party Politburo, whose members hold the prestigious jobs and make the important economic and social decisions. Merely shifting the power base from an authoritarian board of directors to an authoritarian Communist Party does not make a factory more democratic, or for that matter "socialist."

This does not imply that there may not be wide shifts and changes within the Communist Party structure during the next 50 years, but if Communism is not to become completely irrelevant and obsolete during the next few decades, it must gradually change its goal from one of nationalization to one of democracy. There must be more industrial democracy, social democracy, economic democracy, and political democracy in all of the Communist countries, including China — and far more of all of these in the non-Communist world.

Communism cannot continue its present model and survive during the next few decades. It frustrates too many of its citizens with its present inefficiencies and repressions. Its change is inevitable, though the possibilities or the extent of that change are still unclear at the moment. Perhaps the need to make Communism into a more efficient and satisfying society than exists in the non-Communist world may be one of the chief motivating factors leading to change. The gradual replacement of the bureaucrats who have served since Stalin's day may be another. Certainly a growing recognition of the need for political change may take place among the younger bureaucrats and junior staffs of the industrial, scientific, educational, informational, police, and military organizations.

The Communist economic structure cannot return to what was originally its base, and even modern "capitalism" as a revitalized means of making Communist industry more efficient is completely out of the question politically as well as socially. It would be virtually impossible to divide Soviet industry, for example, and sell ownership in its organizations to private individuals, or to turn banks over to pre-Communist ownership. Too much has been built up through hardships and taxation of the Russians and other peoples to permit a return to what existed before the Five-Year Plans were started. The Communists need to build their future society upon the basis of their existing nationalized industries, banks, communications, distribution centers, and transportation.

There are, however, opportunities to develop new cooperatives out of most of them, or to encourage decentralized staffs working together to take over most of the functions of manufacturing, servicing, and informing. Newspapers, radio and television stations will need to be turned over to non-Party cooperatives. But the cooperatives must be far more democratic in organization than any present-day economic units. They must be egalitarian, open to suggestions as well as continuous reform, and there must be built-in inhibitors preventing the growth of oligarchies and machine political blocs. These again represent problems that men in the next few decades must attempt to resolve.

And so, as we move toward the end of the century and try to peer into the next one, it does seem that we are moving slowly though definitely in the direction of a cooperative, democratic, consumer-organized society, in which the emphasis is less upon private-corporate and party-governmental concentrated power and more upon the role of most individuals assuming greater responsibility for the efficient running of their work units within society; and at the same time participating in those decisions which decide the management of the larger segments. The emphasis will also be less upon greater leisure time and more upon the citizen spending his non-working hours becoming better informed. An educated citizenry is a prerequisite in the smooth functioning of a complex Industrial and Scientific civilization.

◊　◊　◊　◊　◊

We are moving in the direction of greater human rights, a better understanding of the implications and practices of democracy, a greater political and social awareness and participation of the citizens in government in all of its phases. We and the Communist world are both moving in the same direction, though who will move first and fastest into the new democratic society of the future is still a matter of conjecture. But there is little doubt that this trend is now emerging.

The content of the future democratic society may well differ from one area to another, from one region, and even from one nation to another. We are still centuries away from the One World concept, politically and socially, though here again perhaps in the Fourth or the Fifth civilizations this could become a reality. We are becoming a closer-knit world, a more cosmopolitan one, and certainly a better-informed one. Although many may be pessimistic about the chances of our generation resolving many of the tensions that exist between us, few would deny that in the long run the outlook for such solutions is optimistic.

Men have the possibility to be around for a long time to come. They will certainly continue to accumulate knowledge, develop a greater awareness of themselves and the physical and biological universes they inhabit, and move inexorably in the direction of creating a society that will become with each succeeding generation a less frustrating one. Men have been and are continuing to be their own worst enemies, and perhaps only the future can resolve the problem of how men can continue to run their various societies with more sophistication, efficiency, and humanitarianism.

Although we may underline the problems faced by the developing and the Communist nations, we must also remember that we in the developed area of the non-Communist world are by no means shining examples of democratic, humanitarian, or egalitarian behavior. Too much wealth and political power are gathered in the hands of too small a percentage of the population. Our organization of men is still inefficient and inhumane, as will become clearer from the vantage point of the next century. We have a long way to go to develop our enormous human potential, to create a more pleasant society for most inhabitants, and to build a world that is completely democratic in all of its aspects. The differences between ourselves and the more authoritarian societies are quite often more a matter of degree than of kind. Authoritarianism and the repression of opinion sap at the foundations of traditional institutions of power in the United States as well as in the Soviet Union. Men take their official positions personally as they consider their vested authority as also conferring upon them more power to control and manipulate others. Although we are more democratic than the citizens who live in totalitarian states, we are in fact not as free as we think we are or as we undoubtedly will be in the next century.

Still, in terms of trends that exist today, it will be difficult to turn us in the direction of the totalitarian political regimes. We have no other way of going than toward greater freedom, a more sophisticated awareness, a more individual responsibility, more participation by the citizenry, and a stronger forging of the links that tie all of us to one another. While men may become depressed at times over the swirling changes occurring in our world at present, those who can perceive even dimly the outlines of the evolving future find it difficult to be pessimistic. Emerging intellectual tools for coping with change provide a future potential for resolving problems that baffle us at the moment. The story of mankind has been an optimistic one thus far. By all standards, it must also be seen as a success story. We have little doubt that future generations will see it as such, even as they look in despair at how little we accomplished in our lifetime.

Although it is difficult to compare separate centuries, we may assume that what bothers men in one era might be resolved in another. At the moment, the short-range outlook may appear pessimistic, but in the long run men have always created improved social, economic, and political worlds. The present trend, I believe, is toward greater autonomy for the human personality. There can be no conclusion to the story of mankind, but at least we can end the story at this point on an optimistic note.

SELECTIVE BIBLIOGRAPHY

Thousands of books have been written on the incomplete story of man. It would be impossible to compile even a fair list, but out of the hundreds and hundreds which the author has read the following titles may be useful.

1. Adams, R. N., *The Second Sowing: Power and Secondary Development in Latin America* (San Francisco, Chandler, 1967).
2. Akamatsu, Paul, *Meiji 1868* (New York, Harper and Row, 1968).
3. Alimen, H., *The Prehistory of Africa* (London, Hutchinson, 1957).
4. Anderson, Robert T., *Traditional Europe* (Belmont, Calif., Wadsworth, 1970).
5. Aso, Makato and Ikuo Amano, *Education and Japan's Modernization* (Tokyo, Ministry of Foreign Affairs, 1972).
6. Appadorai, Angadipuram, *India: Studies in Social and Political Development, 1947-1967* (New York, Asia Publishing House, 1968).
7. Bacon, Edward, *Archaeology: Discoveries in the 1960's* (New York, Praeger, 1971).
8. Barbour, Violet, *Capitalism in the Seventeenth Century* (Ann Arbor, U. of Michigan Press, 1963).
9. Basham, A. D., *The Wonder That Was India* (New York, Grove Evergreen, 1959).
10. Beard, Miriam, *A History of Business* (Ann Arbor, U. of Michigan Press, 1962-1963), 2 Volumes.
11. Beasley, W. G., *The Meiji Restoration* (Stanford, Stanford U. Press, 1973).
12. Bell, Daniel K., *The Coming of Post-Industrial Society* (New York, Basic Books, 1973).
13. Bendix, Reinhard, *Work and Authority in Industry* (New York, Harper and Row Torchbooks, 1963).
14. Bernal, J. D., *Science in History* (New York, Hawthorn Books, 1965).
15. Berneri, Marie Louise, *Journey Through Utopia* (New York, Schocken Books, 1971).
16. Bibby, Geoffrey, *Four Thousand Years Ago* (New York, Alfred A. Knopf, 1961).
17. _____, *The Testimony of the Spade* (New York, Alfred A. Knopf, 1956).
18. Bloodworth, Dennis, *The Chinese Looking Glass* (New York, Farrar, Straus, Giroux, 1967).
19. Bohannan, Paul, *Africa and Africans* (New York, Doubleday, 1964).

20. Bordes, Francois, *The Old Stone Age* (New York, McGraw-Hill, 1968).
21. Braidwood, Robert J. and Gordon R. Willey, *Courses Toward Urban Life* (Chicago, Aldine, 1962).
22. Braidwood, Robert J., *Prehistoric Men* (Glenview, Illinois, Scott Foresman, 1967).
23. Brocher, Karl D., *The German Dictatorship* (New York, Praeger, 1970).
24. Brumberg, Abraham, Ed., *In Quest of Justice* (New York, Praeger, 1972).
25. Buckingham, Walter, *Automation* (New York, Mentor Books, 1961).
26. Buer, Mabel C., *Health, Wealth and Population in the Early Days of the Industrial Revolution* (New York, Howard Fertig, 1968).
27. Butterfield, Herbert, *The Origins of Modern Science, 1300-1800* (New York, Collier Books, 1962).
28. Edwards, E. S., et al, *Cambridge Ancient History* (Cambridge, England and New York, Cambridge U. Press, 1970). Volume I.
29. Childe, V. Gordon, *Man Makes Himself* (New York, New American Library, 1961).
30. _____, *New Light on the Most Ancient East* (London, Routledge, 1952).
31. Clark, Grahame, *World Prehistory* (New York, Cambridge U. Press, 1969).
32. Clark, Grahame and Stuart Piggott, *Prehistoric Societies* (New York, Alfred A. Knopf, 1967).
33. Clark, J. Desmond, *The Prehistory of Africa* (New York, Praeger, 1970).
34. Clubb, O. Edmund, *Twentieth Century China* (New York, Columbia U. Press, 1972).
35. Cochran, Thomas C., *The Age of Enterprise* (New York, Harper and Row Torchbooks, 1961).
36. Coe, Michael D., *America's First Civilization* (New York, American Heritage, 1968).
37. Cook, R. M., *The Greeks Until Alexander* (New York, Praeger, 1962).
38. Coon, Carleton S., *Caravan: The Story of the Middle East* (New York, Holt, Rinehart and Winston, 1961).
39. _____, *The Origin of Races* (New York, Alfred A. Knopf, 1962).
40. _____, *The Story of Man* (New York, Alfred A. Knopf, 1955).
41. Crombie, A. C., *Medieval and Early Modern Science* (Garden City, N. Y., Doubleday Anchor Books, 1959).

42. Daniel, Glyn, *The First Civilizations* (New York, Thomas Crowell, 1970), 2 Volumes.
43. Davidson, Marshall B., ed., *The Horizon Book of Lost Worlds* (New York, Doubleday, 1962).
44. Davies, John Paton, Jr., *Dragon by the Tail* (New York, Norton, 1972).
45. De Burgh, W. G., *The Legacy of the Ancient World* (Baltimore, Penguin, 1953).
46. Emery, W. B., *Archaic Egypt* (Baltimore, Penguin, 1961).
47. Fainsod, Merle, *How Russia Is Ruled* (Cambridge, Mass., Harvard U. Press, 1963).
48. Feuer, Lewis S., *The Scientific Intellectual* (New York, Basic Books, 1963).
49. Fitzgerald, C. P., *The Birth of Communist China* (Baltimore, Penguin, 1964).
50. Forbes, R. J. and E. J. Dijksterhuis, *A History of Science and Technology* (Baltimore, Penguin, 1963), 2 Volumes.
51. Foster, George M., *Traditional Cultures and the Impact of Technological Change* (New York, Harper and Row, 1962).
52. Frankfort, Henri, *The Birth of Civilization in the Near East* (New York, Doubleday Anchor, 1960).
53. Friedrich, Paul, *Agrarian Revolt in a Mexican Village* (Englewood Cliffs, New Jersey, Prentice-Hall, 1970).
54. Fromm, Erich and Michael Maccoby, *Social Character in a Mexican Village* (Englewood Cliffs, Prentice-Hall, 1970).
55. Frye, Richard N., *The Heritage of Persia* (New York, Mentor Books, 1966).
56. Gabel, Creighton, ed., *Man Before History* (Englewood Cliffs, Prentice-Hall, 1964).
57. Galbraith, John Kenneth, *The New Industrial State* (Boston, Houghton Mifflin, 1967).
58. George, Dorothy M., *London Life in the 18th Century* (New York, Capricorn Books, 1965).
59. Ginzberg, Eli, *The Development of Human Resources* (New York, McGraw-Hill, 1966).
60. Granet, Marcel, *Chinese Civilization* (Cleveland, World Meridian Books, 1958).
61. Granick, David, *Managerial Comparisons of Four Developed Countries: France, Britain, United States and Russia* (Cambridge, Mass., M.I.T. Press, 1972).
62. —————, *The Red Executive* (New York, Doubleday Anchor Books, 1961).
63. Grant, Michael, *The World of Rome* (Cleveland, World, 1960).
64. Gurney, O. R., *The Hittites* (Baltimore, Penguin, 1954).
65. Hagen, Everett E., *On the Theory of Social Change* (Homewood, Illinois, Dorsey, 1962).

66. Hall, John Whitney, *Japan from Prehistory to Modern Times* (New York, Delta Books, 1971).
67. Hall, John Whitney and Richard K. Beardsley, *Twelve Doors to Japan* (New York, McGraw-Hill, 1965).
68. Hawkes, J. and L. Wooley, *Prehistory and the Beginning of Civilization* (New York, Harper and Row, 1963).
69. Heilbroner, Robert L., *The Future as History* (New York, Grove Evergreen, 1961).
70. Henry, Jules, *Culture Against Man* (New York, Random House, 1963).
71. Herskovits, Melville J., *The Human Factor in Changing Africa* (New York, Alfred A. Knopf, 1962).
72. Hodges, Henry, *Technology in the Ancient World* (New York, Knopf, 1970).
73. Hollander, Paul, *American and Soviet Society* (Englewood Cliffs, Prentice-Hall, 1969).
74. Holmes, Lowell, *Anthropology: An Introduction* (New York, Ronald Press, 1972), Revised edition.
75. Hsu, Francis L. K., *Clan, Caste and Club* (Princeton, New Jersey, Van Nostrand, 1963).
76. —————, *Under the Ancestors' Shadow* (New York, Doubleday Anchor, 1967).
77. Huizinga, J., *The Waning of the Middle Ages* (New York, Doubleday, 1954).
78. Hutchinson, R. W., *Prehistoric Crete* (Baltimore, Penguin, 1962).
79. Hyde, H. Montgomery, *Stalin, the History of a Dictator* (New York, Farrar, Straus and Giroux, 1972).
80. Jacobson, Julius, ed., *Soviet Communism and the Socialist Vision* (New Brunswick, New Jersey, Transaction Books, 1972).
81. Karnow, Stanley, *Mao and China* (New York, Viking, 1972).
82. Kebschull, Harvey G., *Politics in Transitional Societies* (New York, Appleton-Century-Crofts, 1968).
83. Klineberg, Otto and Marisa Zavalloni, *Nationalism and Tribalism among African Students* (New York, Humanities Press, 1969).
84. Lahontan, Baron de—R. G. Thwaites, editor—*New Voyages to North America* (New York, Burt Franklin, 1905), 2 Volumes.
85. Levi, Carlo, *Christ Stopped at Eboli* (New York, Farrar Straus, 1947).
86. Lewis, I. M., *History and Social Anthropology* (New York, Harper and Row, 1970).
87. Lewis, John P., *Quiet Crisis in India* (New York, Doubleday Anchor, 1964).

88. Lewis, Oscar, *Five Families (New York, Basic Books, 1962).*
89. Linton, Ralph, *The Tree of Culture* (New York, Knopf, 1955).
90. Lipset, Seymour Martin and Reinhard Bendix, *Social Mobility in Industrial Society* (Berkeley and Los Angeles, U. of California Press, 1964).
91. Lloyd, Seton, *Early Anatolia* (Baltimore, Penguin, 1956).
92. Locke, John, *Travels in France, 1675-1679* (Cambridge, Cambridge U. Press, 1953).
93. Lopez, Robert S., *The Birth of Europe* (Englewood Cliffs, Prentice-Hall, 1967).
94. _____, *The Commercial Revolution of the Middle Ages, 950-1350* (Englewood Cliffs, Prentice-Hall, 1971).
95. Mabogunje, Akin L., *Urbanization in Nigeria* (New York, African Publishing Co., 1969).
96. Mantoux, Paul, *The Industrial Revolution in the 18th Century* (New York, Harper Torchbooks, 1961).
97. Metraux, Guy S. and Francois Crouzet, eds., *The Nineteenth Century World* (New York, Mentor Books, 1963).
98. Middleton, John, ed., *Black Africa: Its Peoples and Their Cultures* (New York, Macmillan, 1970).
99. Mills, C. Wright, *The Marxists* (New York, Dell, 1962).
100. Mongait, A. L., *Archaeology in the U.S.S.R.* (Baltimore, Penguin, 1961).
101. Mueller, Herbert J., *Freedom in the Ancient World* (New York, Harper and Row, 1961).
102. Mumford, Lewis, *Technics and Civilization* (New York, Harcourt Brace, 1963).
103. _____, *The Myth of the Machine* (New York, Harcourt Brace, 1967).
104. Murdock, George P., *Africa: Its Peoples and Their Cultural History* (New York, McGraw-Hill, 1959).
105. Nakane, Chie, *Japanese Society* (Berkeley and Los Angeles, U. of California Press, 1970).
106. Needham, Joseph, *Science and Civilization* (London, Cambridge U. Press, 1956).
107. Norbeck, Edward, *Changing Japan* (New York, Holt, Rinehart and Winston, 1965).
108. Ottenberg, Simon and Phoebe Ottenberg, *Cultures and Societies of Africa* (New York, Random House, 1961).
109. Paddock, William and Paul Paddock, *Famine 1975* (Boston, Little Brown, 1967).
110. Papanek, Gustav, *Pakistan's Development* (Cambridge, Mass., Harvard U. Press 1967).
111. Peterson, Frederick A., *Ancient Mexico* (New York, Capricorn Books, 1962).
112. Piggott, Stuart, *Ancient Europe* (Chicago, Aldine, 1965).

113. Piggott, Stuart, *Prehistoric India* (Baltimore, Penguin, 1950).
114. _____, ed., *The Dawn of Civilization* (New York, McGraw-Hill, 1961).
115. Reynolds, R. L., *Europe Emerges* (Madison, U. of Wisconsin, 1961).
116. Reischauer, E. O. and J. K. Fairbank, *East Asia: The Great Tradition* (Boston, Houghton Mifflin, 1960).
117. Reischauer, E. O., *Japan: Past and Present* (New York, Knopf, 1953).
118. Rice, Edward F., *Mao's Way* (Berkeley and Los Angeles, U. of California Press, 1972).
119. Richman, Barry M., *Industrial Society in Communist China* (New York, Random House, 1969).
120. Ritvo, Herbert, ed., *The New Soviet Society* (New York, The New Leader Press, 1962).
121. Rodnick, David, *Essays on an America in Transition* (Lubbock, Caprock Press, 1972).
122. _____, *Introduction to Man and His Development* (New York, Appleton-Century-Crofts, 1966).
123. _____, *The Strangled Democracy: Czechoslovakia 1948-1969* (Lubbock, Caprock Press, 1970).
124. Rothberg, Abraham, *The Heirs of Stalin, 1953-1970* (Ithaca, Cornell U. Press, 1972).
125. Roux, Georges, *Ancient Iraq* (Cleveland and New York, World, 1964).
126. Selden, Mark, *The Yenan Way in Revolutionary China* (Cambridge, Harvard U. Press, 1971).
127. Seligman, Ben B., *Most Notorious Victory: Man in an Age of Automation* (New York, The Free Press, 1966).
128. Sinai, I. R., *The Challenge of Modernization* (London, Chatto and Windus, 1964).
129. Singer, Charles, E. J. Holmyard and A. R. Hall, *A History of Technology* (New York, Oxford Press, 1958), Volume I.
130. Singer, Milton, et al, eds., *Structure and Change in Indian Society* (Chicago, Aldine, 1969).
131. Singer, Milton, *When a Great Tradition Modernizes* (New York, Praeger, 1972).
132. Sjoberg, Gideon, *The Preindustrial City* (New York, The Free Press, 1965).
133. Snow, Edgar, *The Long Revolution* (New York, Random House, 1972).
134. _____, *The Other Side of the River* (New York, Random House, 1961).
135. Solomon, Richard H., *Mao's Revolution and the Chinese Political Culture* (Berkeley and Los Angeles, U. of California Press, 1971).

136. Sorlin, Pierre, *The Soviet People and Their Society* (New York, Praeger, 1969).
137. Stone, P. B., *Japan Surges Ahead: The Story of an Economic Miracle* (New York, Praeger, 1969).
138. Tagliacozzo, Giorgio, ed., *Giambattista Vico* (Baltimore, Johns Hopkins Press, 1969).
139. Talmon, J. L., *The Origins of Totalitarian Democracy* (New York, Praeger, 1960).
140. "The Encyclopedia Brittannica Conference on the Technological Culture," *Technology and Culture* (Detroit, Wayne State U. Press, 1962).
141. Thrupp, Sylvia L., *The Merchant Class of Medieval Europe* (Ann Arbor, U. of Michigan Press, 1962).
142. Tsurumi, Kazuko, *Social Change and the Individual* (Princeton, Princeton U. Press, 1970).
143. Tucker, Robert C., *The Marx-Engels Reader* (New York, Norton, 1972).
144. _____, *The Marxian Revolutionary Idea* (New York, Norton, 1970).
145. Tyler, Stephen A., *India: An Anthropological Perspective* (Pacific Palisades, Calif., Goodyear, 1973).
146. Uchendu, Victor S., *The Igbo of Southeast Nigeria* (New York, Holt, Rinehart and Winston, 1965).
147. Wagley, Charles, *An Introduction to Brazil* (New York, Columbia U. Press, 1963).
148. Wallerstein, Immanuel, *Social Change: The Colonial Situation* (New York, John Wiley and Sons, 1966).
149. Ward, Robert E. and Dankwart A. Rustow, *Political Modernization in Japan and Turkey* (Princeton, Princeton U. Press, 1964).
150. Wheeler, Sir Mortimer, *Early India and Pakistan* (New York, Praeger, 1959).
151. White, Andrew Dickson, *A History of the Warfare of Science with Theology* (New York, The Free Press, 1965).
152. White, Lynn, Jr., *Medieval Technology and Social Change* (London, Oxford U. Press, 1963).
153. Wilson, Dick, *The Long March* (New York, Viking, 1971).
154. Wiser, William and Charlotte Wiser, *Behind Mud Walls, 1930-1960* (Berkeley and Los Angeles, U. of California Press, 1963).
155. Wittfogel, Karl A., *Oriental Despotism* (New Haven, Yale U. Press, 1957).
156. Yoshino, M. Y., *Japan's Managerial System* (Cambridge, M.I.T. Press, 1968).

Index

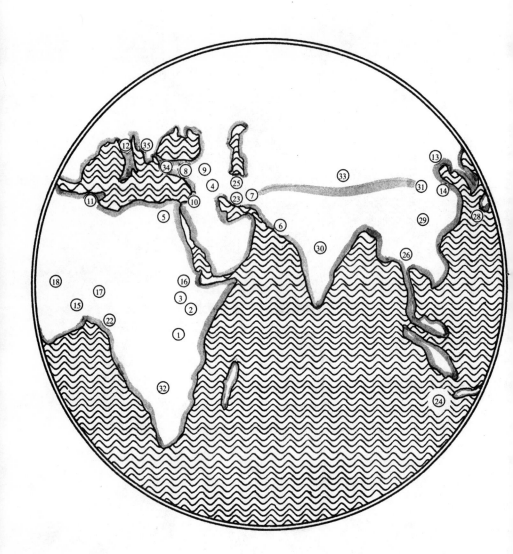

1. Olduvai
2. Lake Rudolph
3. Omo River
4. Sumerians
5. Egyptians
6. Harappans
7. Tepe Yahya
8. Anatolia
9. Hurrians
10. Phoenicians
11. Carthaginians
12. Etruscans
13. Choukoutien
14. Shan Empire
15. Songhai
16. Axum
17. Mali
18. Ghana

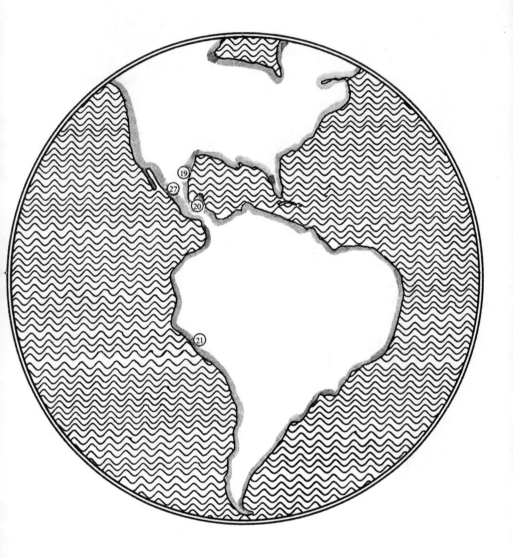